POLITICAL VIOLENCE IN TURKEY, 1975-1980

Contemporary Turkey

BIAA | BRITISH INSTITUTE AT ANKARA
Understanding Turkey and the Black Sea

The *Contemporary Turkey* monograph series is a joint initiative by the British Institute at Ankara (BIAA), internationally renowned for its support of independent academic research, and leading publisher of Middle East and Turkish Studies I.B. Tauris, an imprint of Bloomsbury Academic.

The series publishes cutting-edge research monographs and edited collections from a new generation of scholars working on modern Turkey across the social sciences and humanities. In bringing to light new data and insights directly from the field, this series is distinguished by its emphasis on innovative approaches that challenge established ways of examining Turkey.

Series Editor:
Ceren Lord, University of Oxford, UK

Advisory Board
Sevgi Adak, The Aga Khan University, UK
Pınar Bedirhanoğlu, Middle East Technical University, Turkey
Zerrin Özlem Biner, SOAS, University of London, UK
Martin Stokes, King's College London, UK

Published Titles
The Politics of Education in Turkey: Islam, Neoliberalism, and Gender, Zühre Emanet
Architectures of Emergency in Turkey: Heritage, Displacement and Catastrophe, edited by Eray Çaylı, Pınar Aykaç and Sevcan Ercan
Political Violence in Turkey, 1975–1980: The State at Stake, Benjamin Gourisse
Mobility and Armenian Belonging in Contemporary Turkey: Migratory Routes and the Meaning of the Local, Salim Aykut Öztürk
Police Reform in Turkey: Human Security, Gender and State Violence Under Erdogan, Funda Hülagü
Turkey and the Global Political Economy, edited by Mehmet Erman Erol, Görkem Altınörs, Gönenç Uysal

POLITICAL VIOLENCE IN TURKEY, 1975–1980

The state at stake

Benjamin Gourisse

I.B. TAURIS
LONDON • NEW YORK • OXFORD • NEW DELHI • SYDNEY

I.B. TAURIS
Bloomsbury Publishing Plc
50 Bedford Square, London, WC1B 3DP, UK
1385 Broadway, New York, NY 10018, USA
29 Earlsfort Terrace, Dublin 2, Ireland

BLOOMSBURY, I.B. TAURIS and the I.B. Tauris logo are
trademarks of Bloomsbury Publishing Plc

First published in 2014 in France as *La violence politique en Turquie*
by Karthala Editions
This edition published 2023 by I.B.Tauris, an imprint of Bloomsbury Publishing
This paperback edition published 2024

Copyright © Karthala Editions, 2023

Karthala Editions has asserted its right under the Copyright,
Designs and Patents Act, 1988, to be identified as Author of this work.

Series design by Adriana Brioso
Cover image: Former leader of Nationalist Movement Party (MHP) Alparslan Turke, 1980.
(© AA/Anadolu Agency/Getty Images)

All rights reserved. No part of this publication may be reproduced or
transmitted in any form or by any means, electronic or mechanical, including
photocopying, recording, or any information storage or retrieval system,
without prior permission in writing from the publishers.

Bloomsbury Publishing Plc does not have any control over, or responsibility for,
any third-party websites referred to or in this book. All internet addresses given in
this book were correct at the time of going to press. The author and publisher
regret any inconvenience caused if addresses have changed or sites have
ceased to exist, but can accept no responsibility for any such changes.

A catalogue record for this book is available from the British Library.

A catalog record for this book is available from the Library of Congress.

ISBN: HB: 978-0-7556-4647-0
PB: 978-0-7556-4643-2
ePDF: 978-0-7556-4646-3
eBook: 978-0-7556-4645-6

Series: Contemporary Turkey

Typeset by Integra Software Services Pvt. Ltd.

To find out more about our authors and books visit www.bloomsbury.com
and sign up for our newsletters.

CONTENTS

List of illustrations	vi
Acronyms and abbreviations	vii
Introduction	1
Chapter 1 THE STATE AT STAKE	9
Chapter 2 MOVEMENTS IN CONFLICT	33
Chapter 3 THE ACCUMULATION AND CIRCULATION OF RESOURCES	57
Chapter 4 CAPTURING PUBLIC RESOURCES AND POLITICIZING THE STATE	85
Chapter 5 THE SPREAD OF PROTEST MOVEMENTS	107
Chapter 6 THE ESCALATION IN VIOLENCE	121
Chapter 7 THE EFFECTS OF VIOLENCE ON POLITICAL CONTESTS	139
Conclusion	167
Notes	170
Outline chronology of events (1961–1980)	203
Bibliography	209
Index	221

LIST OF ILLUSTRATIONS

Figure

6.1 Number of deaths per month (1 January 1977–12 September 1980)   124

Tables

3.1 Party Revenue and Expenditure between 1975 and 1979 (in TL)   58
6.1 Monthly Average Number of Victims under Each Government   125
6.2 Number of Deaths by Province (1 January 1977–12 September 1980)   130
6.3 Socio-professional Categories of Victims of Fighting   136

ACRONYMS AND ABBREVIATIONS

ADÜTDF	*Avrupa Demokratik Ülkücü Türk Dernekleri Federasyonu*, Democratic Federation of Turkish Ülkücüs Associations in Europe
ADYÖD	*Ankara Demokratik Yüksek Öğrenim Derneği*, Ankara Higher Education Democratic Association
AP	*Adalet Partisi*, Justice Party
AYÖD	*Ankara Yüksek Öğrenim Derneği*, Ankara Higher Education Association
BÜD	*Büyük Ülkü Derneği*, Association of the Great Ideal
CGP	*Cumhuriyetçi Güven Partisi*, Republican Reliance Party
CHP	*Cumhuriyet Halk Partisi*, Republican People's Party
CKMP	*Cumhuriyetçi Köylü Millet Partisi*, Republican Villagers Nation Party
CP	*Cumhuriyetçi Parti*, Republican Party
Dev-Genç	*Devrimci Gençlik Federasyonu*, Federation of Revolutionary Youth
Dev-Sol	*Devrimci Sol*, Revolutionary Left
Dev-Yol	*Devrimci Yol*, Revolutionary Path
DGD	*Devrimci Gençlik Derneği*, Revolutionary Youth Association
DGDF	*Devrimci Gençlik Dernekleri Federasyonu*, Federation of Revolutionary Youth Associations
DİP	*Demokrat İşçi Partisi*, Democratic Labour Party
DİSK	*Devrimci İşçi Sendikaları Konfederasyonu*, Confederation of Revolutionary Trade Unions of Turkey
DÖB	*Devrimci Öğrenci Birliği*, Revolutionary Student Union
DP	*Demokrat Parti*, Democrat Party
ETKO	*Esir Türkleri Kurtarma Ordusu*, Enslaved Turks Liberation Army
FKF	*Fikir Kulüpleri Federasyonu*, Federation of Opinion Clubs
GSB	*Genç Sosyalistler Birliği*, Young Socialist Union
GÜT	*Genç Ülkücüler Teşkilatı*, Ülkücü Youth Organisation
HK	*Halkın Kurtuluşu*, People's Liberation
HY	*Halkın Yolu*, People's Path
İGD	*İlerici Gençlik Derneği*, Progressive Youth Association
İYÖD	*İstanbul Yüksek Öğrenim Derneği*, Istanbul Higher Education Association
İYÖKD	*İstanbul Yüksek Öğrenim Kültür Derneği*, Istanbul Higher Education Cultural Association
MC	*Milliyetçi Cephe*, Nationalist Front
MDD	*Milli Demokratik Devrim*, National Democratic Revolution
MHP	*Milliyetçi Hareket Partisi*, Nationalist Movement Party
MİSK	*Milliyetçi İşçi Sendikaları Konfederasyonu*, Confederation of Nationalist Workers Unions
MLSPB	*Marxist Leninist Silahlı Propaganda Birliği*, Marxist Leninist Armed Propaganda Union
MNP	*Milli Nizam Partisi*, National Order Party

MP	*Millet Partisi*, Nation Party
MSP	*Milli Selâmet Partisi*, National Salvation Party
ODTÜ	*Orta Doğu Teknik Üniversitesi*, Middle East Technical University
Pol-Bir	*Polis Birliği*, Police Union
Pol-Der	*Polis Derneği*, Police Association
SDP	*Sosyalist Devrim Partisi*, Socialist Revolution Party
TEP	*Türkiye Emekçi Partisi*, Labour Party of Turkey
THKO	*Türkiye Halk Kurtuluş Ordusu*, People's Liberation Army of Turkey
THKP-C	*Türkiye Halk Kurtuluş Partisi-Cephesi*, People's Liberation Party-Front of Turkey
TİİKP	*Türkiye İhtilalci İşçi Köylü Partisi*, Revolutionary Workers and Peasants Party of Turkey
TİP	*Türkiye İşçi Partisi*, Workers Party of Turkey
TİT	*Türk İntikam Tugayı*, Turkish Revenge Brigade
TKP	*Türkiye Komünist Partisi*, Turkish Communist Party
TKP-ML/ TİKKO	*Türkiye Komünist Partisi – Marxist Leninist/Türkiye İşçi Köylü Kurtuluş Ordusu*, Communist Party of Turkey – Marxist-Leninist/Workers and Peasants Liberation Army of Turkey
Töb-Der	*Tüm Öğretmenler Birleşme ve Dayanışma Derneği*, Association for Union and Solidarity between Teachers
TÖS	*Tüm Öğretmen Sendikası*, Turkish Teachers Union
TSİP	*Türkiye Sosyalist İşçi Partisi*, Socialist Workers Party of Turkey
Tüm-Der	*Türkiye Memurlar Birleşme ve Dayanışma Derneği*, Association for Union and Solidarity between Officials in Turkey
TÜT	*Türk Ülkücüler Teşkilatı*, Turkish Ülkücüs Organisation
TYO	*Türk Yıldırm Ordusu*, Turkish Thunderbolt Army
ÜGD	*Ülkücü Gençler Derneği*, Ülkücü Youth Association
Ülkü-Bir	*Ülkücü Öğretmenler Birliği Derneği*, Ülkücü Teachers Union Association
Ülkü-Han	*Ülkücü Hanımlar Derneği*, Ülkücü Women Association
Ülkü-Köy	*Ülkücü Köylüler Derneği*, Ülkücü Villagers Association
Ülküm	*Ülkücü Kamu Görevliler ve Memurlar Derneği*, Ülkücü Public Sector Workers and Officials Association
Ülküm-Bir	*Ülkücü Kamu Görevlileri Güçbirliği Derneği*, Public Sector Worker Forces Union Association
ÜOB	*Ülkü Ocakları Birliği*, Union of Ülkü Hearths
ÜOD	*Ülkü Ocakları Derneği*, Association of Ülkü Hearths
ÜYD	*Ülkü Yolu Derneği*, Association of the Ülkü Path
VP	*Vatan Partisi*, Fatherland Party
YTP	*Yeni Türkiye Partisi*, New Turkey Party

INTRODUCTION

The military coup of September 1980 occurred in the wake of five years of ever increasing violence in Turkey, over which time the country had been affected by an unparalleled level of social mobilization. In the run-up to the coup all the social actors concerned described the country's political, economic and social situation as one of generalized chaos.[1] Altercations between militants from extremist left-wing and extremist right-wing organizations were resulting in an increasing number of victims.[2] By 1977 the *Milliyet* newspaper was referring to a 'situation of street warfare'.[3] 'Darkness and anarchy are taking hold everywhere'.[4] The media, together with certain intellectuals and politicians,[5] condemned the reign of anarchy and terror being exerted by radical organizations[6] that were accused of dividing the country into two irreconcilable camps. City neighbourhoods and rural areas were under the territorial control of militias, who acted as local substitutes for the public authorities, or else exploited their collusive relationship with protagonists in official arenas in order to expand their legal and illegal activities. The state was losing control of whole swathes of its territory, which was subjected to the domination of radical armed groups, who alone were able to ensure the inhabitants' security against units from the opposing side.

Assassinations, bombings and gun battles were a daily occurrence in a situation reminiscent of the Weimar Republic in the aftermath of the elections of 14 September 1930, described by Sebastian Haffner as somewhere 'between "peace and stability" and "civil war" (there were no barricades, but every day meaningless and childish brawls and gunfights, attacks on party offices, and regularly also killings)'.[7] Over the summer of 1980 confrontations between antagonistic radical groups were leaving at least twenty people dead across the country as a whole every single day. Civil war seemed inevitable. In 1978 the Nationalist Movement Party (Milliyetçi Hareket Partisi, MHP), the main political organization on the far right, accused the 'communists', supported by the government of the centre-left Republican People's Party (Cumhuriyet Halk Partisi, CHP),[8] of preparing for such an eventuality,[9] notably by establishing strongholds where the forces of law and order were unable to go.[10] Far-left organizations for their part called on people to rise up 'against fascist terror'[11] so that 'the blood of the dead shall not remain on the ground'.[12] In the provinces militarized radical groups threatened and intimidated state officials. In October 1978 the Nationalist Movement, following a tried-and-tested tactic to destabilize the government, called for martial law to be declared.[13] It obtained this on 26 December of the same year after the massacre in the town of Kahramanmaraş, where its own units played an active role, in which 111 people were killed.

Ever since 1974 Turkey had had a string of governments in quick succession.[14] The balance of power in the Turkish parliament had resulted in a series of short-lived, fragile coalition governments. Each handover of power led to the replacement of many of those working for the public authorities, whose staff belonged to rival organizations mobilizing in support of whichever party their members owed their appointment to. As of November 1979 a minority government was running the country, while the state of martial law declared in an increasing number of provinces failed to restore order. In 1980 the system of party political alliances prevented the election of the country's president for several months. Institutional politics was in a state of deadlock. The country was hit by an unprecedented economic crisis and the State, obliged to run up massive debts, turned to international financing bodies on several occasions. With galloping inflation the Turkish lira was repeatedly devalued. But against such a backdrop the adjustment programme drawn up under IMF auspices by the government, and presented on 24 January 1980, did nothing to halt the economic collapse. Inflation and unemployment shot up. In the summer of 1980 Turkey looked like it was on the verge of bankruptcy. The dominant feeling amongst the population was that the country was in chaos and ungovernable.

Interpretations of the Turkish crisis

This Turkish vision of the situation may be found in many literary and academic works on the topic, which present 1975–1980 as a period when the state and political system failed, being unable to rise to the challenge posed by the mobilization of antagonistic radical groups whose clashes were instrumental in bringing about an anarchic, pre-revolutionary situation. This explanatory model, though of seductive simplicity, is highly debatable. It assumes that the resources and positions of the protagonists in the conflict were in some way equal. The state, seen as the arbiter of social interplay, is said to have been temporarily knocked out of play, as violence became an autonomous, generalized mode of interaction. But each of these assertions is open to challenge once we actually look at the activities of the conflicting groups. It is thus necessary to assess the limits of such an explanation and identify which aspects it fails to account for.

The supposed symmetry in actors' positions and resources

The various accounts produced about the period portray the conflicting radical movements as being on an equal footing.[15] It is argued that the country was 'divided in two'[16] and in the grip of terror and anarchy exerted by groups enjoying comparable levels and types of resources, pursuing similar means of action and posing a comparable threat of destabilization to the political and economic system.[17] But observation in fact shows that the protagonists had highly unequal means at their disposal. While the activities of the *ülkücü* action system were coordinated by the MHP,[18] far-left movements were largely uncoordinated and undisciplined. This asymmetry had a major impact on the sort of "trophies" each side set their sights on. The ülkücüs' goals were all primarily national and involved holding key positions in public institutions. Hence the MHP's unexpected participation in the coalition government set up in 1975[19] enabled ülkücü trade unions and associations to expand their influence in state-owned companies and the public sector. Equally, ülkücü sections managed to defy left-wing municipalities thanks to the ülkücüs' collusive relationship with members of decentralized state bodies appointed via the intermediary of the MHP (police officers, court personnel etc.). Far-left organizations, deprived of direct access to state and governmental positions, mobilized around local and sector-specific objectives, such as the shelving of a projected law, the resignation of a university rector, the overturning of dismissal procedures in a publicly owned company and so on. But despite this marked asymmetry in the means and resources the movements could mobilize, tilted heavily in the ülkücüs' favour, the commemorative and academic literature has conjured up a far left able to seize power by revolution or by calling a general strike.[20] This dominant account tends to grant legitimacy to the military intervention of 12 September 1980 by presenting the coup as a necessary evil to end the anarchy prevailing in the country.[21] And so the only way to visit afresh the crisis Turkey went through in the second half of the 1970s is to leave this account to one side.

The supposed autonomization of violence

The second postulate put forward in the literature is that violence became autonomous. It is said that the radical movements built up their structures in step with the escalation and propagation of their violent activities, with state institutions being powerless to do anything to halt this. However, and contrary to a widespread belief, the intensity, rhythm and places where these violent activities were carried out tended to follow the fluctuating balance of political power, shifting with the varying positions held by each protagonist. Analysis of these organizations' violent practices therefore needs to be embedded within broader analysis of the entire range of tactical activities deployed by the rival groups. The shift to violent forms of action, ranging from intimidation to mass massacre, depended on the positions of the various groups mobilized, but recourse to such practices brought about a shift in the balance of power within any given sector (politics, trade unionism, associations, the economy etc.) and thus offered a way of accumulating a new set of resources inaccessible via conventional means. Thus territorial control, won by ülkücü militia and activists making intermittent use of violence in local arenas, was used by the MHP as a bargaining chip in its negotiations with governments, threatening a generalized conflagration if it failed to obtain the positions it was demanding in the apparatus of state.

The increasingly widespread use of violence is in fact revelatory of a change in the rules for winning access to resources.[22] This work therefore focuses on the ways in which the mobilization of radical groups was instrumental in modifying the rules governing contests played out in political and state arenas. This implies conducting a comparative sociology of state, party political and protest milieus, and leaving to one side the postulates generally put forward in the sociology and history of the Turkish state.

The state supposedly knocked out of play

The Turkish state is generally described as an autonomous body distinct from Turkish society.[23] It is said to dominate social relations and be endowed with rational-legal administrative control enabling it to exert its monopoly over physical and symbolic violence across its territory and to impose order and regulations on an amorphous, non-organized society.[24] In this account the rationalized functioning of public institutions in Turkey is attributable to the legal codes and regulations borrowed from European states. Mustafa Kemal is said to have 'invented modern Turkey'[25] by importing a Western model of government and building a nation-state[26] on the 'ruins' of the Ottoman Empire.[27] The endurance of the Republican state is thus said to be linked to the stability of the autonomous corps of administrative personnel standing outside social and political conflicts, as well as to the regular intervention of the army to right any disruptions to the equilibrium of state.[28] But such an analysis, in which the crisis of the second half of the 1970s is presented as a direct consequence of the defeat or failure of the state, fails to provide any convincing explanatory model. The state, confronted with radical mobilization and the uptake of physical violence within the repertoire of action, was no longer able to assume its 'role' as arbitrator or its 'function' as the interlocutor for social forces. This leads to the image of an 'outsider' state, a *tertius gaudens*[29] temporarily knocked out of the contest. The 1975–1980 sequence of events is thus presented as a hiatus, brought to a close by the military intervention of 12 September 1980, and the concomitant re-establishment of the monopoly over the legitimate exercise of physical and symbolic constraint across most of the country. It is said that since this crisis was exceptional, the mechanisms at work simply cannot be identified.

Such a conception also perpetuates the vision of a state field comprised of a unitary body acting in accordance with interests and rationales external to those of social forces. But what we actually see on looking at the interaction between the two spheres of society and State in Turkey fails to correspond to any such view. Public institutions during the 1970s were the privileged locus for rivalry between the antagonistic radical movements, as well as the site for conflictual interactions between officials who politicized their professional practices so as to lend their support to the party whose electoral victory would ensure they retained their position.[30] The state was thus central, both as a locus for antagonistic mobilizations and as a stake. And yet, at the same time, it was overwhelmed in its monopoly of legitimate physical violence for it was unable to oppose the militarized sections of the conflicting movements. The Turkish people understood this and placed themselves in the hands of radical organizations to whom they looked to ensure their protection and to redistribute public resources to their benefit.

If we are to understand the set-up within Turkey during the second part of the 1970s, then we need to place the state at the heart of our analysis of social and political conflict and see it as the stake and arena for mobilizations, not as an actor in some way distinct from them. The state was never out of play between 1975 and 1980. Quite the contrary, in fact, for its institutions, together with the practices, beliefs and representations of their members and users, were absolutely central to the processes constituting the crisis. It operated at the heart of the contest, and the resources and positions it offered or claimed to control formed the stakes over which antagonistic mobilizations fought – notably because they represented the sole means of access to most social, economic and political resources, at least up until the economic liberalization of the early 1980s.

Questions and hypotheses

An analysis of the processes at work in Turkey during the second half of the 1970s will enable us not only to solve a historical enigma but also to address a larger theoretical problem. I hope that the attempt to understand the reasons why violence occupied an ever larger place within the Turkish political field over this period will contribute to the analysis of situations of prolonged political crisis in which the state loses its capacity to exercise its monopoly over legitimate violence. To this end I will be testing a series of hypotheses, where the links between them will help put forward a global model explaining the Turkish crisis. The first of these hypotheses is that mobilizations and state dynamics actually worked in tandem to trigger the processes driving the crisis.

Since the early years of the Republic, the ruling parties had appropriated state resources and positions that they could redistribute in the form of public-sector jobs, contracts, benefits and allowances, and policy programmes benefiting their social and economic partners. This work analyses how public resources were actually captured in practice and, in the specific context of the 1970s that is of interest here, examines how new collective actors (the ülkücü organizations and to a lesser extent the far-left movements) adopted the routine practices of overlap and accumulation traditionally implemented by the governing parties.

The second hypothesis is that the resources to which the ülkücüs had access not only gave them an advantage in the contest opposing them to their rivals but also was a way of influencing the course taken by the contest. The Nationalist Movement could draw on a high degree of coordination between its sector-specific organizations, on the control the MHP exerted over its allied organizations (which it virtually ran), not to mention its significant funding capacities stemming from its structure and from its involvement in several governments between 1975 and 1978. Far-left organizations, on the other hand, were divided, curbing the strategic potential of the mobilized groups and preventing the use of cumulative national or multi-sector tactics.

On gaining access to the central institutions of state the ülkücüs further benefited from their ability to influence the course of the contest. Once in government, the MHP set up ülkücü organizations in all the public institutions where it was able to interfere in appointment proceedings. In public institutions affiliated with ministries run by the MHP, any personnel who refused to join would find themselves marginalized.[31] This drive to extend its influence in public institutions resulted in an increasing number of sites where it was in confrontation with left-wing and far-left organizations, as well as in the division of realms of institutional rivalry into two polar opposites. The ideological conflict systematically transpired in conflicts of interests, the defence of which required coordination across different sectors. Within this context the Nationalist Movement was able to draw on its position within multiple fields and the strong degree of coordination between its component parts in order to win the upper hand over its rivals in each sector-specific conflict. The practices that the Nationalist Movement used to capture state resources thus meant it was able to strongly influence how and when it traded blows with extremist left-wing organizations, being able to determine both the rhythm of this encounter and the shape the conflict took.

The actions of the two radical movements together with their mobilizations within the state politicized the practices of government officials, hence – and this is the third hypothesis – bringing about the de-objectification of state institutions, via which the social relationships within these institutions lost 'their externality, their impersonality, and their automatically being perceived as such'.[32] In certain state-run educational establishments ülkücü students were certain to be awarded their diplomas, whilst in others the word 'cheating' would be systematically written across their exam scripts. Policemen in charge of restoring order in the event of altercations between rival organizations took sides instead. Court personnel interceded in favour of defendants of similar political sympathy, and certain hospitals would only tend to those who belonged to one or other of the two movements. Members within a given institution would insult each other, fight and use their skills to marginalize those from the adverse association. Each public institution became a realm for competition between coalitions based on different interests, representations and practices. Within this context the state served more as an arena for confrontation than as a network to consolidate public authority, and the institutions, transformed into the strongholds of one camp or the other, ended up working against each other.

This leads to the hypothesis that it was the activities of radical groups *within* the state which led to the intensification and propagation of physical violence, clearly showing changes in the rules governing the contests played out in political and state arenas. Violence became a routine form of political action used to accumulate resources. The forces of law and order did not have the means to restore security and were unable to cope. In addition to this they were extensively infiltrated by radicals, who then provided activists with special privileges and various ways of getting around rules. There were an increasing number of armed conflicts in the streets, and students fought on a daily basis. There were armed units specializing in intimidation and elimination operating at various scales, that of the district, town, province or country as a whole. In Central Anatolia militias served the local interests of one or the other of the conflicting groups by imposing political homogeneity within neighbourhoods, intervening in economic flows and obliging inhabitants to take part in their activities. Entire sectors were wrested free of state authority and controlled by armed militants. Violent action became a lever to accumulate resources and instruments for wielding power. It flourished in the interstices generated by the state's shortcomings. But it did not occur *in spite of* the state, for violence became entrenched via contacts between groups and the apparatus of state. Later on we shall see how the forms, rhythms and intensity of violence were associated with the balance of power between antagonistic coalition networks operating at different levels of public action. The resources acquired by winning national office made up for a lack of local resources. Violence thus peaked in zones where the Nationalist Movement was in the political minority at precisely those times when it was able to draw on the support of the administration.

It is thus impossible to argue that there was any systematic link between marginality and the recourse to violence. Most of the time it was when the MHP was able to make public-sector appointments that local ülkücü sections turned to violence, as the support they could draw on from representatives of the Nationalist Movement working in decentralized state bodies enabled them to go head-to-head with municipal authorities. And so what may be observed is a continuum running from violent activities to more conventional ones. The legal and the illegal, the state and the criminal became entangled and caught up with one another, modifying the balance of power in the political, trade union and economic spheres. Locally, the action of militias sometimes led to the departure of populations known to lend their electoral support to the opposing camp – this is what happened, for instance, in the towns of Kahramanmaraş, Çorum and Malatya, where ülkücü militias attacked Alevi populations. Units deployed in most of the cities around the country saw to it that local leaders from opposing organizations were eliminated. Attacks and blind shootings sought to intimidate the opposing camp and break up their mobilization in places where they assembled and were in a position of force, such as cafés, coffeehouses, bookstores, party and association premises or university buildings and halls of residence. Violence could also be part of a larger tactic to win access to resources. The high degree of coordination within the Nationalist Movement meant the MHP was able to wield the threat of its militias in its negotiations with the political authorities.[33] Thus when the Justice Party (Adalet Partisi, AP) formed a minority government in November 1979, the MHP negotiated positions within the apparatus of state in exchange for its conditional parliamentary support – and it would seem that the AP accepted in order to avoid a wave of violence similar to that which had hit the previous government on taking office. Legal and peaceful activities to accumulate resources and gain access to power thus combined with illegal and armed ones, where these mutually reinforced one another and expanded the tactical opportunities available to the actors involved.

Plan of the book

The first chapter analyses the historicity of the practices of overlap and accumulation, stretching back to the Ottoman Empire, and implemented by coalitions of actors seeking to penetrate the apparatus of state, so as to flourish and draw on its resources in order to entrench their positions of domination. It examines the interactions going to make up the state field in Turkey and identifies the mechanisms of co-optation, collusion, alliance and circumvention that contradict the 'traditional' vision of the Turkish state as a unified body able to impose its will. It shows how transformations to Turkish society and its political economy in the 1960s and 1970s resulted in a redistribution of opportunities to win access to resources, providing new actors with the possibility of taking part in these practices of overlap and accumulation against the backdrop of institutional gridlock and parliamentary paralysis.

The second chapter compares the emergence and development of the ülkücü and far-left movements. This comparative approach is pursued in the third chapter, which examines the types and levels of social, political and economic resources enjoyed by the two movements. Observation of power relationships and of the modes of accumulation, circulation and allocation of resources brings out the inner workings characterizing the pronounced asymmetry that favoured the Nationalist Movement in the contests opposing it to far-left organizations, as well as the ways in which this difference influenced the types of activities deployed by each protagonist to capture public resources.

The fourth chapter describes how the activities used by the conflicting movements to capture public resources affected how the contest actually functioned. The MHP's participation in government provided the Nationalist Movement with the opportunity to intervene in public-sector recruitment processes and thereby reinforce its organization, but whenever far-left groups wanted to influence the distribution of public resources, they could only draw on their social movement and its operating in lieu of local institutions (be this negotiated substitution or else taken by force). It is argued that the confrontation between these tactics to access resources led to the de-objectification of public institutions, where this may be seen in the politicization of the practices of their members and the perceptions users had of them.

Chapter 5 looks at the effects of tactical ploys implemented by the ülkücüs working within the state to diversify the sites they held. The increasing number of ülkücü mobilizations within state arenas forced the far-left groups into a series of adjustments, leading to the homogenization of their demands, agendas and forms of mobilization. The activities implemented by the Nationalist Movement within public institutions would thus appear to have exerted a decisive influence on the way rules, practices and representations became increasingly less sector-specific.

Chapter 6 shows how violence became a mode of political action in Turkey during the late 1970s and a means to accumulate resources, before the seventh and final chapter turns to an examination of how the contests being played out within political and state arenas were transformed by the escalation and generalization of violence, up until the coup of 12 September 1980.

Chapter 1

THE STATE AT STAKE

The traditional picture of the Turkish state as an autonomous and unified body with the means to impose its order on a non-organized society does not stand up to analysis. The categories of the 'centre' and the 'periphery' do not in fact correspond to anything tangible, and the externality certain historians view as characteristic of the relationship between state and society turns out to be largely overstated. In addition to this, any such picture tends, firstly, to ignore the paltry institutionalization of state roles and, secondly, to sweep to one side the mechanisms of devolution and discontinuity that have repeatedly surfaced in the history of the configurations of the state in Turkey. At any one time the chances are that its officials constitute but the visible part of a larger corps, and so we need to apprehend the relationships public institutions and their personnel have with economic and social elites in terms of interdependencies, alliances and means of circumvention – and this at all levels throughout the administration.

So what is needed is to pay greater attention to the interactions between the protagonists in official arenas and the individuals, groups and institutions making up their environment, that is to say study the retroaction of the populations' initiatives on the state just as much as the state's action on its populations.[1] When we do so what we see is far removed from the image of some unified, dominant body standing apart from society, and we may rather observe the common interests and multiple positions turning state arenas into a set of positions to be conquered, where these positions make it possible to accumulate resources that can then be converted in other realms. The Turkish state has been particularly 'permeable' to sociopolitical divisions and external interests. A large number of individual and collective actors (tribal leaders, provincial notables, political parties and so on) – whilst only occasionally penetrating the structures of state – have maintained lasting relationships with it and have needed to accommodate its political and administrative ramifications.[2] This chapter examines how ever since the days of Empire these actors have managed to continually adapt to reconfigurations within the state. Instead of being 'peripheries' constituted in opposition to or in spite of the state, they have learnt how to 'play with' the situation, entering into agreements with its representatives (and on occasions opposing them), for maintaining a relationship with the state offers guaranteed access to a large range of resources. They are in no way 'passive objects of a process of dependency'.[3]

This chapter starts by analysing the historical regularity with which dominant social actors have used practices designed to capture public resources. It is impossible to understand the forms taken by these practices of accumulation in the 1970s unless their historicity is entered into the equation. It then examines the social and economic transformations affecting the country since the early 1960s, as well as the impact these had on the means used to capture and redistribute resources. The economic crisis that hit Turkey in the second half of the 1970s diminished state resources, whilst, in parallel to this, the traditional collusion between established elites and protagonists in official arenas was swept away under the joint effects of the urbanization of society, the proletarianization of the economy and the expansion of markets. These transformations impacted on the effectiveness of delegating social control – the means by which the state has historically ensured its legitimacy in the provinces. Finally we shall see how the means of coercion available to the state were insufficient in this context for it to repress social conflict effectively, opening up new scope for manoeuvre by the mobilized radical movements.

The state's limited autonomy

Though public arenas and private interests have been visibly interwoven ever since the Empire, the protagonists, means deployed and paths taken have changed continually depending upon the period and system of government.

The interpenetration of the state and social spheres

Penetration of the Ottoman provincial system of state Suraiya Faroqhi, in her studies of 'political initiatives' by social groups in the sixteenth-century and seventeenth-century Ottoman Empire, shows that the Sultan's subjects, far from passively undergoing the positions adopted by the Porte,[4] developed 'political initiatives' (resistance, circumvention, agreements and so on) intended to expand their scope for manoeuvre. Michael Meeker argues that, from the second half of the eighteenth century onwards, state representatives came to arrangements with local elites and especially the Aghas, landowners with sufficient resources to protect themselves from central government interference and win recognition of their hegemony. The governors sent by the central state[5] had no choice if they were to maintain order and exert even indirect control over the raising of taxes: either they passed via the intermediary of Aghas or else they entered into conflict with them. On occasions Aghas exerted almost total sovereignty over a territory (such as a valley), collecting taxes, amassing troops and arresting those who infringed the law.[6] In the early nineteenth century many had armed troops and the wherewithal to negotiate positions in the provincial administration of the Empire.[7]

In 1839 a phase of state centralization started, one of the objectives of which was 'to extend central government control to all aspects of Ottoman life in the provinces'.[8] Up until the late nineteenth century this reorganization (*tanzimat*) led to an increase in bureaucratic regulation. Tax reform was one of the main issues of the tanzimat. Tax farms were abolished, and fiscal rents were collected by governors or palace representatives.[9] In 1864 the law on the provinces bolstered the spheres of competence of provincial governors.[10] But these measures had little effect on the scope for manoeuvre available to local notables. Reşat Kasaba[11] sees the tanzimat as a means for state institutions to come to accommodations, notably with regard to non-Muslim social groups living in port towns, which were undergoing rapid economic expansion and building up links with Europe. He argues that state representatives, wishing to preserve their authority, adapted to the demands put forward by these groups, and that this may be seen in the way they drew up and devised these reforms. Thus notables often managed to benefit from the new bureaucratic regulations introduced by the tanzimat, becoming indispensable for obtaining certain official certificates – such as passports, marriage certificates, certificates to build a mosque or place of business and property deeds – and they were quite prepared to sell their services for exorbitant prices. In addition to this, the reforms did not prevent officials from maintaining their alliances with local elites. Meeker describes how in the mid-nineteenth century numerous foreign and palace representatives were surprised on discovering that local notables in the province of Trabzon were able to manipulate and even subvert the rules and decisions taken by the central and provincial administration.[12]

But this situation is not that surprising if we consider that state officials in the provinces did not have the troops needed to maintain order or confront the Aghas' armed men. Carrying out the most elementary functions of provincial government involved having people in a position to raise armed troops, and the Aghas, irrespective of whether they were officially appointed or not, often held positions in the local military hierarchy. But local notables also had to ensure they had contacts in the provincial administration, together with its backing in order to safeguard their positions, especially their economic position. As the Ottoman state extended its control over its provinces, they went on to 'negotiate and oversee the incorporation of lands within the bosom of the state'[13] whilst deploying tactics to penetrate the provincial state system. Thus local notables and officials, rather than hailing from two distinct political systems, actually formed the two sides of a single governmental structure, up until the proclamation of the Republic in 1923.[14]

The non-differentiation between party and state rationales under the single-party regime

The proclamation of the Turkish Republic in 1923 marked a new phase in the reforms to the Ottoman administration which had been in progress since 1839, not some clean break.[15] Prior even to its advent purges had been conducted against the 'dual loyalty' of former Ottoman bureaucrats.[16] On 1 October 1922, the Turkish Great National Assembly passed a law temporarily suspending all public-sector administrative staff. Each minister was able to select his personnel from amongst former imperial officials and new bureaucrats accredited by the Kemalist authorities.[17] At the CHP convention in 1927 it was decided that the appointment of officials in charge of social, political and economic affairs and cultural agencies, as well as village mayors (*muhtar*), was to be conducted with the agreement of party inspectors (*müfettiş*). Party personnel thus became intertwined with the civilian bureaucracy.[18] As of 1936 provincial governors were appointed to head the party's provincial sections.[19] Holding a position in public administration continued to offer a way to accumulate resources at all levels of the administration. In addition to having secure employment, public officials were comparatively well paid and, if they ran into difficulty, their salaries were topped up with gifts of coal, clothing, sugar, fat and rice. 'For a family or an individual to slip back from ruling group status, however humble, to peasant status, however high, [was] regarded as disaster, and all possible measures [were] taken to avoid it.'[20] The state was prized for everything it could offer the families constituting the ruling group. Hence members of parliament frequently resigned in order to become judges, prosecutors, provincial governors, sub-governors or else to run state monopolies. In the district of Of, in the province of Trabzon, family clans exerted strong control over their respective communities and lands. During the final decades of the Ottoman Empire, two rival families had laid hold of the administrative positions open to local elites. When Meeker arrived in the province in the 1960s, the opposition between them no longer took the form of agreements with local administrators or raising men at arms but was rather played out by lining up behind the banners of national political parties and relying on family members to control local electoral, associative and administrative posts.[21] By adopting the rules of the Republic in this way they had retained their control over the public institutions and political organizations in the two main towns in the district. Better still, the highly centralized nature of the new regime, in conjunction with its increasing number of political and administrative positions, opened up possibilities for establishing holds in the central institutions of state. Cemil Koçak has shown that local notables were one of the main groups to win seats in parliament during the single-party period: 'Generally, the economically and socially powerful people in the region would become parliamentarians. ... Especially in areas of the country where a feudal agricultural structure prevailed, wealthy landowners were consistently sitting in Parliament as MPs.'[22]

How practices to capture public resources continued under the multi-party regime

There is nothing surprising about party appropriation of state resources under a single-party regime. But these practices did not come to an end in 1945 when a multi-party system was introduced or with the first change in government when the Democrat Party (Demokrat Parti, DP) took office in 1950. Instead it modified them. Thus when the DP took power in 1950, CHP officials were fired and the administration taken under the control of the government. Each new government, in order to avoid having to suffer from the actions of officials from the ranks of the parties now in opposition, distributed the public offices it controlled to its supporters.²³ In Ankara the state would appear to have been permeable to the political forces that were now in government, and it was exposed to tactics deployed by political parties to instrumentalize it and subject it to their own interests. Since the parties in power controlled appointments and promotions, they had an effective way of recompensing their supporters, as well as securing the backing of the administration now won over to their cause. Although access to public administration jobs was governed by law, and had been opened up as of the early years of the Republic (on the basis of a battery of exams and competitions), a veritable spoil system emerged which became institutionalized despite being illegal. Against the backdrop of an economic policy seeking to replace imports (by creating large public enterprises) and to steer economic activity (via five-year plans between 1962 and 1977), controlling state institutions became a central if illegal strategy to socially entrench political parties.

Up until the victory of the DP in the 1950 elections, the CHP operated uncontested to infiltrate the machinery of state, selecting and controlling officials at all levels of the administrative hierarchy. These practices of party political governance of public administration continued after 1950, though they became less visible. One of the first tasks of the Democrat government was to ensure that the bureaucratic elite did not have the means to hinder its action.²⁴ To this end it took a series of steps guaranteeing it could influence the training and careers of public administration cadres. Thus law 6185 passed in 1953 curbed the budgetary autonomy of universities and made it possible to fire university staff who had published texts of a political nature. Law 6422, which came into effect on 25 June 1954, provided a means of purging them, introducing obligatory retirement (at the government's request) for university staff who had effected twenty-five years of service. Lastly, law 6435, also passed in 1954, increased state control over its administrative personnel, since all government employees could henceforth be stripped of the post by the authority which had appointed them without any course for appeal. Law 6435 also authorised the Ministry of Education to suspend university professors 'if that is deemed necessary'.²⁵ The government made excessive use of these legal measures. New universities were set up where Democrats appointed those won over to their cause. This was the case at the Middle East Technical University (ODTÜ), which was founded in 1956 and soon became known as the 'Democrats' University'. More generally, the DP strove to weaken sectors that were likely to oppose its actions by setting up duplicate structures staffed by its supporters and operating alongside hostile administrations.

The coup on 27 May 1960 led to the DP being shut down and the physical or political elimination of its leaders. The return to civilian rule in 1961 did not, however, put an end to the practices of party control of the administration.²⁶ The case of Turhan Kaya, the sub-governor of the district of Çamlıdere in Ankara Province, is illustrative of how these practices in fact continued. In June 1963, on being informed that he was to be transferred by the new CHP-led coalition government to a district in the province of Kahramanmaraş, he refused the new position. Over the course of several weeks his resignation provided the Turkish nationalist press with an opportunity to wage a campaign against the political pressures brought to bear on the administration.[27] Between 1963 and 1980 the number of officials in public administration rose from 450,000 to 1,400,000.[28] An increasing number of candidates were attracted by this status despite inflation causing a rapid drop in their purchasing power.[29] İlkay Sunar argues that this drop led to a corresponding drop in the prestige of public administration positions and incited officials to indulge in fraudulent practices such as taking bribes.[30] Kalaycıoğlu makes a similar observation, speaking of a system in which meritocracy became an exception.[31]

Metin Heper suggests that the coalition governments which came to power after the coup of 12 March 1971 reshuffled the public administration to an extent that was unparalleled in the history of the Republic.[32] Party members from the series of government coalitions that succeeded one another up until 1980 appointed their supporters to government agencies and administrative institutions.[33] They thereby introduced party political rules and means of assessment. These strategies to place party cadres in public office (*kadrolaşma*) introduced lines of political division within the institutions of state and were a factor in their politicization. The national press for that matter regularly referred to government purges and public administration appointments. On 5 January 1978, the CHP took office after having won the support of a handful of MPs who had hitherto supported the Nationalist Front government.[34] On 3 February, the *Milliyet* newspaper announced a first wave of transfers of forty provincial governors,[35] as well as the removal of the Istanbul chief of police who had been appointed by the previous government.[36] A few days later the governor of Istanbul and the head of General Directorate of Security were also replaced.[37] On 13 February, twenty-six governors were transferred to the central governors' office – to which unassigned governors were attached – while seventeen others previously posted there were now appointed to the provinces.[38] In July 1978, the CHP government laid hold of the police hierarchy, with a series of transfers and appointments of commissioners, chief commissioners, heads of provincial Police Directorates and cadres working in various services in the largest towns around the country.[39] Thirty-eight sub-governors were transferred,[40] and over 11,000 contract teachers, recruited during the three years when the previous coalition government had been in office, were fired from their posts in primary schools.[41] On 12 November 1979, Süleyman Demirel and the Justice Party formed a minority government. Demirel rapidly proceeded to make numerous public administration appointments, and 220 sub-governors were replaced as soon as he arrived in power.[42]

The idea here is not to suggest that all positions in the administration were commandeered by the ruling parties, nor that there were no mechanisms intended to guarantee a minimum degree of autonomy within the public sector. The situations differ here from one part of it to another. The procedures to control certain administrations and set them apart (such as the army or diplomatic corps), especially with regard to recruitment, stand in sharp contrast to the very extensive opening up of other institutions which were thus less autonomous (such as the Directorate of Security, the Ministry of Customs and Monopolies, the Ministry of Health and so on). But all the sources consulted confirm that practices to capture public resources continued. Positions of power continued to act as positions to accumulate resources, via which their beneficiaries implemented tactics to appropriate entire sectors of the public sector and other state resources, which up until 1980 owned most of the means of production and exchange.

Subcontracting out the maintenance of law and order

The image of the Turkish state as standing apart from its environment and imposing its order on society does not stand up to scrutiny of the bargaining between state officials and social groups (tribal chieftains, elites of local notables, political parties and so on). Observation of the means used to maintain order and to exert legitimate violence reveal collusion between official protagonists and private actors from various backgrounds (landowners, tribal chieftains, bandits, criminals and mafia networks). The fact that the state handed over its function of maintaining order is suggestive of a state with little means of coercion, an image far removed from that of one that is omnipresent. The forms taken by this delegation of its functions and the beneficiaries differ from one time and place to another, but the handing over the exercise of physical violence is a historically continuous fact.

The Ottoman and Turkish states, rather than eliminating the more subversive elements operating within their territory, often preferred to incorporate them within their structures. Karen Barkey has shown that as of the early seventeenth century the consolidation of state control was less a matter of repression than of making deals with the 'bandits'.[43] The state used bandits operating in rural regions (the *efe* or *eşkıya*) and in towns (the *kabadayı*), either acting individually or in bands, in order to maintain order and protect the population.[44] Rather than endeavouring to wipe them out, local and provincial authorities progressively entrusted them with certain functions in administration and in maintaining order. According to Bilginer, some were employed by officials as informers or as undercover agents in the Porte (especially in intellectual movements during the reign of Abdülhamid II).[45] Up until the creation of the Ottoman police in the second half of the nineteenth century, they worked to maintain order in the towns of the Empire and exerted control over the urban territories, before then either being incorporated into the new police structures or else eliminated.

In the Kurdish regions the states made use of a different type of actor. In the late nineteenth century Sultan Abdülhamid set up 'tribal regiments'[46] – the Hamidiye – 'thereby transforming the Kurdish tribes into allies of the State',[47] conferring certain of his prerogatives on them. In so doing the Sultan had numerous objectives: 'ensuring border security against the Russians, reinforcing the tribes and Aghas against the *eşraf* and *ayân* (urban circles of notables), containing the Armenian nationalists, and accelerating the integration of the Kurds (and Arabs) into the Empire in the name of Muslim solidarity'.[48] Gilles Dorronsoro reckons that, depending upon the period, the Hamidiye corps numbered between 30,000 and 60,000 men at arms. Despite their alliance with the state, these regiments drew most of their resources from their predatory activities (against shopkeepers, Armenians, urban populations and so on),[49] which were sometimes so extensive 'as to considerably disrupt economic mechanisms' within the region.[50] This delegation of the state's functions was used once again during the 1980s in the south-east of the country when the war with the PKK was raging (Partiya Karkerên Kurdistan, the Kurdistan Workers' Party). As of 1987 village militias were set up in the Kurdish regions in order to support the counter-insurrection strategy being conducted against the PKK. These *geçici köy korucuları* (temporary village guards) were placed under the authority of the minister for the interior, received payment and were provided with arms and uniforms.[51] Unlike the Hamidiye they were civilian organizations composed of volunteers, whose members were on the state payroll.[52] These militias were seconded by the *gönüllü korucu* (voluntary village guards) 'made up of unpaid volunteers affected to the passive defence of the village, [which could] be set up by the municipal council with the prior agreement of the sub-governor (*kaymakam*)'.[53] The total number of *korucu* in 2005 is reckoned to have been 89,000 men at arms.[54]

These arrangements between state officials and civilians may be observed throughout the country and dating back to the last years of the Empire at the least. When the Committee of Union and Progress came to power in 1908, it set up a secret organization – Teşkilat-i Mahsusa – placed under the direct authority of the war minister, Enver Pacha, and operating as an intelligence service for the regime.[55] Philip Stoddard suggests that whilst the upper echelons were comprised of army officers, the lower echelons were full of doctors, intellectuals, engineers and journalists who traded their services against payment,[56] alongside whom were a large number of criminals and outlaws from the minorities making up the Empire and whose skills and knowledge of the 'milieu' were of interest to the regime. According to Stoddard, the organization had up to 30,000 members during the First World War. It was officially shut down in 1918 with the collapse of the Union and Progress government, but its activities continued during the early years of the Republic. The same type of collusive relationship may be observed after the Second World War. For instance, the 'special war division' (Özel Harp Dairesi)[57] – the stay-behind unit of the Gladio network established by NATO to counter communist penetration of Western bloc countries – drew on civilian organizations to develop its activities. Certain authors thus state that Özel Harp Dairesi worked in collaboration with militias close to the MHP in order to eradicate the most radical left-wing groups in the 1970s.[58]

Thus the subcontracting out of the maintenance of order to actors who were on paper not part of the state did not come to an end with the proclamation of the Republic. These collusions and collaborative agreements continued to exist in the 1970s and up until the 1980 coup, linking certain sectors of the state to militias from the Nationalist Movement. Élise Massicard's study of the 'gangs in uniform' of the 1990s shows how 'security institutions used militia men and reconverted right-wing activists as their armed wing to carry out underhand operations in the "special war" conducted against the PKK. In exchange they were remunerated with rigged public contracts and enjoyed legal protection – that only officials could provide them with – as well as logistical backup'.[59] Massicard identifies a series of collusive links stretching back to 1970, and regularly updated and reinforced, between institutional, political and criminal circles. Within these collusive relationships know-how about violence was exchanged against social resources (such as immunity and state protection) provided by institutional actors, as well as economic resources, leading to the development of criminal activities.[60]

Throughout the history of Republican Turkey, there have been visible collusive relationships linking representatives from official state arenas to individuals and groups external to them. These have taken on various specific forms and involved different actors depending upon the period, context and goals of those involved. The rapid overview sketched out here shows the many mechanisms used in delegating the monopoly over legitimate physical violence, after which the actors involved were sometimes integrated within state arenas or else eliminated in the wake of changes in alliance. This picture builds up a convincing case for the historicity of the porous frontiers of the Turkish state. It also sheds light on how the state depended on these agreements to maintain its control over certain populations and certain parts of its territory.

Socio-economic transformations (1960–1980)

The socio-economic transformations affecting Turkey in the early 1960s upset the old balances which had enabled the state to impose itself 'as a skilful arbitrator able to negotiate promotion and coercion and, above all, to accommodate the complexity and multiplicity of the Anatolian provinces'.[61] The country's rapid urbanization went hand-in-hand with the proletarianization of its economy,[62] encouraged by the proactive policy to replace imports implemented by various governments. These changes modified the distribution of resources, meaning that collusive relationships that had previously granted the state legitimacy over its territory now fell into obsolescence. The ability of the public authorities to negotiate social control and coercion with its 'traditional' interlocutors was gradually imperilled, and the capacities even of these interlocutors diminished as the local economy underwent transformation. What we are now going to try to understand is how the economic and social transformations affecting the country encouraged the emergence of new actors capable of contesting the position of the traditional elites (local notables, the 'historical' party political elites and so on).

Economic performance and orientation

The Kemalist's adoption of economic dirigisme Whilst the Ottoman Empire's economic policy had been characterized throughout the nineteenth century by its openness to foreign capital, the 'Kemalist's development strategy'[63] discouraged foreign trade and investment. Commercial activities had historically been largely carried out by non-Turkish populations, who acted as the machinery for the penetration of the Empire by European capital. Henceforth the state sought to take control of virtually all means of production and exchange. As of 1923 economic growth became a priority, in accordance with the principle of self-sufficiency,[64] and the non-Turkish groups gradually lost their economic positions. The national reconstruction programme promoted the setting up of banks and credit institutions to finance economic development. The Agricultural Bank, founded in 1899, was expanded and strengthened to provide farmers with loans and technical support, the İş-Bankası was set up in 1924 to organize and support private companies and the Industrial and Mining Bank of Turkey was established in 1925 to finance and manage public industrial establishments.[65] The founding of the Sumerbank in 1933 was a first step towards state capitalism, conceived of as a means to respond to the global economic crisis.[66] The new bank financed and controlled industrial companies set up under the first five-year plan (covering the period 1934–1939), whilst others saw to the development of mining activities and energy production. Five-year plans and public investment were the favoured instruments for igniting economic growth.[67] A national bourgeoisie emerged who profited from this virtual nationalization of the economy, obtaining market monopolies via the creation of public companies, exclusive import licences, very lucrative contracts to subcontract state construction projects and loans from the public banking sector on very favourable terms.[68].

The nationalization of the economy came to a halt during the 1950s. The Democrat Party was now in power, and it promoted liberal measures, transferring public company assets to private capital. Bilateral agreements were signed with European countries and the United States, and international capital injected into the economy. In parallel to this, the government set up a vast agricultural support programme (based on modernization, subsidies etc.), the aim of which was to boost farm productivity in order to finance the import of manufactured consumer goods by exporting agricultural produce.[69] However, and contrary to a widely held idea, the Democrats did not liberalize the economy left, right and centre, since it also set up public companies in the manufacturing, transport, irrigation and mining sectors to support production. During the second half of the 1950s the average annual growth rate in industrial output stood at 4.3 per cent, whilst that for agriculture reached 1.8 per cent.[70]

Domestic savings to replace imports (1962–1977) Up until the second half of the 1970s the growth of the Turkish economy was supported by the industrialization of the country. Three Five-Year Plans (1963–1967, 1968–1972 and 1973–1977)[71] were implemented in succession to direct and encourage activity. The average annual growth rate reached 6.4 per cent under the first plan, 6.7 per cent under the second and 7.2 per cent under the third.[72] Whilst the average annual growth rate for agriculture stood at 3.3 per cent up until 1977, that for manufacturing industry was over 10 per cent.[73] The overt protectionism of economic policy was accompanied by tax relief and cheap credit.[74] Public companies provided investment in infrastructure and useful intermediary goods (such as steel, aluminium and petrochemicals) at below cost price.[75] The Turkish economy was restructured around the industrial sector, which absorbed the majority of investment, followed by the construction sector, transport and communications.[76] Agricultural output's share of GDP dropped from 38.4 per cent in 1962 to 23.3 per cent in 1977, whilst that of the industrial sector grew from 22.3 per cent to 31.5

per cent. Over the same period the proportion of the working population in the agricultural sector dropped from 77 per cent to 61.8 per cent, that in the industrial sector rose from 7.2 per cent to 11 per cent and that in the service sector jumped from 15.1 per cent to 25.6 per cent.⁷⁷ Up until 1976 activity was buoyed aloft by strong domestic demand, and the industrial sector could draw on high levels of saving as a privileged means of financing its activity. But in late 1976 Turkey was hit by the effects of the oil crisis. Its growth suddenly stopped due to the marked contraction in world trade.

Imports replaced by a ballooning current account deficit (1977–1980) The late 1970s may be described as a period of negative import substitution financed by ballooning current account deficits.⁷⁸ The balance of payments was affected by weak exports and rapidly worsened when OPEC quadrupled its oil price. Although the country resisted the first oil crisis fairly well, it was hit hard by the second, and between 1972 and 1978 the external debt ratio went from 13.1 to 26.7, with three-quarters of this debt being comprised of short-term borrowing. The annual rate of inflation, which had stood at 14 per cent between 1970 and 1972, hit triple figures by the end of the decade.⁷⁹ Wages dropped, leading to rapid erosion of domestic demand and savings. The unemployment rate soared, reaching 14.8 per cent of the working population in 1980.⁸⁰ In early 1978 the government needed to call on the financial backing of OECD (Organization for Economic Co-operation and Development) countries, while at the same time restructuring external debt held by its long-standing creditors.⁸¹ It therefore presented an IMF (International Monetary Fund)-coordinated stabilization programme focusing on boosting exports.⁸² The Turkish lira was devalued by half (losing 23 per cent of its value in March 1978 and 44 per cent in June 1979), a system was introduced to reimburse export taxes so as to improve the balance of trade, and the country's debt restructured under OECD oversight. But this stabilization and adjustment package did not reverse the trend, and GDP growth was negative as of 1979.⁸³ In August 1979 some 254 international banks took part in the restructuring of $2.6 billion of Turkish debt, overseen by the IMF.⁸⁴ At the same time they extended $400 million in new loans to Turkey. On 24 January 1980, new stabilization and adjustment programmes were adopted under the aegis of the IMF,⁸⁵ the World Bank and the OECD in order to reduce inflation and redress the balance of payments.⁸⁶ In June the IMF granted Turkey an additional loan of $1.65 billion, at the time the largest ever made by the Fund. In July Western governments added an additional $3 billion. By the end of the summer Turkey's external debt stood in excess of $17 billion, of which $4.8 billion was held by private banks, $8.2 billion by governments and $4 billion by international financial institutions.⁸⁷

These transformations to the Turkish economy triggered profound social change. The growing industrialization fed into the flight from the countryside, draining large numbers of poor workers towards the outskirts of the major industrial towns, and the state's traditional interlocutors lost control over a whole swathe of economic and political resources they had hitherto controlled.

Social transformations

Rural exodus, the proletarianization of the economy and the shift towards the tertiary sector During the 1960s and 1970s the proletarianization of the economy continued, together with the shift towards the tertiary sector. The industrial sector accounted for 7.9 per cent of the working population in 1962 and 4.7 per cent in 1978, whilst tertiary sector employment rose from 6 per cent to 13 per cent over the same period, with agriculture – which had accounted for 77 per cent in 1962 – dropping to 60.9 per cent in 1978. The country thus underwent urbanization,[88] with the urban population increasing from 18.5 per cent in 1950 to 40 per cent in 1978.[89] Industrialization was concentrated around the major urban centres in the country, leading to the exodus of the rural peasantry who swelled the ranks of poor workers in the *gecekondu* (slums). This exodus was encouraged by the demand for labour in the urban and industrial centres, as well as by the comparatively low level of agricultural pay, the mechanization of agriculture and the dearth of available land.[90]

The speculation that accompanied urbanization drove up property values. In Istanbul certain plots of land which had been bought for 50 lira in 1949 ($17.80) were worth 50,000 in 1965 (nearly $5500),[91] whilst in Istanbul, Izmir and Ankara rents increased by a factor of 2.5 between 1955 and 1965, meaning that low-income populations had to allocate over one-third of their budget to renting their accommodation.[92] For many of the country dwellers flocking to the urban centres the solution was gecekondu, a cheap but illegal sort of housing:[93] a census in 1955 counted 50,000 of them, or 3.5 per cent of dwellings in Turkey. But in 1972 there were 700,000, accounting for 22.4 per cent of the total number of dwellings.[94] In the late 1960s 45 per cent of the population living in Istanbul, 65 per cent in Ankara and 35 per cent in Izmir resided in gecekondu neighbourhoods.[95]

The towns were also attracting more and more students. Between 1960 and 1977 the number of students in vocational colleges rose from 180,000 to 436,000, whilst the number of university students increased from 65,000 to 340,000.[96] Facilities had to be significantly expanded for these new students, new teachers needed to be trained and the overall structure of the higher education system had to be redesigned. The number of teachers working in vocational colleges rose from 8,333 in 1960 to 22,728 in 1977, whilst the number of teaching staff in universities went from 4071 to 16,981. The state launched a university building programme, raising their number from six[97] in 1957 to seventeen[98] in 1977. Since the new students came mainly from Turkey's rural regions, residences (*yurt*) were built to house them. In the city of Istanbul there were twenty-one residences in 1979, each able to house between 100 to over 2000 students.[99] Each residence was meant to group together students from the same region (thus at the University of Istanbul the Sivas *yurdu* had students from the province of Sivas, the Rize *yurdu* those from Rize and so on), enabling new arrivals to meet former acquaintances and socialize more rapidly. The residences were where students spent much of their time, sleeping, eating, relaxing, and studying there. The Atatürk student campus (Atatürk Öğrenci Sitesi) in Istanbul was home to over 2000 students and there were canteens, restaurants, a library, a tennis court, a sports hall, 'social' activities and a cinema auditorium there.[100] Students generally had very little purchasing power and divided their time between the university and the residence where they found the facilities they needed for life in the city of Istanbul.

The departure abroad of over 1 million Turks during the 1960s and 1970s was an additional factor modifying the circuits of economic accumulation and relationships of domination. Professional migration acted as an intake of oxygen, helping to fuel the Turkish economy. Foreign currency sent from Germany, Belgium and France provided substantial sources of revenue for families who had stayed behind, and they were often reinvested in purchasing plots of land, setting up small businesses or opening shops.

All of these transformations loosened the traditional collusive relationships binding social elites to actors from the state field, impacting on the effectiveness of delegating social control, a means hitherto used by the state to acquire legitimacy over its populations and territory.

Transformations to structures of economic and social control The state's privileged interlocutors gradually lost their grip over the circulation and allocation of economic resources. There were an increasing number of coffeehouses in the villages, offering a number of clans and families the opportunity to build up their own circles and clienteles.[101] Professional migration, entrepreneurial ventures and commercial activities no longer operated at the scale of the district or province, but at the national or international level due to the progressive expansion and differentiation of markets throughout the second half of the twentieth century, which now operated independently of control by traditional local notables. All these transformations were instrumental in the emergence of new economic and political actors, who tended in turn to build up their own clientele networks and contest the role played by traditional elites in controlling and redistributing public resources.[102] New social groups (workers, students and the gecekondu populations) were the target of intense mobilization and politicization campaigns conducted by organizations wishing to compete in political, trade union and economic contests.

The restructuring and deadlock of institutional politics

Between 1950 and 1980 the political field was slowly restructured, as shown by the shifting balance of power in the Turkish parliament. In the 1950s the CHP and the DP alone garnered over 90 per cent of the votes in each general election. In the 1950 general election they won 484 out of the 489 parliamentary seats, 534 of the 541 seats in play in 1954 and 602 of the 610 seats in 1957; the Nation Party (Millet Partisi, MP) and the Republican Nation Party (Cumhuriyetçi Millet Partisi, CMP) shared the few remaining seats. The Democrat Party came first in each of these three elections, comfortably ahead of the CHP with 339 more seats than its rival in 1950, 460 in 1954, and 246 in 1957.

Several factors explain this balance of power. The victory of the Democrat Party in 1950 after twelve years of İsmet İnönü's presidency and twenty-seven years of CHP power may be interpreted as the price exacted on the CHP after having been worn down by its long term in office. These were the first truly free elections held in the country, for the first elections held under the multi-party system in 1946 took place only a few months after the setting up of the Democrat Party, which had been hindered by the Kemalist apparatus of state, much of which still backed the CHP. In 1950 the new party could draw on broad support, won over the course of several years in which economic policy had resulted in strong inflation, in a context in which salaries were not indexed. The victory of the Democrat Party was thus partly due to the CHP losing its legitimacy with its hitherto loyal supporters – the Anatolian bourgeoisie, those with local economic power, and public-sector workers. After this initial electoral victory, the Democrat government transformed itself into what Hamit Bozarslan describes as a 'muscular authoritarian power'.[103] The electoral laws were changed, rival political parties shut down and the opposition subjected to particularly virulent media campaigns. As of 1957 the Democrat Party looked like it wanted to re-establish a single-party regime. The press was muzzled and political meetings outlawed.[104] The increasingly harsh repression conducted by the Democrat Party, together with its religious policy that ran counter contrary to the principles of the Kemalist revolution (the reintroduction of prayers in Arabic and the opening of Koranic schools and religious education establishments), pushed young military officers to set up a National Unity Committee; this took power on 27 May 1960, proceeding to ban the Democrat Party, arrest and physically eliminate some of its leaders, and draw up a new constitution which was passed by the constituent assembly on 27 May 1961.

With the shutting down of the Democrat Party, the CHP won the first general elections after the introduction of the new regime, held on 15 October 1961. Four parties shared the seats in parliament. The CHP only did marginally better than its direct rival, the Justice Party (Adalet Partisi, AP), winning 1.9 per cent more of the vote and 15 additional seats in parliament. İsmet İnönü thus had to resign himself to forming a coalition government. Although the military intervention in 1960 had tilted the balance of political power, it had not discredited Democrat personnel. Four years later the CHP turned in the worst electoral performance in its history – winning 28.7 per cent of the vote – and the AP won the elections of 10 October 1965 with 52.87 per cent of the vote. In 1969 the AP won the elections again (with 46.55 per cent of the vote and 256 seats). Although not performing as well as it had done in 1965, it still managed to extend its lead over the CHP.

The balance of power between the parties over the course of the 1960s presents three particularly striking phenomena. First, the AP's monopolization of the Democrat Party's legacy, winning in 1965 and 1969 similar shares of the vote to its predecessor, and managing to establish itself as an abiding political force on the Turkish right. Second, the rapid collapse in the CHP's electoral performance: whilst in 1961, on the strength of the aura conferred by participation in the constitutional process and its support for the 'progressive' coup of 1960, it managed to win 36.7

per cent of the vote in 1961 (1.6 per cent more than in 1954, its lowest score of the previous decade), over the course of the next two general elections its vote dropped by nearly 10 per cent. These setbacks weakened İsmet İnönü, who was increasingly powerless to defend his dominance of the party, and notably in the face of the challenge from Bülent Ecevit, the young secretary general in favour of taking up centre-left ground, something which the old leader refused to do. Thirdly, the political developments over the decade and in particular the emergence of new political parties led to a dispersal of votes. Whilst the two main parties had won over 90 per cent of the vote in 1950s, they only attracted 71.5 per cent in 1961, 81.6 per cent in 1965 and 74 per cent in 1969. The number of parties with seats in parliament thus rose from four in 1957 to eight in 1969.

Amongst these new parties, the TİP (far left) and the Nationalist Movement Party (Milliyetçi Hareket Partisi, MHP, nationalist far right, founded in 1969 by Alparslan Türkeş on the bases of the CKMP, whose leader he had been since 1965) had particularly active relays in several social sectors (especially factories and universities) where there were regular mobilizations and increasingly radical means of action, including physical confrontation and even clandestine armed activity. Confronted with this radicalization, and with the emergence of an Islamist political option based on the National Order Party (Milli Nizam Partisi, MNP), created by Necmettin Erbakan, an AP renegade, the army intervened once again in 1971. It sent an ultimatum to the AP government, which complied without batting an eyelid. The army did not dissolve parliament, but set up several interim governments composed of selected politicians and other ministers picked for their technical skills, until a general election was held in October 1973.

İsmet İnönü had been the target of internal dissent due to the CHP's lamentable electoral results since the early 1960s, and to his refusal to oppose military intervention, and in 1971 he resigned from the party leadership. Bülent Ecevit, who won the elections to succeed him, repositioned the party on the centre-left (*ortanın solu*) of the political spectrum and led it to victory in the elections of 14 October 1973, winning 33.3 per cent of the vote and 185 seats in parliament, ahead of the AP in second place, with 29.8 per cent of the vote and 149 seats. Throughout the 1970s the CHP was the main political force in the country – though it never won enough seats to govern on its own. In the wake of the 1973 elections the number of potential coalition partners was limited, and it was with the Necmettin Erbakan's National Salvation Party (Milli Selamet Partisi, MSP, Islamist right wing) that it came to agreement in 1974, forming a first coalition government. That same year the government decided to intervene in Cyprus in order to protect Turkish Cypriots after the coup there led by Nikos Samson, with the support of the ruling junta in Athens. Although condemned by NATO, this decision was almost unanimously welcomed in Turkey. Ecevit, who was head of government, understood the interest of capitalizing on the political gains from this intervention, and resigned in order to prepare early elections – which he was sure to win hands down – and enable the CHP to govern alone. But the MSP, aware that this posed a threat to its own positions in government, chose to back the AP project to form a sufficiently broad coalition government to command a parliamentary majority. After lengthy negotiations a Nationalist Front government (Milliyetçi Cephe hükümeti) won a parliamentary vote of confidence, combining the AP, MSP, MHP and CGP, united by their staunch anti-communism and desire to marginalize the CHP. The governing parties further chose to make use of the communist threat – a credible one given Turkey's geopolitical situation and the growing number of people drawn by far-left extra-parliamentary movements – and over the course of several campaigns accused the CHP of being a pro-Soviet, communist, revolutionary party. The MHP, whose electoral manifesto was underpinned by its anti-communism, managed to exact a high price for its participation in government, winning two ministries even though it only had three seats in parliament. The balance of parliamentary power made it an essential ally for the AP. The MHP was also crucial to the AP because the AP did not have a youth movement and could not face leftists on the streets, whereas the MHP could. The MHP took advantage of its place in government to distribute a series of sinecures and resources to its activists and supporters, thereby reinforcing its organization and enabling it to step up its activities and present itself as the champion of anti-communism in Turkey.

The CHP made further progress in the general elections of 1977, winning 41.4 per cent of the vote, giving it 213 out of the 450 seats in parliament. Ecevit then tried to form a government, but was unable to win a vote of confidence. The AP and the MHP had also strengthened their positions in these elections, unlike all the other parties, which had either collapsed or been weakened, such as the MSP which lost half of the seats it had held in the previous parliament. Negotiations conducted by the CHP came to naught, given that there were so few non-CHP MPs who were prepared to support a government headed by Ecevit.[105] Thus the party which had won the elections with over 40 per cent of the vote was prevented from forming a government, as the distribution of seats in parliament enabled the AP to form a second Nationalist Front with the support of the MHP and MSP. This new government, which won a vote of confidence in September 1977, had a slender parliamentary majority, being able to rely on 229 out of 450 MPs. And so the system shifted from a two-party system in the 1950s to a bipolar multi-party system, with the two main parties never managing to form a majority government on their own.

This situation led to the breaking of alliances and the forging of new ones. In January 1978 Ecevit won over MPs from the ruling parties in exchange for ministerial positions, enabling him to form a coalition government on 17 January 1978 with the CGP and the Democratic Party (Demokratik Parti). But the economic situation rapidly worsened; the oil crisis hit the country hard, inflation rose and there were street demonstrations against the continuous rise in prices and erosion of people's purchasing power. Ecevit reacted by entering into more international agreements. Turkey thus became the country to receive the second most help from the USSR (after Cuba)[106] – something the opposition parties seized on to accuse the government of 'selling the country out' to foreign interests, and especially the USSR, while relations with the United States were taking a sharp turn for the worse in the wake of the intervention in Cyprus. The change in government was welcomed favourably by far-left organizations, most of whose members had voted for the leader of the CHP after three years of Nationalist Front government and the exactions of nationalist groups working with the support of certain state sectors. Ecevit was furthermore accused by the MHP of opening the doors of the public administration to members of radical left-wing associations, whose entryism was condemned in repeated media campaigns. Yet far-left groups did not profit directly from the sinecures at the CHP's disposal, which had to start by distributing the public positions it now had at its disposal to its numerous supporters. And given how widespread anti-communist sentiment was, any rapprochement with radical groups risked being electorally counter-productive.

In addition to this, the proclamation of martial law in an increasing number of provinces – in the aftermath of the massacre by ülkücü elements in the town of Kahramanmaraş in December 1978 – increased the control the military exerted over institutional politics, precluding Ecevit from entering into any formal agreement with radical organizations. And then the international situation in the late 1970s prevented him from being too close to the far left. Though the intervention in Cyprus in 1974 had been followed by an American arms embargo, this had been lifted in 1978. Regional rifts – in particular the Iranian revolution – together with the United States' concern lest the activities of far-left groups in Turkey should run out of control brought the country back into the Western fold. Thus although on taking power the CHP worked to markedly improve the situation of far-left organizations – who had been the principal targets of the previous government – by orchestrating a drop in police harassment and withdrawing the official support accorded to ülkücü militias and organizations when the MHP had been government, it did not go so far as to enable them to gain access to the resources or positions available within the apparatus of state.

The arrival of the CHP in power was accompanied by increasingly fierce confrontation between radical groups. The government was unable to ensure the security of populations in the face of exactions committed by ülkücü organizations close to the MHP, which increased their violent activities in order to maintain a climate of permanent insecurity. It was also hit by the degradation in the economic and social situation, until the CHP lost the November 1979 by-elections. It was then the turn of the AP to form a new government, but neither the MSP nor the MHP agreed to take part, apparently betting on the economic and social conditions continuing to worsen. The CHP was also opposed to forming a broad national unity government, and so finally a minority AP government won a vote of parliamentary confidence with the support of its former allies, but it was threatened with collapse every time the CHP tabled a motion of no confidence. The balance of parliamentary power rapidly led to the paralysis of institutional politics, peaking in April 1980 when parliament failed to elect a new president. In July, after 96 rounds of voting, no candidate managed to garner enough votes to be elected.

It was against this backdrop of progressive political deadlock that the conflict between radical groups escalated, exactly when the means at the state's disposal meant it was unable to step in to maintain order and social peace.

Maintaining order in practical terms

During the 1970s the worsening economic conditions compelled governments to engage in difficult financial arbitrations. The administration struggled to obtain the necessary resources to provide uninterrupted public service. Working conditions within the administration worsened as ministry budgets were cut, whilst the political parties used public employment as a means to maintain their electoral clienteles, hard-hit by the effects of the economic crisis. The institutions in charge of maintaining order did not have the means at their disposal to contain the social conflict, while movements led by radical trade union and political actors took on unparalleled scale. Over the course of the 1970s the police, like many other public institutions, became a privileged site for mobilization and competition for the conflicting movements, whose modes of action became ever more radical. Soon the forces of order were overrun. The Directorate of Security suffered from a severe lack of human, logistical and material resources, as well as shortcomings in its internal disciplinary mechanisms.

The lack of professionalization among agents

As of the 1960s the Directorate of Security needed to recruit an increasing number of policemen in order to cope with the increases in urban populations. There was no shortage of candidates for public-sector employment given the economic crisis, as journalist Ertuğrul Akbay suggested in a report published in *Polis Magazin* under the title 'The hidden face of the Turkish police' in early 1980:

> Many policemen today chose the profession not out of vocation but in order to be able to eat. The majority of them would change jobs on the spot if they found another job. Only the high level of unemployment in the country prevents this from happening. These people's ideal is not to be policemen but to have a job.[107]

The case of Sıtkı Öner, a former secretary general to the left-wing police Association Pol-Der, shows how easy it was to become a policeman in the 1960s.[108] In July 1964 a friend told him about a recruitment campaign. One month after sending in their applications the two friends were informed that they had been appointed to the Ankara Directorate of Security (Emniyet Müdürlüğü), without having to pass the slightest entrance exam or receive any kind of training. It is probable that the two new recruits received political backing on joining the police, something which was current practice at the time, as suggested by police officer Nahit Dündar:

> Recruitment has got worse in the country. On joining the organisation [the police] individuals are pushed towards party politics. Nowadays the competition and entrance exam have become formalities. The people to be recruited contact party organisations, who provide them with documents certifying that they have 'passed the public-sector employment exam'. ... Exam committees generally serve reasons other than those for which they were set up. Whereas these

committees are meant to be composed of specialists, what you see are people appointed for their political views who recruit as they see fit. The composition of examinations committees should only be carried out by competent people within the institution.[109]

This politicization in access to police careers established rival forms of legitimacy – between the norms prescribed by the position and the norms used by political forces in a dominant position within the institution – leading in turn to the politicization of policemen's practices and interactions.

Any professional training that did exist was inappropriate and insufficient, and policeman took up their jobs without having acquired the know-how or behavioural skills stipulated by the institution. Up until 1979, when programmes to build training centres were launched, the police were apparently largely uninterested in professionalizing personnel.[110] Professional knowledge was learnt on the job, by reading manuals or copying others. Sıtkı Öner observed:

> Like most police officers I started out without having received any kind of training. I tried to learn by modelling my behaviour on my elders and I simply read a few books about the job.[111]

In 1980 Hasan Fehmi Güneş, a former CHP Minister for the Interior, admitted that 'between 1966 and 1973 we gave out uniforms and the right to bear arms to 14,000 people who had not received the slightest training, and said "now you are policemen", and sent them to their suicide'.[112] Although the majority of police officers did receive two or three months' instruction in a training centre, it was regarded as unsatisfactory by police cadres and police associations. The Istanbul head of police himself questioned the length of training dispensed in police academies:

> Being a policeman is a tough job. A policeman needs to know the law and see to it that it is applied. And he needs to know how to use an arm. Two months training is not enough for that. That is why the police officers who arrive here don't have the necessary know-how. So we try to teach them whilst they are on duty. When we have managed to train them to respond to the situation they are confronted with, they are sent out to other provinces and we have to start all over again. And that isn't the fault of the personnel, but of the system.[113]

Over the course of the 1970s, which were marked by the escalation of radical groups' activities, the lack of professionalization amongst the police made it particularly difficult to maintain order.[114] Thus Commander Bölügiray deplored the lack of training received by policeman placed under his orders during the period of martial law in December 1978,[115] their ill-preparedness and their ignorance about their powers and duties.[116] Bölügiray refers to men in lamentable physical condition, in poor health and too old or too fat. He developed 'refresher' programmes, and made an increasing number of interventions at police provincial headquarters in Adana in order to reassert the principles of the institution, which to his mind were severely tainted by police practice: 'it is above all your duty to show your respect for your uniforms. ... Particularly in police stations and places where you are on duty, or when a patrol carries out checks.'[117] But such attempts were isolated. The lack of guidance received by new recruits who were obliged to learn the tricks of the trade alongside their elders made it impossible to implement any unified professional habitus. The Turkish police failed to propose the negative rites ('seeking to remove a certain number of civilian properties from the novice') and aggregative rites ('whose purpose is to signify the belonging of the decivilianised novices') needed to propagate to all new recruits a shared 'way of acting and behaving' as a police officer.[118]

The lack of police means

The difficulties encountered by the police were in no way limited to the question of the lack of professionalization of police officers. It also suffered from a general lack of means that prevented officers from learning 'rules of conduct seeking to instil norms of collective order'[119] and consequently the propagation of a habitus specific to the institution.

In addition to the radicalization of modes of protest, the police were confronted with the diversification of the arenas of mobilization and confrontation. The police now had to ensure the security of property and people within universities, high schools, factories and public institutions. In 1970 the police numbered 21,478 officers, whilst the urban population it was in charge of stood at 13,066,631 inhabitants, working out at about one policeman per 608 inhabitants.[120] By the end of the decade the situation had got worse. In 1979 in the town of Adana there were 850 policemen for 700,000 inhabitants[121] (or one policeman per 823.5 inhabitants). In addition to this, the police were divided equally between day and night duty, reducing the number of officers available at any one time to 425 (which works out at one officer per 1647 inhabitants). This number is no doubt an overestimate – since certain officers were ill, suspended, affected to intelligence duties or else in training – and the number of policemen who could be could be called upon at any one time may be put more reasonably at around 300,[122] of whom over 100 were affected to protecting provincial governors, public prosecutors, personnel working in the justice system, foreign residents and official buildings that might be targeted in attacks. The lack of police officers was such that in the run-up to the coup of 12 September 1980 the General Directorate of Security considered calling on retired policemen. The situation was a cause for particular concern in the province of Adana, where in one district of the town there were 50,000 inhabitants for only thirty active policeman (divided into two groups of fifteen), some of whom were affected to administrative tasks and bodyguard duties, meaning there were only seven officers in charge of maintaining order.[123] This personnel shortage made the daily task of policemen more complicated. For example, they were unable to remove slogans, drawings and insults daubed on the walls of the towns and villages. In order to make up for the lack of officers, mobile police stations resembling caravans were set up and placed in the more troubled neighbourhoods so as to ensure a semblance of order. But the two policemen in charge of a mobile police station were unable to leave their caravan without protection, and so unable to intervene directly on-site in the event of receiving a complaint.

The police also suffered from a lack of facilities, equipment (handcuffs, gas masks, arms etc.) and financial resources. The picture Bölügiray sketches of police stations gives some idea of the poor working conditions of the police officers:

> The police stations in the provinces and districts that I had to inspect were all very different, some being installed in houses, others in the basements of blocks of flats, and they were often extremely dirty … Dirty walls, dirty chairs and tables, with the holes in broken windows patched up using newspaper and pieces of cardboard. As for the toilets … It was incomprehensible! … So basically the policeman working in these places were housed as prisoners might be.[124]

In his report about the Turkish police Ertuğrul Akbay describes a similar situation at the Eyüp police station in Istanbul:

> All the police stations in Turkey are in a similar state of utter disrepair. According to a report by the Development Directorate, Eyüp police station is liable to collapse at any moment. … But the dilapidation of Eyüp police station, and that of other police stations, does not stop there. When it rains, water flows into the station. There is a permanent fire hazard due to electric circuits catching fire. In addition to this not all rooms have electricity … Candles are used for lighting. … And what heating is there for policeman on duty in police stations? In many stations it is possible to have heating if the neighbours help. Eyüp station is lucky. There are a lot of charitable Muslims in the Eyüp Sultan area. The neighbourhood provides a bundle of firewood and a scuttle of coal on winter days. … Policeman from Eyüp go and arrest suspects on foot, as is the case in many other police stations. Means of transport exist, but most of the time they only move if pushed. There is no room for holding suspects in custody, only a waiting room.[125]

In Bölügiray's description of them police stations are unhealthy places,[126] and the policeman were not always safe there. These infrastructural shortcomings are compounded by problems with equipment. According to a survey carried out by the *Milliyet* newspaper, 'policemen's arms are no match for those of the individuals they have to confront, in terms both of the models and of their firepower'.[127] There were also only a very limited number of megaphones, speakers and sirens.[128] During strikes or protest marches the police had cameras to photograph participants for police records, but they did not have any zoom lenses, rendering the operation pointless since the policemen preferred not to get too close to the demonstrators.[129] Inhabitants tuned in to internal radio communications between policemen, bearing in mind that the police did not use coded language.[130] Given that it was not possible to buy fuel, police vehicles were sometimes immobilized, and the stations had to negotiate loans from the local petrol stations. And when means were available, the lack of professionalization of police officers meant they were unable to use them.[131] This was the case with the water cannons (Adana had two vehicles equipped with a water cannon, one of which worked). The situation was similar for the most basic equipment used by the police on a daily basis. The Directorate of Security did not always provide them with uniforms, and when they did receive one they had to pay for it to be patched up – meaning they did not all wear the same uniform and dressed as best they could. Commander Bölügiray tells how one day, in the winter of 1979, when going around the streets of Adana, he noticed that two policemen in charge of a 'mobile police station' (*mobil karakol*) were not out patrolling.[132] They explained to him that they could not do so because of bad weather, only having canvas shoes – that they bought with their own money – short-sleeved shirts, no overcoats and no rubber boots. On enquiring into the situation with those in charge at the local police station, he learnt that equipment generally arrived one or two seasons late. The working patterns imposed on police officers were also a source of discontent and demands. An officer having to carry out twelve hours on duty per day was often only relieved after twenty-four hours, and overtime was rarely paid.[133] And if an officer fell ill he was unable to take any leave.[134]

It would thus appear that the police was an institution with low levels of professionalization, exposed to the influence of political parties (which intervened in the appointment of police officers), and with insufficient human and material resources to carry out its function of maintaining order. Low pay, the lack of professionalization of officers and the insalubrious condition of many police stations, together with local tactics to solicit the population's generosity, all hindered the assertion of a unified internal order within the institution, capable of acting as a source of values, and separate from contingencies external to the police's function of maintaining order. This situation prevented the establishment of respected internal discipline, as well as the implementation of principles pertaining to an institution operating independently of social and political division. This state of internal disorder encouraged individual and collective strategies of self-preservation, which were then instrumentalized by the rival police associations during the second half of the 1970s.

*

The image of the state which emerges from these observations is of a fluctuating set of interests and positions, whose protagonists partook in many transactions, and whose very institutions were stakes in perpetually renewed negotiations. The vision of the social order and the state order as a dichotomy – which never fully manages to avoid the tendency to naturalize these two entities – would thus seem to need discarding, to be replaced by an analysis of the fluctuating forms taken by this dialectic between society and state. Whereas many authors believe they can see an autonomous and differentiated entity, observations show to the contrary that the state acquired its legitimacy by practices of co-optation, collusion and circumvention. Looking at the transactions binding social forces and state officials over the long term brings out the historical continuity of the practices of interpenetration between the social and state spheres. The upheavals affecting the Turkish economy since the 1960s, together with urbanization and the proletarianization of society, led to a redistribution of the positions of accumulation and power, enabling new collective actors to mobilize resources, and populations who now operated independently of the control of traditional elites. The resulting transformations in the balance of political power offered opportunities for hitherto unexplored coalitions, resulting in the paralysis of institutional politics, in a context in which the public authorities did not have the means to put an end to the conflict opposing antagonistic radical movements. In order to understand how these radical movements managed to insert themselves within social and political contests, we shall now turn to how they emerged and developed their structures.

Chapter 2

MOVEMENTS IN CONFLICT

The conflict between the Turkish far left and far right in the 1970s was markedly asymmetrical. The Nationalist Movement's strategy to access power, which it implemented as of 1975, was based on participating in electoral contests, infiltrating state arenas, and using physical violence. The high level of coordination amongst ülkücü units enabled the MHP to draw on the entire movement as a multi-sector mobilization force. The far-left organizations opposing it were dispersed, with very low levels of integration. Their action system included political, associative and trade union organizations that were largely uncoordinated, and they frequently competed against one another whilst intermittently coming together to denounce 'fascist' exactions. The two systems did not have the same possibilities at their disposal for accessing resources in the contest opposing them, and the reasons for the differences in their technical capacities need to be sought in the ways they were structured.

The structuring of the two conflicting movements was linked to the types and levels of resources available to their cadres. On the far left, cultural capital was valued as a distinctive resource. Intellectuals, academics, students, and leaders had sufficient cultural capital to adopt tactics of political differentiation, and in particular to emancipate themselves from existing organizations by setting up a journal or an organization. Most of the time challenges to the existing structure led to defections, and the dissidents preferred to try to make a go of things in an organization that they controlled rather than be subjected to the decisions of a leadership whose legitimacy they did not recognize. This is why no party-type entity other than the Workers Party of Turkey (Türkiye İşçi Partisi, TİP) managed to accumulate significant political resources between 1965 and 1971.

On the far right the situation was very different. Alparslan Türkeş, the leader of the Nationalist Action Party, was an ex-army colonel. After the coup of 27 May 1960 he was against handing power back to the civilians, and embodied the hard line adopted by part of the junta. On entering politics he drew on networks he had built up during his military career to establish high levels of discipline in the party he ran. Differentiation was frowned upon within the Nationalist Movement, with discipline and loyalty being valued, and defection and dissidence repressed. Intellectual capital did not entitle one to speak out; what counted was holding one of the positions approved by the leader, who acted as the Nationalist Movement's guide.

The power relations structuring the two conflicting movements had an influence on their repertoires of action. In order to understand the pronounced asymmetry between the tactical activities used by the two antagonistic systems, this chapter will conduct a comparative analysis of how they emerged and subsequently developed.

The radical left

As of 1961 the Turkish far left underwent profound restructuring. Party political, student, professional, and cultural organizations were established, and their social base expanded to a hitherto unparalleled extent, up until the 1980 coup. They were united by their common rejection of 'fascism' as embodied by the ülkücüs, of economic liberalism and of American imperialism, and their members were in regular contact with each other. But there was significant disparity between the calls for unity amongst progressive forces, with each group acting as the herald, and a low level of coordination amongst their activities, not to mention the increasing tendency towards splits in the far-left action system.

The Workers Party of Turkey

Thanks to the possibilities opened up by the new constitution,[1] a handful of trade union leaders[2] who had broken with the powerful Türk-İş trade union confederation founded the Workers Party of Turkey (TİP) on 13 February 1961. Their political and social trajectories differ significantly from those of the historical figures on the Turkish left and of the supporters of the Turkish Communist Party (Türkiye Komünist Partisi, TKP) with whom they disputed the legitimacy to defend the interests of the working class. Up until the creation of the TİP the Turkish far left was composed of small groups and banned for lengthy periods.[3] It was made up of several hundred individuals who tended to be intellectuals rather than trade unionists. Most of them had fallen foul of the law and were obliged to operate clandestinely due to the regime's hostility to all forms of communist ideology, and they belonged to networks of members of the former TKP (founded on 10 September 1920 in Bakou). The twelve trade unionists who set up the TİP had very different profiles to those on the 'traditional' Turkish far left. With the exception of Kemal Sülker, they were all officials from trades union affiliated to the Türk-İş confederation.[4] None of them had previously held any political position, and only one of them (İbrahim Güzelce) had already been a member of a political party. The TİP, wishing to place its activities on a legal footing, argued for a middle way between capitalism and socialism – a 'non-capitalist path'.[5] In foreign affairs it was opposed to Turkey's membership of NATO, but was careful not to call for any rapprochement with the USSR, refusing to be labelled as communist and instead preferring to promote its working-class composition.[6]

Between 1961, when it was set up, and its being banned by the junta after the coup of 12 March 1971, the TİP gradually established itself as the main actor on the Turkish far left despite its heterodox positions. It entered parliament in 1963 when Niyazi Ağırnaslı became a member, who until then had been a senator for the Nation Party (Millet Partisi, MP). In the 1963 local elections it presented candidates in nine provinces, winning 36,000 votes.[7] But it was with the general election of 10 October 1965 that it was confirmed as the key actor on the far-left, winning 276,000 votes (3 per cent of the total cast), giving it fifteen MPs. These good results legitimized its decision to follow the parliamentary and legalist approach. It also encouraged it to step up its mobilization and to diversify the sites where it had a hold.

TİP members set up new trade union and student organizations. On 17 December 1965 the party grouped several student organizations together to form the Federation of Opinion Clubs (Fikir Kulüpleri Federasyonu, FKF), whose leaders it selected. The FKF, though statutorily external to the TİP, initially acted as the party's youth wing. Its members were behind several protest movements, conducted independently or with other organizations (and in particular the DİSK trade union confederation, established in 1967). In a very short space of time other left-wing movements tried to take control of it. Most of the 1960s student leaders of both legal and underground groups passed through the ranks of the FKF, which acted as a key forum for socialization in left-wing ideas and a place for accumulating activist know-how – often reinvested in setting up or taking part in other groups as of 1968, when the Federation was rent apart by ideological and strategic debate.

In 1968 the party counted 12,695 members,[8] but was able to mobilize a far larger base of sympathizers. It did this on numerous occasions, coordinating its activities with those of the DİSK trade union confederation, which in 1967 (its first year of existence) already numbered over 65,000 members.[9] From 1967 to 1970 DİSK, the TİP, and the FKF (renamed Dev-Genç in 1969) worked to propagate and coordinate protest movements in universities and factories, as well as those conducted by agricultural labourers and small-scale farmers. Students ran village meetings during the summer of 1970 in the east of the country and on the Black Sea coast, and joint demonstrations were organized to defend trade union rights (Dev-Genç and DİSK set up a joint security unit in 1970), resounding to cries of 'Long live the working class' (*Yaşasın işçi sınıfı*), 'AP power is not our power' (*AP iktidar, bizim iktidarimiz değildir*) and 'Death to fascism and all reactionaries' (*Tüm gericiler ve faşizm kahrolsun*).

Dissent and division

During the second half of the 1960s factions opposed to the ideological line adopted by the TİP leadership endeavoured to take control of the party. The National Democratic Revolution (Milli Demokratik Devrim, MDD) – headed by Mihri Belli, who had a long track record as a far-left cadre – refused to recognize the validity of the TİP's line of taking part in electoral contests. The social and political resources of 'traditional' leading figures on the Turkish left enabled them to set themselves up as rivals to the new party, and the younger members of the associative environment broke free at the end of the decade, calling for a less legalist approach.

Behice Boran and Sadun Aren, MPs and members of the TİP's central executive, decided to work together to promote a line opposed to that of Mehmet Ali Aybar, the TİP leader and the criticisms of Leninism he was formulating to legitimize his strategy of winning power via parliament. They launched a journal called *Emek* (*Labour*) to spread their ideas amongst activists, and got Aybar to resign after the general elections the following year, when the party encountered its first electoral setback, winning 2.68 per cent of the votes cast yet losing all but two seats in parliament due to alterations in the electoral system. Aybar was replaced by M. Ali Aslan, Şaban Yıldız, then Behice Boran, shortly before the military intervention of 12 March led to the party being banned.

It was within this context of an internal power struggle that the TİP lost control of the FKF. At the party congress in March 1968, Aybar managed to get a young university assistant called Doğu Perinçek elected as head of the Federation, but not without provoking tension and confrontations, with certain clubs refusing to recognize the authority of the new leader. Perinçek, who when elected had the backing of the TİP leader, embodied the 'legitimist' movement, opposed to the MDDists Deniz Gezmiş, Mahir Çayan and Yusuf Küpeli, whose influence steadily grew. But very soon he announced publicly that he had been won over to the ideas of the MDD, leading to his being immediately replaced by Zülküf Şahin, a legitimist, before then being excluded from the Federation. Perinçek's team took advantage of the nascent popularity of the deposed leader to establish its own structure, the Revolution Force (Dev-Güç), which operated under the wing of the MDDist movement up until early 1970, when it started publishing a journal called *Proletarian Revolution Enlightenment* (*Proleter Devrimci Aydınlık*, PDA) and transformed itself into the Revolutionary Workers and Peasants Party of Turkey (Türkiye İhtilalci İşçi Köylü Partisi, TİİKP).[10]

And so over the summer of 1968 protests by the FKF movement against the presence of the American sixth fleet anchored in Turkish waters were conducted in a dispersed manner. During protest marches certain young activists acquired a degree of notoriety amongst left-wing student milieus. Such was the case of Deniz Gezmiş, who was very active at the Istanbul Law Faculty. In October of the same year Gezmiş left the FKF and together with a few friends set up the Revolutionary Student Union (Devrimci Öğrenci Birliği, DÖB), calling for an end to the legalist approach championed by the federation. The MDDists managed to take control of the FKF at its congress in January 1969, and they celebrated their victory with chants of 'Long live people's wars' (Yaşasın Halk Savaşları).[11] Over the course of the following weeks DÖB members rejoined the federation. The FKF's legalist approach – as embodied by its pro-TİP leaders – had reached the end of the road. In order to make clear its shift in ideological stance, the federation changed its name, becoming the Federation of Revolutionary Youth Associations (Devrimci Gençlik Dernekleri Federasyonu, Dev-Genç). Certain members of the new leadership (including Deniz Gezmiş and Mahir Çayan) called for violent action to put an end to the regime's contradictions.[12]

In their desire to move away from all forms of conventional action they set up underground organizations to conduct urban and rural guerrilla operations.

They were encouraged in this by the publication in Turkish of several works about the theories and strategies of guerrilla action. In 1967 Doğan Özgüden, a journalist and member of the TİP central committee, founded a journal called *Ant*, as well as a publishing house of the same name. Up until the late 1960s it brought out Carlos Marighella's *Manual of the Urban Guerrilla* (translated into Turkish the year it was published in 1969), texts by Che Guevara setting out his theory of *foco*, and the better-known works about guerrilla strategy by the Cuban Alberto Bayo and the Venezuelan Douglas Bravo.[13] The ideological positions of the underground armed organizations which emerged at the time were based on one of the various revolutionary theories disseminated in the country. Whilst the People's Liberation Army of Turkey (Türkiye Halk Kurtuluş Ordusu, THKO), which started operating in autumn 1969, championed Che Guevara's theories of rural guerrilla activity, Mahir Çayan (a student at the Ankara Faculty of Political Science) established urban guerrilla as the privileged form of action for the People's Liberation Party-Front of Turkey (Türkiye Halk Kurtuluş Partisi-Cephesi, THKP-C), which he founded in 1971.[14] The Communist Party of Turkey – Marxist-Leninist/Workers and Peasants Liberation Army of Turkey (Türkiye Komünist Partisi – Marxist Leninist/Türkiye İşçi Köylü Kurtuluş Ordusu, TKP-ML/TİKKO), which distanced itself from Perinçek's Maoist TİİKP in 1972, deeming it took too legalist a line, devoted its activities to preparing a revolution which, according to the classical Maoist vision adapted to Turkey, was to start in the poorest rural provinces (and especially the Kurdish provinces) before then spreading to the rest of the country. These revolutionary armed groups never had more than a few dozen members each, mainly students from the large universities in the country (the Ankara Faculty of Political Sciences and Istanbul University). Their cadres knew each as they had held the same leadership positions in the FKF or Dev-Genç, where they had cut their teeth and acquired a certain renown and had also attended the same universities. Up until their elimination in the 1971 coup they disputed the legitimacy to represent the true revolutionary path in Turkey, respectively embodying each of the major guerrilla theories in vogue in the late 1960s.

The coup of 12 March 1971 and the ebb in mobilization

The army, in a communiqué sent to the Justice Party government on 12 March 1971, demanded that the prime minister resign. The new government it then set up was composed of ministers selected for their 'technical skills' and representatives from the main political parties. Martial law was proclaimed in April 1971 in eleven provinces – including the provinces of Istanbul, Ankara, Izmir and Adana.[15] To justify its intervention the army referred to how the Demirel government was 'driving [the] country into anarchy, fratricidal strife, and social and economic unrest'.[16] Youth organizations and left-wing journals were shut down, political meetings banned, and the activities of trade unions and professionals organization suspended. On 20 May 1971 the Constitutional Court decreed that the National

Order Party (Milli Nizam Partisi, MNP) be dissolved, accusing it of Islamism. Two months later the TİP was also obliged to cease all activity. The army proceeded to arrest hundreds of politicians and figures from the trade union movement,[17] including the leaders of the TİP, the MNP and DİSK. The leaders of the armed revolutionary movements were either eliminated by the forces of order or else executed after summary trials. 147 academics were fired for having taken part in activities deemed subversive (mainly editorial activities) and some of them were imprisoned.

The coup amounted more to a military veto against the routine operation of institutions than to any real suspension of political activity.[18] The Erim government had thirty-five articles of the 1961 Constitution amended, as well as adding provisional articles designed to increase the army's leeway and enable them to consolidate their control over politics. The army thus intervened to carry out moderate alterations to the constitution.[19] Although it amended certain articles and introduced martial law, it did not impose a new constitution or dissolve parliament.[20] In addition to this, some of the organizations shut down by the military courts were able to continue their activities under a different name. This was the case for example of the Union of All Teachers (Tüm Öğretmen Sendikası, TÖS), which suspended its activities on 20 September 1971 when an amendment to the 1961 Constitution forbade public-sector trade unionism, before resuming its activity, as an association, called the Turkish Teachers Union (Türkiye Öğretmen Birliği, TÖB),[21] founded on 3 September 1971.

The army's intervention was openly and almost unanimously criticized by all political bodies. But it was only over the course of the early months of 1973 that the parties represented in parliament formally opposed the army, collectively refusing to elect as president of the Republic the candidate put forward by the military, General Faruk Gürler, head of the joint chiefs of staff. Several factors led to this confrontation between civilians and the military, as well paving the way to an outcome which favoured the political parties, who on this occasion worked together. On 18 May 1972 Bülent Ecevit took over the leadership of the CHP after İsmet İnönü – the former president of the Republic of Turkey and prime minister under Mustafa Kemal – retired from political life. Ecevit, who followed a centre-left political line (*ortanın solu*), beat Kemal Satır, the candidate from the right wing of the party, who later went on to found the Republican Party (Cumhuriyetçi Parti, CP). Under Ecevit's leadership the CHP championed civil liberties, and repeatedly denounced the grip exerted by the military over political life, as well as deploring that it was underrepresented in the so-called 'transitional' governments. Süleyman Demirel, the leader of the AP and victor in the 1969 elections, apparently feared that the outcome could be fatal to his party, as had been the case for its predecessor, the DP, whose activities had been banned in the aftermath of the 1960 coup.

The two major parties saw the presidential elections of 1973 as an opportunity to oppose the generals.[22] Whilst Cemal Gürsel, who had been elected thanks to the support of the coup leaders of 1960, and his successor, Cevdet Sunay, were both seen as progressive presidents who respected the legal political contest, the generals' candidate for the 1973 presidential election, General Faruk Gürler, and signatory to the 12 March communiqué, was an interventionist. If he were to be elected it would amount to civilian recognition of military influence over political life. After a tussle between the parties and the generals – who had parliament surrounded by tanks – it was Senator Fahri Korutürk, a former navy commander who was elected, paving the way for a return to normal in political. Two weeks before the general elections in October 1973 the army lifted martial law. These elections were a success for the CHP, which won 33.3 per cent of the vote and went on to found (on 7 January 1974) a coalition government with the MSP, the conservative Islamic party created by Necmettin Erbakan after the MNP had been shut down.

Competing organizations (1973–1980)

Political parties On 14 May 1974 parliament passed the general amnesty bill tabled by the government. The activists and leaders of DİSK, the TİP and far-left associations were released from prison. The first political parties were formed a few months after the amnesty, student associations sprung up, and DİSK resumed its activities. The ideological and strategic debates which took shape amongst the former TİP cadres resulted in the setting up of four, and then five, political parties.

The first party headed by members of the now defunct TİP to be set up after the normalization of political life was the Socialist Workers Party of Turkey (Türkiye Sosyalist İşçi Partisi, TSİP). It was founded on 20 June 1974 by a group of former MDDists headed by Ahmet Kaçmaz, before then splitting a first time when a faction opposed to the leadership managed to take control of the party's weekly journal *Kitle* (*The Masses*),[23] and then a second time in 1978 when some of its younger cadres, who were critical of its pacifism and legalism, decided to found the Turkish Communist Party/Union (Türkiye Komünist Partisi/ Birlik, TKP/B).[24] But the biggest obstacle to the TSİP's attempts to monopolize socialist representation in Turkey was not so much these internal divisions as the appearance of other parties emerging from the ashes of the TİP and the MDD. Four parties sprang up in the early months of 1975: the Fatherland Party (Vatan Partisi, VP), founded on 21 January by supporters of Hikmet Kıvılcımlı;[25] the Labour Party of Turkey (Türkiye Emekçi Partisi, TEP), founded on 23 February by Mihri Belli;[26] the TİP, refounded on 1 May by Behice Boran and Sadun Aren;[27] and the Socialist Revolution Party (Sosyalist Devrim Partisi, SDP), founded on 30 May by Mehmet Ali Aybar.[28] In ideological terms the TSİP, the VP, the TEP and the TİP were characterized by their pro-Soviet attitude, whereas Mehmet Ali Aybar was still seeking to pursue a specifically socialist line – 'smiling socialism' (*güler yüzlü sosyalizm*). Doğu Perinçek also took advantage of the general amnesty to start publishing the *Aydınlık* weekly once again and to launch another journal in 1975, *Halkın Sesi* (*The Voice of the People*), supporting the TİİKP, which was unofficially up and running once again after the release of its members.

Only the TİP managed to move beyond the status of political minnow and establish itself in a large enough number of provinces to take part in the 1977 general elections, winning 0.1 per cent of the vote (with 20,565 votes, as against

276,101 in the elections held on 10 October 1965). The other parties only took part in local elections and on a sporadic basis. The change in CHP leadership, its position on the centre-left of the political spectrum and its work to politicize the working class together with its anti-imperialist and 'anti-fascist' stances (on several occasions Ecevit was targeted in attacks carried out by Nationalist Movement activists) would appear to have deprived the new far-left parties of any distinct political space. Without any electoral resources, none of them could offer members sufficient recompense to be sure of their loyalty, and nor could they capture representation of the far-left's symbolic assets in the political contest.

Professional organizations and trade unions The situation in the trade union field was markedly different. The DİSK confederation, whose activities were in effect suspended after the arrest of its leaders in the wake of coup, saw its membership numbers progress from 88,650 in late 1970 to 270,000 in 1973, before rising to nearly 600,000 in 1976 (at which time Türk-İş had 700,000 members), managing to impose the principle of one union per sector on its affiliated unions.[29] In the light of the social and economic policies pursued by the Nationalist Front government, in power as of 1975, DİSK lent its support to the CHP in national elections. It organized several demonstrations to display the unity and mass of the working classes grouped together under its leadership. On 1 May 1976 it organized a demonstration to celebrate Labour Day, the first of its kind in Turkey for fifty-one years. It repeated the operation the following year, with a meeting on Taksim Square in Istanbul drawing over 500,000 people. It was attended by all the student, political and associative organizations in Istanbul that were 'socialist', 'anti-imperialist' and 'anti-fascist'. In some regards DİSK was the most consensual force within the far-left action system, conducting its campaigns to improve workers' living conditions at the same time as the struggle against 'fascism' (as embodied by the Nationalist Movement), against American imperialism and hence against Süleyman Demirel's Justice Party, viewed as its Turkish ally.

In the public sector, where all union activity had been banned since the constitutional amendments introduced in the aftermath of the 1971 coup, sector-specific organizations to defend the interests of public-sector workers were set up in the form of associations. The largest of these in terms of membership numbers were the Association for Union and Solidarity between Teachers in Turkey (Türkiye Öğretmenler Birleşme ve Dayanışma Derneği, Töb-Der) and the Association for Union and Solidarity between Officials in Turkey (Türkiye Memurlar Birleşme ve Dayanışma Derneği, Tüm-Der). The first of these, set up on 3 September 1971 to replace the Union of All Teachers, numbered 670 branches and over 200,000 members teaching in primary schools, middle schools and high schools. Though it initially backed the CHP and its choice of a centre-left political line, several of its sections subsequently became more radical,[30] and it started presenting itself as a rampart against the 'fascist transformation' of teaching. The second of the two, which defined itself as 'anti-fascist', had nearly 300 branches and over 100,000 members prior to the coup of 12 September 1980,[31] drawing its membership from various sectors in public administration. In May 1975 the Police Association

(Polis Derneği, Pol-Der) was set up. According to its secretary-general, it numbered 17,000 police officers in 1977.[32] It was founded by CHP sympathizers, but its members gradually adopted more radical positions, waging a physical and ideological struggle from within the institution against 'fascist' officials, and when out on the streets adopting practices to protect students and activists from left-wing organizations against the violence perpetrated by ülkücü militants and police officers sympathetic to the ülkücü movement. Many other associations were set up within the public sector, especially in higher education, the vast majority of which were only active within a given university or faculty, such as ODTÜ's Association of Lecturers (ODTÜ Öğretim Üyeleri Derneği) and its Association of All Teaching Staff (ODTÜ Tüm Öğretim Elemanları Derneği). On occasions these associations (comprised of assistants, lecturers and professors) combined forces with left-wing student associations, and in their tussles with the administration were forever threatening that their members would resign. These sector-specific organizations tended not to coordinate their actions but acquaintanceship ties were built up between their members and cross-sector support was not rare. Thus when the Pol-Der Association organized a meeting in memory of Cevat Yurdakul, the head of the Adana Directorate of Security and Pol-Der member assassinated by an ülkücü militant on 20 September 1979, an enormous crowd gathered in Ankara made up of members from far-left political parties, public-sector associations and student-based extra-parliamentary organizations. Equally, when a bomb placed by ülkücü activists exploded at Istanbul University on 16 March 1978, demonstrations condemning 'fascism' drew individuals from most of the public-sector associations (as well as students and members of political parties). So whilst these associations formed part of a far-left action system, this system only operated on an intermittent and non-coordinated basis.

Extra-parliamentary movements When the Ecevit government passed the amnesty law in May 1974, student associations had been outlawed for three years. However, dormant networks up of Dev-Genç sympathizers and second-rank cadres had continued to disseminate their leaders' writings.[33] Their (clandestine) activities had retained a base of sympathizers, who were quick to mobilize in the wake of the amnesty on returning to university in 1974.[34] The normalization of political life in the autumn of 1973 also encouraged the setting up of local student associations, which took advantage of the return of the cadres from the student movements of the previous decade to coordinate and step up their activities. Up until 1980 these extra-parliamentary groups went through a period of unprecedented expansion. But the massively increased scale of the movements they ran also led to an increasing tendency towards splits, based on ideological positions and interpersonal quarrels.

The Istanbul Higher Education Cultural Association (İstanbul Yüksek Öğrenim Kültür Derneği, İYÖKD) was set up in November 1973.[35] It drew on the CHP's arrival in power to take part in the campaign for the amnesty of imprisoned and exiled activists. Its leadership was composed of five pro-THKP-C members, one pro-THKO member and one MDD sympathizer. The heirs to the TİKKO and the representatives of the new TSİP, finding themselves sidelined, left to set up their own bodies, the Revolutionary Youth Association (Devrimci Gençlik Derneği, DGD) and the Young Socialist Union (Genç Sosyalistler Birliği, GSB). The İYÖKD published the first issue of its review, *İleri* (*The avant-garde*), on 18 November 1974, but was shut down in February 1975, accused of clandestine activity. It rapidly regrouped under the name of the Istanbul Higher Education Association (Istanbul Yüksek Öğrenim Derneği, İYÖD). When it announced it was holding its first congress, this encouraged students from other universities to set up their own associations. Former Dev-Genç members presided over their founding in Ankara, Izmir, Erzurum, Adana, Bursa, Sakarya and Erzurum. Drawing on the acquaintanceship ties uniting their leaders, these associations launched a joint review in December 1975, called *Revolutionary Youth* (*Devrimci Gençlik*), before fusing in August 1976 to create the Federation of Revolution Youth Associations (Devrimci Gençlik Dernekleri Federasyonu, DGDF).[36] In May 1977 the DGDF published the first issue of its journal, *Revolutionary Path* (*Devrimci Yol*, better known by its abbreviated form, *Dev-Yol*), adopting this as the federation's name the following month. Dev-Yol henceforth emerged as the principal far-left movement in the country, and its non-official youth wing, Dev-Genç, became the most powerful student organization in Turkey.

However, the centralization of far-left student associations was only a partial process. Firstly, other organizations emerged on the far left over the same period, and secondly, despite operating under a common acronym, the level of discipline and coordination within the organization was in fact extremely low. Halkın Yolu (People's Path) was a group run by former members of the THKP-C sections in Istanbul, Izmir, Trabzon, Denizli and Kars. It was set up in 1974, publishing the *Militan Gençlik* (*Militant Youth*) review, before bringing out the *Halkın Yolu* review the following year. It was explicitly in favour of armed combat and focused its activities on rural zones. In early 1976 the Halkın Kurtuluşu (People's Liberation) group appeared, publishing a review of the same name, and endeavouring to embody the Maoist legacy bequeathed by the Gezmiş THKO (which had acted as the main source in Turkey of Enver Hodja's so-called 'Albanian' theses at the end of the decade). The Turkish Communist Party (TKP) – which had been banned from operating in Turkey but continued to be run from East Berlin by a handful of individuals making up its 'External Bureau' (*Dış Bürosu*) – set up a youth organization called the Progressive Youth Association (İlerici Gençlik Derneği, IGD). Doğu Perinçek, who was still ploughing a lonely furrow between Maoism and nationalism, also had a few supporters in the universities, who spread the ideas published by the group in *Halkın Sesi* (*The People's Voice*). The DGDF (and subsequently Dev-Yol) also encountered internal opposition, led by former THKP-C members who in 1976 set up their own organization, Kurtuluş (Liberation), officially due to a difference over the interpretation of the writings of Mahir Çayan, the THKP-C leader who had been assassinated by the forces of law and order in 1972. Then in spring 1978 the Istanbul section of Dev-Yol split from the organization and set itself up as Devrimci Sol (Revolutionary Left).[37]

The splintering continued to increase. By the end of the decade there were over thirty organizations operating at regional or national level with membership ranging from a few dozen to several thousand sympathizers. Given the size of the numbers involved, there is no way of assessing the number of legal and clandestine associations and organizations that were active in any given university or town. They were initially concentrated in universities but rapidly diversified their mobilization sites and expanded their recruitment. Mahmut explained why setting up Dev-Yol (in which he was a cadre) was seen as a way to prevent DGDF activities being limited to universities:

> 'We felt that many young people in Dev-Genç needed to open up to the people, open up to society. Because the fascists held the neighbourhoods we therefore felt there was an internal war. So we adopted the name Dev-Yol with the purpose of creating something bigger than the DGDF. We made this initiative public in 1977 and the first issue of *Dev-Yol* came out in May.'[38]

The status of these organizations was ambiguous. It is true that they were represented in the universities, and throughout the 1970s the DGDF and then Dev-Yol (via its youth wing, Dev-Genç) won large majorities in student council elections at the Middle East Technical University (ODTÜ-ÖTK) and many faculties in Istanbul.[39] But they did not have any official status, and, as the MHP reverted to its strategy of confrontation with far-left organizations, the forms of mobilization they used became less and less conventional (drawing on illegal activities, physical altercations, assassinations, and so on). Mahmut observed:

> There was no membership system at Dev-Yol ... It was half legal, half illegal, there wasn't even a leader, even though we all knew who was in charge. There were hierarchies, of course, but nothing official, there were leaders ... But legally there weren't. ... In Dev-Yol there was Ankara and the provinces. In certain neighbourhoods and even certain provinces it wasn't very organised ... Not really bureaucratic, but in important provinces Dev-Yol sent out important people, people who could be counted on.[40]

These organizations all militated against 'fascism' and for a 'democratic university' whose students were to take part in decision-making, whilst differing ideologically in taking as their model Leninism (the South American path), Maoism or the Albanian regime. These organization's sympathizers and activists – there were no official members – defined themselves primarily as anti-fascist. Their audience grew uninterruptedly. By the end of the decade *Dev-Yol* was selling 100,000 copies, Kurtuluş's was selling 70,000 and those of the TKP were running at 20,000 copies.[41]

Clandestine armed groups Most of the far-left clandestine armed groups which emerged over the course of the 1970s were set up by former students who had become politicized within Dev-Genç before leaving the country to join

Palestinian training camps in Lebanon and escape justice in the aftermath of the coup of 12 March 1971. On returning, they specialized in carrying out irregular violent tasks drawing on their military know-how and bound together by their shared experience. In so doing they presented themselves as the direct heirs to the martyrs of socialism eliminated by the 1971 military regime. These groups resembled the organizations with more conventional repertoires of action in their tendency to splinter, and in the localized and sometimes territorialized nature of their activities. The clandestine groups of the far-left, just like its political parties and associations, suffered from a low degree of coordination.

After the coup of 12 March 1971 individuals close to the THKP-C and THKO left for the Palestinian training camps in Lebanon where the first members of these groups had established contacts as of the summer of 1969, organizing several waves of departures until they were arrested or killed. Lebanon acted at that time as a sanctuary for all those afraid of being arrested by the junta. Gülten Çayan, Mahir Çayan's wife, moved to a Palestinian camp in Lebanon ahead of the military intervention, where she thought about setting up an organization initially devised as a relay for the THKP-C abroad, and subsequently as the heir to its legacy. When the last imprisoned activists were released in the spring of 1974, some of them left the country to join her. She then set up Organisation X (X Örgütü). All the founders of the clandestine armed groups of the decade passed via the Palestinian camps between 1971 and 1975, learning how to use weapons and make improvised bombs, and building up friendships within X Örgütü before returning to Turkey to set up their own armed splinter groups. X Örgütü was initially conceived as an organization to unite what remained of the various revolutionary forces that had been operating before the coup, but it became primarily somewhere activists passed through to acquire training, before then returning to Turkey and founding their own small group in an attempt to monopolize the legacy of the illustrious martyrs to the cause.

In 1975 a group of former students led by Hasan Basri and İlker Akman published a pamphlet under the title *The Urgent Problems of the Turkish Revolution* (*Türkiye Devriminin Acil Sorunları*), in which they reasserted the need for armed struggle. The 'Urgent Ones' (Acilciler), as they styled themselves, started doing bank hold-ups and assassinating far-right activists, mainly in the province of Hatay. In 1976 certain members of the group took advantage of the financial windfall from a successful hold-up to leave the organization and set up Revolutionary War (Devrimci Savaş). Another group called the Marxist Leninist Armed Propaganda Union (Marxist Leninist Silahlı Propaganda Birliği, MLSPB), a band of guerrilla fighters who had trained in Lebanon, started operating on Turkish soil in 1975. It was soon joined by the Kasabalılar,[42] militants specializing in bank hold-ups in the province of Manisa, before several of its members split in 1976 to form the Path of the Front (Cephe Yolu) and the Warriors (Savaşçılar). These were the only clandestine armed groups to specialize in violent activities, and they had very few links with the radical extra-parliamentary movements. On the far left there was a clear discontinuity between legal activities and illegal ones, between violence and more conventional approaches, and in this it differed from the Nationalist Movement, whose structure encouraged continuity across its activities as part of a more global strategy to gain access to positions of accumulation and power.

Antagonisms and altercations

DİSK emerged as the only far-left trade union confederation. But in other fields radical organizations often had rivals. Each political party and each extra-parliamentary group had at least one journal, and antagonisms were initially expressed via articles and editorials, where these press attacks sought primarily to delegitimize and stigmatize rivals by labelling them as 'social fascists', 'opportunists', 'revisionists' and so on. The position taken up by Dev-Yol towards pro-Soviet political parties is illustrative of this tendency. The 15 May 1977 issue of *Devrimci Yol* criticized the influence exerted over the DİSK leadership by the TKP, accusing the confederation of revisionism for supporting the CHP in the upcoming general elections.[43] But it also refused to back the TİP for these elections, describing it as a 'reformist and revisionist organisation perverting the struggle against fascism'.[44] The 1 June 1977 issue directly attacked the TKP and its youth wing, described as an organization that was 'in it for the money' and which took advantage of its position of strength within DİSK to oblige workers to join the İGD (the TKP's youth association).[45] Dev-Yol also criticized Maoist organizations. Responding to the denunciation in the *Halkın Kurtuluşu* journal of the 'opportunist-revisionist tactics and positions of the *Devrimci Yol* journal regarding the elections' of June 1977,[46] *Devrimci Yol* published a long article seeking to show how '*Halkın Kurtuluşu* [was] politically lost and confused'.[47] In addition to its recurrent criticism of members of the Maoist group headed by Doğu Perinçek, described as an 'opportunist profiteer',[48] *Devrimci Yol* did not pull any punches when it came to attacking *Halkın Yolu*, another Maoist group it roundly condemned for dishonesty.[49] Each of these left-wing journals competed with its rivals to win legitimacy to embody the true path of revolution. Thus the *Halkın Sesi* (People's Voice) journal, for instance, the mouthpiece of the Perinçek group, continually criticized the ideological positions and electoral tactics of pro-Soviet groups and political parties. On 15 April 1975 it denounced 'the betrayal of the workers of Epengle [a textile factory in Istanbul] by the TSİP revisionists',[50] and then three months later accused the TSİP of being 'the most right-wing' party in Turkey after its journal *Kitle* had attacked it in an article headed '*People's Voice*, or the voice of an association in the struggle against communism?'.[51] When activists from the TKP's youth association criticized activists from the TİP, which was also pro-Soviet, *Halkın Sesi* supported the TİP and denounced the attack by the 'revisionists from the İGD [the TKP's youth organisation]'.[52] This did not prevent it from calling on people not to support the TİP in the 1977 general elections, describing it as the 'Russians' lackey'.[53] Perinçek's journal also criticized the Dev-Yol 'leftists', accused of 'dividing the youth at the Istanbul Technical University'[54] and exhorting it to come clean about its crimes.[55]

These divergences resulted in incessant disagreements and quarrels amongst activists, not to mention regular altercations between pro-Soviet and Maoist groups, and even within movements. According to Mahmut, 'the Maoists were divided along the lines of the internal divisions within the Chinese regime, arguing over the same problems'.[56] Yet physical violence would not appear to have been a generalized means of settling conflicts between different movements. In places where the ülkücüs were in a position of force, the activists from various left-wing organizations came together and rallied under the banner of anti-fascism, which acted as the prime framework for their activities. But though it is difficult to arrive at an exact estimation of the number of victims of internal altercations within the far left, out of the 1200 portraits brandished aloft in 2005 at a demonstration held by the 1978 Generation Association (*Yetmişsekizliler Derneği*)[57] in memory of the victims of the events of the 1970s, forty-eight were activists killed in altercations between left-wing groups.

The nationalist far right

Far-right nationalist milieus also underwent a period of profound restructuring during the 1960s. As of 1965, the Republican Villagers Nation Party (Cumhuriyetçi Köylü Millet Partisi, CKMP), renamed the Nationalist Action Party (Milliyetçi Hareket Partisi, MHP) in 1969, set up a whole range of associations and anti-communist, nationalist trade unions whose activities it coordinated in order to form what may be described as an integrated, centralized action system – the Nationalist Movement, which rapidly captured representation of anti-communist symbolical assets and established itself as the main actor on the Turkish far right up until the coup of 12 September 1980.

How the MHP originated

The takeover of the CKMP carried out in 1965 by a small team headed by Alparslan Türkeş was officially approved at the Adana Congress of 8 and 9 February 1969 when the party changed its name, becoming the Nationalist Action Party. Within a few years Türkeş, a former army colonel, had managed to evict the party's long-standing leaders by appointing a core group of supporters to key positions, many of whom he had met during his military career. The placing of members of this small group within many pan-Turkish and anti-communist associations meant that the party enjoyed the support of the most influential people within Turkish nationalist circles.

On joining the CKMP in 1964 Alparslan Türkeş turned his back on his military career, which had been considerably shaped by his political preferences, and opted for a more conventional form of political activity. When the army had taken power in May 1960 he had been a colonel. He was an important member of the junta through to November 1960, and acted for a few months as undersecretary to the prime minister. Türkeş embodied a radical line on the Milli Birlik Komitesi

(Committee of National Union, MBK), and was supported by certain of its youngest and lowest-ranking members. This group was opposed to any rapid return to civilian government, which, in the aftermath of 27 May, amounted to establishing the CHP in power, whose political positions they did not share. Cemal Gürsel, the head of the Milli Birlik Komitesi, arbitrated in favour of the moderates. He proceeded to remove fourteen members of the MBK on 13 November 1960, who were retired and sent on diplomatic postings abroad.[58] On returning to the country in 1963, Türkeş sought to join the AP, but ran into hostility from its leadership who were not eager to count among its members the hardline representative of the Committee of National Union. On resigning from the army, Türkeş enjoyed very considerable prestige in nationalist circles, and was recruited by the CKMP as inspector general to the party, in charge of identifying those who had remained loyal to its former leader, Osman Bölükbaşı. This position enabled him to weed out numerous potential rivals for the position of party chairman. He was joined at the CKMP by several close supporters, including some of the fourteen members of the Committee of National Union who had been forced out in November 1960 (Muzaffer Özdağ, Rıfat Baykal, Ahmet Er, Dündar Taşer, Mustafa Kaplan, Fazıl Akkoyunlu, Şefik Soyuyüce, Numan Esin and Münir Köseoğlu), all of whom were active in various nationalist associations, and who worked actively to expand Türkeş's influence within the party.[59]

Within just over a year the small team had conquered virtually the entire party leadership. At the extraordinary congress held on 31 July and 1 August 1965 Türkeş was elected party chairman, winning 698 votes to the 516 cast for the outgoing chairman, Ahmet Oğuz;[60] Muzaffer Özdağ, Türkeş' right-hand man, was elected deputy secretary general.[61] In reaction to this, six MPs left the party, together with the minister for defence (Hasan Dinçer, MP for Afyon) and the minister for village affairs (Seyfi Öztürk, MP for Eskişehir), followed a few days later by İrfan Baran, a former minister of justice and MP for Konya.[62] With the departure of the last members of the old guard, the team headed by Türkeş was able to extend its control over the organization with greater ease. Whilst in the 1965 general elections this restructuring led the party to suffer an electoral setback – dropping right back to only 2.2 per cent of the vote – at each subsequent general election it did progressively better. In 1969 it became the MHP, winning 3 per cent of the vote and a seat in parliament in the elections held on 12 October 1969, followed by 3.4 per cent of the vote and three seats on 14 October 1973, and then 6.4 per cent and fifteen seats on 5 June 1977.

At the CKMP Congress held in November 1967, the party adopted the national-socialist doctrine of the 'nine lights' as presented by Türkeş in a work he had written in 1965.[63] He started being referred to as 'Başbuğ', meaning leader in old Turkish.[64] The ruling team gradually replaced pan-Turkism with the defence of Islamic values, leading it to drop the wolf as the party's symbol in favour of three white crescents on a red background. In the light of the increasing mobilization by the far left and the electoral success of the TİP, the cadres of the future MHP decided to adopt an anti-communist and anti-separatist line. In a speech given in 1967 Türkeş asserted, 'Within our universities a nationalist youth front has risen up against communist rioters'.[65] In 1966 a network of youth associations – the Ülkü Hearths (Ülkü Ocakları) – was set up to support the action of the party's youth sections and constitute a civilian support force. These 'hearths' were the most dynamic sections in the Nationalist movement. Though statutorily independent of the MHP, being devised as non-official youth sections, they were in charge of the Nationalist Movement's non-conventional activities and throughout the 1970s ran the counter-mobilization against left-wing movements. In the summer of 1968 commando camps were set up to train cadres for anti-communist militias[66] who went on to eliminate several left-wing activists up until the coup of 12 March 1971. The Turkish political classes' fear of the activism of far-left splinter groups meant that party members suspected of exactions could act with relative impunity. They were thus left largely undisturbed in the wake of the coup of 12 March 1971, which the party openly supported.

Setting up an environment of associations

The increasing electoral success of the TİP, the hegemonic position acquired by far-left student associations in certain faculties and the emergence of DİSK within the trade union field encouraged the MHP to position itself as a counter-mobilization cause in those sectors where the left was operative. As of 1966 the new leadership set up a series of nationalist and anti-communist associations, which it controlled by financing their activities and appointing trusted people to run them. It thereby deployed a strategy to build up fronts in all those sectors where the left was mobilizing. It displayed organizational skills unknown on the far left and managed to establish a highly coordinated structure in which the division of labour was overseen by the party, which had the means at its disposal to impose a strong degree of discipline.

The party set up youth associations in universities and institutes of higher education. Though local at first, these soon fused into larger structures. In March 1966 the first Ülkü Hearth (Ülkü Ocağı) was set up in the Law Faculty at Ankara University on the initiative of Namık Kemal Zeybek, the chairman of the CKMP's youth wing. Other hearths opened later that year in Ankara University's faculties of languages, history and geography (DTCF), agriculture (Ziraat Fakültesi), teaching (Eğitim Fakültesi) and political science (Siyasal Bilgiler Fakültesi).[67] That same month, two other student associations, the Turkish National Youth Association (Türkiye Milli Gençlik Derneği, TMGD) and the Turkish Nationalist Youth Organisation (Milliyetçi Türk Gençlik Teşkilatı, MTGT), were established in Ankara. On 29 February 1968 the Ülkücü Youth Organisation (Genç Ülkücüler Teşkilatı, GÜT) was founded; by the time it was shut down during the period of martial law in late 1971, it numbered 348 branches.[68]

Ülkü Hearths sprang up in most of the faculties and universities in Ankara, Istanbul and Izmir. In 1969, once again under the impetus of the MHP, they started coordinating their activities within the Union of Ülkü Hearths (Ülkü Ocakları Birliği, ÜOB). This was founded in April under the patronage of Alparslan Türkeş,[69] and held its first general council in Ankara on 15 November 1970. This process of coordination between the activities of the MHP and the ülkücü associations ran into hostility from certain groups. Fifty or so young members of the CKMP's Izmir section left the party in 1969 to set up the Energetic Development of National Activity group (Nasyonel Aktivite Zinde İnkişaf, NAZI).[70]

Although the Nationalist Movement was largely spared by the coup of 12 March, the clubs were shut down in late 1971. But other associations were then created in provinces not under martial law. The Turkish Ülkücüs Organisation (Türk Ülkücüler Teşkilatı, TÜT) was created on 15 February 1972 in Çankırı, the Association of the Great Ülkü (Büyük Ülkü Derneği, BÜD) on 22 December 1972 in Kayseri, and the Association of Ülkü Hearths (Ülkü Ocakları Derneği, ÜOD) was set up in Bursa by MHP representatives on 15 September 1973. Associations which were the fruit of local initiatives such as the BÜD and the TÜT soon joined the ÜOD structures.[71] Throughout the 1970s the party was able to draw on the ÜOD in its ideological and physical combat with left-wing organizations. Remzi Çayir, a ÜOD member from 1978 onwards, explained the relationship between ülkücü youth associations and the party in the following terms:

> The MHP youth wing was the ülkücü associations ... The MHP youth sections were just something official. Because building up relationships between associations and political power was forbidden ... Otherwise the real youth sections were the ülkücü associations.
>
> *But when you were a member of an ülkücü association did you become a party member?*
>
> 'No, it was a shared identity. But afterwards, all ülkücüs ended up joining the party.'[72]

When the CHP government dissolved the ÜOD in 1978, the Nationalist Movement immediately set up a new structure called the Ülkücü Youth Association (Ülkücü Gençlik Derneği, ÜGD).[73] Although in some cases the party cadres were replaced, no changes were made to the leaders of the youth sections or to Türkeş' youth advisers – the true leaders working 'in the shadows' of the various ülkücü youth associations. A similar series of events took place on 9 March 1980, when the ÜGD's provincial sections had to close down due to the new period of martial law. The organization was dissolved but reappeared under the name of the Association of the Ideal Path (Ülkü Yolu Derneği, ÜYD), based in Nevşehir in a province unaffected by martial law. In his indictment, the prosecutor describes the activities of these ülkücü organizations and their relationship with the MHP in the following terms:

> The association worked to establish a totalitarian and centralist regime, illegally, by turning itself into an armed organisation that eliminated anybody who did not share its political views. That is why the Association rapidly and illegally set up organisations in schools, neighbourhoods, streets, halls of residence (*yurt*) and State offices. [The party] orchestrated the separation between communists and ülkücüs in these places, oversaw the running of its allied associations,

gathered information, trained assault teams (*vurucu timler*), and held seminars to train ülkücü activists so as to establish its dominance.[74]

MHP activists were encouraged to set up ülkücü associations in their place of work. Sometimes the party established ties with existing associations, offering personnel or financial support, before then taking control of them. The Confederation of Nationalist Workers Unions (Milliyetçi İşçi Sendikaları Konfederasyonu, MİSK) was set up on 23 June 1970, a few days after DİSK's display of force against a proposed alteration to trade union law. It was initially composed of two unions, Plastik-İş and Türpek-İş, numbering only 4,766 members in 1971, but it started to attract more between 1975 and 1978 when the MHP was one of the parties in the Nationalist Front governments. By 1979 it had nineteen affiliated trade unions, totalling 285,496 members.[75] MİSK had close ties to the MHP, which controlled the composition of its executive board. During the 1970s many professional associations were set up for workers, craftsmen, journalists, lawyers, decorators, economists, engineers and academics, all organized along corporatist lines.

In the public sector the party set up ülkücü associations to defend the interests of public-sector workers in reaction to the left-wing associations which, with the gradual normalization of political life, were now beginning to emerge. The Ülkücü Teachers Union Association (Ülkücü Öğretmenler Birliği Derneği, Ülkü-Bir) was set up in 1975 to counter the activism of Töb-Der in secondary schools. The same year a group of police officers and MHP sympathizers formed the Ülkücü Police Union (Ülkücü Polisler Birliği, Pol-Bir) to resist the takeover of Pol-Der – the only existing police association – by a group of police officers close to the CHP. The mission of the Ülkücü Public Sector Workers and Officials Association (Ülkücü Kamu Görevliler ve Memurlar Derneği, Ülküm) was to provide a framework for all those working in the public sector, as was that of the Public Sector Worker Forces Union Association (Ülkücü Kamu Görevlileri Güçbirliği Derneği, Ülküm-Bir),[76] which replaced it when it was shut down on 7 March 1979.[77]

Ülkücü cultural associations sprang up in many different places. The Ülkücü Villagers Association (Ülkücü Köylüler Derneği, Ülkü-Köy) organized many evening gatherings and concerts of traditional music, as well as distributing free meals. Associations in Trabzon worked to develop the town and improve its appearance (*Trabzon kalkındırma ve güzelleştirme dernekleri*); associations for music lovers (*müzik severler derneği*) were set up in seven neighbourhoods in Bursa, and nine neighbourhoods in Elazığ became home to cultural associations. In other towns the network was even denser, with twenty-five active neighbourhood associations in Kayseri. An Ülkücü Women Association (Ülkücü Hanımlar Derneği, Ülkü-Han)[78] was also set up.

Although all of these associations directed their attention solely to organizing concerts, meetings, meals, readings and lessons on how to play traditional Turkish musical instruments, their function as intended by the MHP leadership was always the same: to lead local inhabitants, workers, employees and public-sector staff to the party, and get them to participate in financing its activities by raising contributions or calling for donations. This division of labour by the party can only properly be understood, however, by examining the power relations structuring the Nationalist Movement.

Party political control of the Nationalist Movement

Party mechanisms for controlling the movement The large number of reports, accounts and letters found at the party's Ankara headquarters after the 1980 coup gives an idea of the sheer extent of interaction between the executive board and the entire Nationalist Movement, together with the influence that the party exerted over it. It was members of the party's executive board and their local representatives who appointed and removed provincial cadres and national leaders of ülkücü unions and associations, coordinated the transfers of money between associations and local sections and provided for the various needs of individual organizations.

The systematic presence of a party representative at meetings of ülkücü associations provides a first indication of the extent to which the Nationalist Movement was interconnected with party organizations and associations. Party bodies were in charge of controlling the activities of associations at each level (local, provincial and national) and of transmitting the party's orders. The movement's national leaders were regularly called to party headquarters or to the offices of the youth wing's leadership. In the provinces, meetings were held to coordinate the activities of the various local organizations. It was the head of the local (provincial or district) MHP section, seconded by the party's local youth section heads, who chaired the interviews to which were summoned ÜOD, ÜGD and ÜYD section heads, their board members, neighbourhood section heads, representatives in schools and student residences and those in charge of local professional organizations.[79] In even the smallest ülkücü association, reports were drawn up at each level of the hierarchy assessing people on the preceding below, and these were sent to the local or provincial party manager, or else directly to Türkeş' youth advisers.[80] For instance, in a letter sent by Ali Haydar Yangın, the BÜD head in the province of Kahramanmaraş, to Ramiz Ongun, who at the time was the general chairman of the party's youth sections, Yangın refers to his disappointment with the head of the BÜD's Göksün section, and requests that he be replaced.[81] The police found countless such reports from all the ülkücü organizations when it searched the party's headquarters.

The party stepped up its control over the Nationalist Movement as of 1975. On arriving in government, the MHP had direct access to public resources, and was thus able to reinforce its control over ülkücü organizations, ensuring their pliancy by distributing the resources and positions it now controlled to their members. The party's access to public resources is the reason behind the growing centralization of the Nationalist Movement. In addition to this, the increasing number of altercations between ülkücü activists and those from the far left – that the party encouraged so as to maintain a climate of social tension that it hoped to turn to its advantage by presenting itself as a credible solution for re-establishing order – obliged it to coordinate the activities of ülkücü associations even more closely. It needed to manage the supply of weapons and material to militants, oversee the defence of ülkücüs standing trial and where necessary provide for imprisoned activists and their families.

It was only comparatively later on, in 1977, that the party established a stable mechanism to control and liaise with the Nationalist Movement's organizations. On 21 July, Gün Sazak, Türkeş' right-hand man, was appointed minister of customs and monopolies in the second Nationalist Front government. On taking up this position, he recruited party activists and members of ülkücü associations, appointing twenty-odd young cadres to positions on the Council of Customs Controllers, most of whom had been local or national leaders of either the party or of nationalist associations.[82] These cadres appointed other activists, facilitated relationships between the party and its sections in Europe and acted as intermediaries between party personnel and its members working in the ministry. Within several months the Ministry was transformed into a veritable MHP stronghold. When the government was overthrown in January 1978 the minister left his job and the controllers had to resign, on which the party absorbed them within its structures and appointed them to oversee relations with the ülkücü associations. All of them were offered a job as regional head of the ülkücü *Hergün* newspaper, but in actual fact they were in charge of controlling, financing and driving the activities of ülkücü associations in the various parts of Anatolia. They were thus central to the relationship between party headquarters, its sections and its environment of associations and trade unions. These 'instructors' (*eğitimci*), as they were henceforth called, were initially in charge of running seminars in the provinces, and they continued to associate with Gün Sazak and draw up activist training programmes with him.[83] They acted as the relays for party headquarters, transmitting its orders, pooling donations and orchestrating the distribution of resources within the Nationalist Movement. Ramiz Ongun, a former head of the party's youth wing, acted as the leader of this little group up until his departure on military service in early 1979, when he was replaced by Türkmen Onur.[84] When martial law was proclaimed in late December 1978, most of these instructors were called back to Ankara. From then on they were placed in charge of the training programmes at party headquarters reserved for the most promising members of the Nationalist Movement, where they trained and identified those who would go on to act as their substitutes and hold seminars in the Anatolian provinces.[85]

These various elements are indicative of efforts by the party to homogenize and control the Nationalist Movement, rather than of any existing homogeneity. They also emphasize the risks of a split within the movement and fears for its unity given its rapid growth. Indeed, by 1975, the total number of Ülkücüler exceeded tens of thousands. Between 1975 and 1977, there was a sharp spike in the number of violent confrontations between the ülkücüs and the leftists, too – so sharp indeed that Türkeş could not cope with events on the ground anymore, given the lack of communication at the time. Under those circumstances, it may be considered that he had to agree, willy-nilly, to devolving decision-making powers to instructors, who would each oversee a number of cities. Some of the instructors, such as Ramiz

Ongun, were also said to have accumulated power to challenge Türkeş in the future. In other words, there were also potential centrifugal forces within the MHP and the Nationalist Movement as well. It was only by drawing on organizational skills acquired during previous military and political experience that Türkeş's entourage was able to rely on a set of relays– in this case the instructors– while managing to maintain a sufficient degree of homogeneity to support its political mobilization efforts. The setting up of ülkücü bureaus in local arenas, with the goal of managing and guiding the ülkücüs' mobilization in their daily life, is another indication of the daily efforts made by the party leadership to order and control the movement.

Ülkücü bureaus It is not possible to apprehend the relationship between the organizations within the Nationalist Movement by looking solely at the control the party exerted over ülkücü organizations. Over the course of the 1970s the Movement established bureaus (*masa*), hybrid structures which were statutorily autonomous or else without any official legal existence, run both by party members and ülkücü associations. They were thus not part of the party structure, but their composition was carefully monitored by local party cadres in cooperation with local Nationalist Movement organizations. Some served to organize and mobilize ülkücüs, such as the schools bureau (*okullar masası*),[86] which helped establish ülkücü structures in schools and universities. It was in charge of collecting fees and contacting teachers to ensure the movement students passed their exams or entrance exams; it was funded by the halls of residence bureau (*yurtlar masası*), which helped ülkücü students living in a hall of residence to establish an organization there and take political control of it. The *gecekondu* district bureau (*gecekondu semtler masası*) coordinated all of these activities and pooled revenue from neighbourhood associations, obtained by selling reviews, insignia, posters and meals, as well as by bringing pressure to bear on shopkeepers to make a financial contribution to the Nationalist Movement. The social works bureau (*sosyal faaliyetler masası*) helped needy ülkücüs and coordinated activities relating to Ramadan, such as collective meals to break the fast. The education bureau (*eğitim masası*) sent out seminar programmes devised by the team of educators and organized decentralized training programmes. Finally the legal bureau (*hukuk masası*) provided the party and ülkücü associations with legal expertise, as well as supporting ülkücüs who had been imprisoned for armed activity. It drew up dismissal requests, distributed bribes, approached personnel working in the courts in question, provided lawyers, gave financial support to the families of those who had died for the cause, catered to the needs of imprisoned ülkücüs[87] and provided ülkücüs wanted by the police with places to hide. An organization bureau (*teşkilatlandırma masası*) was established in order to coordinate the activities of these bureaus and local ülkücü associations (the neighbourhood, women, school, student residence and business organizations).

The movement's economic ventures The Nationalist Movement could also draw on a certain number of businesses to run its cultural and publishing activities. The first such business, the Printing and Newspaper Operations Company (Matbaa ve Gazete İşletmeciliği Anonim Şirketi), whose role was to distribute ülkücü publications, was created in 1972. All its shareholders were members of the party hierarchy.[88] It was seconded in its task by the Hergün Journalism Company (Hergün Gazetecilik Anonim Şirketi), founded on 12 June 1975, which brought out certain of the Movement's newspapers and journals (and notably the *Hergün* newspaper), as well as offering column space to announce upcoming party and ülkücü association congresses, meetings, and other events.[89] On 15 June 1979 the party decided to centralize the activities of the company's operating under its wing, grouping them into the Sedaş Press, Publishing, Distribution, Filmmaking, Tourism, and Trade company (Sedaş Basın, Yayın Dağıtım Filmcilik, Turizm ve Ticaret Anonim Şirketi),[90] which now oversaw the Nationalist Movement's main companies: the Hasret Publishing and Distribution Enterprise (Hasret Yayınevi ve Dağıtım İşletmesi) and Soydan Printing Press (Soydan Matbaası), which published and distributed virtually all ülkücü writings, as well as its posters and campaign posters; the Şöhret Advertising company (Şöhret Reklam), in charge of selling advertising space in ülkücü publications; Başak Offset (Başak Ofset), a printing press and film production company; the Elif Concert and Organisation Bureau (Elif Konser ve Organize Bürosu) and the Töre, Arts, Sport, Folklore, Tourism, and Education Association (Töre, Sanat, Spor, Folklor, Turizm ve Eğitim Derneği, TÖMFED) which programmed concerts and plays, sporting activities, and folklore events for the Movement; the Maltepe Sports Club (Maltepe Spor Kulübü); and the Burçak Restaurant (*Burçak Lokantası*), which prepared and distributed meals for imprisoned ülkücüs. In addition to this the Çelik-İş Industry and Trade Company (Çelik-İş Sanayii ve Ticaret A.Ş.), created and controlled by the MİSK-affiliated Çelik-İş trade union, provided union members with cheap meals and clothing. The Istanbul-based ANDA Publishing and Distribution Company (ANDA Yayın Dağıtım Şirketi) was in charge of a certain number of ülkücü publications.[91] The party directly controlled two foundations, the Foundation for Historical and Islamic Research (Tarih ve İslam Araştırma Vakfı), founded on 25 October 1979 to 'disseminate and promote knowledge of Islamic culture', and the Education and Social Security Foundation (Sosyal Güvenlik ve Eğitim Vakfı).[92] On the strength of this vast set of companies, foundations and bureaus, the Nationalist Movement enjoyed a level of integration that was unparalleled in pre-1980 Turkey.

Moving into and controlling migration space The activities of the Nationalist Movement were not limited to national arenas but also extended to migrant spaces. As Olivier Grojean has observed, together with Erbakan's MSP the MHP was one of the first parties to 'be aware of the importance of the Turkish migration space: they rapidly realised that including the diaspora in their electoral strategy in Turkey could boost the level of internal consolidation'.[93] The drive to mobilize the diaspora started in 1965.[94] Prior to the founding congress of the German branch of the party on 9 April 1973,[95] the MHP did not have any official organization in Europe. Up until that date 'cultural associations (Kültür Dernekleri), Turkish centres (Türk Merkezleri), Turkish hearths (Türk Ocakları), and Islamic cultural centres (İslam Kültür Merkezleri) had sprung up ... with varying degrees of autonomy, and united by their proximity to the MHP'.[96] In 1973 the party established a MHP-European council (MHP-Europarates).[97]

The party was then able to draw on its national network of associations to identify and contact sympathizers or activists settled in Germany. As early as 29 November 1972 the MHP secretary general had already launched a mobilization campaign in Germany, asking ülkücü associations and the party's district and provincial sections to 'send party headquarters lists of names and addresses [of ülkücüs] in their region who had gone to work abroad', so as to forward them to party contacts in Germany.[98]

An Ülkücü Youth Association (Ülkücü Gençlik) was founded in 1976, grouping together 111 organizations and some 26,000 members in the Federal Republic of Germany.[99] The party took advantage of its involvement in the Nationalist Front governments (from 31 March 1975 to 22 June 1977, and from 21 July 1977 to 5 January 1978) to further its relations with associations based in Europe. Thus 'teachers close to the movement, and confirmed activists even, were appointed important positions in Turkish consulates and embassies in Europe, sometimes blurring the boundaries between the State domain and the political party domain'.[100] In 1978 a decision by the Turkish Constitutional Court obliged the MHP to cease all party political activity abroad,[101] compelling it to draw more extensively on associative networks in Europe whilst maintaining a clandestine party structure in Germany.

In Germany the MHP was able to draw on a certain degree of benevolence from CDU and CSU cadres who wished to establish a rampart against far-left mobilization amongst the Turkish community. On returning from a trip to Turkey, Heinz Schwarz, the CDU interior minister for Rhineland-Palatinate, told the press that the ruling Nationalist Front coalition 'brings the guarantee that Turkey will not fall under the influence of Soviet factions'.[102] And when Türkeş met the CSU leader Franz Joseph Strauß in Bavaria in April 1978, the two agreed on the need to work together to counter the spread of communism amongst Turkish immigrants. The MHP founded the Democratic Federation of Turkish Ülkücü Associations in Europe (Avrupa Demokratik Ülkücü Türk Dernekleri Federasyonu, ADÜTDF) or Turkish Federation (Türk Federasyonu), a few weeks later, on 17–18 June 1978, in Schwarzenborn in Rhineland-Palatinate. This had '220 associations in Europe, 170 of which were in Germany, and over 33,000 members'.[103] There were no doubts about the degree of proximity between the party and the federation since it was Türkeş himself who nominated its chairman, Lokman Kondakcı,[104] before then replacing him in February 1979 with Serdar Çelebi, an MHP member registered in the Şişli district of Istanbul,[105] and member of the Council of Controllers at the Ministry of Customs and Monopolies from 13 October 1977 to 19 April 1978.[106] The Turkish Federation may thus be considered as the MHP outpost in Europe. It drew on funding sent by the MHP and took part in the party's work to mobilize for electoral victory in Turkey. The presence of the MHP and ülkücü associations in Europe was thus, as Olivier Grojean has observed, part of a 'veritable strategy for electoral victory "back home": the migrant space was included within the realm of Turkish politics, constituting a new province as it were, or more specifically a new Turkish constituency, even though it had its own specific qualities (being comparatively wealthy, extraterritorial, and with links to many different Turkish provinces, etc.).'[107]

*

In the conflict opposing the two movements the far left acted in dispersed manner, whereas the MHP coordinated and controlled a vast set of mobilized organizations in order to facilitate its access to power. On the far left the sites for recruitment, together with the trajectories, capitals and multiple social positions of the leaders, fostered individual initiatives and encouraged differentiation. Within the Nationalist Movement the value placed on resources of authority meant it brought together individuals whose profiles had been approved by the party machinery or its associative representatives, directly recruited by the team of party leader Alparslan Türkeş. It would thus appear to have been highly integrated and centralized around the MHP, unlike the far-left action system, which was spread out thinly, with very low levels of integration, operating in a largely uncoordinated manner, and with internal rivalry within each sector. What we now need to do is study the effects that these specific structuring processes had on each of the two systems, and on the ways in which they accumulated and allocated resources.

Chapter 3

THE ACCUMULATION AND CIRCULATION OF RESOURCES

Studying the two action systems' positions and resources[1] casts light on the tactical opportunities available to the Turkish far left and far right during the 1970s. The structure of the Nationalist Movement and the MHP's unexpected involvement in government between 1975 and 1978 enabled it to pursue a national strategy to gain access to power, whilst the general shortage of resources on the far left and its splintering into rival and largely uncoordinated organizations exacerbated the tendency to pursue individual and local strategies. This chapter assesses how these two action systems' tactical capacities were fashioned by the means they used to accumulate and redistribute resources. It then looks at the work conducted within each action system to homogenize their habitus, where this was systematic on the far right but less rigorous on the far left. It closes with an examination of how the systems invested their political identities in the conflict, as well as the ways in which the adversarial relationship binding the two movements together legitimized their mobilization, thereby enabling them to expand their social bases.

Dissimilar economic resources

The different structures of the two antagonistic movements influenced their mechanisms for accumulating and circulating resources. Whilst the ülkücü movement had a global system for funding its sections, far-left organizations were obliged to be self-financing and they experienced recurrent resource shortages.

The circulation of resources within the Nationalist Movement

MHP financial accounts show that it increased its revenue and expenditure continuously over the period 1975–1979. Its revenue went from $89,158 to $285,783 dollars,[2] whilst its expenditure increased fivefold, from $74,994 to $380,034.[3] The electoral progress made by the party in the 1977 general elections meant it was able to draw on greater levels of public financing than in the past. Between 1976 and 1977 its revenue doubled, going from $91,081 to $186,339. In 1978 it received $136,088 dollars in State funding, making up over 72 per cent of its annual revenue.

The party took advantage of the increase in funding attendant upon its electoral success to exert greater control over the organizations in the Nationalist Movement by providing them with the revenue they needed for their everyday functioning. Its participation in the Nationalist Front government as of 1975 already placed it in a position of strength in its relationship with various ülkücü organizations, and the doubling of its finances after 1977 further reinforced its central position within 'its' movement, extending its domination a notch further. It became what Doug McAdam, Sidney Tarrow and Charles Tilly refer to as the ülkücü movement's 'broker', defined as a body that 'reduces transaction costs of communication and coordination among sites, facilitates the combined use of resources located at different sites, and creates new potential collective actors'.[4] It is thus not possible to conceive of the activities of the MHP independently of those of the ülkücü organizations.

The MHP presided over the circulation and allocation of financial resources within the movement. It was the instructors sent out to the regions – the brokers within the Nationalist Movement – who were in charge of distributing the sums of money that the party transferred to its organizations. The 'brokers' themselves were very well paid, receiving between TL7500 and TL13,000 per month depending on whether they were married or single (that is to say, in 1978, between $300 and $520). Between February 1978 and September 1980 the party distributed TL6,353,000 in all ($90,757 at the 1980 exchange rate) to its instructors[5] and provided them with a sum of TL1,110,000 ($15,587), with which they bought six vehicles. They were also allocated funds to cover their expenses and to help local associations as they saw fit.[6] On several occasions the party's secretary general noted in his diary requests from representatives and ülkücü associations,[7] and several documents show that funds were transferred to ülkücü youth associations.[8] It is for instance known that in 1977 the party's treasurer general received an order to transfer TL75,000 ($4201) to Muhsin Yazıcıoğlu, who was chairman of the ÜOD at that time. On 31 May 1979 Türkeş ordered the transfer of an identical sum for 'the youth of Istanbul', and Mehmet Deryal, the ÜYD treasurer, received TL10,000 ($519) on 29 December 1979. Activity reports from the party's provincial sections refer to numerous donations made to the local sections of ülkücü associations.[9] This money enabled them to pay their rent or buy material, run cultural activities and lay on entertainments, and was also used to meet the needs of members who were in prison.

As of 1977, the party had sufficient money to finance and therefore control the ülkücü organizations. They were not, however, totally dependent on financial

Table 3.1 Party Revenue and Expenditure between 1975 and 1979 (in TL)[10]

	1975	1976	1977	1978	1979
Revenue	1,258,911.16	1,486,442.03	3,326,167.35	4,701,613.78	10,202,478.60
Expenditure	1,058,928.82	1,407,528.81	3,534,226.28	5,147,490.21	13,567,246.25[11]

transfers from the party, and a cross-financing system was gradually set up by which the better funded organizations in the Nationalist Movement helped the poorer ones. Companies also lent their financial support to the activities of the ÜGD and then the ÜYD: ANDA gave them over TL800,000[12] in *zekat* and *fitre*,[13] whilst TÖMFED, Hasret and the Burçak restaurant made several transfers to cover their operating costs.[14] This was to support the Nationalist Movement's youth movements, which found it hard to obtain the funds they needed to look after their imprisoned members and those who had gone into hiding. These youth organizations could also draw on regular help from other ülkücü unions and associations. The ÜGD activity report for the period from 19 March to 14 October 1979 shows that Ülküm undertook to transfer it TL60,000 ($1273.88) per month, that it received TL158,000 ($3354.56) from Ülkü-Han, and TL20,000[15] ($424.62) from Ülkü-Tek. The MİSK trade union confederation also helped with funding, directly transferring money to the ÜGD (TL142,000 – $5680 – between 19 March and 14 October 1978) and then to the ÜYD (TL425,000 – $6071.42 – between 21 March and 20 July 1980), as well as providing them with fabric to be sold on.[16]

Whilst the party helped fund ülkücü organizations, the lattice-like structure it established within the Nationalist Movement also helped fund MHP activities. Ülkücü associations were tasked with collecting and selling animal skins – an activity which in 1979 brought them TL2,325,000 ($65,126) across the country as a whole.[17] They pooled the *zekat* (1/40 of annual income that the Islamic religion decrees be distributed to the poor) and the *fitre* (alms at the end of Ramadan), and sent them to the party treasurer general,[18] to whom they are also regularly transferred money brought in by their cultural activities and entertainments. Thus the Women's Ülkü Hearths Bureau (Ülkü Ocakları Kızlar Masası) gave the party the TL2177 it collected from holding a 'Grey wolf night' (*Bozkurt Gecesi*) on 5 July 1974,[19] and the ÜOD regularly handed over the money it made from its musical evenings.[20] In 1980 the ÜYD treasurer[21] called for small businesses (such as coffeehouses, restaurants, grocery stores, peddlers and so on) to be set up in the neighbourhoods in major towns, and asked the treasuries of the association's local sections to step up their activity with local businessmen and entrepreneurs. The MİSK trade union confederation was also called upon to contribute. In the companies where it was in a position of force it could oblige management to make a direct financial contribution to the party. Associations, companies and trade unions were also called upon to assist ülkücüs who had been imprisoned or fallen on hard times, along with wounded ülkücüs and the families of those who had lost their life for the cause, who received regular visits from delegations from the party's local sections and ülkücü associations who came to ascertain whether they had enough money to meet their needs. If they did not have the financial wherewithal, the local sections would find a job in businesses ran by its sympathizers for the men in the family.[22] The legal bureau (*hukuk masası*) centralized all of the services provided to ülkücüs who were imprisoned or else awaiting judgement, providing any legal and judicial expertise required by activists, working with lawyers to prepare for trial and paying their fees, approaching members of the courts who were to judge ülkücüs in order to buy an acquittal, and working with the Burçak restaurant to supply imprisoned activists with food and clothing and to meet their families' needs. As the months passed the bureau's budget exploded, with expenditure rising from TL89,825 ($3522)[23] in March 1979 to TL603,547 ($16,906)[24] by January 1980.[25] Although the entire Nationalist Movement helped finance the bureau, it was the party, via the intermediary of its instructors, that provided most of the funding. Three instructors –Türkmen Onur, Ramiz Ongun and Mehmet Ekici – were allocated to oversee relations with the bureau, which between 1 January 1978 and 15 February 1979 received TL357,000 ($14,280) from them just for the maintenance of imprisoned ülkücüs.[26] The bureau also received financial support from the party to pay the fees of the Nationalist Movement's lawyers.[27]

Between the late 1976 and 1980 the party launched several fundraising campaigns in order to finance its electoral activity, refurbish its headquarters in Ankara and support needy ülkücüs' families. All of the ülkücü associations and trade unions in Turkey and Europe were called upon to make a contribution. In early 1976 Türkeş announced the launch of the 'A thousand lira from 10,000 people' campaign (*On bin kişiden 1000 lira kampanyası*). This involved 'setting up a 10 million lira election fund [$560,224] in order to be ready for the elections and be in a position to cover any expenditure incur[red]'. Two bank accounts were opened to pool these funds. The campaign was a comparative failure. According to a report drawn up for the MHP trial, TL1,060,353 ($59,403) was paid into the first account, and TL2,017,693 ($113,036) into the second.[28] The sums collected also had to be used to renovate party headquarters, a project for which a specific campaign was launched (raising TL1,283,330 – $71,895), enabling the party to allocate TL1,683,330 ($94,304) to this refurbishment.[29]

Ülkücü associations abroad were also called upon to participate. Several bank accounts were opened in Germany in the name of Alparslan Türkeş,[30] and local representatives of the party or the Turkish Federation regularly paid in some of the membership fees they recevied. Enver Altaylı, the head of the MHP's European council, had an account with Deutschbank, into which some DM225,000 were paid[31] before being handed over to Türkeş. The Turkish Federation had an account in Germany with DM175,000 on it, and it is known that Türkeş received DM70,000 in cash from the head of the Federation in a hotel in Bonn during a visit there in 1977. Money was normally transferred by wire or postal order. Thus the leaders of the Association of the Great Ideal in Berlin (Berlin Büyük Ülkü Derneği) transferred TL27,900 ($1563)[32] to the account of the secretary general of the party in Turkey in order to support families of ülkücüs killed in an altercation with far-left activists in 1977.[33] The MHP made sure that it received this money, and did not hesitate to remind association cadres of their obligation to send it. Thus in 1975 the MHP treasurer wrote to Orhan Yılman, a cadre at the Turkish workers association in the Netherlands, reminding him that 'all members have to pay their fees' and that the association's cadres 'need to make sure that these membership fees are sent regularly to the MHP'.[34] This money came mainly from selling flags, emblems, calendars and journals, or from a share of the membership fees paid by party and association members in Europe. However, and even though it is not possible to do any more than conjecture given how scarce the sources are, the scale of resources the party withdrew from the migrant space suggests it might have received external financial support. The MHP was the fiercest opponent of the far left in Turkey, and benefited from the benevolent attitude the German political parties had towards it – in particular that of the CDU minister of the interior in Rhineland-Palatinate, and of the head of the CSU in Bavaria who wished to turn Bavaria into a rampart in the joint struggle against the spread of communism amongst Turkish immigrants in Germany.[35] When viewed from this angle, and given the international context of the Cold War, the possibility cannot be wholly excluded that it received external financial support to counter the progress of far-left mobilizations in the migrant space and in Turkey.

The MHP's capacity to provide the Nationalist Movement with support on multiple fronts may thus be explained by the material and financial resources at its disposal. Study of how these were accumulated and allocated brings out the redistribution mechanisms enabling it to extend its influence over ülkücü organizations and help them to develop their activities. But it also brings to light the shared interests and cross-subsidizing that encouraged the circulation and pooling of political, economic and social resources within the Nationalist Movement.

The self-financing of far-left organizations

Within the far-left action system no single organization controlled sufficient resources to be able to establish itself as broker. Left-wing political parties were deprived of public funding due to their electoral weakness, and so they relied on activists' membership fees as their main source of revenue. As for the extra-parliamentary organizations, they had no official legal existence, and did not have enough members to be able to regularly raise membership fees, especially as there was no formal distinction within their ranks between permanent members, activists and sympathizers. But the radical organizations still needed to pay their 'professional revolutionaries' who were mobilized full-time. The far left was thus obliged to make do with the dispersed, irregular, and haphazard resources at its disposal, a factor contributing to the comparative lack of integration of its action system. This would also appear to have been one of the reasons why the far left was unable to aggregate the interests of the various mobilized groups. The modes of organization and the comparative lack of coordination between radical left-wing organizations prevented them from accessing certain resources (especially public resources) and meant they had difficulty financing their activities. And the modes of economic accumulation impacted in turn on the organizational structure of their action system.

Publishing activities were one of the main sources of finance for far-left organizations, all of which had one or several journals. The TİP published *Yürüyüş* (*March*), the TEP brought out *Emekçi* (*Worker*), the TSİP had the weekly *Kitle* (*The masses*) and the monthly *İlke* (*Principle*), the TİKP produced

Halkın Sesi (*Voice of the People*) and then *Aydınlık* (*Brightness*), whilst the TKP published the monthly *Ürün* (*Production*). Little information is available about the number of copies each of these journals sold, making it hard to estimate how much these activities brought in. According to Ergun Aydınoğlu, although the Fatherland Party (Vatan Partisi) only had 500 activists, average sales of its journal were 5000 copies.[36] The monthly *Ürün* states in its January 1979 publication that each issue sold 21,000 copies (amounting to TL42,000–$1647).[37] Publications by extra-parliamentary groups reached a wider public. *Devrimci Yol* sold up to 100,000 copies[38] of its fortnightly journal.[39] Mustafa, a former Kurtuluş leader in Antalya province, referred to sales of 15,000 copies of its monthly *Kurtuluş Sosyalist Dergi* (*Socialist Liberation Journal*), and 45,000 copies of its weekly *Haftalık Kurtuluş* (*Weekly Liberation*).[40] The groups used their publications to announce the launch of fundraising campaigns. In its issue of 3 February 1978 *Devrimci Yol* informed its readers that 'the resistance campaign against fascist oppression and high prices' (*Faşist Zulme ve Pahalılığa Karşı Direniş Kampanyası*) had enabled Dev-Yol to collect TL210,352 ($8414.08).[41]

Revenue from the sale of these publications went to the central bodies of extra-parliamentary groups and parties, whose local representatives were thus obliged to finance their activities unaided. The sale of publications made this possible, for whilst they sent the journal's editor the 'official' amount for the number of copies sold, they only rarely sold journals at their cover price. Tevfik, a former Dev-Yol member, told:

> There were people who sang traditional songs, and who collected money that way. Journals were sold, and if for example it cost one lira it might be sold for three lira, it depended on the means of the person buying it.[42]

These publications were on sale in certain bookshops, but activists and sympathizers were in charge of selling them where they lived and at their place of work or study. It was a matter of calling on the generosity of colleagues, fellow students or neighbours to help finance the cause. This call on people's generosity was a key means of local financing. Kutay, a former Dev-Genç activist, confirmed this:

> 'We approached people but giving was voluntary. We went to the parks, cafes, and restaurants "we are revolutionaries, we need money", and people could give to us.'[43]

'How did you actually go about it?'

> 'For instance, there were ... *gecekondu*, *varoş* (suburbs) at the time, *gecekondu* where there were factories. Well we went to the factories or to the *varoş*, selling newspapers, doing propaganda, or organising things, we went to the burials of friends and left-wing activists.'[44]

Local sections organized sales, and used the revenues to finance the organization's activities in the neighbourhood or university in question. Tuncay, a former Dev-Genç activist (the Dev-Yol youth wing), explained it in these terms:

> We sold *köfte*, books, things to eat, and we collected money. … We sold bracelets for one lira. We would say 'buy a bracelet against imperialism' and that way we collected money.[45]

Unlike the situation in the MHP, which often provided the equipment needed for armed operations, left-wing activists and sympathizers were obliged to club together and use their savings to buy a weapon. This is what Mahmut explained, a former Dev-Yol national cadre:

> Some students would pool their savings to buy an arm together, or, to give another example, a peasant would sell a cow to buy an arm. But there were an awful lot of arms in Turkey.[46]

Activists used all possible opportunities to obtain financial support from the population. Collections for the cause were held at comrades' weddings and funerals, and the sale of journals, posters, pamphlets, drawings, poems and handmade jewellery helped cover daily expenses.

The members of extra-parliamentary and clandestine armed groups also used less conventional means of financing, notably theft and racketeering. According to İrfan, the founder of Dev-Sol:

> Journals do not bring in much money, we got money by controlling legal organisations … The money came from places of work, from hold-ups, or we stole from certain people who had illegal earnings, who didn't declare their earnings to the tax authorities, and who could not therefore file a complaint about the theft.[47]

Certain organizations set up teams specialized in bank hold-ups, and in what the Kurtuluş group called 'business activities' (*ticari işler*). Mustafa explained it in the following terms:

> I took part there in 'business activities', which consisted especially in holding up banks. Kurtuluş often used this method to collect funds, we did between forty and fifty hold-ups in 1985 alone, the last one was at the Bank of Pakistan … It was a sort of expropriation (*kamulaştırma*).[48]

In the neighbourhoods in big towns and in the villages where left-wing groups were in a position of strength, pressure was exerted on the population to make a financial contribution to the cause. This practice was not generalized throughout the country, nor was it specific to left-wing extraparliamentary organizations, since ülkücü associations also used it wherever possible.

The financing of the activities of left-wing organizations did not benefit from any coordination between the political parties, associations and student-based groups. The various organizations themselves only made a marginal financial contribution to the activities carried out by their own sections. Locally activists had to devise ever more initiatives to obtain adequate funding for their activities, leading to splits, and so further weakening the integration of the far left's action system.

Institutional fashioning and activist cultures

Activist training

Within the Nationalist Movement the doctrinal education of activists was systematic and carried out centrally by the MHP. On the far left, and especially in the extra-parliamentary groups, any such education was delegated to local sections that were in charge of teaching activists a few elements of doctrine. All the radical groups set up partisan schools and seminars intended to homogenize their members' practices and ideological positions. These seminars provided activists with what Nathalie Ethuin, writing about French Communist Party schools, has described as 'a framework of thought able to formulate and give meaning to' their condition.[49] In these places for the diffusion of collective norms, they sought to model the identity of the activists, who familiarized themselves with doctrine and integrated the precepts that were meant to guide their behaviour.

Between 1965 and 1980 the MHP was continually honing its training system. In the early years of Türkeş' leadership, when the party did not yet have any centralized training system, it was the activists with the most cultural capital who ran local reading seminars. Teachers who belonged to the movement organized reading sessions of nationalist authors and gave lessons about Turkish nationalism. Thus Battalion Commander Tahir Bilir, who taught national security at the Gümüşhane high school, singled out the students who were most interested in what he had to say and advised them to read nationalist authors, or else invited them to meetings he held at home. One of his students explained:

> His passionate words captivated us for one hour per week. He insisted on Turkish nationalism, the Turkish nation, and its enemies. We were influenced by what he told us about the enemies of the Turkish nation, about communism, Zionism, and the Freemasons. He explained what Dev-Genç was doing in the cities. We saw them as the symbol of communist activity in Turkey. When we thought about what Dev-Genç, the TİP, and their sympathisers were doing, our hatred for the CHP increased. ... We saw that Mr. Tahir supported Türkeş and the MHP. He gave us some of his books and advised us to buy certain others, which we devoured and thanks to which we learned a lot. We tried to spread his ideas around us, and we used them to oppose left-wing teachers. Some friends took out a subscription to *Devlet* and we started reading all its issues.[50]

According to Ömer, who joined an ülkücü youth association in 1969, Ülkü Hearths leaders gave young militants reading advice ('they gave us books, they said "read these books" and we read them ... Books about language or religion, for example').[51] According to a study carried out by Mustafa Çalık with 114 activists from Gümüşhane province, they systematically read party newspapers and journals such as *Devlet* (*The State*), *Töre* (*Morals*) and *Bozkurt* (*Grey wolf*), as well the writings of the party leader, Alparslan Türkeş. Those surveyed also stated they had read *Dokuz Işık* (*The Nine Lights*), *Milliyetçi Türkiye* (*Nationalist Turkey*) and *Türkiye'nin Meseleri* (*Turkey's Problems*), three books by Türkeş.[52] Whilst it seems unlikely that they read all the books they cited, the answers collected by Çalık clearly show that there were certain 'essentials' in the ülkücü ideological and literary repertoire. Gradually the party's cadres set up seminars, whose exact form and programmes were devised by party headquarters. As of 1978 the way the training system was organized became more complex and efficient, partly thanks to an increase in the MHP's revenue in the wake of the 1977 general election. The person in charge of the MHP's educational activities was Namık Kemal Zeybek, who worked at party headquarters. He was assisted by thirty-seven provincial educators in charge of devising and implementing programmes. According to Mehmet Şandır, the educator in charge of Istanbul province from 1977 to 1980, the seminars took place in the evenings over the course of a fortnight or month, or else in the daytime over one or two weeks.[53] A course of 'ongoing training' was also available, with two seminars per week. The first seminars were held in Istanbul and Ankara, before spreading to all the provinces where the MHP was present. Alparslan Türkeş himself gave seminars for handpicked MHP students. Whilst 100 or so educators were paid, the others were volunteers. A letter sent by a local cadre from an ülkücü association to Namık Kemal Zeybek gives an idea of the sort of qualities the party was looking for in its educators:

> This friend was arrested in 1975 as a witness to the Töb-Der incidents in Amasya, and was sentenced to ten years in prison. He spent nearly six years in prison at Ankara, Amasya, Tokat, Niğde, and Ceyhun. ... But he is a brave, respectful, humble, moral believer. At the moment he is in the village of Karaköprü in Amasya. He could be very useful to our cause by working in our educational operations.[54]

These seminars were for all members of ülkücü associations, grouped together by level of educational attainment and their position within the movement's hierarchy. 'First level' training involving five lessons a day for six days was for 'basic activists', with the emphasis being placed on history, Nationalist and anti-communist ideology, and disciplinary rules. Another programme was run for cadres, training them in the cut-and-thrust of debate, in organization and mobilization, and in how to manage activists properly, with attendees sitting a test at the end. There was a third programme for 'intellectuals', comprising six days on the history of the Turks (where they first appeared, their conquests, Islamization, the Ottoman Empire, and the Turkish Republic), two days studying Islam, two about the Nationalist doctrine of the 'nine lights', two further days on the ideology and history of communism, plus one day on international politics and four days of primarily practical (as opposed to theoretical) training in organization, debating and management. Whilst not all ülkücü activists attended the seminars, all sections within the Nationalist Movement followed the programmes drawn up by the educators in Ankara, and the education bureau (*eğitim masası*) oversaw the running of training courses in neighbourhoods, where its representatives picked the most promising young ülkücüs to attend them.

Activists were also encouraged to follow the courses run by Koranic schools that were close to the Nationalist Movement. These courses were virtually obligatory for imprisoned activists since the party made sure that courses in prayer, religious reading and explanation of the Koran were run in all prisons where ülkücüs were incarcerated. Prisons were also considered as good places to train and fashion activists, who were housed together in cells and had their own internal hierarchy.[55]

Far-left organizations also provided their militants with training, though this was not as systematic and centralized as it was in the Nationalist Movement.[56] This often took the form of seminars run by local section members, but without any real national coordination. These seminars were held in party buildings, at an activist's home, in a university residence, a bookshop or a coffeehouse.[57] They too were all about viewing the history of the country in the light of ideology, reading the great doctrinal texts and learning how to act in accordance with the behavioural norms promoted by the group:

> 'Tell me how these seminars were organised.'
>
> 'There were, say ... four per month, we worked on the classics of Marxism, some read books and gave explanations on a specific subject we talked about, we compared different ideas, and examined them in the light of what happened in our daily lives.'[58]

Most of the time training consisted simply in reading lists. The way Dev-Yol trained its activists is symptomatic here of the practices of far-left groups. Like other extra-parliamentary movements, there was little coordination between Dev-Yol's central bodies and its provincial structures. Seminars were set up on the basis of local initiatives and were not controlled by the organization's national cadres, who merely published a set of texts in its journal along with advice for activists who wished to offer improvised training courses. Thus in its first issue the journal listed 'points to be considered in educating the masses' ('Kitle eğitiminde dikkat edilmesi gereken noktalar').[59] In particular those running seminars were asked to 'set aside their intellectual penchant' and 'avoid thinking of themselves as teachers', instead placing themselves on an equal footing with their students and not presenting any visible signs which might ostracize them in the eyes of the audience:

> You need to dress in a normal and ordinary way (not only for educational activities, but in everyday life). Women wearing short clothing and men with

beards and long hair produce a negative effect. Women should not use make-up. Use everyday language in discussions. It is a mistake to use modern Turkish (öztürkçe).[60]

They were to 'show unlimited respect to the masses' and 'behave in a very respectful manner towards those who believe in tradition, religion, and custom', without being in any way offensive. Patience was also required, for 'the influence exerted by reactionary ideologies over the centuries cannot be wiped clean in a few hours'. The organization wanted its teachers to act as models for their activists, and required that they put the ideology they taught into practice. The article adds that those attending a seminar were to organize other seminars in turn. In order to fully understand the importance Dev-Yol attached to running seminars, it needs to be remembered that these were one of the privileged means of involvement in far-left groups. Students were often invited by classmates to attend a seminar held in a cafe near the university or else in one of its residences. After this initial contact, the person running the seminar would encourage them to join their ranks and make contact with the group's representative in the university, or else directly entrust them with their first tour of armed duty in a neighbourhood controlled by the group. The journal was used as a platform for diffusing seminar programmes and reading recommendations, and to publicize the position adopted by the group in the theoretical debates animating the far left in Turkey. An article in the first issue of *Devrimci Yol* insisted on 'the importance of Marxist theory and learning this theory'.[61] A list of works was drawn up for reading and commentary in seminars. The pantheon of communism was of course on the programme, with books by Marx, Engels, Lenin, Stalin and Mao Zedong. As Dev-Yol wished to embody the THKP-C heritage, the three volumes of Mahir Çayan's *Uninterrupted Revolution* (*Kesintisiz Devrim I-II-III*) were also obligatory reading. Certain chapters in Maurice Cornforth's *Reader's Guide to the Marxist Classics*, published by Sol Yayınları in 1975, were also recommended. That same year the journal also started running its 'A few theoretical questions' section (*Bazı teorik sorunlar*) with a long article published under the title 'On teaching Marxist philosophy',[62] which acted as a guide for teachers, accompanied by a list of Marxist philosophical works to study in seminars. In July 1977 the journal published a text about 'political economy and education'[63] that listed works for study. In September it gave a presentation of 'historical materialism' (*tarihsel materyalizm*). The question of the state was the subject of an article called 'The Marxist theory of State' ('Marxist devlet teorisi') published in the 15 January 1978 issue, whilst there was a lengthy article in the 21 February 1978 issue about 'imperialism' (*emperyalizm*)[64] in the 'Education' (*Eğitim*) section, which sometimes featured in the journal.

These articles helped activists position themselves within the far left's internal debates. They indicated the attitude to be adopted, and provided the right turns of phrase to be used in daily discussions and polemics with members of radical organizations. In an article called 'The non-capitalist path: a negation of Lenin's theory of revolution'[65] the journal lambasted 'nationalist-revisionist' regimes following a middle course between socialist and capitalist economic models. Elsewhere it positioned itself against the TKP and its theory of 'advanced democracy', denouncing it as revisionist.[66] Between 15 July and 1 September 1977 it published three long articles called 'Position within the disintegrating socialist system in the split between China and the Soviets (I, II, and III)',[67] in which it set out its stance in the ideological debates structuring the far left. Up until the aftermath of 12 September 1980, *Devrimci Yol* regularly published in-depth special reports (about the 'Kurdish issue',[68] colonialism[69] or the fight against fascism,[70] for instance), together with articles about the wars of national liberation of the late 1970s. It provided analysis of revolutionary movements in Honduras,[71] Chile,[72] Nicaragua[73] and Iran,[74] denounced the military coup of 5 July 1977 in Pakistan[75] and gave biographical sketches of the great figures of international socialism.[76]

According to Haldun, the Dev-Genç seminars he attended in Istanbul were based mainly on reading and analysing the texts indicated by the journal. He insisted on the important role played by the seminars as a point of entry to the group:

> In fact at the beginning we called them sympathisers, and when they became sympathisers they already had to take part in education classes, they read Marxist literature I mean ... But wholly Stalinist.[77]

This was in fact the way he had joined Dev-Genç:

> In any case, we had no political knowledge to begin with, and so the first education thing we went to was pro-Chinese ... We became pro-Chinese, we got into it, especially at the age of fourteen or fifteen ... At school it started with friendships too, of course. For example I was friendly with Rüşen and we ... I don't know how but we started mixing with student movements, we started reading books, we were pretty left wing, and at that moment I think I had ... I don't even know if it's because of him, we were in contact with an organisation outside the school ... Dev Genç, and so there were seminars for high school students at the end of the week, on Saturdays or Sundays, and so he and I started going there, both of us, and of course, there, there were lists of books to read and all that.[78]

The representatives of Kurtuluş also held seminars based on reading the classics of Marxist literature:

> We also did educational work, we read Marxist books, in Antalya for example there were eight education groups, including five for workers ... There were classes on political economy, philosophy, and its *fundamental* principles.
>
> 'But what did you talk about in these education classes? What did you do?'
>
> 'Books by Marx, such as *Wages, Price, and Profit*, Marx and Engels ... *Anti-Dühring* ... After these books we moved onto Lenin, *Imperialism, State, and Revolution* ... We also read Dimitrov, *To vanquish fascism* ... As for novels, we read the Russian, English, and French classics, those which explained the

revolution. Gorki ... There was also Ilya Ehrenburg, *Fall of Paris* ... Books about Vietnam, about the war of resistance ... We read *Les Misérables* by Victor Hugo too.'[79]

The purpose of reading and analysing these works in seminars was to provide activists with a framework for interpreting political events in the contemporary world. But not all activists attended the seminars, and many were largely uninterested in analysing these texts. Tamer, who was in charge of running several seminars in a Halkın Kuruluşu section, observed:

> I gave seminars, but for many people Marxism, Leninism, didn't really matter, what mattered was being revolutionary, being against inequality, that was what mattered. ... People didn't read much, what mattered was what they did in practice, responding to the fascists, taking up arms, fighting, it wasn't necessarily for the socialism.[80]

Not all activists followed training, and many of them spent more time confronting MHP activists than in doctrinal training. It is worth noting that many of them only had low cultural resources.

It was not only the activists in extra-parliamentary movements and far-left parties who had clearly differentiated relationships to cultural and ideological assets. The same division of organizational labour may also be observed in the Nationalist Movement, along with the same multiple types of motivation and involvement. Certain groups introduced measures to prepare for violent action. As of the summer of 1968 the MHP established 'commando camps' in various provinces and constituencies around Turkey in order to provide physical and ideological training for members from its youth wing (MHP Gençlik Kolları), as well as from the Union of Ülkü Hearths (Ülkü Ocakları Birliği), the Ülkücü Youth Organisation (Genç Ülkücüler Teşkilatı) and the Turkish National Student Union (Milli Türk Talebe Birliği). A report presented to Prime Minister Süleyman Demirel in 1970 refers to twenty-two 'commando camps' held throughout Turkey between the summer of 1968 and that of 1970. These camps were sometimes set up with the help of Türkeş' top aides, and were modelled along the lines of military camps. Each camp took in groups of between 10 and 150 young activists at a time, and sometimes more, for a period of between fifteen and twenty days.[81] Their purpose was to provide the most committed activists with training in physical combat against communist students at university or school, and only a minority of activists attended them;[82] there is no proof that they continued to operate after 1970. For that matter the MHP even denies that these camps existed. According to Mehmet Şandır, who was an instructor in the province of Istanbul at the time:

> There were commando camps, but no violence at all, no, no ... They were camps ... Like Scout camps, with sports, hiking, seminars ... We never did anything against the State, it was the communists who were against the State.[83]

Although reserved for a minority of activists, these camps were nevertheless based on MHP values and modelled around a military aesthetic (as indicated by the fact of running camps), religion (with the five daily prayers and discussions about religion), physical culture (walking and combat sports) and political activity (with debates about topical events and the acquisition of organizational know-how).

Far-left groups did not have this type of set-up. In 1977 the *Milliyet* newspaper referred to the setting up of training camps in the Taurus Mountains by Perinçek's TİİKP in 1971,[84] but this was apparently an isolated case. Prior to the coup of 12 March 1971 certain activists went to join the Palestinian camps in Lebanon to receive military training there. On returning they shared what they had learnt but on an informal basis:

> *And what about left-wing groups, did they train or not? Were there camps like the ülkücü training camps?*
>
> 'No, all that was done in a fairly ... improvised manner ... I don't know, but they went to train abroad for two or three months, as I did ...'
>
> *'Yes, you had a certain level of know-how ...'*
>
> 'Yes'
>
> *'But did you help, did you provide people with training or not?'*
>
> 'No, I dropped that. They went to train with guns ... I don't know, in the Belgrade Forest near Istanbul for example.'[85]

However, local groups did sometimes set up training locally:

> There were no training camps, but I think that organisations did training in the countryside, for ten days or so, with equipment, where the guy who had gone to Palestine, and so who knew ... But I didn't ... I didn't experience that.[86]

But the vast majority of ülkücü and far-left activists did not receive training in violent action. It was often when on guard duty that they learned how to use a weapon:

> Officially, the neighbourhood didn't exist at that time, it was when the houses were being built ... As it was known for being a left-wing neighbourhood, far-right people came from time to time to carry out attacks, and so the whole neighbourhood was held by activists. But they weren't necessarily activists from there. If you have a neighbourhood with five, six places, perhaps eight places you needed to guard, then there was a guard system. People from the neighbourhood ... People in charge of the neighbourhood, people from there, the guy knew everybody, but activists from ... I don't know, from the high school or university came after school in the evening and they were told 'you're on from 2 to 4 o'clock, you from 4 to 6', and that way there were guards, there

was the person in charge who came with another eight people, who went over things with them and left the others. And so there were armed guards, it was also a way to … Introduce the activists to a certain discipline …. In any case when you were on guard duty you were in charge of that, you knew you weren't going to just fire it just like that, but well … You learnt it on the job … When the people in charge got together they gave reports on the activists, in fact they were called sympathisers at first.[87]

Guard duty functioned as a rite of passage to join the group, in which people went from the status of sympathizer to that of an activist in the eyes of their peers.

The development of antagonistic ethoses

It is in the most routine practices, in a group's usage of a 'silent pedagogy of bodies in action'[88] that individuals may be observed in the act of conforming to the power relationships in which they are caught. This section looks at how social and cultural practices become vectors fashioning individuals to an institution, and how these practices take on distinctive characteristics when used within a conflict.

Ways of talking Antagonistic radical groups promoted their own specific ways of talking about politics and modes of resistance. Joining a group meant acquiring its vocabulary and passwords. Having a specific language diffused across an organization and mastered by its members made several things possible. In addition to building up a strong bond between those who spoke it, it also acted as a principle of political recognition and of identifying the Other. The use of a specific vocabulary was part of the ordering of the world carried out by the mobilized groups, which – as the French Communist Party once did – worked to build up '"separate" symbolic realms' thanks to which socialist and ülkücü identities 'mirrored one another in their singularity'.[89] Within the Nationalist Movement Alparslan Türkeş was called *Albayım* (my Colonel) or *Başbuğ*, a term which literally means leader but was only employed for the leader of the MHP, and close in meaning to that of *Duce*, *Caudillo* or *Führer*. Ömer, who was a young ülkücü activist at the time, remembers having been corrected by Türkeş himself when, on joining the Nationalist Movement, he had not yet mastered the group's 'passwords':

'Alparslan Türkeş … The first time I saw him I was very young … He got cross for some reason or other, I can't remember why he got cross … Türkeş … I had called him "amca" [uncle] … Do you know what that means?'

'Yes, "amca" is like "ağabey" [elder brother] but …'

'Yes, that's right … But I was very young, I must have been fourteen …'

'So what were you meant to call him, "my head" [başkanım])?'

'No, Başbuğ, Başbuğum …'[90]

Activists were called *ülküdaş* (companions of the ideal) or *gönülveren* (those who give their heart). Though left-wing armed groups sometimes used the term *militan*, most of the time it had negative connotations, associated more with underground activity by a member of a party or association that normally used conventional means, and in the Nationalist Movement, it was used only in a pejorative sense. More generally ülkücüs used a vocabulary that drew on 'old Turkish' (*eski türkçe*). The Turkish language had been continually evolving ever since the 1928 language reform, and the Turkish Academy of Language (*Türk Dil Kurumu*) was in charge of modernizing it by 'Turkifying' certain European words and inventing other new ones which were meant to replace vocabulary that sounded Arabic or Persian.[91] As of the late 1960s the MHP accused the academy of being left-leaning, and refused to use the 'pure Turkish' (*öz türkçe*) that it was establishing. All the party's publications used a very large proportion of 'old Turkish', and activists used an outdated vocabulary. This refusal of modern Turkish was indicative of far more than mere linguistic nostalgia. It associated the speaker with a set of conservative political positions, tending to establish him in opposition to the great reforms of the Republic. Ülkücü sociolects were also built up in contrast to the linguistic practices of the far left, which privileged modern Turkish. Each group and each party had their own 'passwords' enabling members to identify each other.[92] Rather than using *hoca* (teacher) and *bacı* (elder sister) as Halkın Kurtuluşu members did when addressing each other,[93] Dev-Yol preferred the word *arkadaş* (friend),[94] whilst *yoldaş* (comrade) tended to be reserved for talking with activists from other left-wing groups. According to Tamer, in Halkın Kurtuluşu 'we didn't use the word "boss", it was totally forbidden, if you said "boss" people would hit you, it was a word to be used ironically for other groups'.[95]

The realms of meaning thereby mobilized were indicative of different ways of conceiving of the social order, with the use of modern Turkish indicating that one adhered to less conservative political ideas and values than those who used vocabulary from old Turkish. Language, by laying down 'the legitimate political terms and issues',[96] became established as an instrument for political classification and identification, just like clothing and bodily practices, which were laden with undeniable polemical value.

Clothing and bodily practices Each of the two movements set up clothing and bodily practices deemed legitimate, compliance with which was policed by peers. Ülkücüs had long, crescent-shaped moustaches,[97] dark suit and formal footwear. They did not have beards or sideburns, and wore an MHP rosette on their lapel. The rosette for party members was three white moons on a red background, whilst that for members of ülkücü associations was a wolf and three white moons on a red background. The way of dress embodied the values championed by the Movement. By adopting it one became the living model of ülkücü identity, suggesting a specific set of gestures. Socialist activists, on the other hand, had short moustaches (rarely going further than the corner of the mouth), fatigue jackets, loose-fitting trousers (in canvas or corduroy) and sports shoes:

There were instructions about how to dress. Wearing American clothes was forbidden, you had to be dressed like people in the neighbourhood where you were working. In the winter we wore corduroy trousers and a parka ... A fatigue jacket. Shoes ... Sports shoes, cheap ones, sports shoes to be able to run. We had moustaches down to our lips.

'What about the ülkücüs?'

'They wore suits, with heeled shoes.'[98]

'Did left wingers have specific types of dress?'

'Yes, a brown-coloured fatigue jacket, green corduroy trousers, military shoes, moustaches a bit like Stalin's. Right-wing people had longer moustaches and a hat.'[99]

'We didn't wear Levi's, so as not to look wealthy.'[100]

These bodily and dress codes became components in the identity configurations specific to each of the two movements, as were religious practices too.

Religious practices Ülkücü activists were required to attend lessons in the Koranic schools in their neighbourhood. A document stipulated that 'ülkücüs and sympathisers shall attend the religious seminars given by the religious leaders in the neighbourhood. We must ensure that ülkücüs attend Friday prayers. Organisation leaders will perform the five daily prayers. A room shall be set aside for prayer in each association'.[101] On the far left, on the other hand, atheism was de rigueur. Adnan, an ülkücü activist, explained how these religious practices took on meaning within the conflict:

Everything our left-wing teachers said was contrary to our beliefs. There were things we couldn't accept, such as the fact that man descended from the apes and not from Adam, that there was no difference between the sexes, and that resurrection did not exist. So we went to see the teachers (*hoca*) from the mosque to talk with them about this ... They read us verses from the Koran which spoke about these things. Who do you think we were going to believe? The verses in the Koran, or the teachers with their suits, who were foreign to us? We couldn't give up on the verses ... None [of the left-wing teachers] prayed or fasted. And outside school, anyone who didn't fast or who didn't go to the mosque on Friday wasn't viewed as a Muslim. ...] Their moustaches were short and they had long hair ... A bit below the back of the neck. We weren't used to that ... We couldn't accept it ... We knew that Alevis had short moustaches and we Sunnis didn't like that at all, to tell the truth we hated and despised them.[102]

Several factors account for this identification between Alevis and left-wingers. Firstly, Islam, after having been rejected on the grounds that it was a rival ideology to nationalism, was taken up as of the early 1970s as a central element within ülkücü identity, which promoted the Hanafi Sunni model and sought to monopolize political representation of it. Alevis were thus not a core electorate for the party. In addition to this, left-wing groups drew extensively on Alevi cultural references – going so far as to view the Alevi revolts under the Ottoman Empire as proto-communist movements – and re-appropriated a whole range of Alevi symbols.[103] In the late 1960s Alevi folksongs were sung at the funerals of assassinated activists, and the groups tended to take up the watchwords of the Alevi cultural heritage, chanting them during meetings and often giving them a new twist. Thus the expression *Enelhak* ('I am God') – for which the Sufi mystic Mansur-al Hallaj was sentenced to death – was transformed during protest marches to *Emek-Hak* ('Work-Justice'), and Pir Sultan Abdal's Love of God (*Hak aşkı*) became Love of Justice (using the same formulation, *Hak aşkı*). Musicians close to far-left circles such as Ruhi Su, Zülfü Livaneli, Rahmi Saltuk and Sadık Gürbüz put the poems of Pir Sultan Abdal to music, which Selda Bağcan and Cem Karaca then adapted to pop-folk rhythms, thus promoting their dissemination.[104] These borrowings from Alevi historical references meant that in the ülkücü vision of the world the radical left was identified with Aleviness.

Cultural practices The two action systems promoted different cultural productions, issuing from opposing political and intellectual traditions. The MHP took care to organize cultural activities in each of its sections. A circular sent out by the party in 1980 to ülkücü associations called on ülkücüs to 'make contact with famous people in order to organise "evenings" during which concerts and plays are to be performed'.[105] Readings were held regularly of works by nationalist authors such as Necdet Sevinç, Nihal Atsız and Dündar Taşer, and musical evenings of traditional songs were a common occurrence in ülkücü association locales and in coffeehouses run by sympathizers, as were film screenings about the war of independence or the emancipation of the Turks, and documentaries about the origins and history of the Turkish people. The far left organized collective cultural practices too. Left-wingers went in groups to the cinema and to attend theatrical performances by socialist troupes. The works tended to have pronounced political connotations ('in Turkish cinema we watched left-wing filmmakers, Yılmaz Güney, his films from the 1970s, *Arkadaş*, *Yol*. Films about the mines and workers', Mustafa explained).[106] Popular music (*halk müziği*) was listened to extensively ('we were against Ottoman music').[107] These cultural activities were policed by peers, in the same way as dress and bodily practices were. Within this context activists were strongly encouraged and sometimes enjoined to adopt the 'legitimate' cultural references. Tevfik, a Dev-Yol activist, admitted that he 'liked Elvis, but didn't say so because it was American',[108] and hence forbidden by his organization. It was only in private, when staying with his parents, for example, that he indulged this taste.

Consumption practices Activists' consumption practices were also laden with political meaning. Neither the ülkücüs nor far-left activists bought foreign cigarettes. In the left-wing Halkın Kurtuluşu group 'we smoked filterless Bafra or Birinci. Cheap cigarettes. We kept our money for the organisation and didn't smoke American brands … We used to say "İç Birinci ol devrimci" ("Smoke a

Birinci, become a revolutionary") when offering someone a cigarette'.[109] According to Kutay, filtered cigarettes were forbidden in Dev-Yol because they cost more than filterless Turkish cigarettes ('they used to say "use your money for the struggle" ... ').[110] Ülkücüs too only smoked Turkish cigarettes.[111] There is no doubt that American cigarettes symbolized foreign imperialism, both on the left and on the right, and cultural goods labelled as 'American' or deemed imperialist were banned within both movements. The consumption of alcohol was also forbidden in the Nationalist Movement, and breaking this law led to expulsion and hostile reactions from one's peers. All the ülkücüs activists I encountered said they did not drink alcohol, and at the various evenings I attended held by the MHP's Ankara section I never observed any consumption of alcohol, suggesting that this could well have already been the case in the 1970s. Although the consumption of alcohol was formally condemned on the far left, numerous accounts provided by former activists suggest that it was tolerated, and during field surveys I observed that it was quite normal amongst many former activists. For the movements' cadres the use of alcohol was an important issue, for it was associated with the social representation of the socialist or ülkücü activist, and hence with the group image. Organizations severely punished any members caught inebriated, generally via physical punishment.

Relationships between the sexes Organizations within the Nationalist Movement prohibited all sexual and affective relationships between unmarried activists. Keeping the sexes apart underpinned all the norms governing sociability. The Islamic moral codes championed by the Movement further accentuated this structural exclusion, as did the values of honour and virility prevalent within it. The situation on the left varied from one organization or section to another. For Metin 'it was very puritan. If you met a girl and had a relationship with her, if you slept with her, then you had to marry her otherwise you were thrown out of the party. ... And of course you couldn't be homosexual'.[112] The people I spoke to referred to a culture or philosophy of the elder sister (*bacı kültürü* or *bacı felsefesi*). According to Tamer,

> it was very difficult with girls, I fell in love ... Well ... I had a girlfriend and I was severely criticised. I said "it's not love with a fascist, she's a revolutionary", but I was suspended for a week from the seminar I worked in, and I had to apologise and no longer see the girl again, you know, it was an elder sister culture (*bacı kültürü*).[113]

Power relations The symbolic worlds and behavioural norms that activists had to incorporate on joining either movement were further reinforced by mechanisms to control and fashion them as individuals, where these mechanisms sought to secure their loyalty and ensure they complied with the models promoted by the movement. The power relations established by the two action systems were disciplinary in kind, and were used to control activists and get them to integrate group norms. But unlike far-left organizations, the Nationalist Movement had mechanisms to instil the correct activist ethos, leading to greater homogenization in practices and habitus. There were very high levels of discipline, with a centralized system of permanent collective appraisal based on sending regular reports to party headquarters. Normalization was thus part of a specific mode of functioning in which the group itself checked that each of its members conformed to ülkücü values. This involved being quiet and silent (*sessiz*), introverted and withdrawn (*kapanık*), well-mannered (*efendi*) and even-tempered (*sakin*).[114] Activists were invited to incorporate a whole series of ways of behaving and acting, with measured gestures, controlled hair length and carefully policed language. These were mechanisms to appropriate an ülkücü body animated by principles which, when put into practice, signified that one was part of the collective body. A circular sent out by the ÜYD leadership stipulated the attitude to be adopted with local inhabitants in neighbourhoods where ülkücü organizations were present:

> In order to win over the hearts of neighbourhood inhabitants it is important, for instance, to carry the shopping bags of the elderly on their way back from the market and to accompany them back to their home.[115]

Religious practice was also carefully controlled, and activists were encouraged to attend Koranic classes in their neighbourhood:

> Our ülkücüs and sympathisers must be obliged to attend religious seminars given by the religious leaders in the neighbourhood. We must ensure that all ülkücüs attend Friday prayers. Organisation leaders shall perform the five daily prayers. A room shall be set aside for prayer in each association.[116]

Activists were obliged to follow rules of conduct in their interaction with their daily environment:

> We need to try to solve problems relating to electricity and water in the neighbourhoods. We also need to make sure that houses in the neighbourhood have a book by a religious teacher, and try to gain access to these houses via their younger members. Care must be taken to ensure that the young people with whom we are in contact do not distance themselves from their family. It is essential to talk with people at the mosque before and after prayers, and to sit with them in the cafes and listen attentively to what they have to say. It is essential not be in anyway disrespectful.[117]

The description given by Yusuf of how young ülkücü activists in the province of Gümüşhane behaved suggests that these behavioural rules were applied:

> One day they invited me to the association. I went. There were lots of very interesting talks. There were some people like me who were a bit older, and weren't part of the association. They showed great respect towards us. They had us sit down in the rows at the very front. They were all extremely well brought up and respected custom … And then in the association there was discipline and

a love of respect. ... There were people who knew a lot more than we did, they were cultivated men, but they showed us respect, they said we were older than them ... I saw all that, and I also saw young left-wingers ... But they were true young Turks ... Educated, respectful, cultivated ... [118]

Ülkücü organizations also exerted physical control over their activists who lived, relaxed and worked in an ülkücü environment with which they had many strong ties. Activists' friends and family were often members of an ülkücü organization, which sometimes provided for their needs. This meant that the price to be paid for betraying the Nationalist Movement, for leaving it or for not conforming to its values was very high indeed.

On the far left, activists were subject to less stringent control. Whilst the norms of the group were upheld by all members, as amongst ülkücüs, left-wingers more readily transgressed behavioural rules, and sanctions tended not to be meted out. As was the case amongst ülkücüs, far-left activists devoted a considerable amount of time to group activities and spent much of their life with other members of their group. According to Nejat:

It was all the time ... All the time. We were together all day long. We didn't have much money but we shared everything ... I would bring the cheese, you would bring the bread ... Someone else would bring the olives ... That is how it was. We didn't have much money, but we shared everything.[119]

Activists also had shared leisure activities. This was another opportunity to pool their goods:

In spring when we went on picnics with 100 or 200 people we gave each other presents, especially books, and played football or volleyball. We brought food from home, a bit more than necessary for one person, and we shared everything.[120]

The power relations that operated within extra-parliamentary movements and far-left parties were less restrictive than those amongst ülkücüs. It was far easier to become involved, and also far easier to leave; there was also more dissent at national or local level, as indicated by the large number of local groups who would start by joining national organizations and then break away from them. When activists decided to set up their own structure they did not encounter any obstacles. Whilst defection amongst ülkücüs was punished by ostracism and sometimes physical discipline, far-left activists could leave their organization without thereby breaking off the ties they had with their former comrades. Inconstancy was a recurrent feature on the left for that matter. Several of the individuals I spoke to had migrated from one group to another: İrfan left Dev-Yol when its Istanbul section set itself up as Dev-Sol, for which he became one of the leaders, before then returning to the ranks of his former organization without being made to suffer in any way for his 'misguided' action; Ergun, a member of the pro-Soviet Fatherland

Party, became a Trotskyite in 1979 and distanced himself from the organization, without thereby losing his friends there; and Metin left the TİP in 1978 to set up his own group. In each case the price to be paid for leaving was far less than that within the Nationalist Movement.

Political identities and the uses to which they were put

The ways of behaving and acting required by members of the two conflicting movements were based on strongly differing value systems, and we have so far looked at their existence and the mechanisms to disseminate them. This section will now discuss how they were put into practice in order to understand how these two bodies of symbolic assets, values and cultural practices were mobilized within the conflict.

The adversarial relationship between the two movements developed over the course of the second half of the 1960s. The first declarations of hostility came from the MHP leader. As soon as Türkeş took over as party chairman, the party directed its principal attacks against communism. It thereby reproduced a tactic adopted by pan-Turkish circles in previous decades, seeking to instrumentalize a danger which had acquired an unprecedented topicality and potential for mobilization since the beginnings of the Cold War, and perhaps especially since the setting up of the Turkish Workers Party in 1961. Thus the MHP leadership drew on anti-communism as an ideological instrument for rallying the Turkish nationalist far right to the party and to expand its electoral base.

When Alparslan Türkeş took over the leadership of the CKMP in 1965 he already enjoyed a modest degree of notoriety within the media, together with a certain level of esteem amongst pan-Turkish circles. He had been involved with pan-Turkish journals and associations as of the 1940s. In April 1944 he had taken part in a demonstration in support of Nihal Atsız, a figurehead amongst pan-Turkish and pan-Turanian circles, who had been put on trial for accusing certain of the regime's academics of carrying out clandestine communist activities. In an open letter to Prime Minister Şükrü Saraçoğlu, published by Atsız in his *Orhun* journal, he divulged the names of certain of these academics, and called on the prime minister to react decisively against these underground circles. The government reacted sharply to Atsız's letter. The country was in the process of hastily revising its international agreements in the light of the military collapse of Nazi Germany, so the regime seized the opportunity to harden its position against pan-Turanian circles who were in favour expansion within Central Asian countries where there was a Turkish-speaking majority, a position which was severely frowned upon by the upper echelons of government. *Orhun* was banned and Atsız was given a suspended four-month prison sentence. During his trial protest marches were staged, attracting extensive media coverage. On one occasion several dozen pan-Turanian activists (including Alparslan Türkeş) gathered in front of the court buildings and burnt the works of Sabahattin Âli, who taught at the State Conservatory in Ankara and was one of those Atsız accused of clandestine communist activity. İsmet İnönü himself, the then president of the Turkish Republic, condemned these 'racist' (*ırkçılar*) 'Turanians' (*turancılar*).[121] Several pan-Turkish journals were shut down (as was the case for *Orhun* on 1 April, for *Kopuz* on 16 May, and for *Çınaraltı* on 27 May 1944) and their editors arrested, such as Ali İhsan Sâbis, who ran the German language publication *Türkische Post*. Pan-Turkish circles were hit by a wave of arrests, and on 7 September 1944 twenty-three people were put on trial in Istanbul, including Alparslan Türkeş. The trial lasted until 29 March 1945, but the ruling was overturned by the military Court of Appeal, giving rise to a second trial starting on 31 May 1947, at which all the accused were acquitted.

These were the final stages in the events establishing anti-communism as a central value amongst pan-Turkish and pan-Turanian circles. The events of 1944 together with the media coverage they attracted enabled Alparslan Türkeş to come to public attention. In 1950 an article he published, 'Pan-Turkism and the Turkish Union' (*Türkçülük ve türk birliği*), earned him the gratitude of pan-Turkism's best-known champions. In the immediate aftermath of the 1960 coup, when he was a colonel in the Army, it was he who went on the radio to announce the military intervention. He was duly appointed to the position of undersecretary to the prime minister. In the Committee of National Union, he was one of the hardline representatives of those opposed to a return to civilian rule he was sidelined and sent abroad. On returning to Turkey in 1963 he joined the CKMP and drew on his networks in pan-Turkist and pan-Turanian circles, which were strongly anti-communist in the early 1960s, in order to build up a position of force within the party. Given the international context, in which the USSR was exerting its domination over the Soviet republics in Central Asia, where there was a large proportion of Turkish speakers, anti-communism became one of the party's main symbolic assets.

This ideological stance was also electorally strategic. The setting up of the Turkish Workers Party and its first electoral successes, together with the intensification in far-left worker and student movements, pushed the CKMP and then the MHP to the fore as the main counter-protest force opposing the 'threat' posed by the radical left – in addition to which anti-communism went down well with much of the electorate. The fact that Turkey had a border with the USSR led some people to fear that far-left organizations might acquire too much political influence; equally, Turkey's participation in the Korean War in the early 1950s had given rise to numerous media campaigns emphasizing the sacrifice of Turkish soldiers for the liberty of the Korean people who were exposed to Chinese and soviet imperialism. Communism, in the eyes of part of the electorate, threatened the country with division, and was an ideology that could lead to separatism. Thus the MHP was able to expand its electoral base and increase its number of activists by designating communism as the 'greatest enemy of the Turkish nation'.[122]

In a 1965 book, called *Turkey and The Nine Lights* (*Dokuz Işık ve Türkiye*), in which Türkeş sets out his political agenda, particular emphasis is placed on the threat that communism is said to pose for Turkey:

> I have said that communism is the greatest enemy of the Turkish nation and the Turkish homeland. The events which started a few years ago in our country provide the most vivid examples of this. The boycotts which have started in our universities, the sit-ins, fights, street protests, and bank hold-ups, the shooting of activists and policemen, the kidnappings – this is what has been done to the nation by its greatest enemy. That is why I said that communism is the greatest danger and the greatest enemy.[123]

He then goes on to identify it as the direct adversary of the Nationalist Movement:

> I have said that the greatest enemy today of the Turkish homeland and Turkish nation is communism. And communism is the principal enemy (*baş düşmanı*) of the Nationalist Movement. We champion a doctrine that is 100% local and 100% national because we know that no foreign ideology is able to solve Turkey's main problems.[124]

The party progressively placed the eradication of far-left groups at the centre of its political manifesto, in accordance with the line embodied by its campaign posters in 1977 ('The Nationalist Movement against Communism. Vote for the Crescent, not for the pipedreams of the Communists').[125] The rhetoric Türkeş drew upon in his essays and speeches sought to legitimize the path adopted by the MHP, arguing that the nation was endangered by an enemy within, meaning the mobilization needed to be stepped up:

> The communists do not recognise either homeland or nation. They take working-class domination as their starting point. Their ideal is the worldwide elimination of all classes except the working class, in a bloody revolution, and the introduction of the dictatorship of the proletariat. …. The communists foment conflict based on fear and hatred. They direct their limitless hatred against all those who are not in the working class. … According to communism, property must disappear, the right of ownership is no longer to be recognised, and everything is to belong to the State. … We are the enemies of communism not only because it is a rotten ideology, but also because it is an instrument of colonisation deployed by the greatest enemy of Turkishness – Russia.[126]

This threat also legitimized certain forms of non-conventional action, and meant the party could view itself as providing the state with civilian support in the struggle against the communists:

> It is the Grey Wolves (*Bozkurtlar*) who have thwarted the communists' plan to take possession of our universities, and who have saved the country from even greater disaster. They have died, they have been slandered, but they have not given in. The fight put up by the Grey Wolves has played a major role in eliminating communists from universities. Many martyrs have sacrificed their lives for this happy outcome.[127]

On the far left the key lever to mobilize people was anti-fascism. Every student, trade union and political organization drew on it to proclaim its rejection of ülkücü values, identified with those of fascist regimes in Europe. It was a matter not only of mobilization but also of defending workers' and students' interests, as well as promoting social progress against imperialism and especially against fascism and hence the MHP,[128] the enemy within who needed to be eliminated for the revolution to come to pass. Each event was used as an opportunity to denounce the MHP's fascism. At the funeral of Ertuğrul Karakaya, killed by gendarmes on 8 June 1977, the ODTÜ Dev-Genç section pasted up a poster proclaiming, 'Death to fascism, Long live our struggle' (*Kahrolsun faşizm yaşasın mücadelemiz*).[129] When the Ankara section of the Revolutionary Women's Association (Devrimci kadınlar derneği) was set up in 1978 by Dev-Yol activists, this was announced with a poster proclaiming, 'The Ankara Women's Association is open. DEATH TO FASCISM. Ülkü Hearths are the instruments of fascism and must be shut down' (*Ankara kadınlar derneği açıldı. KAHROLSUN FAŞİZM. Faşizmin maşası ülkü ocakları kapatılmalıdır*). The slogans chanted at meetings and protest marches also revealed the adversarial relationship to ülkücüs. Activists would gather to cries of 'Shoulder to shoulder against fascism ... One fist, one heart ... ' (*Faşizme karşı omuz omuza ... Tek bir yumruk, tek bir yürek ...*), or 'Let's fight fascist terror' (*Faşist teröre karşı savaşalım!*).[130]

The collective behavioural norms and values mobilized by the conflicting groups acted as political markers. They announced that an activist belonged to one of the two camps and made it possible to identify the 'enemy', as Celalettin, an ülkücü activist, explained:

> We gradually realised that many of our teachers were left wing. We established criteria for determining whether such-and-such a teacher was left wing. We asked questions such as 'Do you believe in the existence of the sexes?' or 'Do you think it right that there are boycotts and sit-ins in the universities?', or else 'Do you think that Nazım Hikmet is a patriotic poet?'. Those who did not recognise the existence of the sexes, who supported the boycotts, or who showed a liking for Nazım Hikmet could easily be classified as left-wing, and then we tried to argue against them whenever we could. And these teachers gradually became more and more severe towards us. If they tackled religious topics they would speak about religion and believers as if they were mocking them. ... The teachers we called communists said they were progressive revolutionaries and actually Ataturkists. ... But they claimed that the greatest problem with Turkish society was religious ignoramuses and sectarians. ... In our eyes the greatest proof that they were communists was that they criticised American imperialism and America's colonisation of Turkey, and said we should leave NATO, but they didn't have a word to say against the Soviet Union.[131]

Young activists in high schools learnt how to identify the political positions of their teachers:

> After a few weeks at high school I realised that our teachers talked to us about lots of things I didn't know about. About NATO, for example, and America. By joining NATO we were now policed by America. In order to become a truly independent country once again we had to leave NATO. Our literature teacher never spoke to us about the authors and works we had enjoyed at primary school or in middle school. ... According to our literature teacher the main particularity and most important thing about Mehmet Akif was his stance against imperialism. But for us, national poems and poems about independence were what we liked best. We knew he was religious but it was the first time we had heard anyone say he was anti-imperialist. Our literature teacher sometimes read us poems about deprived people, without telling us who they were written by ... One day, during break, a friend who knew a lot about politics observed that the style of the poet our teacher was reading resembled that of the communist poet and traitor to his country, Nazım Hikmet. In order to instil left-wing ideas in us our teacher tried to influence us with poems by Nazım Hikmet. ... Most of us thought our friend was right. He said what we all secretly thought. We reacted this way against a lot of our teachers.[132]

Ways of dress and the style of haircut and facial hair provoked the same adverse reactions amongst members of the opposing camp:

> We learned from articles published in the newspapers that left-wing anarchists had long hair, beards, and sideburns. I was frightened of and strongly disliked students I had seen the previous summer in our region. The boys had long hair like girls and curly whiskers. Those were more or less my political and ideological ideas and feelings when I started at the Gümüşhane high school in the autumn of 1971.[133]

These practices constituted two separate political identities, and thus acted as levers that could be used to mobilize groups and activists within the conflict.

*

Whilst the two conflicting action systems each built up unity by constructing antagonistic political identities, they did not have the same type or same level of resources. As of the second half of the 1960s the MHP set up an environment of associations whose purpose was to channel the electorate towards the party. Internal power relationships within the Nationalist Movement and the resources to which it had access enabled it to instil a high level of conformity amongst its members. The way individuals were shaped by its institutions was closely monitored, unlike on the far left, where the mechanisms to get activists to conform were less strict. Thus whilst the identification of a common enemy was sometimes the only cohesive element within groups on the far left, the ülkücüs could base their formatting efforts on a whole range of practical and discursive mechanisms that were produced and monitored by the organizations, and reinforced by the resources flowing from the party's place in government.

Whilst the MHP and ülkücü organizations mobilized to gain access to central power, the left-wing organizations nearly all sought to win local and sector-specific trophies. Thus the MHP drew on its antagonism with the far left as a symbolic asset that could be cashed in with voters, with the existence of a communist 'threat' legitimizing its tactic to win power based on the three-pronged strategy of *electoral participation – capturing State resources – armed violence*. Its purpose was to stand up to the drift towards anarchy – firstly by implementing a conservative nationalist policy agenda, secondly by evicting left-wing public-sector workers in order to replace them with ülkücüs who would act guard the integrity of the Turkish State and thirdly to fight in the street alongside the forces of law and order. Whilst far-left mobilizations were predominantly sectorial and tended to be local, the Nationalist Movement was able to privilege a global set of tactics to gain access to central power and resources. Analysis of the crisis processes at work in the second half of the 1970s needs to take into account this difference in the strategic dispositions of the protagonists. The next chapter shows how the dispositions of these antagonistic radical organizations came into play in the ways they defined and implemented their respective modes of action.

Chapter 4

CAPTURING PUBLIC RESOURCES AND POLITICIZING THE STATE

Hospitals in the region separated into two camps. There were those which cared for the right-wing sick and wounded, and those which tended to left-wing patients. Prior to admission the question of political preference was asked. Those who gave the wrong answer were not accepted.[1]

Base! A friend is waiting outside the hospital, he is wounded. We are at the police station.

Take the wounded to hospital …

'Base! This hospital only takes left-wing patients. They don't look after our friends.'[2]

In 1975 organizations from the two action systems carried out a series of activities targeting the resources of public institutions. These activities may be divided into three broad fields – penetrating central and municipal institutions, collective mobilization within these institutions and acting in the stead of the public authorities. The MHP's participation in the March 1975 government enabled the Nationalist Movement to penetrate central and decentralized state institutions by capturing their 'authority resources'. Far-left organizations were for their part excluded from these collusive networks granting access to the distribution of jobs, and instead had to count on collective mobilization within state institutions to dominate their internal power relationships on an intermittent basis. Whilst the ülkücüs' action repertoire also included collective mobilization, this was just one of the means they were able to draw upon to capture public resources. As for replacing the public authorities, the two movements did this whenever they were in a position to establish local control via violence, for it was a matter of occupying the ground in places where the writ of public authority largely failed to hold.

Activities by the radical organizations to capture resources contributed to the de-objectification of the state. They brought into question 'the exteriority and impersonality of social relationships, as well as their automatically being perceived as such',[3] where these features tend to consolidate the state via the practices of its members and social actors' perceptions of it. Officials started to politicize their professional practices based on which of the two movements they belonged to, obliging the population to place themselves in the hands of mobilized groups in order to receive their protection or else to benefit from the redistribution of the public resources they held. In the first chapter we saw how it was a routine occurrence for governing parties in Turkey to penetrate the state, a phenomenon which was institutionalized, even though it was illegal. The de-objectification of the state during the second half of the 1970s did not therefore stem from its being penetrated by the conflicting movements (primarily by the Nationalist Movement). It instead had far more to do with the way these groups captured public resources as part of a larger, global strategy, including multi-sector mobilization and recourse to intermittent violence.

This chapter looks at the ways in which activities to capture resources were a factor in the de-objectification of the state. For reasons of clarity, and in order to better deconstruct the complex mechanisms at each level of the state and of its operation, it starts by describing the activities the MHP conducted when in government to penetrate the country's central institutions. It then looks at the effects these activities had in law and order, especially the police, which was highly exposed to social and political forces, as seen in Chapter 1. This brings out how competition between rival organizations led firstly to the politicization of police practices, and secondly to the de-objectification of the police institution in the eyes of the populace. Lastly, it analyses the various ways in which public resources were captured in local arenas, providing insight into how these activities brought about a general transformation in the rules governing the games played out in state and political arenas.

Acceding to government as a way to obtain state positions

Acceding to government enabled political parties in Turkey to influence the selection of public-sector personnel. This is exactly what the MHP did when it was part of two coalition governments – the first between 31 March 1975 and 22 June 1977, and the second between 21 July 1977 and 5 June 1978 – and then during the period of minority government under the Justice Party in November 1979.[4] The following sections analyse the situation that enabled the party to see this through successfully, before examining where, when and how it acted to capture resources, and identifying the paths via which it managed, if not to control certain public institutions, then at least to extend its influence over them. It then examines the extent to which this served its half-legal/half-illegal strategy to gain access to power that it pursued over the course of the second half of the 1970s.

Penetrating central institutions

The presence of the MHP within the two so-called 'Nationalist Front' coalition governments (Milliyetçi Cephe, MC) enabled it to build up influential networks within the state by placing its activists in key positions, and especially – though not uniquely – in institutions attached to the ministries it ran. It was, given its electoral results, disproportionately successful in doing this, as the political situation singled it out as the key partner for the AP, the main right-wing party. Despite winning only 3.4 per cent of the vote in the general election of 14 October 1973, bringing it three seats in parliament, declarations by MHP leaders and the demands of its members established it as the champion of anti-communism. The elections were actually won by the CHP, the major centre-left party headed by Bülent Ecevit, which garnered 33.3 per cent of the vote and 185 seats in parliament, with the Justice Party arriving in second place with 29.8 per cent of the vote and 149 seats. But neither was in a position to govern alone. When a first coalition government led by the CHP collapsed, it was the turn of AP leader Süleyman Demirel to broker a deal enabling him to assume power. The first Nationalist Front government was thus formed;[5] the MHP exacted a high price for its involvement, winning two ministerial roles (with Alparslan Türkeş as deputy prime minister and Mustafa Kemal Erkovan as minister of state). In the general election of 5 June 1977 the MHP won 6.4 per cent of the vote and sixteen seats, after a campaign period marked by social unrest.[6] Süleyman Demirel and the AP were obliged to form a coalition government once again, the second Nationalist Front government (ikinci Milliyetçi Cephe), which was in office from 21 July 1977 to 5 January 1978,[7] and in which the MHP ran five ministries.[8] In November 1979, after nearly two years of CHP government, the MHP once again won influence in public institutions in exchange for parliamentary support for the AP government. It thus did well out of the balance of power between the major centre-left and centre-right parties, establishing itself as a crucial partner for the AP.

When in government the MHP found it easiest to place its activists in the ministries it ran. On 21 July 1977 Gün Sazak, Türkeş' right-hand man, was appointed minister of customs and monopolies. On being appointed, he recruited Nationalist Movement activists to work in the ministry. Over the course of several months the ülkücü cadres he had placed got other activists appointed in turn, facilitated relations between the party and its sections in Europe and acted as an interface between party cadres and the activities of the ministry, gradually transforming it into an MHP stronghold. To be recruited, one simply had to go to one of the institutions attached to the ministry with a letter of recommendation signed by the minister, Alparslan Türkeş, or by a party cadre.[9] Most of the time controlling the positions in the upper echelons of the targeted institution was sufficient for those holding them to then be able to pursue a recruitment policy favouring party members. This is what happened when Ağâh Oktay Güner, MHP minister for trade in the second Nationalist Front government, appointed Abdurrahman Sağkaya as managing director of the vast Antbirlik textile factory in Antalya. Sağkaya immediately launched a large-scale programme to recruit ülkücüs in the province.[10] The same thing happened at the ministry of health when its minister, Gökçek, appointed party sympathizers as directors in several hospitals, tasked with recruiting healthcare and other personnel from amongst local MHP supporters.

The Ministry of the Interior together with the General Directorate of Security which it ran were privileged targets for the MHP, which strove to short-circuit the institution's recruitment procedures and place a large number of activists in them.[11] The MHP worked to get certain members appointed to the police by sending lists of activists and sympathizers to the relevant authorities. Sometimes it conducted isolated initiatives. For instance, on 3 September 1980 a commissioner working in the Izmir Directorate of Security wrote to the chairman of the MHP to request that an individual, presented as a member of the party, be appointed to the Intelligence agency.[12] Other documents suggest that this practice was indeed overseen by the party. The minutes of a meeting found at party headquarters laid down the proceedings for entering police training colleges. The minutes specify that 'with regard to the exams to be held on 19 April 1980 to enter the police courses at Orta K [*open to those with middle school diplomas*] and Lise K [*open to those with high school diplomas*], the necessary procedures need to be completed at least fifteen days beforehand. The list will be taken to party headquarters' with the party leadership then seeing to it that its candidate lists reached the relevant people.[13] Over one quarter of the activists with MHP backing joined the police in this way. Thus between 4 April and 24 November 1980, out of a total of 590 individuals listed on a party document, 155 were appointed police officers with the approval of the Ministry of the Interior, and many of them passed the entrance exam even though they did not obtain the required mark.[14]

The institutions of the Ministry of Education (high schools, universities, colleges of further education, teacher training colleges and so on) were also privileged points of penetration – even though the military prosecutor appointed by Martial Law Command in the provinces of Ankara, Çankırı and Kastamonu no doubt overestimated the MHP's grip over education when stating in his indictment that 'gradually all the educational institutes [*eğitim enstitüleri*] came under its control, becoming "liberated ülkücü education institutes" [*Kurtarılmış ülkücü eğitim kurumları*] in the party jargon'.[15] But the discovery of blank diplomas waiting to be filled out and of correspondence between party cadres and officials working for the Department of Education shows he was right in asserting that 'there have always been MHP officials in the Ministry of Education who were working for the benefit of the MHP, not that of the State. The MHP leadership organised this undertaking. On joining the Ministry sympathisers sought to take control of appointments. And as soon as sympathisers were appointed to a school, they sought to set up an ülkücü organisation'.[16] In addition to this, ülkücüs at higher education establishments (and often those in high schools too) regularly enrolled students who were party members or sympathizers. In so doing the MHP once again short-circuited recruitment procedures. A report into the activities of the party in the province of Kayseri between 18 and 26 March 1980 describes how the MHP made sure its young activists had access to local education institutes. It tells how its local bodies worked to help activists enter the Kayseri State Academy of Architecture and Engineering (Kayseri Devlet Mimarlık Mühendislik Akademisi, KDMMA):

The Head of the Kayseri residence informed us in November 1979 that seventy-five people were going to be awarded places at the KDMMA. In a meeting chaired by Yıldız we drew up a pre-enrolment list ... Pre-enrolments opened on 18 March ... 420 points were required in science. On 21 March this requirement was lowered to 395 points. On 21 March we came to an agreement with the head of the KDDMA as follows: either the number of points of our candidates would not be made public, or else the number of points obtained by our candidates would be shown as higher than those of the other people who had applied.[17]

Ülkücü officials thus enabled young activists to enter certain higher educational institutes without having to meet the entry requirements. They also guaranteed that they would be awarded their diplomas.[18]

The Nationalist Movement demanded that ülkücü associations be set up wherever activists worked. Every two weeks the section heads of ülkücü associations were summoned to Ankara for seminars in which the doctrine and means of infiltrating institutions were discussed. More generally, there were modules about this in training sessions provided by the party, with one session for instance on 'The importance of education in the ülkücü movement, education in our enclave activities, education in penetrating crowds, and education once again in conquering the State', and another called 'Infiltration (*kadrolaşma*), the creation of mass movements (*kitleleşme*), and State control (*devletleşme*)'.[19]

Party members standing trial were accused of having infringed several articles of the Constitution, various regulations,[20] and the law on political parties[21] that had been introduced to ensure the autonomy of the state. But what is of interest to us here is not so much the illegal character of these infiltration practices, as the way in which recruitment processes were circumvented and party political rules imported into the administration. Acquaintanceship and political bonds became the two principles for being appointed to the public sector, working against the full legal arsenal endeavouring to protect the frontiers of the state, to separate officials from their class, religious and territorial ties, and to inculcate the values of public service via deep socialization to the state. On the strength of the government positions it held, the MHP was able to replace the legal rules overseeing access to public sector employment with its own ways of promoting certain individual profiles. By short-circuiting the legal means of access to public-sector employment, the MHP prevented public administration from being constituted as an autonomous sector – though it was not the only party to act this way.

Whilst numerous documents used in the prosecutor's indictment indicate that the party organized state penetration when it had access to government posts and during the final Demirel government, others indicate that this approach was not systematic, or else clearly show the difficulties the MHP encountered in entrenching its presence in the state whenever the left won power. Not all ülkücüs working in the public sector were permanent officials, many of them being employees who lost their jobs whenever the government changed political sides. Thus a large number of MHP activists were expelled from public institutions when the CHP returned to power in January 1978. And though ülkücü permanent officials did not lose their posts, they were marginalized or else penalized in the wave of transfers enacted by the new government. After the Association of Ülkücü Officials (Ülkücü Memurlar Derneği, Ülküm) was shut down in October 1978, Yusuf Okumuş, the head of the Ülküm-Bir association which replaced it, informed Türkeş of the new difficulties he was encountering in the province of Ankara:

> Before [Ülküm] was shut down we could count on the membership fees paid by between 1000 and 2000 members in Ankara. ... The number of members has risen constantly since we started our activities. But with the state of martial law we paused our activities. ... We encounter two types of difficulty in opening sections. We try to find people who are honest and intelligent about the current situation. We are careful not to attract more problems than we already encounter. The people we had chosen to open sections were transferred, at least to some other place in the province. We look for officials who are able to channel the ülkücü movement. ... For the reasons mentioned earlier some are hesitant and reserved. This means we are too. Despite the current government, morale is good amongst our members in Ankara and the province. But all they are expecting is another wave of transfers.[22]

A letter sent by a law student in the province of Hatay to the head of the MHP on 29 July 1980 reveals the difficulties encountered by ülkücüs wishing to work in the public sector when the CHP was in government. The student explains that his commitment to the MHP had meant he was unable to follow the 1979 training programme to become a district sub-governor (*kaymakam*), and that he had had to sit exams to become a lawyer. He then continues:

> My Başbuğ, there are 135 districts without a sub-governor (*kaymakam*). Most of the current sub-governors are left-wing and they will not appoint us. Because I am MHP ... Başbuğ, I want to become a sub-governor (*Kaymakam*) because I think I could be more useful in this position.[23]

The MHP, sidelined from power, found it hard to find officials able to represent it in state institutions, and its members, after having been marginalized by the representatives of the new government, saw the doors to public-sector jobs closing shut. The party lost a whole range of resources which had previously enabled it to maintain a support network. The unfortunate candidate for sub-governor was all too aware of this situation, but the letter he sent to Alparslan Türkeş shows that party members had incorporated the fact that the way to access jobs in public administration was via the party.

Additional benefits attendant upon penetration

The numerous advantages the Nationalist Movement drew from its activities to capture resources show just how central the practice of penetrating the state was to party strategies in Turkey. The MHP, in circumventing legal administrative procedures and appropriating the resources of ministries and administrations, was in effect privatizing public resources. Whilst this was a feasible strategy and one that it partially implemented when in government, it was not possible when in opposition. When in power the posts it controlled in the public administration offered the MHP a formidable means of recompensing its supporters and electoral clienteles. This provided it with the manpower it needed for its political activity. At certain periods the MHP had at its disposal a wide range of posts that it was free to distribute as it pleased, thereby rewarding its most promising or faithful activists (as was the case for the members of the Supervisory Committee of the Ministry of Customs), and negotiating support in exchange for state resources (by promising to promote officials who swore allegiance to it, for instance). But to continue to exert its control over those appointed to the positions it distributed, it had to maintain its hold over these positions. When recruiting it was thus careful to get those appointed to sign an undated letter of resignation, which would be sent to the person's superior at the first misdeed. It was thus virtually impossible to attempt to free ride or to shrug off party oversight.[24]

On taking up their job the new recruits acted as party informers. The following extract from a report (from an unspecified department) shows for instance how ülkücü officials provided information about the balance of political power in their place of work:

> Information report on the situation in our regional headquarters [*bölge*]. ... The situation of the fifty-one people working in the department is as follows: nine ülkücüs, seven MSP, ten AP, six members of left-wing organisations. The others are mainly CHP or else neutral. None of our eight ülkücü friends are managers, they are all administrative officials. Conclusion: the number of personnel in our new headquarters will shortly be doubling. In order to be sure of influencing our office we need more members amongst the appointees. We need to be sure that we have at least a few friends among the managers to be appointed shortly (for example the director, or deputy director).[25]

Files found at MHP party headquarters contain names, first names and places where serving policeman worked in the cities around the country, accompanied by information about their political ideas. According to the prosecutor, these reports prove that as of '1976 and 1977 police officers and officials working at the Ankara Directorate of Security produced subjective assessments based on the political preferences of their colleagues, specifying whether they were left or right wing. Suggestions were added to these assessments'.[26] These informant activities were also carried out in higher education. A search carried out at the home of Şadi Somuncuoğlu[27] on 15 September 1980 discovered a list of names of teaching staff at the Faculties of Law and Economics at Istanbul University, the Medicine Faculties at Cerrahpaşa and Çapa, and the faculty of Dentistry at Istanbul Technical University, classified into 'positive' and 'negative' categories. The positive signs accompanying a name (*, **, ***) corresponded to: ***Totally worthy of trust, nationalist; **Worthy of trust; *May make concessions when needed or else perhaps be converted – whilst those who were suspected or known to be associated with left-wing movements or ideologies were designated by #, ##, or ###. The same search also produced two pages copied from the Law Faculty's Who's Who, with the title 'Who's Who – get to know the teachers at the Law Faculty', containing indications about each teacher. It is stated for instance that one teacher 'shuttles back and forth between communism and socialism without managing to make up his mind'.[28] In a letter to the leader of the MHP, the head of judicial services in Hakkari province writes that 'personnel working in Hakkari judicial services have been classified by political ideas and beliefs, [and] this assessment is based on reliable sources'.[29] A letter sent to the MHP leader by an activist working at the Ministry of the Interior provides an illustration of these activities:

> The governor of … is a classic bureaucrat. He does his duty at all times. He displays genuine qualities as a member of the public administration. He is not an enemy of the MHP. The governor of … comes from a Sunni CHP family in Sivas. He is worthy of trust on subjects relating to the nation and morality. He may be considered as close to anti-MHP milieus. He needs to be approached and attempts made to win him over in a thoughtful and moderate manner. The governor of … was a Kurdist in his youth, but has changed over the years. He joined the MSP to become a governor. Then he moved over to the AP. His goal is to enter parliament. If the MHP were to make him an offer he might well accept it. … If approached intelligently he may be used.[30]

On the strength of the work it conducted to collect information about personnel in public institutions, the party was able to assess the extent of its influence, identify individuals to approach and detect officials hostile to ülkücüs – whom it then endeavoured to marginalize. Having support within institutions was also a considerable advantage at election time. A letter sent to Alparslan Türkeş on 30 June 1980 by Nihat Ülkekul, an inspector at the General Directorate of Security, gives the following information about his activities:

> As a State official, and in compliance with the law as befits my position, I wish to be under your orders and work for the country and the MHP. To this end, and with the upcoming period of electoral campaigning, I want to help the MHP in every way I can so as to help it secure a fine victory. My activities are currently devoted to the electoral campaign. If the decision is taken to organise any elections, I will step up my work for this purpose.[31]

Lastly, the Nationalist Movement was able to draw on its personnel working as officials in order to circumvent legal procedure in a whole range of sectors. When local ülkücü associations were shut down by the legal system, party cadres used their networks within the provincial administration to get the decision overturned. This is what happened after the first ülkücü hearth in Bornova was shut down, in February 1978, when the head of the Izmir section requested – and obtained – the support of the governor of the province.[32] Thanks to its positions in public institutions the MHP was able to protect its activists by intervening in legal proceedings or else by contacting police stations. Apart from when the CHP was in government, local ülkücüs sections often contacted party cadres (be they leaders or elected representatives) in order get them to intervene at the relevant police station to obtain the release of members who had been arrested.[33] Ömer Tanlak, a reformed MHP activist, describes how he was released after having been arrested for a gun battle in a cafe in the district of İsmetpaşa in Ankara:

> The next day we went into town. A search was being carried out in the cafés, and an arm was found on a friend we called Hikmet the soldier [*Asker Hikmet*]. The police rounded us up and put us in a vehicle. Before getting in Hikmet the soldier said to the café owner, who was the mayor [*muhtar*], 'tell Necati Paşa' [i.e. Necati Gültekin, the party general secretary]. They took us to the Anafartalar police station. Two hours later they released us.[34]

The same Ömer Tanlak, referring to his activist work at Etlik high school in Ankara, provides precious information about the support he and his friends received from the headmaster, who was a member of the Ülkü-Bir association; Tanlak says that as of 1977 he lent them his own weapon to carry out operations outside school, and provided them with protection inside it.[35] Sometimes the party was able to secure the support of people placed very high up in the administration. Notes taken by the MHP general secretary show that an unnamed Head of Security was thanked in a meeting of the MHP executive board for intervening to get arms permits issued to certain party activists.[36]

Politicizing institutions – the law and order sector

> *But what were the police doing?*
>
> 'Well – I don't know. We had a good relationship with Pol-Der … We had their support, they let us get on with things. But in the Army too we had the support of revolutionary officers. It was a revolutionary situation, you know.'[37]

The institutions tasked with maintaining law and order were especially exposed to activities to capture their resources, in particular because controlling them considerably reduced the risks associated with mobilization. In the Directorate of Security there were antagonistic associations of police officers, resulting in the politicization of officials' working practices. We thus need to understand how the representatives of law and order, in carrying out their functions, were led to act in ways that differed depending upon their political position. This stage of the argument is fundamental for understanding the concrete ways in which state institutions ended up functioning more as arenas for rivalry and conflict than as networks to consolidate the authority and legitimacy of the state.

The army largely unaffected by resource capture

It is difficult to assess the extent to which the Turkish army was permeated by the lines of political division structuring the other public institutions during the second half of the 1970s, given that there are only fragmentary sources about the subject. It would appear to have been shielded from political influence thanks to its separation from the civilian bureaucracy in the coups of 27 May 1960 and 12 March 1971, and the introduction of measures and regulations specifically dedicated to ensuring its financial autonomy. The setting up of the Armed Forces Assistance Fund (Ordu Yardımlaşma Kurumu, OYAK) in the 1960s provided military personnel with a way of being rid of oversight by the political authorities.[38] And indeed the financial autonomy and selection procedures of the armed forces meant they were less exposed than other institutions to penetration activities by ülkücü or far-left groups.

During the 1970s a rapprochement nevertheless took place between the army and radical groups. Certain measures taken by Commander Bölügiray on arriving in Adana in 1979 suggest that the battalions stationed in the town were politicized. In particular the insistence with which he reminded the troops of their duty to remain neutral suggests that this had not hitherto been fully respected:

> The most important principle in our mission is to remain neutral. Never mind your personal convictions, we have to be neutral in carrying out our functions. If we maintain this stance then we will be able to put an end to the anarchy and terror throughout the country. ... Do not allow the honour and reputation of the Army to be sullied on any occasion.[39]

A bit later, on learning that soldiers were in contact with local party leaders, he immediately dismissed the culprits, and reminded his second-in-commands that 'the purpose of martial law is to defend the entire people, irrespective of where they come from, against anarchy and terror, and to act as a support to the State. There can be no Army party or ideology. Our party, our ideology, is Ataturkism'.[40]

In his thesis about the 'incident' at Kahramanmaraş,[41] Burak Gürel observes that NCOs were 'divided along political lines'. Thus students from the Harbiye military school spontaneously protested against the Kahramanmaraş massacre, observing 'a minute's silence for the victims of the massacre and then [chanting] anti-fascist slogans'.[42] In addition to this, officers publicly complained about the 'ideological influence' of recruits.[43] It is thus more than likely that the stated neutrality of the army – made credible a posteriori by its intervention on 12 September 1980 – actually concealed a process of politicization. The available sources indicate, however, that any such politicization occurred on an irregular basis and affected only a minority. This was something the MHP, which had been hoping to draw on support from the military apparatus, realized to its regret in the wake of the 12 September 1980 coup. No sector in the army protested against the line laid down by the Military Staff. But things were different in the police, which was more exposed to the influence of political forces.

The police

The Pol-Der association (Polis Derneği, Police Association) was founded on 17 May 1975. It resulted from the change in leadership of the Orta(k)lılar Derneği (so called after the specific training course, *Orta(k)*), an association of ranked police officers whose leader had resigned at the previous general congress. The elections held to appoint a new leadership were marked by opposition between a group of policemen composed of CHP and far-left sympathizers (including Kasim Ulusoy, İsmet Hoşça and Sıtkı Öner) and another group composed of ülkücüs. For the latter this conflict was part of the Nationalist Movement's overall strategy of seeking to expand its sites of mobilization. The Ulusoy faction won. The new team renamed the association Pol-Der, and altered its statutes to open it up to all police officers irrespective of rank. It wished to establish it as a model for a 'people's police' (*halkın polisi*) and denounced the demands of the 'fascists', the abuses of power by the recently formed Nationalist Front government and the torture used against members of 'progressive' organizations by certain policemen. It also militated for the ministry to treat policemen better, demanding a wage increase for policemen, the reintroduction of effective training and improved working conditions. In 1975 the association asserted its stance was apolitical,[44] but the first issue of its journal defended the right to not obey orders[45] – a position viewed by the new Nationalist Front government as a declaration of hostility. In 1976, after having failed once again to win control of the association, ülkücü officers founded Pol-Bir (Polis Birliği, the Police Union) – whose main demand was quite simply the shutting down of Pol-Der, which it accused of supporting communism and separatism.

The police thus became an arena for rivalry between associations with opposing demands. By politicizing their discourse they put forward antagonistic models of the role of a police officer, based on the worldviews they were promoting. The role laid down by the institution gradually disappeared behind the categorizations imported by these associations, giving rise to differentiated police practices. Policemen – prior even to considering themselves as members of the forces of law and order – adopted a position 'against the fascists' or as 'enemies of the communists'. Internal sociabilities were badly affected. Nurhan Varlı provides an account of these changes, describing how in the Hacettepe police station in Ankara 'the left/right divergences had reached a point where it was impossible to trust anyone.'[46] One morning her commissioner caught her reading *Cumhuriyet*, the major centre-left newspaper, and she was subjected to disciplinary proceedings.[47] After numerous appeals she was transferred to the town of Artvin (in the north-east of Anatolia), where she encountered a comparable situation to that prevailing in Hacettepe, with the police station divided into two opposing camps. The officers there were won over to the ülkücü cause, and to be allocated a prestigious posting (to the political unit, for instance) they had to display their ideological proximity to the Nationalist Movement. Left-wing police officers were ostracized, marginalized and condemned to secondary tasks, such as public order (*asayiş şubesi*).[48] Professional careers were becoming politicized since the principles governing transfers and promotions related to the ideological positions of the officers concerned.

Professional sociabilities were also subject to officers' political choices. On-duty police officers insulted each other, fought and abandoned all semblance of neutrality in restoring order. Police officers in Adana, on being sent out to a fight between antagonistic groups, would take position within the ranks of those present.[49] Excerpts from conversations between police officers confirm this polarization ('Base here. A gunbattle has broken out in the street. ... Teams 315 and 320 go there immediately!'. 'Fascist dog! You've become a man and now you're giving orders?'. 'Communist bastard! Traitor! Son of a ...'),[50] as does the hasty departure of the new head of Security in September 1979 on receiving death threats ('Fascist dog, what do you think you're doing here? Get out or else we are determined to eliminate you').[51] Association members were the first victims. In his memoirs Sıtkı refers to the case of a Pol-Der member who, on attending a festival organized in tribute to Yunus Emre in Eskişehir,[52] was stopped by ülkücü policemen, bludgeoned, and then tortured in the local police station when his colleagues learnt that he belonged to the left-wing association.[53] Even the most routine professional practices were politicized. Witnesses tell how police teams called out to a dispute would turn against the plaintiffs, or else allow the culprits to escape.[54] A sub-lieutenant at the gendarmerie in Adana says he saw police officers relieve far-left militants of their weapons so as avoid taking them into custody.[55] Nevzat Bölügiray, the Martial Law Commander in Adana, notes how policemen in the town treated individuals differently depending upon how they dressed, whether they had a moustache or not, and the newspapers they read.[56] In late 1979 he dismissed six officers who on attending seminars run by Devrimci Yol had informed its members of upcoming police operations.[57] The Kahramanmaraş massacre is a good example of the politicization of the practices of police officers. During the incidents there between 22 and 25 December 1978,[58] in which the Alevi population was attacked by part of the Sunni population directed by members of local ülkücü organizations, the police effectively took part in the massacre either by turning a blind eye (as members of Pol-Bir did) or else by encouraging acts of vengeance (as certain Pol-Der members did).[59] These acts of insubordination and indiscipline became increasingly frequent since provincial Directorates of Security did not have the means to prevent them. Bölügiray recounts a discussion he says he had with one of his subordinates about the increasing number of acts of indiscipline in the Adana police:

'There are more and more acts of insubordination, what measures have you taken to improve discipline?'

Sir, we are putting together a file about undisciplined officers and we will be sending it to the provincial disciplinary council.

'Fine, and what sanctions will be meted out?'

None.

'What? How come?'

'Because the provincial disciplinary council has not operated since 1977. That is why no disciplinary measures are taken against this type of police officer.'[60]

Cevat Yurdakul, the Head of Security in Adana and a Pol-Der member, was assassinated on 20 September 1979; over 300 police officers, mostly from the association, gathered in the gardens of the Directorate of Security, wholly deaf to orders enjoining them to disperse, chanting: 'Down with fascism! No to martial law, death to fascism!'. Despite the arrival of the governor of the province exhorting them to calm down and go back to work, they attacked the buildings of the Directorate of Security before then dispersing. A bit later on police cars drove around Adana calling on the population to attend the ceremony organized by Pol-Der members. In the evening police officers barricaded themselves inside police stations in protest, and Commander Bölügiray called in the army to evict them. In the wake of these incidents 221 police officers were suspended, 14 imprisoned and 54 transferred out of the district. At Yurdakul's burial in Ankara, police officers formed a cortege and brandished placards bearing political slogans: 'Fascist assassinations will never win out against patriotic policeman, down with fascism, long live our combat!', 'We will continue our friend's struggle ... Our association lost a valiant combatant with Yurdakul's assassination'. Fights broke out between protesters (police officers, students and trade unionists), and the forces of order were called in to oversee the cortege.

This political bipolarization upset the maintenance of law and order. Such was Commander Bölügiray's distrust of 'partisan' and 'activist' police officers that he did not warn the Adana police when large-scale operations were being prepared by the army.[61] In the late 1970s the Turkish police no longer provided its members with a set of specific unified, coherent norms. Mobilization by the associations pushed certain police officers to redefine their role along ideological lines that were external to the institution, forming the backdrop to the tumultuous cohabitation of differentiated and irreconcilable practices and representations. Rivalry between police organizations was a factor in politicizing the practices of police officers, which tended towards their being de-objectified as a unified set of practices. But it would also appear to have de-objectified the police in the eyes of the population, who no longer considered it to be functionally and politically distinct from the radical groups. They thus now started turning to the armed sections of the two action systems to ensure their security, participating financially in their movements or else joining the non-militarized sections of their organizations.

Replacing the public authorities

In certain villages and neighbourhoods groups replaced the public authorities. This situation may be explained firstly by the fact that the public authorities were sometimes almost wholly unrepresented, and by the obstacles encountered in establishing any state presence there. Throughout the second part of the 1970s state representatives were the target of repression, pressure and intimidation by radical groups wishing to appropriate certain of their prerogatives. These physical threats, together with the numerous changes in government, led to a rapid turnover in those representing the public authorities. Hamit Bozarslan argues that the state was sometimes

> simply absent ... Niğde had six governors in succession between 1975 and 1980. Over the same period there was a change in governor four times in Ordu, seven times in Çorum, four times in Malatya, six times in Elazığ, four times in Erzincan, five times in Maraş, five times in Kars, four times in Erzurum, four times in Diyarbakir, and so on and so forth. In 1980 there was no governor in Urfa, and there were only sub-governors in towns such as Siverek, Besiri, Sirnak, and Uludere.[62]

The replacement of the local public authorities included the privatization of municipal services. It was thus not only by drawing on public services that the mobilized groups managed to win political and economic control over urban and rural zones but also by replacing those services.

Holding municipal office

The town of Fatsa provides a particularly interesting case of the overlap between public services and political forces, for it shows how far-left groups, deprived of access to central resources, had to draw on mobilization by activists in order to oppose state representatives, especially within local electoral arenas. Fatsa is a district capital on the Black Sea coast, in the province of Ordu. For the far left it is a highly symbolic place, as it was in this district (at Kızıldere) that Mahir Çayan and his fellow THKP-C members – far-left icons in the 1970s – were eliminated by the forces of law and order in 1972. The Dev-Yol group was thus particularly active here. The town was a traditional CHP stronghold up until the general elections of 14 October 1979 when it was won by Dev-Yol member Fikri Sönmez, running as an independent candidate. His victory meant that the organization controlled all municipal jobs and was in a position to defy the governor of Ordu province.

Once in office the new municipal team imposed a singular management model. Several testimonials indicate the municipal personnel were not fired when the team took up office. Most of the people questioned by Pertev Aksakal for his work about the 'Fatsa Commune' stated that municipal employees were able to keep their jobs provided they did not hinder the action of the new municipal majority and that they abandoned their corruption practices.[63] This does not appear to be wholly accurate, however. Whilst municipal personnel retained their jobs, they were placed beneath the direct control of Dev-Yol cadres and the people's committees (*halk komiteleri*) that were put in place in the days following Sönmez's arrival in office. In addition to this, municipal committees (*belediye komiteleri*) composed of those sympathetic to the new mayor were set up alongside official municipal posts, thus depriving municipal personnel of any real role in managing the town. Ahmet Özdemir, who worked at the Public Relations Directorate (Halkla İlişkiler Müdürlüğü), describes these committees as units in charge of settling inhabitants' problems in direct liaison with the mayor.[64] The role of the people's committees was to devise and implement municipal policy in the seven neighbourhoods of the town, with each neighbourhood being divided up into eleven zones in which elections were held to vote for committees comprising between three and seven members. All parties were allowed to put forward candidates, with the exception of the MHP whose representatives were chased out of town on the day following the municipal elections,[65] and all inhabitants of voting age were allowed to take part in the vote. But the new municipal team[66] were not happy with the results of the first election, and they held a second vote, giving their backing to selected candidates, the vast majority of whom were elected.[67]

The people's committees laid down the rules for life in the neighbourhoods. According to Hamit Bozarslan, they 'banned the consumption of alcohol and outlawed gambling; they also decided to carry arms in order to defend themselves'.[68] Their members intervened in economic flows in the town. In late 1979, when the shopkeepers had run out of supplies of cooking oil, members of the people' committees and resistance committees (*direniş komiteleri*) – units set up to enforce order in the neighbourhoods – confiscated the stock of the local Fiskobirlik oil production factory and distributed it to the population. The town authorities also controlled trade in hazelnut shells, which the population used as heating fuel in winter. They obtained the financial backing of the cement factory, the water supply and distribution company, and the local port, after having threatened to shut them down and take over their assets. It also set up a bus and collective taxi service (*dolmuş*), enabling them to recruit Dev-Yol sympathizers and increase its revenues. It regularized building norms and got the owners of illegally erected buildings to pay taxes.

This parallel organization was comprised of hundreds of people,[69] with committees controlled by Dev-Yol set up alongside all the public institutions. The people's committees replaced the neighbourhood mayors (*muhtar*) and judicial institutions, the resistance committees replaced the police and the municipal committees replaced the municipal personnel. The people's committees arbitrated in the event of intra-community, family and neighbourhood disputes,[70] whilst the resistance committees patrolled the neighbourhoods to maintain order in town.[71] The 'Fatsa Commune' existed for several months, throughout which period the police, gendarmerie and justice system did not intervene in the town on a single occasion.

The 'liberated' municipality of Fatsa came to an end on 11 July 1980,[72] when three gendarmerie commando squads, troops from Ordu Province Commandership, a mechanised infantry battalion and policemen entered the town, with the support of three assault vessels anchored facing the port, in order to 'retake control of the liberated zones' in the words of Prime Minister Demirel.[73] During this operation dozens of masked individuals guided the forces of law and order through the streets of the town and checked inhabitants' ID papers.[74] It is known that four of them were former members of the ülkücü residences in the town.[75] When the leader of the CHP, Bülent Ecevit, called this collaboration a 'fascist occupation', the Demirel government refused to divulge the names of the ülkücüs present during the operation; the Nationalist Movement responded via a pamphlet distributed in town: 'Brave Turkish nation, heroic inhabitants of Fatsa. From now on we shall riposte to the martyrdom of all those who follow our ideals in the villages with [several executions] in town.'[76] On 11 July the ülkücüs returned to the town,[77] taking over from the resistance committees to maintain order. The subsequent exodus this time round was of the population suspected of association with the Dev-Yol municipal authorities.

The 'Fatsa Commune' is not an isolated example. In several other towns MHP or far-left municipal office-holders used militias to exert control over the urban area. In Elazığ and Erzincan, for example, the MHP used threats, violence (with beatings, the destruction of shops, and assassination attempts), racketeering and extortion to prevent the Alevi population (suspected by the MHP of being idealistically affiliated with the left) and activists from left-wing organizations from entering the town centres. In Kars the links between the CHP municipal authorities and left-wing groups enabled the latter to take over certain neighbourhoods in the town, exert control over them via armed guards and politically homogenise their population. In October 1978 the local police chief stated it was no longer possible to enter the neighbourhoods controlled by far-left organizations without endangering the life both of the inhabitants and of his troops.[78]

This patchiness of public authority explains the ease with which parties and organizations winning municipalities office in Fatsa and other towns in Anatolia were able to shake off the tutelage of the State so as to monopolise and take control of all the local resources. Winning municipal office was a major stake for the ülkücüs and for left-wing organizations, which were the only ones to replace the State in this manner, turning the towns they conquered into 'liberated zones' (*kurtarılmış bölgeler*). The MHP used its municipal strongholds to settle certain personnel there who had lost their position in government or central institutions.

The 'liberated zones'

In certain neighbourhoods mobilized groups took advantage of the comparative absence of the ruling parties and of the lack of public institutions to establish their control and win recognition as the local interlocutors for the municipal and governmental authorities. It is this replacing of public authorities that we are now going to analyse, based on observation of the situation in the May Day neighbourhood in Istanbul (Bir Mayis Mahallesi) from 1977 onwards.[79]

The setting up of 'liberated zones' In the 1950s the demand for labour in the country's great industrial centres and the mechanization of agriculture led to the widespread exodus of the rural population. The migrants amassed in the outskirts of the larger towns, building housing in what gradually became new outlying neighbourhoods. Up until the late 1970s the governments and public authorities viewed these neighbourhoods as zones to be eradicated rather than as territories to be incorporated within their field of action.⁸⁰ This is why there were frequently no public institutions there, and why the police – or the gendarmerie when they were built outside the scope of the town authorities – only rarely set foot there other than to evacuate and demolish them.

This was the prevailing situation in the Mustafa Kemal neighbourhood up until 1977, when a committee comprised of activists from local left-wing groups took control and renamed it 'May Day neighbourhood'. This was one of the fourteen neighbourhoods in the town of Ümraniye, in the district of Üsküdar, in the Asian part of Istanbul. The neighbourhood had sprung up without official sanction in the early 1960s when a group of migrants had settled near the Ümraniye stone quarry.⁸¹ But the town's population had grown from 22,969 inhabitants in 1970 to 71,954 inhabitants in 1980,⁸² and given its limited financial means, there were no public services.

As of the second half of the 1970s left-wing groups devoted much effort to establishing their presence in zones inhabited by populations issuing from the rural exodus, who were well disposed to their rhetoric of defending workers. The Halkın Kurtuluşu, Halkın Yolu, Halkın Birliği and Partizan groups had a strong presence in the May Day neighbourhood. In May 1977 they held elections there for a people's committee (*halk komitesi*) comprising eight members,⁸³ which, in Şükrü Aslan's words, 'was going to constitute a non-official decision-making centre in the neighbourhood by organizing all aspects of the inhabitants' lives'.⁸⁴ The committee was the non-official seat of local power, and it became the main interlocutor for the public authorities. It homogenized the population by exerting pressure on the inhabitants and selecting new arrivals on the basis of political preference,⁸⁵ and established order by using armed guards – all of whom were activists – who were also in charge of protecting the frontiers of the neighbourhood:

Were these neighbourhoods well-known?

'There were well-known neighbourhoods such as Ümranye, Kağıthane, which have now become ... not even slums anymore in fact ... Now they are in fact part of the town, but, well, I used to know them, I watched them as they developed and were built up. For example it was people from Kars who came, who didn't have any money, we used to help them build houses, honestly, I mean, it was a matter of exchange, you helped people settle in town, you dug the pipes. But, well, gradually things got built.'

Were people asked to become part of the group? Were the services given free of charge or was something expected in return?

'In any case when we took control of the neighbourhood it meant that these people depended on you, the State was not there. Officially the neighbourhood didn't exist at that time, it was when the houses were being built ... I don't know, because it was known as a left-wing neighbourhood there were sometimes far-right people who launched attacks, so the entire neighbourhood was held by activists. There was a guard system. ... So there were armed guards.'⁸⁶

The committee drew up neighbourhood planning rules with the help of activists from other left-wing groups, members of the Union of Chambers of Turkish Engineers and Architects (Türk Mühendis ve Mimar Odaları Birliği, TMMOB), and students studying town planning, engineering or architecture.[87] Over the course of its few months' existence, it ran projects to build schools, kindergartens and parks,[88] controlled the allocation of numerous lodgings and drew on contributions from the population to obtain the funds they needed to carry out these projects, thereby becoming a central economic actor in the neighbourhood.

The existence of this liberated zone attracted widespread coverage in the Turkish press, as did the autonomy enjoyed by the people's committee in running it. The second Nationalist Front government (which took office on 21 July 1977) decided to intervene together with the Istanbul municipal authorities. On 2 September 1977 bulldozers were sent into the neighbourhood.[89] This triggered altercations between left-wing groups and the forces of law and order, leaving 5 people dead and 47 injured (of whom 38 were civilians), with 138 people being taken into detention. Once this extensively reported intervention was over, the public authorities again lost interest in the neighbourhood. The people's committee promised to rebuild the blocks of flats which had been demolished, financing the works with campaigns orchestrated by far-left journals. However, the committee was dissolved in January 1979 due to internal dissent and the neighbourhood divided up into five zones (A, B, C, D and E), each of which (apart from zone C) was controlled by a radical group (zone A being controlled by Halkın Kurtuluşu, zone B by Halkın Yolu, zone D by the Partizan group and zone E by Halkın Birliği).[90]

The demolition operations and division of the neighbourhood into distinct zones brought to a close the phase of infrastructure building launched by the people's committee. There was still no school or hospital in the neighbourhood, no access to running water, and it only had electricity thanks to illegal hook-ups to the municipal infrastructure. There were no transport links with neighbouring areas. The far-left groups, faced with the impossibility of dealing directly with the public authorities, set up a committee of old hands (*yaşlılar komitesi*) comprising five members, one from each of the five zones in the neighbourhood. This committee very soon emerged as the main interlocutor for the public authorities and embedded its positions of dominance within the neighbourhood by obtaining approval for the infrastructure projects it was calling for.

This form of territorial control may also be observed in other neighbourhoods of Istanbul,[91] as well as in Ankara[92] and many other towns around the country. Thus Hamit Bozarslan describes a comparable situation in Kars, where the ülkücüs managed to control two neighbourhoods – before being chased out of town, and returning sporadically to carry out surprise attacks.[93] In Ardahan, which at the time was part of the province of Kars, the Porters' Association (Hammallar Derneği), a group of 200 to 300 workers close to far-left movements, 'controlled in the name of the people whichever State and private institutions it wished'.[94] Ülkücüs in Sivas hemmed the Alevi population into the neighbourhood of Alibaba.[95] Neighbourhoods in the hands of antagonistic groups sometimes bordered each other, and their frontiers were controlled by militias who oversaw population flows between the liberated zones. In the district of Pazarcık, in Adana, the road from Kahramanmaraş to Malatya was divided lengthwise by a green line marking the frontier between two opposing zones. Activists were stationed on either side of this line drawn along the asphalt,[96] and armed altercations frequently broke out.[97]

When groups managed to impose their order over neighbourhoods in large towns, they implemented a range of activities which were theoretically the remit of the public authorities. They homogenized populations along political or community lines, occasionally had housing built and oversaw its allocation, arbitrated in intra- and inter-community disputes within the neighbourhood, and used coercive means to have various taxes paid, thereby enabling them to entrench their activities within the territories under their control. By redistributing the sums they pooled via taxation they became key economic actors and were able to set up veritable militias.[98]

Social control in liberated zones Groups carried out spatial demarcation and regulated the cultural assets available in the neighbourhoods they controlled. The walls of buildings in 'liberated zones' were covered with stencilled images portraying ülkücü or far-left martyrs, together with slogans, posters and notices. The forces of law and order rarely entered these zones, allowing a whole set of symbols to flourish, which were intended to signify the domination exerted there by the constituted groups.

In Adana, Martial Law Commander Bölügiray sought to combat these clearly visible signs. On 5 September, an NCO told him that in several sectors of the town 'nearly all the walls are covered with Maoist mural journals. Wherever the journal has been posted up there are insults, slogans, and red stars painted everywhere on the walls'.[99] Whilst the commander was surprised that the army did not act to clean them up, he appreciated that the local Martial Law Command could only intervene if the mayors (*muhtar*) told them of the situation in their neighbourhood. But mayors frequently did not have a telephone and had to go to business premises with a phone line, laying themselves open to reprisals. The *muhtars*, out of fear or ideological sympathy, thus allowed groups to mark neighbourhoods with symbols. Sometimes they changed the name of the place, as was the case for Mustafa Kemal neighbourhood in Istanbul which became the May Day neighbourhood,[100] or the neighbourhood in Ankara controlled by the ülkücüs which became Ergenekon (*Ergenekon Mahallesi*).[101]

The inhabitants' cultural practices and mores were also kept under close observation. A whole series of places became 'control towers thanks to their "strategic" position and visibility – such as mosques, ülkücü residences, left-wing associations, restaurants, coffeehouses, and bookshops'.[102] Militia patrolled the liberated zones, acting as morality police, arresting and punishing anyone who failed to comply with the cultural codes intended to signify that one either belonged to or else was close to the dominant local group. Groups in a position of force exerted a high level of social control. It could thus be very risky to venture into an ülkücü liberated zone if one had long hair, was wearing a fatigue jacket, was carrying the *Cumhuriyet* newspaper[103] or displaying any other clearly visible sign of far-left sympathy:

> *Were their neighbourhoods in the towns which were held by the left, with others being held by the right?*
>
> 'Yes it was like that and then if you went … In any case the slums were like villages, everybody knew everybody else, there were slums for example with people from eastern Turkey, it was people from such a town who were there and so, the people in this neighbourhood … If a neighbourhood was known for being held by left-wing or right-wing activists, people could not go into the neighbourhood, if you came from outside perhaps you could enter, but you couldn't enter with a left-wing newspaper, people would have understood who you were.'
>
> *But was it dangerous or …*
>
> 'There was a real risk of being beaten up, and then … Well, people were killed like that. People, for example, who entered a right-wing neighbourhood with a left-wing newspaper, they knew they were going to get their heads smashed in if they ran into any militants.'[104]

Equally it was unthinkable to go around a zone controlled by the far left carrying *Hergün* or *Devlet*, journals published by the Nationalist Movement. A document sent out to all local ülkücü sections gives an idea of how the Nationalist Movement went about imposing cultural homogenization on its neighbourhoods.[105] The text is presented as a list of recommendations to be followed by the local Nationalist Movement[106] and targeting the population of the neighbourhood in question. Members of the Nationalist Movement are invited to act in such a way as to foster uniformity in religious practice and references: 'We must ensure that all the houses in the neighbourhood have a book by a religious teacher, and efforts must be made to gain access to these houses by their younger members.'[107] To build up contact with the younger inhabitants the local sections of ülkücü organizations worked with the bureaus set up by the Nationalist Movement, and especially the local education bureau (*eğitim masası*) and the *gecekondu* neighbourhood bureaus (*gecekondu semtler masası*) which coordinated all of the activities of the *gecekondu* organizations. Ülkücü high school students were to make contact with young people in the neighbourhood in order to advise them about what to read, lend them books and check that the precepts they were preaching were being properly applied. The document states that '[young people] must be given the opportunity to apply what they have read in the Book of Dede Korkut:[108] get them to buy something in a grocer's, observe someone sent into a café, get them to buy bread from a grocer's for the elderly'.[109] Each time activists encountered young people in the neighbourhood they were to 'ask them about what they had got from their lessons, if they had read and liked the books they had been given, and, depending upon their answers, to give them further books'. Young people were considered as an effective way of gaining admittance to families, and much of the ülkücüs' channelling activities were targeted at them. Activists were to 'get them to recite the *bismillahirrahmanirrahim* ["In the name of God, the Most Gracious, the Most Merciful"] from time to time, teach them prayers, organise religious lessons in their neighbourhood, get them to perform the Friday ablutions and accompany them as a group to the mosque for Friday prayers', and also to 'teach [them the] national anthem and get them to play military games, such as singing the national anthem for instance with their chest puffed out, head held high, and a "tough" expression'.

Sporting activities were also organized. Thus 'when an ülkücü knows enough young people, he shall set up teams and organise matches. The winning team is to receive an illustrated Book of Dede Korkut and a book of tales published by the Ministry of Culture'. During training the young sportspeople were to be motivated by invoking 'the characteristics of the Turkish nation'. During competitions, activists were to give 'the little teams they created a name relating to Turkish history, such as *Oğuz Spor* (Oguz Sport), *Ülkü Spor* (Ideal Sport), or *Göktürk Spor* (Celestial Turkish Sport)', and had to 'explain in a language accessible to the youngest players the historical episodes these names referred to'. Competitions were set up between ülkücü teams from different neighbourhoods, with the winning teams being awarded a 'metal cup', whilst ensuring 'that the young people [did] not develop any servitude towards material goods'.

Territorial marking and organizing activities for the population enabled the groups to define which practices and cultural assets were legitimate within the locality. This fostering of uniform mores enabled them to exert social control over the inhabitants, whilst they could draw on their militias or armed guards to put pressure on any individuals who were recalcitrant to the precepts they sought to impose, either forcing them to comply or else expelling them from the neighbourhood. In addition to this, the liberated zones became sanctuaries for activists from the neighbourhood or elsewhere who were able to go and hide there, or spend time and socialize in the mores and practices of the dominant groups.

The liberated zones and the public authorities It was rare for the groups which had managed to turn neighbourhoods into 'liberated zones' to have a conflictual relationship with the public authorities. On the contrary, their presence within the population meant they were often the privileged interlocutors of representatives from official arenas,[110] with whom they entered into many agreements, most of which were tacit, and certain illicit. Many took advantage of their interaction with the public authorities to reinforce their position within the liberated zones and to increase their legitimacy in the eyes of the inhabitants. Once accepted as the public authorities' interlocutors, they no longer had any interest in opposing the state, and if they did so then the representatives of official arenas (the town hall, the sub-governor's office, the governor's office or the provincial Directorate of Security) called in the forces of law and order, as was the case in the May Day neighbourhood, and (under different circumstances) in Fatsa in July 1980. Most of the time the public authorities negotiated with these local actors. In the May Day neighbourhood the committee of old hands, elected in 1979 after the dissolution of the people's committee, took advantage of its status as the public authorities' interlocutor to entrench its positions. On being set up it informed the provincial sub-governor's office of its existence and its readiness to enter into dialogue so as to improve the life of the inhabitants, something which it claimed the Ümraniye town authorities had been unwilling to do.[111] Initial discussions related to establishing a running water supply and building roads through the neighbourhood. In very little time the committee got dispensaries and four primary schools built in the neighbourhood.[112] In spring 1978 a gendarmerie was opened in the neighbourhood, staffed by between twelve and fourteen gendarmes, and a cooperative was set up in September 1979 for purchasing everyday consumer goods.[113]

In most cases this type of local power did not have the resources to put up any lasting opposition to state action, nor was it in a position to replace it as the sole actor in local public action. But its strong territorial presence enabled it to enter into negotiations with the public authorities, win recognition as the sole local interlocutor and, in return, reinforce its control over the liberated zone. Thus in the wake of 12 September it was Hayri Direk, a member of the committee of old hands, who was selected by the ruling junta as mayor (*muhtar*) in the May Day neighbourhood.[114]

*

The two action systems conducted different yet competing activities to capture public resources, leading to the de-objectification of the institutions in which they were present. These institutions thus no longer functioned as sets of comparatively unified practices or as bodies that were socially and functionally distinct from the actors in the political field. The state's weak capacities made it easier for groups to penetrate municipal arenas, whilst also encouraging them to circumvent these arenas, negotiate with the public authorities and act as their substitutes. Ülkücü and far-left groups exerted armed control over the population and territory in 'liberated zones' and positioned themselves within economic flows, channelling these to their own advantage. They established themselves as the main interlocutors for the at-times conflictual negotiations with the public authorities to get them to hand over social and political control over the neighbourhoods. Penetration, mobilization and replacement were in no way separate mechanisms within the Nationalist Movement. When the Nationalist Movement was in government, its access to the central institutions of state facilitated and furthered the efforts of its local sections to replace the public authorities. The high degree of internal coordination within the movement, together with collusion between its 'civilian' sections and its members holding official public posts, enabled it to reap the benefits of its licit and illicit, legal and illegal activities (such as intervening in the economy, racketeering, introducing regulations and setting up militias in its neighbourhoods). The question of the resources at the disposal of the two action systems is thus fundamental. Thanks to its positions in the central institutions of state, the Nationalist Movement was able to coordinate all the activities of its members as part of a global strategy to obtain and retain power. Unlike the far-left action system, it was thus able to operate on the various different administrative and territorial levels of public action simultaneously.

Chapter 5

THE SPREAD OF PROTEST MOVEMENTS

The conflict between the antagonistic movements spread through institutions in an increasing number of social sectors, in what would appear to be a by-product of the Nationalist Movement's activities to capture public resources. The ülkücüs' activities influenced where and how the conflict occurred. They were thus instrumental in exporting the mobilization to multiple sectors and in bringing about a convergence in demands and in the rhythm of events. Ülkücü organizations were set up in public institutions as of 1975, triggering a split into two polar areas of rivalry, with the supporters of the Nationalist Front coalition parties (hence including the Nationalist Movement) on the one hand and the supporters of opposing groups on the other.[1] This split into two opposing poles encouraged the left to coordinate its sector-specific and category-specific mobilizations.

This chapter shows how the far left's demands, agendas and forms of mobilization tended to become more uniform over time as it came into contact with the MHP's practices to penetrate the state. It thus looks at the protest movement against Hasan Tan's appointment as rector of the Middle East Technical University (ODTÜ) in Ankara, a nomination obtained thanks to MHP influence, before then studying the various phases in the industrial dispute at the Tariş cooperative in Izmir in January and February 1980.[2]

Mobilizations specific to the education sector

During the 1960s state-run schools and places of higher education were the sites of specific mobilizations for the two conflicting movements. Yet student and teacher associations only intermittently pursued the same agendas, demands and campaigns, and it was not until ülkücü initiatives started to be implemented that these educational institutions' various users, finding themselves exposed to a similar risk of marginalization should they fail to take part in ülkücü activities, started to pool their actions. It was this new situation of interdependence which caused the protest movements within schools and universities to become aligned.

The homogenization of demands and agendas

State-run schools and places of higher education were one of the Nationalist Movement's privileged sites of mobilization. Ülkücü staff, on being appointed, worked to recruit students, employees and teachers belonging to the movement,[3] and to marginalize and exclude members of rival associations, mainly on the far left. Certain high schools, vocational schools, and training institutes became 'liberated institutions' (*kurtarılmış kuruluşlar*) in which the administrative bodies had the power to remove any individual opposed to their political line, and where party personnel and students close to the movement were able to bring (physical and administrative) pressure to bear on any students hostile to local ülkücü representatives. This tactic of penetrating state-run schools and places of higher education homogenized the demands of categories of users who were in danger of losing their jobs or student status, or else whose security was threatened, thereby encouraging them to synchronize and align their protest movements.

The MHP would appear to have exerted the greatest influence in institutes of education (*eğitim enstitüleri*). By early 1976 it was present on the administration bodies of virtually all of them, and started seeking to alter selection procedures. On 10 November 1976 the AP Minister for Education in the Nationalist Front government denounced irregularities that had come to light regarding entrance exams which had been held despite the opposition of the authorities. After a couple of days of negotiations the MHP had to give way, and on 22 November the exams were re-held. The following year the MHP was able to impose its own rules on entrance examinations thanks to the stronger position it enjoyed within government. On 10 November 1976 the *Milliyet* newspaper announced that at the Atatürk Institute of Education (Atatürk Eğitim Enstitüsü) 'it was the ülkücüs who organised access to examination halls despite the presence of the police'. Militants from local ülkücü associations outnumbered the police and chose which of the 5600 people who came to sit the exam were allowed do so.[4] On 2 January 1979 *Cumhuriyet* denounced the behaviour of Nationalist Movement associations in these institutes, which had become places of ülkücü mobilization where students who were sympathizers to governing parties could enrol without having obtained the required marks in the entrance exam, and where ülkücü groups physically attacked new students and teachers who did not belong to the movement.[5]

In institutes where the Nationalist Movement had an established presence, students, teachers and administrative and technical staff worked to marginalize and exclude members of rival sector-specific associations. Detailed information is available about the tactics to take control of institutes and politically homogenize them for the period of the last Demirel government (November 1979 to September 1980), to which the MHP lent parliamentary support. On 3 April 1980 100 teachers were dismissed from the Buca Institute of Education (Buca Eğitim Enstitüsü) following changes to its administrative team that benefited the MHP.[6] On 4 April teachers who had graduated from the Atatürk Institute (Atatürk Eğitim Enstitüsü) gave a press conference in which they claimed that MHP candidates were being given priority in postings.[7] On 20 April 600 cadres and 1500 public-sector workers, mainly from the Töb-Der Association, were excluded from their ministry or else transferred to subaltern positions.[8] On 27 April ten inspectors from the education directorate were demoted and appointed as teachers in provincial high schools and middle schools.[9] In June the *Teachers' World* (*Öğretmen dünyası*) journal announced that since the Demirel government had taken office, 8000 teachers had been transferred after refusing to join the Ülkü-Bir association.[10]

Whilst teachers who were not part of the Nationalist Movement were afraid of losing their jobs, students were also being subjected to pressure by ülkücü students and personnel. On 4 May 1980 representatives of the Malatya vocational school protested against the favours accorded to Sunni pupils since the appointment of a new headmaster, known for being close to local ülkücü associations. On 11 May pupils from the Genç high school in Bingöl spoke out in a press article against the provocations they were subjected to by teachers who had arrived at the same time as the new headmaster.[11] On 24 July students from the Technical College (Meslek Yüksek Okulu) stated that ülkücüs had received exam questions before the exams, and that all those listed as belonging to left-wing and far-left student associations had had their scripts struck through and the word 'cheating' written across them.[12] It was within this context that the campaigns and demands of left-wing and far-left sector-specific groups progressively started to become aligned.

The coordination of protest at the ODTÜ

The campaign conducted by the ODTÜ's professional, teacher and student associations against the appointment of Hasan Tan as university rector is illustrative of coordination between different university users.[13] Turkish universities were autonomous institutions, but the members of their governing bodies, which elect rectors, are appointed by government cabinets. It is thus not rare for governments to alter governing bodies in order to control the appointment of teaching staff and faculty heads. On 10 August 1976 a cabinet meeting of the Nationalist Front government decided to change the university's governing body.[14] On 22 December 1976 the university's rector, Alyanak, who had been in open conflict with the new governing body since the beginning of the academic year, was forced to resign.[15] On 29 December students protested against the departure of the rector at a demonstration on Kızılay Square in the centre of Ankara. On 5 January students voted for a one-day boycott. On 8 January the representatives of the AYÖD (Democratic Association of Ankara Higher Education Association) and of Dev-Genç made a public call on campus demanding that the governing body resign, but to no avail.[16] On 13 February the governing body elected Hasan Tan, a member of the governing body of the Intellectuals Association (Aydınlar Ocağı) and known MHP sympathizer, as university rector. Tan had been head of the department of social sciences at the ODTÜ for ten years. He had supported a strong line against an initial boycott held in 1975, and was renowned for the disciplinary sanctions he had taken against many students. When it was announced that he had been elected, student organizations called for a boycott of the university, which only came to an end when, after five months of protest, the rector resigned on 22 June

1977.[17] After the first week of the boycott members of teaching staff also launched a wave of protests against what was generally viewed as a political appointment orchestrated by the MHP in order to establish itself within a university where its attempts at entryism had hitherto failed.[18] Thirty of the forty members of the academic board gathered in the university's gardens to announce that they refused to work with the new rector.[19] On 17 February members of the architecture faculty board all resigned, followed immediately by Uğur Ersoy, dean and founder of the İçel campus, and Rüştü Yüce, head of the department of construction engineering, together with his deputy head Turhan Erdoğan, whilst students at the Gaziantep Technical College, a local ODTÜ offshoot, voted to boycott their place of study.[20] On 19 February the boards of the department of physics and the department of chemical, electrical and mining engineering decided to suspend teaching until Tan departed,[21] and 100 or so members of staff from the English department at the post-secondary preparatory schools went to the rector's buildings and observed a minute's silence. Hasan Tan wrote in the press, calling upon teachers not to encourage students to carry on with the movement:

> The reaction is illegal. I do not intend to resign. Those opposed to my being rector are left wing. Furthermore, many lessons have been stopped from taking place over the past month, and public opinion is not informed. For example 156 right-wing students who wanted to attend class were unable to do so. I am an Ataturkist, and I want to bring about national union and the coexistence of differences within universities.[22]

On 22 February 1977 the dean of the faculty of literature and applied sciences, Fuat Bayrakçeken, resigned in protest at this declaration. After this the movement calling on Hasan Tan to resign took on greater amplitude, drawing an increasing number of actors from various backgrounds both within and outside the university. On the same day, student representatives organized a discussion day about 'the process by which education at the ODTÜ is becoming fascist'. Members from the CHP, the Turkish Law Institute (Türk Hukuk Kurumu), the People's Institutes, the Association of Modern Lawyers (Çağdaş Hukukçular Derneği) and Dev-Genç took part in the event. Teaching staff from other universities lent support, such as those from Hacettepe University and 150 teachers from the Beytepe campus who made a joint declaration voicing their opposition to the appointment of Hasan Tan. According to the president of the ODTÜ student council (ODTÜ-ÖTK), several factors explain why these student and teacher protests emerged:

> *Why were they against him?*
>
> 'Well, because we didn't know him. At the ODTÜ we had managed to chase out the fascists after a one-day boycott. In other universities there were attacks, fights, and violence. But not at the ODTÜ. Troublemakers had been expelled. That is why there were no problems in the student movement at the ODTÜ. There were problems with people from outside, but it was clear that Hasan Tan

was going to interfere and meddle in all that. So the teachers were against his appointment. Everybody. All the heads of department resigned. ... Nobody wanted to carry on with the job. Only three people stayed .... The students started to mobilise. His appointment had been on the cards for the past year or two, and we had opposed it saying "Hasan Tan cannot be rector". But in 1977 he was appointed rector. So there was a boycott. In fact it wasn't a boycott, we didn't announce it. ... We said we don't know Hasan Tan, we won't do anything official with him, none of our actions will be official. We went to classes and on leaving the room we performed sketches caricaturing him for instance ... All the teaching staff were against Hasan Tan.'[23]

The emblematic appointment of an MHP sympathizer to the position of rector of the most prestigious university in the country caused the interests of a whole range of users to coalesce and come into focus. For the teaching staff it was another threat from a government, who wished to control the recruitment of university teaching staff, and for the students it was an attempt to assert control over institutions hitherto spared from the MHP's penetration tactics. As for ODTÜ non-teaching personnel, they were afraid of losing their jobs and being replaced by people close to the new rector.

On 23 February Tan announced that 'the University will close for a fortnight to give students an opportunity to think'.[24] At 7:30 am nearly 2500 gendarmes arrived on campus, forbidding anyone from entering, and taking up positions at the entrances to halls of residence in order to evacuate them. Some students had decided to ignore the ban on going on campus and were waiting for buses in the Sıhhiye and Tunus districts of Ankara, but they were picked up by police vans. In response to this 600 members of ODTÜ teaching staff published a declaration calling on the rector to resign.[25] On 2 March the Council of State overturned the decision to shut the university, but it was not possible to hold the end-of-term exams. On 10 March the university's academic board asked that exams be postponed until classes start up again under satisfactory conditions: 'ever since the governing body appointed Hasan Tan rector of the ODTÜ, research and teaching activities have been forced to come to a halt. Confronted with this situation a new exam calendar was drawn up, without it being known who was responsible for this. This university calendar was not presented to the academic board' which threatened to resign en masse unless its demands were taken into consideration:

> Rector Hasan Tan needs to step down in order to find a solution to the difficult situation in which the university currently finds itself, and enable classes to start again. Exams will need to be organised after an appropriate extension to term time, to be determined in the light of the amount of time lost due to the events affecting the university.

The academic board also sent a letter to the Turkish president, Korutürk, in which they demanded that the rector be removed and new elections held, and that the academic board be allowed to put forward candidates for the position of rector. Three deans had resigned since the beginning of the movement, along with twenty-three of the twenty-five departmental heads.[26] On 18 March Tan went to the lecture hall where psychology faculty exams were being held, escorted by three gendarmes and armed policemen. On arriving there he found the only person present was the commander from the gendarmerie who had been sent to invigilate the exam. There were no students and none of the university teaching assistants who had been summoned for the occasion. It was the first time since the ODTÜ had been created in 1956 that such a situation had arisen.[27]

The protest movements triggered by his appointment did not prevent Hasan Tan from nominating MHP sympathizers to the university's administrative and technical services on taking up his post. This manoeuvre was unanimously seen as indicative of the fascization of the university, and it incited the professional, teaching and student organizations to coordinate their activities.

On 25 March 1977, with ever more ODTÜ staff being recruited by Tan, Atilla Burç was appointed director of the university's IT centre.[28] Scarcely had he taken up his position than he removed certain staff in order to place people close to him. On 29 March twenty-six of the thirty-five people working for the centre were fired, all of whom were members of the DİSK-affiliated Sosyal-İş trade union. They were joined by teachers in a demonstration in front of the rector' buildings to voice their disagreement. On 6 April thirteen further employees were fired who were also Sosyal-İş members. The new appointees set up a trade union called ODTÜ-SEN, the Trade Union of ODTÜ Workers and Officials, affiliated to the MİSK ülkücü trade union confederation. This organizational structure enabled them to coordinate their activities on campus.

Little information is available about the degree of organization amongst ODTÜ ülkücüs. The account provided by Ali Yurtaslan and published in the *Aydınlık* newspaper on 23 August 1980 does, however, show that their recruitment was part of a larger tactic to destabilize and take control of the university. But caution is required in making use of this account, particularly since it was published in a far-left newspaper and thus more a matter of making accusations than of reconstructing a sequence of events, and partly because there is no way of checking how true it is. Nevertheless, it suggests that the local Nationalist Movement used its new hold in the university to expand its organization and destabilization activities. Ali Yurtaslan, who was still a student at the Gazi school in Ankara, went to the headquarters of the Ülkücü Workers Association (ÜİD) to ask for help looking for a job. He met Mustafa Sami Barsan, the association's secretary general, who told him that he wanted to recruit 300 people for the ODTÜ, and said to come back together with some of his friends from the Niğde residence where he was living. According to Yurtaslan, Mustafa Sami Barsan said to the band of friends: 'we are going to be 300 people amongst 10,000 communists, and so there will be people killed and people who will kill. Our goal is not to work, but to make the voice of the ülkücü movement heard.' Barsan recommended Yurtaslan to the head of archives at the university, who employed him without asking the slightest question about his qualifications. According to the new recruits, the ülkücüs drew on the support of members of the administration who had arrived with the new rector or else who had decided to support what he did:

At that time the governing body was appointed by the Nationalist Front government. So it supported us. In particular we were supported by Hasan Tan, by Ünal, the head of university administration, by Mustafa Başoğlu, a member of the governing body and head of the Sağlık-İş trade union, by the head of accounts Özcan bey, by Sevim Tapan, head of personnel, by the IBM head Atilla bey, by the head of archives Baha bey, and the budget head Şeref Çağlayan. They said to us 'welcome, we are all working for the same goal'. It was these people who had made our recruitment possible.[29]

Once recruited ülkücü personnel conducted organizational work within the university:

Mustafa Sami Barsan told us that Bedri would be head of all the ülkücüs at ODTÜ. Mustafa Sami also told us that we were going to be divided into groups (*oba*) of ten people. Each group would choose a leader. All the leaders would answer to their superior, who presided over the whole set-up. I became group leader, and I took my orders from Bedri.[30]

As of the month of March, ülkücüs started using violent action against students and personnel protesting against the rector:

Mustafa Sami Barsan came to the school, he called me and a few other people to Ünal bey's office. He told us that IT service personnel were going to be replaced and that our trade union organisations were going to be scaled up. We could use the ODTÜ services as we wished …. When the university opened fights broke out between students and workers. There were lots of armed altercations at the university. We decided to use explosives, and girls helped us. Between 20 and 30 April 3 bombs exploded. One person was killed.'[31]

On 10 May a group of ülkücüs gained access to the university thanks to personnel on campus, and attacked three people near the infirmary, before entering the cafeteria shouting 'The ODTÜ will be your cemetery', 'Get out of the ODTÜ', 'Death to communists'.[32] On 24 May a bomb exploded in front of the archives department, and during the subsequent enquiry the gendarmerie found explosive material in the possession of Mehmet Altaş, an ülkücü employee. On 31 May two students were attacked by workers who had been recruited by Hasan Tan. That same day protest marches drew students, teachers and university employees, who headed to the rector's buildings calling for his resignation and the re-establishment of a free and autonomous university. Teachers published a declaration in the press demanding the right to oversee the appointment of the rector, and denouncing the forced resignation of İlgaz Alyanak, the dismissal of employees and the recruitment of nearly 200 others without any job interview, and the fact that teachers were being targeted in physical attacks. It was signed by 19 of the 29 professors, 45 of the 65 senior lecturers, 186 of the 218 assistant lecturers, 305 of the 343 contract teaching staff and 196 of the 218 teaching assistants.[33]

On 22 June 1977, the day that the new CHP government took office, Hasan Tan presented his resignation to the governing body. Ülkücü employees and teaching staff who had been recruited during his rectorship were meant to stay in their jobs until December,[34] but the governing body decided to dismiss them in the wake of a campaign by teaching associations, trade unions representing technical personnel, associations of student families,[35] student associations and far-left extra-parliamentary movements at the university.

Hence at the ODTÜ it was the recruitment and exactions of ülkücü personnel which pushed the left-wing sector-specific mobilization to align its demands and come together to defend their now convergent interests.

Multi-sector protest movements

The other specific feature of social and political protest movements over the second half of the 1970s was the fact that they were multi-sector. As of 1975 there were an increasing number of sites of protest, and the demands and the rhythm of events tended to become harmonized. To understand how they became aligned, it is important to be alert to how the movements traded blows with one another and to the tactical innovations of those involved. It is not here a matter of describing how protest movements sprang up in the various sectors concerned, where specific mechanisms involving actors with various demands were at work in each individual case. What we shall instead examine is the way in which these became coordinated, and the resultant drop in the specificity of contests being played out within any given sector.[36]

The division of spheres of contest into two polar opposites

In *Sociologie des crises politiques*, Michel Dobry refers to the 'loosening of the link that holds in routine situations between certain sectoral arenas and *the issues* specific to the confrontations taking place there'.[37] In Turkey over the second half of the 1970s this interplay between different spheres of confrontation originated in the setting up of rival antagonistic associations in an increasing number of sectors.

Throughout the 1970s ülkücü organizations were set up and mobilized wherever there were left-wing organizations, whilst also maintaining collusive links with Nationalist Movement representatives working in other sectors. It was as if the MHP had developed a tactic of systematically setting up fronts opposing left-wing organizations.[38] The flow of resources and the central role played by the party incited newly created ülkücü associations to coordinate their actions and demands across different sectors. A document found in the office of the MHP chairman, headed 'Istanbul province organisation' (*Istanbul ili organizasyonu*), shows how the setting up of ülkücü sectoral organizations was part of a party tactic of establishing new holds:

Istanbul province organisation ... Party chairman:

... The head of the province will organise existing associations or those to be created, unofficially linked to the party. The general chairman will issue orders to settle any problems arising in this activity.

... Institutions open to the people:

... A lot of associations need to be created, legally, based on the model of the Ideal Hearths (Ülkü Ocakları) ... and the Ülkücü Workers Union (Ülkücü İşçiler Birliği), and these associations need to be organised by the party chairman.[39]

Other indications further suggest that ülkücü sectoral organizations routinely coordinated their activities.[40] Thus Necati Gültekin, MHP secretary general, made an entry in his diary for 22 October 1976 that 'instructions have been given to use Ülkü-Bir resources to coordinate ülkücü associations' activities'.[41] The 'bureaus' set up by the Nationalist Movement helped with this coordination.

Hence the mobilization of the two movements across multiple sectors did not operate according to the same mechanisms. Rather than arising from some unique process, the increasing number of spheres of mobilization and the local balance of power that may be observed in fact display two distinct mechanisms: 'dispersal' for left-wing mobilizations, which shared out the social sphere in devolved manner following varying rhythms and based on sector-specific issues,[42] and 'diffusion' for ülkücü mobilizations, or transmission, the rhythm and scale of which depended upon the political positions held by the MHP. The party acted as the main 'broker' within the Nationalist Movement. Thanks to the room for manoeuvre and resources conferred on it by the state, the MHP was able to 'reduce transaction costs of communication and coordination among sites, facilitate the combined use of resources located at different sites, and create new potential collective actors',[43] and thus preside over the distribution and coordination of mobilization across numerous different social spheres. At the local level, ülkücü organizations helped each other out and were also able to draw on the Nationalist Movement's organizational structure to expand their activities. When the party was in government they benefited from 'certification'[44] by the public authorities in certain sectors, making it easier to get their demands heard, whilst their members were also able to benefit from favourable treatment by MHP personnel working in those authorities and from the benevolent attitude adopted by local AP political personnel. When it lost its position in government, it paid the price of 'decertification'[45] by the public authorities and lost the positions it had acquired. The spread of ülkücü mobilization introduced new relationships of contest and rivalry, encouraging the division of spheres into polar opposites and contributing to the alignment of demands and agendas. This division into polar opposites was associated on all mobilization sites with two sets of labels, with 'socialist' and 'communist' being opposed to 'ülkücü' and 'fascist'. These two categories of political positioning (and categories of thought and action) became universal, enabling actors to generalize the scope of sectoral demands (relating to pay or career progress for example), and thereby expand the base of the social movements they ran.

'Tariş resistance'

As of 1975 far-left organizations conducted joint campaigns involving people belonging to sister organizations. In each instance, the underlying purpose of defending sector-specific demands or supporting those of other organizations was to denounce the fascism of the Nationalist Front government.[46] Rather than drawing up a list of all the instances in which protest movements became aligned, this section will look at the movement which started in the Tariş agricultural cooperative (İzmir İncir, Üzüm, Pamuk ve Zeytinyağı Tarım Satış Kooperatifleri Birliği) in late January 1980, and which has gone down in history as the 'Tariş resistance' (*Tariş direnişi*).

The Tariş cooperative in the province of Izmir was a grouping of 80,000 producers of grapes, figs, olives and cotton. Like other cooperatives (Antbirlik, Çukobirlik, Trakyabirlik, Fiskobirlik), it had been set up under a 1935 law intended to protect producers from price volatility. The large local landowners and shareholders of these cooperatives held most of the positions in its management bodies, but these were placed under state oversight, and more specifically the oversight of government who appointed their managers, directors and upper management. The government had the power to control these cooperatives since all decisions taken by its management bodies were subjected to approval by the relevant ministry. These cooperatives generated a lot of jobs, and Tariş employed 11,000 people or so in the province of Izmir.

In the 1970s Tariş, like other cooperatives, suffered from relentless changes to its managers and personnel. Whenever a new government took up office the managing director was replaced by somebody else appointed by the new government cabinet,[47] who on taking up his position immediately proceeded to recruit staff chosen from amongst local supporters of the government majority. As one worker explained:

> Each new government fired the managers and replaced them with its supporters. Then, working down the hierarchy, it was the workers who were affected. This meant that some workers were fired each time there was a change in government. Government supporters and activists established themselves in these institutions. This was a self-perpetuating situation, and people working in these factories were forever living in fear of losing their job.[48]

In 1975 the MHP took advantage of its arrival in government to get hundreds of sympathizers employed, transforming the cooperative into an ülkücü 'stronghold' from which groups of activists regularly set out to pick fights with left-wing students from Ege University.[49]

Erdinç Gönenç, appointed managing director of Tariş when the CHP was in power, had been accommodating towards DİSK-affiliated trade unions.

Employees recruited with the support of local MHP and AP sections were fired, and DİSK got a collective agreement signed that was particularly advantageous to workers, who were meant to receive the equivalent of thirty-six months' salary in the event of dismissal. But the change in government led to the arrival of a new managing director in 1979, İsmail Hakkı Gürün, known to be close to the Nationalist Movement. On 18 January 1980, when local ülkücü association and trade union organizations were taking hold of the cooperative once again, and the recruitment of ülkücü employees was in full swing, workers – mainly from the DİSK-affiliated Gıda-İş union – launched a protest movement against management.[50]

Workers from the cotton and olive oil production units went on strike and blockaded the cooperative. The managing director decided to close it, but faced with the workers' refusal to cooperate, he called in the forces of order. On 22 January hundreds of policemen and gendarmes intervened to evacuate premises occupied by the workers. In the olive oil factory five workers and one policeman were injured. Workers from the Çiğli cotton mill resisted for six hours, before being flushed out by the forces of law and order. During these operations three policemen were injured and hundreds of workers taken into custody. Other units went on strike in reaction to this, demanding that they be released and that their physical safety and jobs be safeguarded. The police operation was unanimously interpreted amongst DİSK's ranks as indicative of collusion between newly recruited ülkücü personnel and the public authorities. On 30 January DİSK called for a return to work. But confronted with the determination of the managing director, who for several days stuck with his decision to close the factory to get it evacuated, it decided to continue the strike. The scale of the movement increased on 8 February when DİSK called on 55,000 of its members in the province of Izmir to go on strike in support of those at Tariş.[51] On the same day shopkeepers and craftsmen in Gültepe, Buca and Altındağ stopped work. DİSK members organized blockades and sit-ins, and workers barricaded themselves into the production and storage sites at the cooperative, saying they would not leave until they were guaranteed they could keep their jobs and that the managing director would resign. Most Tariş sites were at a standstill, and demonstrations were organized on a daily basis with chants of 'death to fascism' (*faşizme ölüm*) and 'end the massacre of the workers' (*işçi kıyımına son*).

Thus far the Tariş workers protest movement had been primarily local and trade-union based, but it was soon relayed by the support campaigns that sprang up in other social sectors, driven by professional associations and student organizations which, on becoming involved, took up, reappropriated and transformed the original demands of the movement. On 29 January 1980 the ODTÜ-ÖTK (ODTÜ student council) voted a one-day boycott of the university to display their support for events at Tariş. On 30 January a student was fatally wounded while writing slogans on the walls of the university expressing support for the cooperative workers.[52] On 11 February confrontations broke out between the forces of law and order and a group of demonstrators composed of DİSK trade union members and students from the universities in Ankara. A procession of students in Istanbul joined the trade union demonstrations there in support of the Tariş workers.[53]

In Izmir student demonstrations were a daily occurrence, and students from Ege University joined the blockades. The 'resistance' of the Tariş workers became symbolic of the struggle against the 'fascization' of the state. Mobilizing in support of Tariş was a way for extra-parliamentary movements and public-sector worker associations to denounce the marginalization their members had been undergoing since the AP's return to power.

And so the alignment of these protest movements stemmed from the split of sectoral spheres of contest into two polar opposites, leading to the rapid escalation of the conflict, and enabling each organization to identify its rival and its interlocutors as the objective allies of one of the two opposing camps (in this instance the forces of law and order and ülkücü associations, on the one hand, and the DİSK workers trade unions, on the other). The structural homology of the social sectors involved – itself a side-effect of activities to penetrate the State – was the primordial factor and arguably even the essential precondition for the alignment of far-left protest movements.

At Tariş activities to replace the public authorities also played a role in the way the conflict unfolded. As of 25 January the press was referring to altercations pitting workers against ülkücü employees appointed by the new managing director.[54] Then as of 9 February the conflict spread to the adjacent *gecekondu* neighbourhoods of Çimentepe and Gültepe when far-left groups, who had a particularly strong hold there, decided to launch actions to support the besieged workers. On 10 February the MHP branch in the neighbourhood of Gümüşpaşa was attacked with firearms,[55] and the following day a bomb exploded near the AP provincial section's building, the local MISK representative was shot at and two petrol stations were torched.[56] At Ege University in Izmir student groups were evicted roughly by the police, and sixty students and seven policemen were injured in altercations. Faced with the general radicalization of the repertories of action, the forces of law and order decided to stage a major operation.

On 10 February squads of gendarmes and police reinforcements were sent to Tariş. The plan was for them to intervene in the cooperative over the course of the day, but radical organizations from Çimentepe blocked the Çiğli–Turan road near the cotton mill. There were confrontations between the forces of law and order and groups positioned on the barricades, who scattered to take refuge in the *gecekondu* when armoured formations arrived. The intervention in the cooperative finally took place on 14 February, when nearly 5000 gendarmes and policemen broke up the barricades thrown by the workers and evacuated the site. The operation lasted several hours, during which there were skirmishes between the forces of law and order and armed members from local groups who had been introduced into the factory by the workers. While 1500 people were taken into custody, between 500 and 600 of them managed to take refuge in Çimentepe. The next day the police and gendarmes tried to enter the neighbourhood to make a series of arrests, but they ran into armed resistance from members of radical groups and workers who had taken refuge there. It was only after many hours of fighting that they finally managed to take control of the neighbourhood. The same thing happened the following day in the neighbourhood of Gültepe, which also bordered Tariş, where the inhabitants joined local far-left groups[57] to protect those being sought by the police. Calm only returned to the area around Tariş on 20 February, when martial law was proclaimed in the province of Izmir. It was now the policemen who controlled the insurgent neighbourhoods and maintained order in the vicinity of the cooperative.

*

Wherever ülkücü organizations were set up, a relationship of rivalry and contestation coalesced around a line opposing the 'progressives' or 'socialists' on the one hand and the ülkücüs, nationalists, or 'fascists' on the other. Once this happened, the interests, demands and rhythms of the campaigns run by far-left organizations tended to become more homogenous, leading to a drop in the autonomy of specific sectors, a 'decompartmentalisation … of sector-specific rationales',[58] and the 'linking up of spheres of confrontation'.[59] The setting up of sectoral ülkücü organizations – whose positions were dependent upon those adopted by the party against the backdrop of the shifting balance of political power (depending on whether or not it was in government) – was also a factor causing spheres of rivalry to split into two polar opposites: bringing about the homogenization of far-left interests and incentives, and generating the characteristic motives for mobilizations.

The decompartmentalization of sectoral rationales was not, however, accompanied by any 'avoidance of calculation' nor by any drop in the actors' tactical capabilities. In the same way, the alignment of mobilizations orchestrated by far-left organizations did not result from any 'regression towards habitus'[60] on the part of their members. Taking part in a campaign always corresponded to the wish to modify the local balance of power. It was an opportunity to denounce what was happening to people locally, to publicize sector-specific demands and to generalize them by relaying, reappropriating and transforming the demands formulated by others.

The positions and structure of the Nationalist Movement endowed it with an advantage in the conflict opposing it to the far left, as well as enabling it to influence the course actually taken by the conflict. By coordinating the activities of its various representatives in state arenas and in the street, it managed to use illegal activities and violence as routine methods for interacting, and for accumulating political, economic and social resources.

Chapter 6

THE ESCALATION IN VIOLENCE

Data compiled by Hamit Bozarslan shows that the number of people killed in clashes between radical movements rose from three in 1974 ... to thirty-four in 1975, ninety in 1976, and 295 in 1977. ... [It] went from 1095 in 1978, to 1368 in 1979, and then to 1939 over the first nine months of 1980, before falling to 79 in the months following the coup. Official figures drawn up by the Army [show that] there were 5713 deaths and 18,480 people injured over the period from 1975 to 1980.[1]

Violence was largely the work of radical organizations targeting the opposing camp, and up until 1979 it was only rarely directed against the state and its representatives. Sporadic confrontations between ülkücüs and 'revolutionaries' had started to break out as of the latter part of the 1960s, resuming after the 1971 coup and escalating up until 1980. By the end of the decade the use of violence had become generalized and was now affecting actors who were external to the two action systems. In addition to the insults and occasionally fatal altercations of the late 1960s, assassination attempts, bombings, shootings, gun battles and street fights now occurred; militias and armed sub-units were set up, torture was used, and mass massacres perpetrated.

This situation is sufficient reason for abandoning any 'mechanistic' interpretation of how the action repertoires first evolved and then expanded. It has often been suggested that use of violence correlates to the positions held by mobilized groups,[2] with violence being used to make up for a lack of resources or as a way to forcibly win recognition for demands being ignored by the system.[3] This is the analysis put forward by Charles Tilly, who links the use of violence to the users' status as challengers and to their setting up groups excluded from the polity.[4] This makes violence one element in a whole repertoire of collective action, linked quasi-mechanistically to the structure of political opportunities.[5] In the case of Turkey, however, it was thanks to their positions in state arenas – especially in institutions tasked with maintaining order – that mobilized groups were able to militarize their actions.

This chapter, however, starts with the idea that actors' activities help generate the opportunities at their disposal. It demonstrates how the mobilization and capture of public resources by people from the far-left and ülkücü action systems brought about the preconditions for the use of violence. It sheds light on the rationales governing the deployment of violence over the second half of the 1970s by looking at the timeframes and territorial scope of the violence, together with the social profiles of activists and victims of armed confrontation. As we shall see, the forms of violence and the level of its intensity were linked to the positions the groups held in municipal and national arenas, and to state support they were able to draw upon; equally, we shall see how the generalization of violence became a routine form of political action up until the coup of 12 September 1980, thereby transforming the political context.

The approach that has been outlined here has several limits, stemming from constraints encountered in aggregating the available data. Firstly, the figures that have been used only concern the number of deaths due to clashes between the radical left and radical right. Obviously, this reduces any detailed understanding of the phenomenon, since fewer deaths in a locality do not necessarily mean that there was less conflict than elsewhere. But it is the only variable that the press used in its daily figures.

Furthermore, this part of the argument only takes into account the political dimension, that is, the electoral balance of power in the localities studied. Once again, from a methodological point of view, this reduces social complexity to a single explanatory variable. But electoral results in a given village, district, town or province are the only available data on which we to assess the local balance of power. As argued further on, the intensity of the violence (that is, here, the number of deaths) depended on the interaction between national and local electoral balances of power, and especially on the position held by local MHP sections in electoral power relations. This is not to say that violence was always initiated by the MHP and ülkücüs. But as will become clear, it was when the MHP had the means to penetrate central public institutions but found itself (or its allies) in the minority locally that ülkücü sections adopted more radical practices to forcefully obtain access to resources. While other variables must be factored in to understand the complex workings behind opting to use violence at the local level, the analysis will focus on this variable for reasons of generalization, for it is the sole variable capable of explaining variations in the level of violence over time and across the territory during the second half of the 1970s.

The time frames of violent exchanges

Continuous increase in the number of victims

The annual number of people killed in confrontations between far-left activists, ülkücü activists and the forces of law and order rose continually from 1975 and 1980. The data I have indicates that for a total number of 4001 people killed over the period from 1 January 1977 to 12 September 1980, the monthly average number of deaths rose from 18.4 in 1977, to 70.08 in 1978, and then 99.42 in 1979, before reaching 194 in 1980.

Observations about the corpus

Work on assembling the corpus used here ran into a series of obstacles relating to the scarcity of sources and the ways in which the available data had been produced. There is no exhaustive database on the subject, and so various scattered elements had to be identified, compiled and classified. The figures used here are based on pooling data for the period running from 1 January 1977 to 31 December 1980, as published in the *Milliyet* and *Cumhuriyet* newspapers, coupled with that provided in the daily press review drawn up by the General Directorate for Information and the Press (tasked with preparing press reviews for the prime minister).[6] From 1977 to 1979 the yearly almanacs published by *Cumhuriyet*, *Hürriyet*, *Milliyet* and the *Turkish Daily News* provided lists of individuals 'killed in political incidents' (*siyasal olaylarda ölenler*),[7] and this has also been included in the corpus, as has data from an encyclopaedia produced by an ülkücü publishing house listing all the 'martyrs' (*şehit*) who died in confrontations with far-left groups and the forces of law and order.[8] But not only did media and party political attention fluctuate, it waxed and waned in accordance with different cycles, making it impossible to assemble the information needed to identify all the victims over this period.

In addition to this the various available sources only provide information about the victims of fatal altercations. There is no exhaustive information available on the number of injured, nor about altercations with no victims. Although I am aware that the number of deaths is an imperfect indicator of the level of violence, I have nevertheless decided to use it in order to make some degree of progress. All in all, out of the 2758 victims listed by Hamit Bozarslan for the period 1 January 1977 to 31 December 1979, the identity of 2555 has been ascertained (that is to say 92.6 per cent). The social category is known for 1614 of the victims over this period (that is to say 58.52 per cent). Useable data is available on place of death for 3765 of the 4697 victims for the period running from 1 January 1977 to 12 September 1980 (80.15 per cent), whilst date of death is known for 4001 victims over the same period (85.18 per cent).

In 1977 violent exchanges were causing between four and twenty-six deaths per month (see Figure 6.1). These deaths generally occurred during street fights, brawls and affrays which broke out when groups of activists ran into one another. Exchanges of gunfire along the frontiers of liberated zones also produced victims. The pronounced increase in the number of deaths between April and May 1977 (rising from seven to fifty) is not in fact indicative of an escalation in altercations between antagonist groups, for it includes those killed in the incidents that took

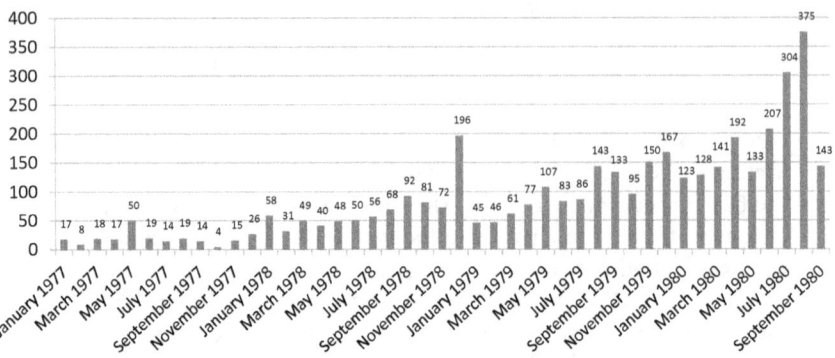

Figure 6.1 Number of deaths per month (1 January 1977–12 September 1980).

place on Taksim Square, in Istanbul, on 1 May 1977, when thirty-four people lost their life[9] as a result an outbreak of panic when gunshots were fired amidst a crowd of 500,000 people who had gathered there for the occasion. The 'incidents' of 1 May 1977 are thus not directly related to confrontations between radical groups, even though all the sources link their victims to the political context of the period.

In 1978 the number of victims was increasing fairly steadily month on month, before rising sharply from 92 in September to 196 in December. This was due to the radicalization of the antagonistic groups' action repertoires; sections of the radical left broke free and went underground, and certain members started carrying out armed attacks on ülkücü representatives. On 17 April 1978 Hamit Fendoğlu, the municipal head of Malatya who had ties with the local sections of parties in the Nationalist Front coalition, was killed along with his two grandchildren and daughter-in-law when he opened a parcel bomb. The next day the AP and MHP staged demonstrations. The crowds marched to cries of 'Ecevit assassin, Ecevit resign' (*Katil Ecevit, Ecevit istifa*), 'Communists to Moscow' (*Komünistler Moskova'ya*) and 'Pol-Der Communist' (*Komünist Pol-Der*), while excerpts from the Koran calling for intransigent treatment of the enemy blared out from the town hall loudspeakers. Fifteen people were injured and three killed in the resultant confrontations and attacks.[10]

Clandestine ülkücü organizations sprang up and militias started to exert armed control over swathes of the country. The most famous of these clandestine ülkücü organizations were set up during 1978 – the Turkish Revenge Brigade (Türk İntikam Tugayı, TİT), the Enslaved Turks Liberation Army (Esir Türkleri Kurtarma Ordusu, ETKO) and the Turkish Thunderbolt Army (Türk Yıldırm Ordusu, TYO). The sharp increase in the number of deaths in December is due to the Kahramanmaraş massacre, in which part of the Sunni population, infiltrated by members of local ülkücü organizations (from the ETKO – whose founding members came from the province – the MHP, and ülkücü associations in the town) attacked the Alevi population, who were supported by local far-left groups. According to official figures, the three-day confrontation (from 22 to 26 December 1978) left 111 people dead, about 1000 injured and hundreds of houses and business premises destroyed. On 1 December 1978 the ülkücü *Hergün* newspaper gave figures for the first eleven months of the Ecevit government, with 4405 'incidents', 943 dead and 5415 wounded – and called for martial law to be declared.[11]

The number of victims dropped noticeably in January 1979. This drop is partly in relation to the heavy toll of Kahramanmaraş the previous month, but is also attributable to the proclamation of martial law on 26 December 1978 in thirteen of the provinces most affected by left/right confrontation (namely Adana, Ankara, Elazığ, Bingöl, Erzincan, Malatya, Erzurum, Gaziantep, Istanbul, Kahramanmaraş, Kars, Urfa and Sivas). But any effect the declaration of martial law may have had rapidly dwindled, with the number of deaths rising once again the following month, before reaching 107 in May and then 150 in December 1979, and this despite the fact that ever more provinces were being placed under army control. According to Mehmet Ali Birand, there were nearly 5,400 wounded in 1979,[12] and 1980 was even worse, with 123 dead in January, 207 in June 1980 and 375 in August. As of July 1980 violent activities carried out by radical groups were leaving no fewer than ten dead each day.

An explanation based on the strategies of those involved in the conflict

Changes in the average monthly number of victims under each government provide a good indicator of certain mechanisms at work in the escalation of physically violent activities. Looking at the number of victims in tandem with changes in government confirms that the positions held by the actors had an influence on their tactics and on the forms of action they undertook. Quantitative data suggests a link between the MHP being in government and the number of deaths, with confrontations escalating only when the party was not in government. This correlation needs to be analysed and nuanced by taking into account the multiple positions held by the Nationalist Movement in various public arenas at the national and local level.

The average number of people killed by violence during the six months of the first Nationalist Front government is higher than that during the two following governments. However, once we strip out the thirty-four deaths at the public

Table 6.1 Monthly Average Number of Victims under Each Government

Nationalist Front I (1 January 1977–21 June 1977)	21.5
CHP (21 June 1977–21 July 1977)	14
Nationalist Front II (21 July 1977–5 January 1978)	15.6
CHP (5 January 1978–12 November 1979)	78.05
AP (12 November 1979–12 September 1980)	187.55

meeting of 1 May 1977 (which all the sources include in their statistics), it is in fact similar. Between 1977 and 1980 the average was at its lowest under Bülent Ecevit, who was prime minister from 21 June to 21 July 1977. But this period needs to be viewed as a brief interlude of parliamentary negotiation, flanked on either side by the two Nationalist Front governments. The CHP did not make sufficient progress in the elections of 5 June to be able to win a vote of parliamentary confidence, leaving the way open to a new Nationalist Front coalition government which went on to remain in power until 5 January 1978. Apart from the month of CHP government, with 14 recorded victims, the monthly average number of deaths was at its lowest during the two Nationalist Front governments, standing at 21.5 during the six last months of the first government, and 15.6 under the second government. Thus it was when the MHP was in government that altercations between extremists left fewer people dead, indicating that changes in the positions held by the MHP led to a modification in the forms of action employed by the ülkücüs, whilst periods when it was not in government coincided with an escalation in the Nationalist Movement's use of violence, which therefore increased at the national level.

The average monthly number of people killed under the new Ecevit government, formed on 5 January 1978, was five times higher than that under the previous government, standing at 78.05 (as opposed to 15.6). It looks as if the MHP's loss of government positions encouraged its members and those of the ülkücü associations to redirect their activities and reconsider their tactics for accessing resources. It would appear that the Nationalist Movement, when in opposition, sought to acquire a dominant position within the anti-communist (and by extension anti-CHP) camp by perpetrating acts of violence against the members of far-left organizations, thereby feeding the climate of general insecurity. This enabled the MHP leaders to denounce the government's inability to maintain order and present itself as the only feasible solution for a return to normal. As of March 1978 ülkücü attacks were attracting prominent media attention, adding to what the press had started calling 'the terror'. On 16 March a small group led by Abdullah Çatlı set off a bomb at Istanbul Technical University, killing seven and wounding forty.[13] On 10 August a group opened fire with a machine gun on a coffeehouse in the Balgat neighbourhood in Ankara, wounding fourteen people and leaving five others dead;[14] in the ensuing investigation it was stated for the first time that ülkücü militants had received training to mount operations to physically eliminate individuals.[15] A few months later in the Bahçelievler neighbourhood in Ankara several TİP members were tortured and assassinated by the same sort of unit as those behind the two previous operations.[16] There are numerous indications that the Nationalist Movement then started arming itself on a massive scale. Press articles refer to an increased number of armed actions and arrests. On 11 July 1978 Bedrettin Cömert, a lecturer at Hacettepe University, was shot dead by ülkücüs.[17] On 7 August three ülkücüs (including the head of a local ÜOD section) opened fire from a car on a public bus in the Mamak neighbourhood in Ankara, killing two people and wounding fourteen.[18] On 8 October thirty-seven ülkücüs were arrested for their part in violent acts carried out in the Aksaray neighbourhood in Istanbul.[19] On 18 September the head of the Şişli MHP youth section in Istanbul was arrested along with three fellow members and charged with the murder of seven people,[20] going on to stand trial for his involvement in thirteen armed operations.[21] A growing number of ülkücüs were locked up for their part in 'commando' activities,[22] and it was proved that in many cases cadres from the MHP and from local and national ülkücü associations had been involved. A 'commando' group operating in Ankara also told inspectors that the heads of the local ÜGD section and MHP youth organization had provided them with the arms they needed to carry out operations planned for the neighbourhoods of and Beykoz and Maltepe,[23] whilst seven ülkücüs admitted that their clandestine armed activities had received logistic support from local MHP cadres.[24] On 27 October 1978 the MHP deputy head in İskilip was arrested in possession of two revolvers, rifles and sticks of dynamite.[25] On 3 December 1978 the Ülkü-Bir head in Elbistan was arrested for having taken part in fourteen armed acts,[26] and then on 10 December the Kadirli ÜGD head in Adana was imprisoned for murder.[27] In July 1979 the head of the MİSK union confederation was arrested together with several of his cadres, accused of having helped make bombs used in certain attacks[28] – something which was subsequently proven in January 1988 when the head of MİSK in Denizli lost both hands when making an explosive device.[29] Although the Nationalist Movement had always had people in its ranks who specialized in physical violence, it was in 1978, on losing access to the central resources of state it had relied upon over the previous two years, that it stepped up its armed activity.

The swings in government led to the replacement of many of those working in devolved state administrations in the provinces, depriving the local MHP sections and ülkücü organizations of the support they had previously received from local ülkücü officials and government employees. The collapse of the Nationalist Front government deprived local ülkücü groups of access to administrative positions and control over recruitment in state-owned companies – or in other words shut them out from a whole set of central resources. Their members were obliged to resort to intimidation and violence to make up for this significant drop in influence. As of early March 1978 units started specializing in maintaining order and large-scale operations. Wherever the MHP had access to municipal resources, and especially in the towns making up its 'fertile crescent' (*verimli hilal*) in Central Anatolia, ülkücü militias worked to entrench their positions and homogenize populations along political and denominational lines. Wherever the party was in opposition, the same militias and groups specializing in armed activity sought to invert the political balance of power (by getting parts of the population to leave or else generating a climate of insecurity) via intimidation, assassination and street fights with left-wing activists.

When the CHP government was overthrown, in November 1979, the MHP declined Süleyman Demirel's invitation to take part in a new coalition government. It nevertheless accorded the AP its conditional parliamentary support, thereby enabling Demirel to form a minority government on 12 November 1979 – and allowing the MHP to reconquer certain positions in central and devolved public institutions that it had held under the Nationalist Front governments. However, the number of victims of left/right fighting under the AP government was far higher than under the CHP government, rising from 78.05 deaths per month to 187.55. This undermines the hypothesis that the use of violence escalated when the Nationalist Movement was deprived of access to public resources – though as we shall see the places with the highest levels of violence were those where the MHP and its allies (the AP and MSP) were in the electoral minority. After nearly two years under the heel of the CHP government, radicalized ülkücü activists now had sufficient room for manoeuvre to be able to bring their activities to fruition, especially in towns controlled by left-wing councils. In implementing its local political initiatives, the MHP was able to draw on the backing of the governor or sub-governor, police superintendents, or high-ranking officials; and if it ran into obstacles, it did not shy away from militarizing its action repertoires and trying out armed confrontation, being assured that party representatives, councillors and officials would if necessary intervene with the appropriate authorities. The escalation in violence around the country is thus largely attributable to armed actions carried out by the MHP and ülkücü organizations. The indictment delivered by the prosecutor at the MHP trial in the wake of the coup refers to a set of reports found at MHP party headquarters in which local members of ülkücü organizations provided accounts of their armed activities.[30] They tell how members of armed units (organized by neighbourhood in the cities) were chosen by MHP youth sections which coordinated their activities, provided them with the equipment they needed for their operations and regularly gave them their instructions.[31] Thus the situation under the last AP government, rather than invalidating the hypothesis of a link between the ülkücüs' use of physically violent activities and the positions held by the MHP, suggests it needs to be nuanced. The data in fact conceals complex mechanisms. Rather than looking solely at the positions held by the party in the central institutions of state, we need to study the situation of actors at all three levels of public action – municipal, provincial and national. As we shall see, it was when the MHP had the means to penetrate central public institutions but found itself (or its allies) in the minority locally that ülkücü sections adopted more radical practices in order to forcefully obtain access to resources. We shall thus be adopting a multi-perspective approach, taking into account how the various levels of public action were entangled, and in this way throw light on the various contexts in which physical violence emerged and spread.

The geographical distribution of violent interactions

In order to test the hypothesis that there is a correlation between violent activities and access to resources, and observe whether and how these two variables interact, I have decided to compare two sets of data: the results of the local elections held on 12 December 1977 and the number of deaths per province. These elections provide a particularly clear indication of the balance of power between political parties, thus shedding light in turn on that holding between the local action systems. These elections were for the general provincial council (*il genel meclisi*), municipal head (*belediye başkanı*) and the town council (*belediye meclisi*). The results obtained in each province thus provide a good means of assessing how strong and how organized each political party was locally, with the MHP being of special interest to us here. They also provide a way of ascertaining the extent to which Nationalist Movement organizations were involved in circuits allocating local public and municipal resources.

For the period running from 1 January 1977 to 12 September 1980 the data indicates the province of death in 3765 cases – though these sources do not tend to specify the exact place. The provinces with the highest levels of violence were Istanbul (935 deaths), Ankara (407 deaths) and Adana (306 deaths). But once this is set against the number of inhabitants per province, the level of violence between 1 January 1977 and 12 September 1980 varies from 27.52 deaths per 100,000 inhabitants in the province of Gaziantep (the province with the highest number of overall deaths, with a total of 199 killed), to 0.20 deaths per 100,000 inhabitants for Adapazarı (ranked 68, with one person killed). The geographical spread of physical violence shows that two zones were particularly affected, the first being southern Anatolia and the South East, encompassing the provinces of Antalya, İçel, Adana, Kahramanmaraş, Kayseri, Gaziantep, Hatay, Malatya, Elazığ, Tunceli, Bingöl, Diyarbakır, Urfa, Mardin and Siirt, situated at between 1st and 29th place on the ranking. The one province not fitting neatly into this otherwise geographically continuous arc is Adıyaman, where the level of violence was comparatively lower, coming 34th in the ranking. The second zone with a comparatively high level of violence lay to the east of the Black Sea, where the provinces sit between 5th and 30th place in the overall ranking. The affected provinces were Samsun, Ordu, Giresun, Trabzon, Rize, Artvin and Kars, with the zone extending inland to Amasya and Çorum. In addition to these two zones, the cities of Istanbul and Ankara were also affected by high levels of violence (coming 4th and 7th respectively in the ranking). The rest of the country was less affected in comparison (ranging from 35th to 68th in the ranking), apart from Eskişehir, Bursa and Manisa (standing respectively at 17th, 21st and 26th). Eleven provinces had less than one death per 100,000 habitants, namely Bolu, Burdur, Afyon, Hakkari, Çankiri, Bilecik, Gümüşhane, Bitlis, Kırklareli, Kastamonu and Adapazarı, coming between 58th and 68th on the ranking.

When we compare the number of victims of left/right confrontation and the results of the 1977 local elections, a strong correlation may be detected between the level of violence and the local position of the MHP and ülkücü organizations as a whole. In provinces where the MHP or one of its national allies (generally the AP and the MSP) controlled a large number of towns, there were relatively few victims. This was also the case in provinces where it did not have any candidate in the municipal elections and where its sections did not have an established presence, irrespective of the results of its allies. The number of deaths was on the contrary higher in provinces where the MHP stood in the local elections but where neither it nor its allies won power.

Places where the MHP was absent

The level of violence was low in nearly all the places where the MHP was largely absent from the elections. The only towns in the province of Bitlis (0.46 deaths per 100,000 inhabitants, 63rd in the ranking) where the MHP had a candidate standing were Adilcevaz, which it won with 36 per cent of the votes cast (which, as we shall see, is the type of local situation in which violence tended not to be used) and Tatvan, where it was the main opposition party to the CHP municipal head. The situation was largely similar in the province of Ağrı (2.12 deaths per 100,000 inhabitants, 44th in the ranking), where it only had one candidate, who won the elections to be municipal head in Taşlıçay. It did not have any candidates in Hakkari (0.79 deaths per 100,000 inhabitants, 58th in the ranking). This correlation between weak levels of MHP presence and low levels of violence may also be seen in the provinces of Van, Muş, Sinop, Muğla, Kırklareli, Bolu and Bilecik, all of which are in the lower third of the ranking of provinces by level of violence.

Table 6.2 Number of Deaths by Province (1 January 1977–12 September 1980)

Province	Number of inhabitants	Number of deaths	Deaths per 100,000 inhabitants
Gaziantep	715,939	197	27.52
Urfa	597,000	157	26.30
Adana	1,240,475	306	24.67
Istanbul	3,904,388	935	23.95
Trabzon	228,026	50	21.93
Elazığ	417,924	71	16.99
Ankara	2,585,293	407	15.74
Kahramanmaraş	738,000	107	14.50
Malatya	574,558	83	14.45
İçel	714,817	93	13.01
Uş'ak	229,679	29	12.63
Ordu	664,290	80	12.04
Diyarbakir	651,233	76	11.67
Samsun	906,381	97	10.70
Kayseri	676,809	71	10.49
Mardin	519,687	52	10.01
Eskisehir	495,097	47	9.49
Artvin	228,026	21	9.21
Hatay	744,113	67	9.00
Siirt	381,503	33	8.65
Bursa	961,639	83	8.63
Tunceli	164,591	14	8.51
Çorum	547,580	44	8.04
Bingöl	210,804	16	7.59
Rize	336,278	25	7.43
Manisa	872,375	62	7.11
Kars	707,398	49	6.93

Amasya	322,806	22	6.82
Antalya	669,357	36	5.38
Giresun	463,587	24	5.18
Izmir	1,973,666	90	4.56
Denizli	560,916	25	4.46
Muş	267,203	11	4.12
Adıyaman	346,892	13	3.75
Edirne	340,732	12	3.52
Kırşehir	232,863	8	3.44
Kocaeli	477,736	16	3.35
Tokat	599,166	19	3.17
Kırıkkale	128,015	4	3.12
Konya	1,422,461	43	3.02
Balıkesir	789,255	23	2.91
Niğde	463,121	13	2.81
Aydın	609,869	17	2.79
Ağrı	330,201	7	2.12
Van	386,314	8	2.07
Tekirdağ	319,987	6	1.88
Erzurum	746,666	14	1.88
Sivas	741,713	13	1.75
Nevşehir	249,308	4	1.60
Yozgat	500,371	8	1.60
Erzincan	283,683	4	1.41
Kütaya	470,423	6	1.28
Isparta	322,685	4	1.24
Sinop	267,605	3	1.12
Çanakkale	369,385	4	1.08
Zonguldak	836,156	9	1.08
Muğ'la	400,796	4	1.00
Bolu	428,704	4	0.93
Burdur	222,896	2	0.90
Afyon	597,516	5	0.84
Hakkari	126,036	1	0.79
Çankırı	265,468	2	0.75
Bilecik	137,120	1	0.73
Gümüş'hane	293,673	2	0.68
Bitlis	218,305	1	0.46
Kırklareli	268,399	1	0.37
Kastamonu	438,243	1	0.23
Adapazarı	495,649	1	

Correlations detectable in other provinces add further detail to these observations. Thus in Siirt the zones where the MHP notched up its best results (whilst still being in opposition) were those with the highest number of deaths. Though it only won 0.94 per cent of the votes cast for the provincial general council, the number of deaths per 100,000 habitants places Siirt 20th in the ranking of Turkish provinces by level of violence. Yet out of the thirty-three deaths recorded in total, nine were in the town of Batman, where the party won 5 per cent of the vote for the town council, and fifteen in the town of Siirt itself, where it won 6.57 per cent – that is, twenty-four out of the thirty-three deaths in the province took place in towns where the CHP won municipal elections. The MHP did not have any candidates standing for election in the other towns in the province. These results confirm that there was a comparatively low level of physical violence in those places where the MHP was not present in municipal arenas.

Places where the MHP was locally dominant

The level of violence was also comparatively low in provinces where the MHP (or its government partners) won municipal office. This is confirmed by the correlations observable in Yozgat and Erzincan, two of the provinces where it obtained its best results in the 1977 local elections. In the province of Yozgat (1.60 deaths per 100,000 inhabitants, 50th in the ranking), the MHP won 24.18 per cent of the votes cast for the provincial general council. Its candidates were elected to be municipal head in nine towns there, including the provincial capital, Yozgat, and Sorgun, the third-largest town in the province in terms of population. The CHP only won twelve of the thirty-two towns in the province, with the AP winning the eleven other towns. The parties in the Nationalist Front coalition thus had access to municipal resources in the majority of the towns in the province, and especially in the larger ones. The MHP obtained 20.32 per cent of the votes cast for the provincial general council in Erzincan (1.41 deaths per 100,000 inhabitants, 55th in the ranking), and won the elections for municipal head in the city of Erzincan with 48.64 per cent of the vote, as well as emerging as the majority party on Erzincan council with 46.25 per cent of the vote. It also won the elections for municipal head in the town of Üzümlü. As for the CHP, it only won the small town of Kemah, where the MHP did not have any candidates standing in either of the two municipal elections. The balance of political power observable in the province of Erzincan thus combines two situations which according to our model exclude the use of physical violence – namely the absence of the MHP in a town won by the CHP, and access to municipal resources in the other towns, including direct access in the provincial capital. In other provinces where the level of physical violence was comparatively low, the MHP was rarely in a position of force; but in places where it did take part in municipal elections, these were won by one of its partners in the Nationalist Front (either the AP or the MSP). The province of Isparta (1.24 deaths per 100,000 inhabitants, 52nd in the ranking) provides a good illustration of this. The AP won all of the towns where the MHP had candidates standing in the municipal elections; its local sections were thus never opposing a CHP governing majority. The same situation also occurred in Gümüşhane (0.68 deaths per 100,000 inhabitants, 62nd in the ranking) where the MHP won 14.57 per cent of the votes cast in the elections for the provincial general council. Although Köse was the only town where it won the municipal head elections, eleven of the fifteen towns in the province were won by one of the parties in the Nationalist Front coalition. Thus violence never emerged as the privileged tactic either of the Nationalist Movement or of far-left groups in places where agreements between the MHP and its national allies meant that the ülkücüs had access to local public resources.

Places where the MHP was in the local minority

The provinces with the highest number of deaths caused by confrontation between radical groups were generally those where ülkücü sections were in the opposition on the town council. The MHP won 13.10 per cent of the votes cast for the provincial general council in Adana (24.67 deaths per 100,000 inhabitants, 3rd in the ranking), which the CHP won with 46.01 per cent of the vote. The MHP had candidates standing for election to five of the thirty town councils in the province. In four of them (Adana,[32] Osmaniye, Ceyhan and Kozan) it was the CHP that won the elections for municipal head and was in the ruling majority on the town council. Thus in four of the five towns where the MHP had candidates standing for election, it failed to win access to local public resources whilst winning seats on the town council. A similar situation may be observed in the province of Elazığ (16.99 deaths per 100,000 inhabitants, 6th in the ranking). The MHP garnered 19.33 per cent of the votes cast for the provincial general council, which the CHP won with 22.40 per cent of the vote. It had candidates standing for election to seven of the sixteen town councils in the province, but did not win any of them. In the town of Ağın it was beaten by the CHP in the elections to be municipal head (winning 45.96 per cent of the votes cast) and in the elections to the town council (with 44.60 per cent). It was also in the opposition on town councils run by the CHP in Keban and Sivrice. Equally, it was in the opposition on the councils of Başkıl, Hankendi, Elazığ and Harput, only here the elections for municipal head were won by independent candidates. It won 7.78 per cent of the votes cast for the provincial general council in İçel (13.01 deaths per 100,000 inhabitants, 10th in the ranking), which was won by the CHP. The MHP stood for election to twelve of the twenty-eight town councils in the province. It did not have any candidate for municipal head in the five towns won by the AP's local candidates – indicating a local agreement with representatives from Nationalist Front coalition parties – instead only taking part in elections to the town council. It was the CHP that won the elections in the seven other towns where the MHP had candidates standing, as was notably the case in Tarsus, a town of over 100,000 inhabitants, where confrontations between the radical movements left fifty-three people dead, out of the ninety-three recorded for the province as a whole. The provinces in the upper third of the ranking are thus those in which the MHP tended to be part of the opposition on the town council, alongside the local sections of other parties in the Nationalist Front coalition.

The Kurdish provinces and the zone to the east of the Black Sea

The correlation between the number of victims and the MHP's electoral results is not observable everywhere. Specific regional logics also came into play. Thus the violence in the Kurdish provinces and those lying to the east of the Black Sea would appear not to have been connected to the balance of power between the radical movements. The fact that the MHP was not present in the provinces of Urfa, Diyarbakır and Mardin (respectively 2nd, 13th and 16th in the ranking) did not prevent there being high levels of physical violence. Hamit Bozarslan, in his article about the militia phenomena in Turkey during the 1970s, describes this area as a zone dominated by the principle of tribal segmentation due to the struggle between the PKK (Partiya Karkerên Kurdistan, Kurdistan Workers Party) and the KUK (Kürdistan Ulusal Kurtuluşçuları, Kurdistan National Liberators) that were competing to monopolize representation of the Kurdish cause. The violence there was due to confrontations that did not involve the far-left and ülkücü groups. To a certain extent Turkish Kurdistan in the 1970s was already a political sphere where endogenous dynamics were emerging that were largely independent of those at work in the rest of the country. This hypothesis is confirmed by the electoral results of the MHP. In the 1977 local elections it did not have a single candidate standing in the province of Mardin. In the province of Diyarbakır it only had one candidate, who ran in the town of Diyarbakır but received virtually no votes. The situation in Urfa was broadly similar.

No correlation would appear to hold between the number of dead and the local positions held by the MHP in the provinces of Samsun, Ordu, Giresun, Trabzon, Rize and Artvin, lying to the east of the Black Sea. All the situations previously described coexisted in this region. The comparatively high number of victims in the coastal provinces, though in part attributable to sporadic armed interactions involving ülkücü activists, was mainly due to confrontations between the forces of order and members of far-left groups. They had taken refuge in this ideally suited mountainous zone and been conducting guerrilla operations there since martial law had been declared in late 1978. The Dev-Yol Armed Resistance Units (Silahlı Direniş Birlikleri, SDB) were at their most active in the coastal provinces bounded by Samsun and Artvin.[33] From early 1980 onwards more and more people joined armed radical groups to train in guerrilla techniques to be put into practice once the army took power – something which was now viewed as certain to occur. Martial law command focused its efforts on these mountainous areas and the number of victims recorded in these provinces was thus not linked to left/right fighting.

Social profiles of the militants and victims

Analysis of the social profiles of the militants and victims in the conflict between radical movements also throws light on how it spread through Turkish society during the second half of the 1970s. In particular it brings out how these groups worked to mobilize people working in public institutions and those living in city neighbourhoods, where they recruited their future activists. Equally, it shows just how diverse the social categories affected by violent activities actually was, thus suggesting a generalized transformation in the informal rules governing political and social contest.

Militants

Only one enquiry has been carried out into the social origin and socio-professional categories of ülkücü and far-left activists. It was conducted by Emin Çölaşan in Ankara prison and involved 162 ülkücü militants and 125 far-left militants, and was published on 18 and 19 April 1979 in *Milliyet*; it was extensively commented on by Doğu Ergil in his book *Terror and Violence in Turkey*,[34] which came out in 1980. It shows that the militants were comparatively young, with 81.5 per cent of the 'revolutionaries' and 76.5 per cent of the ülkücüs in prison being under twenty-five, and only 5.4 per cent and 6.8 per cent respectively of them being over thirty at the time when the study was carried out.

A minority had been brought up in the major urban centres in Turkey, with 29.6 per cent of left-wing militants and 33.9 per cent of militant activists having been born in a provincial capital, as against 46.4 per cent and 45.1 per cent in a village or small town. However, a large majority of them – 74.4 per cent of far-left activists and 66.6 per cent of ülkücü militants – had spent some of their life in a provincial capital. Many had been involved in the rural exodus and had broken their ties with the milieu they originally came from. They became involved with radical groups after arriving in town, where they socialized in institutions (university halls of residence and publicly owned companies) and in neighbourhoods (the *gecekondu*) that had been deserted by the town authorities and the 'traditional' party machinery and where radical groups conducted intense recruitment campaigns.

Militants from both camps tended to come from a similarly modest social background. The fathers of 36 per cent of far-left and 27.8 per cent of ülkücü militants were blue-collar workers, 24 per cent and 21 per cent were public-sector workers, where this is followed by farmers (12 per cent and 17.9 per cent), and then tradesmen (5.6 per cent and 11.7 per cent). Certain professions were comparatively overrepresented. For instance, ülkücüs tended to come from farming families and a larger proportion of their fathers had held religious office or worked in the self-employed professions.

The data collected by Doğu Ergil indicates that 1.2 per cent of the fathers of far-left activists and 12.3 per cent of the fathers of ülkücü militants could not read or write.[35] 73 per cent of the fathers of those in the survey had not completed middle school, 7 per cent had graduated from high school, and 6.4 per cent of fathers of far-left militants and 4.3 per cent of the fathers of ülkücü militants had university qualifications. The socio-professional situation and declared level of studies of militants in Ankara prison shows that most of them had moved up the ladder of educational attainment. The largest category was of those 'who had studied for several years in a place of higher education' (26.4 per cent of far-left militants and 28.6 per cent of ülkücü militants). This was followed by people who had attended high school but left without any qualifications (22.4 per cent and 28 per cent), and then those who had left high school with qualifications (17.6 per cent and 14.9 per cent). These figures shed interesting light on the effect these sorts of institutions had on political commitment and participation in Turkey during the second half of the 1970s.[36] The largest category amongst the imprisoned militants surveyed was quite clearly 'students' (a category which in Ergil's survey included those at high schools and at places of further education). 48 per cent of far-left activists and 54.9 per cent of ülkücü militants were in high school or further education prior to prison. If we add in those who had been studying whilst in employment then the figure rises to 54.6 per cent and 56.1 per cent respectively. The largest number to be involved in armed activity was made up of young men from the rural exodus, separated from their families, available for action and exposed to the mobilization activities of radical groups in state-run schools and places of further education. It needs to be borne in mind however that this data was gathered in a prison in Ankara, and so care needs to be taken before making any generalizations. Whilst this data would seem to correspond to what may be observed in urban centres with large numbers of public institutions, it is partially invalidated by the situation in rural areas, where violence was often carried out by militias composed of individuals recruited in the villages.

The victims

The socio-professional category is known for 1614 of the 2255 victims recorded for the period between 1 January 1977 and 31 December 1979.[37] The data shows that the categories most affected by fighting between radical groups and the forces of order were, logically enough, those directly involved in violent activities (see the following table), that is to say students (588 of the 1614 victims, amounting to 36.43 per cent). The second most affected category – independent workers – accounts for half as many deaths (270 deaths, 16.72 per cent); this is followed by blue-collar workers (251 deaths, 15.55 per cent), secondary school teachers (131 deaths, 8.11 per cent), public-sector workers (119 deaths, 7.37 per cent) – where this category excluded teachers and policemen in the survey – and then policemen (62 deaths, 3.84 per cent).

Table 6.3 Socio-professional Categories of Victims of Fighting

Category	Number	Percentage
Student	588	36.43
Self-employed worker	270	16.72
Blue-collar worker	251	15.55
Teacher	131	8.11
Private-sector worker	119	7.37
Policeman	62	3.84
Child	29	1.79
Watchman	27	1.67
Housewife	18	1.11
Soldier	14	0.86
Barrister	12	0.74
Trade union member	9	0.55

Doctor (academic)	9	0.55
American	7	0.43
Journalist	7	0.43
Retired	7	0.43
Prosecutor	5	0.30
Municipal head	5	0.30
Professor	3	0.18
Pharmacist	2	0.12
Judge	2	0.12
Lecturer	2	0.12
Journalist	1	0.06
Non-commissioned officer	1	0.06
Mayor (*Muhtar*)	1	0.06
Bank manager	1	0.06
Head of the Directorate of Security	1	0.06
Candidate in the senatorial elections	1	0.06

The social categories of the victims became more diverse as the violence escalated and became more generalized. The most affected categories for the period as a whole (1 January 1977–31 December 1979) were those whose members took part in the radical movements. Others were symbolic targets, whilst still others were collateral victims. Participation in violent activities was initially most intense among students, blue-collar workers (who tended to be trade union members), teachers and public-sector workers. However, the proportion of students amongst the victims tended to diminish over time: in early 1978 this number stabilized, whilst the total number of victims increased, so whilst students accounted for 82.35 per cent of victims in January 1977, this figure had dropped to 13.22 per cent by December 1979.

There was also an increase in the number of victims from socio-professional categories that had initially been spared. Whilst up until late December 1977 policemen were only rarely affected by the exactions of radical groups (with three policemen being killed in 1977), as of January 1978 they were losing men nearly every month (with exceptions being April and July 1978, and in January 1979). Sixty-two policemen were killed over the period as a whole. Furthermore, the first victim amongst the nine trade union members was not killed until June 1978, and none of the twelve barristers were killed before August 1978. Equally, whilst no municipal heads (*belediye başkanları*) were killed before April 1978, five had lost their lives to violence by 12 September 1980. Other categories of victims were prime targets for militarized groups, being symbolic figures whose elimination attracted extensive media coverage. This was the case for military personnel and American citizens residing in Turkey, as well as for the candidate to the senatorial elections, the head of the Adana Directorate of Security, Cevat Yurdakul (shot dead by ülkücüs on 29 September 1979), the village mayor, the university professor, the journalist Abdi İpekçi (also killed by ülkücüs on 1 February 1979), the university professors, lecturers and the municipal heads (including Hamit Fendoğlu, the municipal head of Malatya). In each instance their death triggered protests and counter-protests, in turn sparking many reactions in the press.

Lastly, the number of collateral victims rose continually. This was the case as of April 1979 for housewives (eighteen deaths) and children (twenty-nine deaths). It was also the case for self-employed workers – there were no victims in this category prior to December 1977, but the number then rose from two in January 1978 to thirty in December 1979, by which time it accounted for nearly 25 per cent of the victims. The number of public-sector workers killed also increased over time.[38] Between 1 January 1977 and 31 December 1979 119 public-sector workers were killed. As of March 1978 at least one was being killed each month, and by November 1979 they accounted for nearly 14 per cent of victims. As the level of violence increased watchmen (in banks, blocks of flats, hangars, on night-duty and so on) were also killed (a total of twenty-seven over the whole period), and as of April 1979 at least one watchman was killed every month. As the level of violence increased it thus spread through society.

*

The social, spatial and temporal mapping of physically violent activities put forward in this chapter shows a strong correlation between the level of violence and the positions the MHP held in central and local arenas. The level of violence was thus at its highest whenever the Nationalist Movement was deprived of access to municipal and local resources yet could draw on the collusion of ülkücüs working in the public sector. It was because the Nationalist Movement was able to mobilize both local and central resources (by replacing the public authorities and by penetrating the state) that it was able to use illegal and violent means to accumulate resources. Viewed from this perspective, the violence did not occur independently of the balance of power holding in the various arenas of public action, nor of the positions the Nationalist Movement held therein. Public institutions would thus appear to have been external to the escalation in violence in their capacity as autonomous actors, but of key importance as arenas for conflict. The balance of power within each of their various parts determined the level of physical violence and the forms it took. The social categories to be hardest hit were for that matter those whose members attended public institutions, which acted as privileged places for the groups involved in the conflict to recruit members, and as favoured arenas of confrontation. The quantitative data presented in this chapter shows that the violence spread progressively, and that the victims came from increasingly diverse social backgrounds. In order to understand how violence emerged as a routine form of political action and thereby a factor transforming its informal rules (up until the intervention of 12 September 1980, which it helped legitimize), the following chapter looks at the ways in which political contest became increasingly belligerent.

Chapter 7

THE EFFECTS OF VIOLENCE ON POLITICAL CONTESTS

Violence brings into focus the transformations taking place within political contests. Its intensity and rhythm and the context in which it is implemented depend upon configurations arising from the interwoven local and national balances of power. The use of violence contributes to the de-objectification of the state since it enables those behind it to capture additional resources, as well as spreading the feeling of generalized chaos within the population, something to which only military intervention can put an end.

Once violence becomes established as a routine form of action and a standard way of accessing resources, the rules of political contest undergo modification, along with the positions of actors in local and national arenas. In order to understand the mechanisms presiding over this transformation, this chapter looks at the measures employed by radical groups in carrying out their various violent activities, and enquires into their effects. In particular it studies the dynamics that triggered and then presided over the unfolding of the Kahramanmaraş massacre, before then examining its political repercussions. This massacre was the most deadly conflict in 1970s Turkey. On 22 December 1978 part of the Sunni population, overseen by ülkücü units, attacked the town's Alevi population. Four days later, once the forces of law and order had put an end to the confrontation, 111 people lay dead and over 1000 had been injured. All of the processes described in the previous chapters were to be found in the town of Kahramanmaraş. The massacre took place against the backdrop of high levels of politicization amongst staff working for the municipal or provincial authorities. Equally, the CHP were making electoral headway, due notably to the support of far-left organizations and of inhabitants in Alevi neighbourhoods, and this threatened the local resources hitherto available to ülkücü sections. The public authorities had only a patchy presence in the province. In the run-up to the massacre, the town was the scene of outbreaks of violence, with militias patrolling several neighbourhoods, strike units carrying out targeted operations and regular altercations between ülkücüs and members of the far left. The first step in analysing how events in Kahramanmaraş unfolded and in assessing their repercussions is to build up a picture of how the rationales governing resource capture, mobilization, and the de-objectification of public institutions all coalesced in the diffusion and escalation of violence, and how in turn violence impacted on the means to access positions of power and accumulation.

Activities of physical violence and their benefits

The level of violence took on many different forms over time and from one place to another, stemming from the various modes of organization used, and providing access to different resources.

Three types of violent activity may be distinguished: 'daily' violence, 'organized' violence and 'militia' violence. Daily violence was the result of fortuitous encounters and daily interactions between activists from the conflictual groups. Organized violence was carried out by units set up to conduct targeted operations in a town or across the country as a whole. This was more frequently the work of ülkücü sections, given the degree of coordination required, than of those from the far left. Militia violence, which occurred primarily in central and eastern Anatolia, was carried out by urban and rural militias which regularly interfered in jobs markets, economic and migratory flows, and the allocation of housing in territories under their control. These three types of violence were not mutually exclusive. They often coexisted and were sometimes perpetrated by the same individuals.

Daily violence

Daily violence requires few resources and low levels of organization and is carried out in highly localized arenas, flaring up due to chance encounters between antagonistic groups of activists, fights between students at the school or university gates, attacks on people pasting up bills and exchanges of gunfire to control a street corner or bus stop. These altercations were frequent in universities where antagonistic groups existed alongside one another. According to Nejat, a student in the law faculty at Istanbul University and a member of the far-left group Kurtuluş:

> At that time we would sit like that in lecture halls – on one side 30 far-left activists, and on the other about 150 people, non-politicised students and fascists, with a police cordon between the two groups. We were a bit isolated ... In the minority. ... When we entered the university as a group we were surrounded by a police cordon, cut off from the conservatives, reactionaries, and non-politicised students. We were not allowed out of the hall between lectures, and if we did go out we got beaten up.[1]

Celal, who was at that time a student and member of the Fatherland Party (Vatan Partisi), explained that 'fights broke out [between students] every day, and at any time. Schooling was not very important back then, and if a fight broke out somewhere we left school and went there.'[2] All the former students I spoke to confirmed that fights were a frequent occurrence at university. Sometimes there were exchanges of gunfire and attacks carried out by small groups, such as machine-gunning a coffeehouse. Şadi explained how he and a few friends 'attacked the Küllük café' near Istanbul University:

'*Did you fight with ülkücüs from the University?*'

'From the University, yes ... In front of the University ...'

'*And the Küllük café ... Someone blew it up ...*'

'It was one of the fascists' hangouts ... Yes ... We attacked the Küllük ...'

'*Tell me about it ...*'

'We were near the *Küllük*, it was in 1975 I think.'

'*Where was it exactly?*'

'Near the University, really near, opposite, on the other side of the main road ... I think there were about ten of us ... And ... They were all armed of course ... No, we didn't do much, nobody was killed or wounded ...'

'*But ten of you went there ...*'

'Yes, there were about thirty of them.'

'*Armed too.*'

'Yes, armed, of course.'

'*And afterwards?*'

'After you run, of course, towards the University.'[3]

For many activists and sympathizers their experience of violence was limited to being involved in fights, trading insults and – less frequently – exchanging gunfire. The weapons used in this type of situation were not necessarily handed out by the groups, as individuals sometimes saved up money or clubbed together to buy a pistol or revolver from smugglers. According to Mahmut, 'a few students would pool their savings to buy an arm, together, or else, to give another example, a peasant would sell a cow to buy an arm. There were a lot of arms in Turkey'.[4] Activists from both camps would often approach smugglers in city neighbourhoods where arms dealers were known to be found. Chance encounters between members of antagonistic groups regularly caused altercations. In November 1979, in Kozan, on leaving the MHP sectional meeting, a group of ülkücüs ran into far-left activists, and one person was killed in the ensuing fight.[5] There were daily reports of such incidents in the press.[6] More heavily armed activists sometimes attacked more ambitious targets. This is what happened in April 1977 in Çine, when a group of ülkücüs attacked the headquarters of the local CHP and Töb-Der sections, losing one of their members (a high-school student) in the ensuing gun battle.[7] Another comparatively frequent form of attack was to shoot from a car, firing blindly at a predetermined target before fleeing the scene as quickly as possible. The press reported these attacks whenever anyone was killed[8] – which was rarely the case, as they were carried out in haste.

Daily violence also routinely occurred at points of friction between the antagonistic factions, which acted more or less as territorial borders that each side sought to defend by force of arms. It was not a matter of imposing a monopoly over physical violence within a liberated neighbourhood by replacing the forces of law and order – a phenomenon we shall look at later on – but rather of temporarily taking possession of a street corner, bus shelter or crossroads. There were many reasons for doing this, such as commanding a strategic spot to sell publications, or else exerting control over a bench, park or handful of streets in order to stage a show of force. In this type of situation the groups did not replace the public authorities – and indeed they withdrew once the forces of order intervened. They interfered but little in the economic life of the 'conquered territory', merely obliging the local shopkeepers to buy their journals or make a small financial contribution to the cause. There were many different cases on a scale running from total substitution of the state to total absence of activists within a given area. Groups of activists would sometimes lay claim to a stretch of several hundred metres or so of an avenue, with opposing groups appropriating the following section. Thus, according to Celal, in central Ankara

> from Beşevler to Tandoğan it was the far right, then for 500 metres from Tandoğan to Maltepe it was the left, as far as the avenue, but from Maltepe to the bridge it was the right. From the bridge to Kızılay it was the left. … In Yenimahalle the first bus stop was controlled by the left, and the second by the Ülkü Hearths, protected by the police.[9]

The groups controlling these stretches of road or avenue plastered them in slogans and symbols, carried out political ID checks on passers-by, sold their publications and conducted recruitment work. The same thing sometimes happened across an entire neighbourhood, with the borders being patrolled by armed activists. Altercations frequently broke out on the roads and avenues running along the border of controlled zones. According to Metin, 'the thing was to wait for the fascists in the neighbourhoods. If an adjacent neighbourhood was right-wing, we waited for the fascists at the border between the two neighbourhoods, in little groups of three or five people'.[10]

Violence in student halls of residence was also a daily occurrence. Students took it in turn to stand guard and filter people coming into the building. Altercations often broke out between students from different residences. In Fındıkzade on 16 January 1977, students from the Niğde and Sakarya residences fought for over two hours, until one of them was killed, a situation described in the *Cumhuriyet* newspaper as 'street warfare'.[11] A few months later, night-long fights between students from, once again, the Niğde and Sakarya residences, as well as from the Site and Sivas residences in Istanbul, resulted in 460 students being taken into custody.[12] There were also attacks using explosives. For instance, a group of individuals launched an explosive device against the (ülkücü) Adana residence in Ankara, before leaving while exchanging gunfire with its residents who had rushed outside.[13] The frequency of such actions and the fact that they sometimes coincided with others (at least in the cities) can on occasions produce the impression of a general, nationwide flare-up. This was the case on 13 January 1977, when *Cumhuriyet* reported a string of events from the day before: thirteen high-school pupils had been arrested after an altercation at the Karlıova High School in Bingöl; Atatürk University in Erzurum had had to close its doors for an indefinite period after the death of a student; a residence at the Advanced School in Manisa had been dynamited; teachers from the Ortaklar Educational Institute in Aydın had been attacked with bats; and a general fight had broken out at the Başkent School of journalism in Ankara.[14]

Daily violence affected organizations in the two movements in various ways. Intimidation and the use of physical force enabled local sections to seize a wide range of resources. Controlling a street corner was a way of being sure to sell the organization's publications, whilst defending a residence made it possible to house the organization's members there. Activists also found that confronting these ordeals together offered a way of ensuring internal cohesion. Signing up to a form of activism that included physical violence provided a way of playing a concrete part in the revolution that was under way, of combating fascism or defending the country against communism. It generated peer recognition. In far-left groups an individual was only viewed as a true activist once he or she had taken part in the guard duties patrolling the residence or the borders of the 'liberated neighbourhood'. Daily acts of violence also enhanced the status of activists, who displayed their commitment to the group by placing themselves in physical danger for the cause. They also had a performative value, since they provided a way of confirming the danger posed by the opposing side, and hence the need to become physically involved in order to eliminate it. They acted as a mechanism for rapidly building up group loyalty. Violence thus played a major role in the constitution of groups and in maintaining member loyalty.

Organized violence

But other forms of physical violence, such as the sporadic bombings, attacks and aggressions carried out by armed units, followed wholly different rationales. These units were either set up independently of the organizations, as was the case with the MLSPB and Devrimci Savaş on the far left, or else were composed of members selected by the local or national leadership. The activities they carried out necessitated a comparatively high degree of organization. Their members acquired specific skills, and often lived in hiding, carrying out orders and devising plans of action for a district, a town or province, and sometimes for the country as a whole. These units differed from the militias in Central and Eastern Anatolia, with which they sometimes coexisted, for they had but few links with the neighbourhoods where they were based, only interfered intermittently in public life, and did not exert continuous coercive control over urban or rural zones. Kutay told how the Dev-Yol group set up armed units in several towns around the country:

'Dev-Yol had set up a sort of special organisation linked to the central committee, whose members had highly specialised military training. The members were kept separate from the people, from everything, and the sole purpose of this team was armed action. It was very small, perhaps twenty-five people for all of Turkey. A group of five for example would do something in Izmir or in Istanbul.'

'For example?'

'Hold-ups, assassinations in specific fascist centres, against the police, against police stations. Laying bombs, killing fascists. It was the Union of Revolutionary War (Devrimci Savaş Birliği), for very specific actions. Amongst the people, to protect people from the fascists, it was the Union of Armed Resistance (Silahlı Direniş Birliği), which had members throughout Turkey.'[15]

Members of these units lived in hiding, as explained by İrfan, who was one of those in charge of Dev-Sol's armed operations:

When I got out of prison I lived in hiding in various places. ... I had friends in Dev-Sol, Dev-Yol, and in other organisations. I lived in hiding in Istanbul in a simple manner. We didn't go to the cinema or theatre, we didn't eat out, we checked everything, we were very concentrated, always armed, always attentive. I had to live in a very planned manner. I don't think I ate out once on leaving prison. We only went out at night, to carry out the operations we had planned.[16]

In the Nationalist Movement the ÜOD, followed by the ÜGD and the ÜYD, established small units in city neighbourhoods to run targeted actions against individuals, buildings and symbolic places. According to several of my sources, these units were far more numerous than those set up by the far left. In the first months of 1978 underground ülkücü organizations were set up across the country,[17] most notably the Turkish Lightning Commandos (Türk Yıldırım Komandoları, TYK) and the Enslaved Turks Liberation Army (Esir Türkleri Kurtarma Ordusu, ETKO), which were active in Central and Eastern Anatolia.

The Nationalist Movement also opened neighbourhood libraries whose real purpose was to act as headquarters for local armed groups. The ülkücüs extended this metaphor, spinning a coded language in which book titles were used to designate certain weapons, arms, and explosives.[18] Within the Nationalist Movement armed activities tended to be organized by the MHP's central bodies, as attested in a document drawn up by the MHP deputy secretary general in which, after indicating that 'illegal and underground work is an obligation' for the Nationalist Movement, he goes over the 'rules' to be respected in 'underground' work:

All activities must be carried out using the smallest number of men possible. A task which could have been successful with two people sometimes fails because of poor planning, leading to four being involved. ...

Militants must be ignorant of the reasons why another militant has been selected. A fundamental rule is that a militant must know all he needs to know to carry out the task he is chosen for, but other than that he must know nothing further, about the nature of the intervention for example. ...

The discipline of Nationalist militants must be such that they do not seek to find out anything further about what their own operations relate to. They must show no inquisitiveness for matters that do not directly concern them.

Militants taking part in an illegal operation must be separated from militants with whom they usually talk, and placed in a separate environment. ...

Militants must know how to live amongst the people. They must be careful not to behave in a way that is contrary to village life, and in town must not dress differently from others and be careful not to speak differently. ... If wanted by the police or if there is a court sentence against them, they must go into hiding. Under such circumstances they must not tell anybody about their past activities.[19]

The account provided by Mustafa Pehlivanoğlu, who was member of an ülkücü underground armed group based in Ankara, provides concrete details about how the Nationalist Movement organized armed activities. Pehlivanoğlu was arrested in summer 1978 after having been involved in machine-gun attacks on several coffeehouses in the neighbourhood of Balgat in Ankara. During the investigation, he said that he and a few friends had enrolled for Taekwondo classes at Bahçelievler in Ankara in 1976, and socialized in ülkücü circles in the neighbourhood. After several fights with far-left activists he was found guilty of battery and assault and sentenced to twenty-one months in Nevşehir prison. Six months into his prison sentence he received a visit from İsa Armağan and Abdullah Çatlı,[20] two cadres from the Ankara ülkücü youth organization who specialized in armed activities. They told him that they had obtained his release thanks to party supporters working in the judicial administration,[21] and suggested he take part in the activities they ran. On being released he was provided with accommodation in a 'house for single men' in the Karapınar neighbourhood in Ankara, received a salary and started to take part in operations conducted by the neighbourhood unit where he had been placed. He was thus one of the founders of the ülkücü library in Karapınar, which was run by the Dikmen district section of the Association for the Great Ideal (BÜD). As he put it, 'orders and instructions came from the BÜD':[22]

> The organisation had two types of weapon in the base sections (*obalar*) and BÜD sections – members' personal weapons and those of the organisation. The latter were not stocked in the Ankara Club or at Association headquarters, but in the premises of the neighbourhood organisations. When an operation was going to be organised, the Ankara Club (*Ankara ocağı*) and BÜD headquarters sent out instructions to the organisation in question. Once these instructions had been sent, the sections or libraries provided the weapons. The people who

were to take part in the operation went to the Ankara Club, or to the BÜD, took a weapon, then brought it back once they had completed what they had to do. ... The Ankara Club sent headquarters a report about each operation carried out. ... Every week there were meetings at BÜD headquarters attended by the head of each section. ... We were on a lower level and so did not have any direct contact with the MHP.[23]

Pehlivanoğlu stated he had been at the lowest level in the organization for armed activities. He described himself as a mere soldier for the cause. According to him it was the leader of the armed unit, İsa Armağan, who was in charge of liaising with other ülkücü sections:

His role was to carry out leadership and organise operations. İsa was in charge of organising operations and he got the necessary weapons. All the members of our library had a weapon. We blew up a lots of houses belonging to left-wing individuals, threw sticks of dynamite, and fired guns.[24]

For several months the group's activities were limited to the neighbourhoods around Karapınar. Then Pehlivanoğlu was chosen to go and work under the orders of Abdullah Çatlı, who by then was the deputy chairman of the ÜGD:

After a bit we stopped running the Karapınar library, ... we were given jobs at general headquarters. We were placed under the orders of Abdullah Çatlı and carried out assassinations and attacks. İsa Armağan took instructions from Abdullah Çatlı and sent them to us, and together we would carry out the operation. Muhsin Yazıcıoğlu [chairman of the ÜGD] and Şevkat Çetin protected the ülkücüs involved in such operations.[25]

Pelhivanoğlu's account provides information about the various stages in the underground armed work conducted by the Nationalist Movement. Local organizations used the skills of individuals spotted during altercations with the far left or else in clubs for combat sports. Once the local units – or libraries – had been set up, the people running them contacted the local sections of ülkücü associations, whose chairmen liaised with MHP cadres whose task it was to transmit party directives and provide the arms and funding required for underground activities. This type of organization was also to be found elsewhere in the country. In Adana, for example, the deputy chairman of the ÜGD section, called Kütük, was appointed by the party to coordinate the action of small units in the province. He had an office at MHP provincial headquarters, where he was assisted by six other militants, all former members of legal ülkücü organizations. Together they ran most of the Nationalist Movement's armed operations in the province. The information available indicates that they were behind the assassination of Cevat Yurdakul, the head of the Directorate of Security in the province and a member of the left-wing police union, Pol-Der.[26] Other operations attracting less media attention were regularly carried out in the province. Kütük apparently gave the order to avenge the death of an ülkücü, Osman Arıca, whose employer was suspected of having ordered his killing. It would appear that Kütük asked the chairman of the ÜGD section in Kadirli (a district in the province of Adana) to provide two weapons for two ülkücüs to go and kill the employer's father and brothers. Once they had completed their task the two militants are reported to have gone and hid in a place provided for them in Kadirli, before going and reporting to Kütük.[27] Most of the time running targeted operations involved putting together teams of three of four people and providing them with arms in a 'flat for single men' – where they took refuge for a few days on completing their mission before then dispersing, leaving the arms in the flat for other militants to come and collect.[28]

Within the Nationalist Movement, relationships between the MHP and militants thus took the form of criminal political collusion, a phenomenon that may be analysed in terms of 'interactions based on an exchange of services or skills to further convergent interests'.[29] Members of armed units received a salary that was paid by Nationalist Movement cadres or else by a local publicly owned company where the MİSK trade union confederation controlled employee recruitment. In exchange for this, legal ülkücü organizations could use these units to carry out intimidation campaigns, physically eliminate individuals who might hamper their actions or else raise the funds they required for their activities. The account provided by Ömer Tanlak, a reformed ülkücü militant, reveals how these units were tasked with getting recalcitrant businessmen to pay the monies demanded by ideal associations in Antalya. In a press interview he declared:

'We were planning on blowing up a pipework company.'
'*Why were you going to blow it up?*'
'The man did not pay his fees or something like that.'
'*Was it you who collected fees?*'
'Yes it was us.'
'*Was it your chairman who organised it? Did he say "so much from A, so much from B"?*'
'Of course.'
'*So he told you "take 300 from such-and-such a person", and you went and took 300?*'
'He had to give it to us. ... The pipework seller had not paid his latest fees. And he had talked about it to the police, who had arrested one or two people, and so we went round to blow up his store. But I wasn't there. ...'
'*Alright, but were some of those who didn't pay killed? Or targeted in bomb attacks?*'
'From what I know certain were beaten up. Anyway, everyone living in the neighbourhood paid.'
'*You demanded that inhabitants paid fees?*'
'Everybody.'
'*So if an individual was MHP ...*'
'He would volunteer his financial contribution.'
'*And money changed hands.*'

'Yes.'
'*What did you do with this money?*'
'It went to prisons. Cigarettes, food ...'
'*So it went to imprisoned ülkücüs ...*'
'Yes, and we bought arms and ammunition.'[30]

For large-scale operations, instructions were issued orally by the MHP youth section or the chairman of the Ülkü Hearths in the province or town concerned, who would then tell militants to form strike units (*vurucu timler*). According to Tanlak, it was always the Ülkü Hearths who provided the means for carrying out operations, such as weapons and explosive materials:

> The Hearth chairman provided the explosive materials and arms. He would call and say 'there's some work', hand over the material, explain the plan, and then leave.[31]

It was not always the party which gave orders for the operations. A local ülkücü organization could also directly transmit its wishes to Ülkü Hearths – provided it paid the chosen militants or the section they belonged to. Tanlak referred for instance to an operation in which he took part in Antalya that was apparently ordered by Abdurrahman Sağkaya, the director of the Antbirlik factory who had been appointed by the MHP minister for trade in the second Nationalist Front government. On noting that the MİSK trade union confederation had been prevented from distributing its publications in the factory, the director asked the local ülkücü associations to intervene. A strike unit composed of four people attacked a group of factory workers known for their opposition to ülkücü trade unions, killing one of them before then fleeing. According to Tanlak, the assailants left for Ankara, where they were paid by the secretary of MİSK. On learning that the police were looking for them, they took refuge in a flat for single men provided by the Nationalist Movement and made contact with an MHP accountant who provided them with the money they needed to go into hiding.[32] Organized violence thus enabled local organizations to bring about a shift in power relations, and alter them in their favour by intimidating or eliminating individuals hampering local ülkücü activities.

Militia violence

Militia violence, unlike the other two forms of violence, only transpired in certain contexts. It was carried out by militias organized by territory, and with multiple relationships to populations and state representatives. The armed actions they carried out to maintain control over a neighbourhood's population or homogenize it along ethnic or political lines formed but one part of their activities. These amounted to a campaign of territorialized violence, for they were 'capable of taking decisions and carrying out strategies, and acting so as to convert organised force (or violence) into money or other market *resources*, and this in permanent manner'.[33] One of the prime characteristics of militia violence was that it helped territorialize political contest.

The militias' exploitation of divisions between communities Hamit Bozarslan was the first to put forward a framework for understanding the militia phenomenon in Turkey in the second half of the 1970s.[34] He argues that militia violence was deployed in certain parts of the country, as distinct from other forms of violent action observable elsewhere at the same period. He suggests that despite looking overwhelmingly ideological (conflict between radical left and right organizations), the violence in these 'sensitive zones' was closely linked to communitarian dynamics and had a militia aspect. Bozarslan identified several zones that were highly segmented along denominational (Alevi/Sunni) and linguistic (Turkish/Kurdish) lines, where militias were in competition with the state to control municipalities and city neighbourhoods. The first of these subsets, covering the provinces of Çorum, Yozgat, Niğde, Nevşehir, Kırşehir and Ordu, was characterized by the Alevi/Sunni divide, compounded by the opposition between left and right. The second, which Bozarslan calls the 'red zone', covered the provinces of Sivas, Maraş, Malatya, Elazığ, Erzincan, Tunceli and Bingöl, where the Alevi/Sunni denominational divide coincided with the separation into Kurdish- and Turkish-speakers. In the third zone, comprising the provinces of Kars and Erzurum, the political divide followed linguistic rather than denominational lines. In the fourth zone, comprising the Kurdish provinces of Diyarbakır, Urfa and Mardin, and displaying a fairly high degree of linguistic and denominational homogeneity,[35] the emergence of militia structures resulted from the marked degree of tribal segmentation. As seen in the previous chapter, the MHP was largely absent here and the violence was not the work of far-left and ülkücü groups.

Work by radical groups to mobilize the population further politicized ethnic and linguistic divisions. In places where the Sunni and Alevi communities cohabited – an increasingly common occurrence in the wake of the rural exodus – the Nationalist Movement exploited the Alevi presence to leverage the political mobilization of Sunni populations. In the 1970s many Alevi families settled in the new districts of Anatolian towns, where they were stigmatized by the ülkücüs who accused them of Kurdishness, separatism, communism, religious heterodoxy and failing to respect the principles of Islam. According to the Nationalist Movement, their presence posed not just a cultural problem but an economic one too since it skewed the local job market. In the towns of central Anatolia far-left groups therefore did all they could to mobilize the Alevi communities, whilst the ülkücüs treated them as a readily appointed scapegoat to win over Sunni support. Burak Gürel quotes several public speeches, watchwords, and declarations which bring out how the community dimension was exploited for political ends. On 22 September 1978 a tract distributed by the local Muslim Youth (Müslüman Gençlik) organization in Sivas declared: 'Careful Alevis! Don't be used as instruments, learn the lessons of history. You chanted "Shah, Shah" [a reference to the support given by Alevi tribes to the Safavid leader Shah İsmail]. Nowadays you're not running towards the Shah but towards communism.'[36] On 3 and 4 September 1978 MHP militants in Sivas accused communist Alevis of having set off a bomb at the Alibaba mosque. It was immediately decided to carry out a mass attack, in which militias, ülkücü units, and members of the town's Sunni community all took part. The assailants targeted municipal buildings, shops and business premises belonging to CHP sympathizers, and Alevi businesses in the districts of Alibaba, Aydoğan and Çiçekli, where most of the town's Alevi population lived. By nightfall five lay dead and fifty wounded. On the day of the burial of the ülkücü activists killed during the assault, a second wave of attacks was launched against the same neighbourhoods, to the cries of 'Communists and *Kızılbaş* (Alevis) killed our brothers!', 'Muslim Turkey!', 'Death to communists!' and 'Sivas shall be the infidels' tomb!'.[37]

Replacing the public authorities The far-left and ülkücü organizations each mobilized different sides of the denominational and linguistic divide. What we now need to analyse is the extent to which these identifications were linked to militia violence. The zones where this violence occurred were characterized by their denominational and linguistic segmentation, but they were also areas from which the state was largely absent and lacking the means needed to establish its presence there. State representatives had traditionally come to agreements with local notables, to whom they delegated social control:

> In Kurdistan and numerous other towns in Anatolia, the centre ended up being restricted to the *Yenişehir* (new towns), which had been founded to meet the needs of its public employees and were external to the social circuit. So however centralised and powerful the State may have been, it depended largely on legitimisation bodies that pre-existed within society, and coexisted with it. To acquire legitimacy it frequently had to draw on these bodies, to obtain the prior approval of this other legitimacy, and thereby abandon part of the national sovereignty it claimed to embody.[38]

The new actors who emerged in the 1970s were now involved in a contest with these traditional bodies over legitimacy to interact with the centre. First among these were the ülkücü and far-left organizations that drew on physical violence to impose themselves. They were successful in certain places where they exploit the fact that the state had hitherto not needed to build up networks so as to establish its presence there.[39] This enabled them to place neighbourhoods and towns under military oversight, forming 'liberated territories' in which the public authorities sometimes had to negotiate their own withdrawal by coming to agreement with the militias. As Hamit Bozarslan observes:

> And so the links between, firstly, the militias and the State *qua* centre, and, secondly, between the militias and the political system, were not in fact broken; yet conversely, the State's principal prerogatives were completely paralysed or infiltrated at the local level. State employees, hailing from distant places, did not want to stay there or put their life at (genuine) risk. In some cases they ended up admitting they were powerless and entering into strategies of alliance that legitimised the infiltration. ... In other cases the State was quite simply absent.[40]

This absence or withdrawal of the state meant that local arenas (the town, district or neighbourhood) acquired autonomy. Gradually 'town authorities came to replace a seat in parliament as the source of monolithic power'.[41]

Oversight of the population and the monopolization of local resources In order to understand the roles played by militias in intra-community conflict and the indirect benefits they could derive from their activities, it is first necessary to look at how militias originally came to impose their oversight of linguistic and denominational communities in Central and Eastern Anatolia. When ülkücü and far-left groups established militias, they generally renamed the neighbourhood or town they dominated so as to enact its autonomy, as was the case for the First of May neighbourhood in Istanbul, and the town of Fatsa, which became the Fatsa 'commune'. They established armed control over the territory, and this militarization and the first exchanges of gunfire certified the official existence of the militia. At the same time its members exerted political control over the population, forcing the unwilling to obey, raising various taxes and taking control of the allocation of the available accommodation. All the inhabitants were forced to contribute to local solidarity whether they wanted to or not. The younger people were obliged to patrol the limits of the neighbourhood, whilst the population as a whole was compelled to buy from stores run by the militia, to attend the meetings it held and to contribute to its financial upkeep. Coffeehouses, book stores, restaurants and businesses were used to hold public meetings, and cultural, social and economic practices were homogenized. The taxation and redistribution activities carried out by the militia made it a central actor within the local economic field. It was the militia that distributed jobs in the local public companies where allied trade unions were in a position of strength, and the militia which allocated accommodation and selected new settlers in the neighbourhood. The population was placed under its domination. The social link was primarily a coercive one. But it was based on a common interest, since the inhabitants benefited from the protection provided by the militias.[42] And given the context of virtual civil war, the news that there was a new 'liberated' neighbourhood – that is to say one placed under the domination of a militia – soon triggered exchanges of gunfire and sparked off attacks on its inhabitants. To a certain extent, the protection provided by the militias may be compared to racketeering, insofar as the threats against which the militia protected inhabitants stemmed from its own activities, as Charles Tilly observes.[43]

There were multiple ties linking the militias and local populations. Financial and physical involvement in the militia's activities may have been obtained under duress, but the protection the militia provided the population enabled it to impose its 'participation in the war', that is to say attacks on other communities:

> Indeed, the militias managed to get most of the population to take part in the process by making them complicit with what was going on, and winning their silence in the name of protection or of organic ties. Punishing instances of 'betrayal' and obtaining the group's silence about this acted as the best guarantee of their involvement.[44]

The way in which militias managed to associate the populations to their activities no doubt explains how they managed to get them to take part in acts of physical violence perpetrated during the uprisings in Sivas, Çorum, Malatya and Kahramanmaraş. These were the most innovative of the tactical ploys used by ülkücüs in their interaction with left-wing groups – as well as being the most murderous.

The uses and effects of violence – the Kahramanmaraş massacre

As observed earlier, the escalation in activities of physical violence transformed the informal rules governing political contest. Violence emerged as an effective way to accumulate resources – and seemingly viewed as such by those involved – against the backdrop of the de-objectification of the state, henceforth unable to lay claim to the monopoly on violence throughout its territory and to ensure the population's security.

Public institutions that had been infiltrated by activists were no longer able to guarantee the state's authority. They lost control over populations remotely administered via the intermediary of traditional elites, who now found themselves ejected from the contest. Intermittent violence thus came to be seen as a mode of action to be envisaged to ensure one's own protection or else capture resources hitherto controlled by the opposing camp. This is not to deny that armed action followed its own rationales – organizations were out of control, and there was a continual escalation in acts of daily violence. But the levels and types of violence depended to a large extent on the positions the protagonists held in local and national arenas. Thus physical violence was generally only used in situations where access to local resources was under threat. By liberating certain resources, violent activities thus modified the power relations between political groups, trade unions and associations. Hence we need to look not only at the means by which rationales governing state and political contests fashioned violent activities but also at the mechanisms by which violent activities helped transform these rationales, up until the military intervention on 12 September 1980. In order to do so, the next section analyses the dynamics leading to the Kahramanmaraş massacre in late December 1978, and examines its local and national repercussions.

Power relations in Kahramanmaraş

The situation in the town of Kahramanmaraş in the run-up to the massacre was characterized by the progressive exclusion of the Nationalist Front coalition parties from ways of accessing local resources. Whilst the AP retained control of the town in the municipal elections of December 1977 (won by its candidate Ahmet Uncu), the CHP came first in the 1973 general elections (with 32.91 per cent of the votes cast in the province) and those of 1977 (with 34.39 per cent), thus inverting the balance of power, which had favoured the AP (and its predecessor the DP) ever since 1957. The MHP also made considerable progress, going from 1.22 per cent of the votes cast in the 1969 elections, to 15.50 per cent in those of 5 June 1977, when the CHP clearly courted local Alevi support, with three of the top four places on its candidate list going to leading figures from the community (Oğuz Söğütlü, a pharmacist, Hüseyin Doğan, a judge, and Memiş Özdal, a landowner).[45] It notched up its best results in Elbistan and Pazarcık, two districts in the province with a large Alevi population. The victory of the CHP in the 1973 and 1977 general elections opened up access to the public-sector jobs that it now controlled and was thus able to distribute to members of the associations and trade unions that had supported it. This was further boosted as of 1978 when the CHP joined the government. Left-wing associations were then able to draw on the local and national balance of power to win influence, particularly in the police, state-run places of education in the provinces, the Post Office and Telephone company, the Forestry Directorate (Orman Müdürlüğü) and the Highways, Water, and Electricity Organisation (Yol Su Elektrik Teşkilatı).

Since the mid-1970s ülkücü and far-left organizations had been carrying out campaigns in the province, especially in factories and schools. The main far-left organizations there – Halkın Kurtuluşu, Devrimci Halkın Birliği, Halkın Yolu and Türkiye İşçi Köylü Partisi – had been conducting an energetic drive to mobilize rural populations in the province. On 1 May 1977 they staged a turnout of 1500 farmers and agricultural workers to celebrate Labour Day. The following year, over 2000 people attended the meeting organized by the Davutlar Village Peasant Union (Davutlar Köyü Köylü Birliği) and the Pazarcık Cultural Association (Pazarcık Kültür Derneği) to protest against the new agricultural labour law. On 28 October 1978 the demonstrating peasants chanted 'Down with the reactionary labour law!', 'Down with the agreement on social betrayal!' and 'Down with fascism, freedom for the people!'.[46]

The village populations took up arms to protect themselves against incursions by radical units. Trade union conflict in the town of Kahramanmaraş itself centred on the Pişkin mill (Pişkinler İplik Fabrikası), where a MİSK-affiliated ülkücü trade union, the Turkish Textile Workers Union (Türkiye Mensucat İşçileri Sendikası-Türk Mensucat-İş), confronted TEKSİF (Türkiye Tekstil Örme ve Giyim Sanayii İşçileri Sendikası-Textile, Turkish Clothing and Knitwear Workers Union), a member of Türk-İş, the largest trade union confederation in the country. Originally only TEKSİF was allowed to award contracts in the factory. But in April 1976 it lost this right to the ülkücü trade union.[47] In summer 1978 the Textile Union (Tekstil Sendikası), affiliated to DİSK – the far-left trade union confederation – opened a section in the factory, at a time when the CHP – supported by DİSK – was in government. Some of the workers joined this union, triggering altercations in the factory.[48] In reaction to this Abdurrahman Pişkin (the head of the mill and local AP figure) fired eighteen workers belonging to the new union, and then did likewise with the leaders of the resulting resistance movement. As the strike continued, he fired 381 unionized workers, before having to reinstate them when this decision was overturned by the court of justice. He then called upon the services of twenty or so armed men, provided by the ülkücü trade union, in order to maintain order in the factory. A report drawn up by the Kahramanmaraş police on 25 September

1978 states that far-right groups and workers recruited by MİSK and originally from villages in the province were continually provoking workers at the factory,[49] and the number of acts of violence against members of the new trade union rose continually through to the end of 1978. The Textile Union was attacked on several occasions by groups of MİSK, TEKSİF, MHP, Ülkü-Bir and ÜGD members.

Events in the Pişkin factory exacerbated the tensions between members of local ülkücü organizations, on the one hand, and members of far-left organizations and the CHP section, on the other. When the CHP joined the government in January 1978, there was an increase in the number of violent acts against members of organizations sympathetic to it. Most of these involved explosive devices. Bombs were set off on 16 January 1978 in front of the house of İsmail Ünlü, the head of the town's technical art school (Sanat okulu), and on 19 January in the factory of a person known to belong to the local CHP section. On 4 March the house of the public prosecutor was targeted; on 14 March the house of a left-wing teacher was destroyed, as was the Akın Coffee House, an Alevi café. On 26 March 1978 the Tüm-Tis headquarters was attacked (Türkiye Motorlu Taşıt İşçileri Sendikası, Turkish Motorised Transport Workers Union), followed by the CHP offices on 13 April. When the Alevi spiritual leader Sabri Özkan was assassinated by ülkücüs on 3 April 1978, a procession of 5000 people from the Alevi community, joined by activists and sympathizers from far-left organizations and the CHP, marched through the streets of the town chanting anti-fascist slogans.

The arrest in April 1978 of ülkücü militants involved in preparing bomb attacks brought to light the existence of ETKO, an underground ülkücü armed organization. The same day a post office worker died when he opened a parcel addressed to Memış Özdal, an Alevi landowner who had been a CHP candidate in the 1977 general elections. The subsequent investigation established that ETKO members were directly linked to the bomb.[50] Twenty-five suspects were arrested, including a son of the MHP member of parliament, Yusuf Özbaş.[51] The provincial BÜD section, the main local ülkücü youth organization, was shut down. Though tensions continued to run high, they were contained up until the bomb attack on the Çiçek Cinema on 19 December 1978.

The dynamics of the massacre

At 8 pm on 19 December several hundred people converged on the Çiçek Cinema to watch a film called *When Will the Sun Rise?* (by Cüneyt Arkın), in which Turks are portrayed fighting to survive Soviet oppression. The screenings, organized by the town's ÜGD section, had been running since the film came out on 16 December and were proving a great success, taking place in a thoroughly ülkücü atmosphere. At key moments in the film people cried, 'Muslim Turkey!', 'Victory to Islam even if we must spill our blood!', 'Government of murderers!', 'Communists back to Moscow!' and even 'Führer Türkeş!'.[52] At 8:45 pm, when ÜGD members were selling journals at the entrance to the cinema, a bomb went off in the building, injuring seven people. A man spotted running away from the cinema was arrested and temporarily held in the post office building. Nearly 300 people then left the cinema to march through the streets to the chants of 'Muslim Turkey!'.[53] They threw stones at the CHP buildings and at the post office where the suspect was being held, before being dispersed by the police. The following day the Akın café run by Yeni Mahalle, known as a place frequented by Alevis and left-wing sympathisers, was once again the target of a bomb attack, wounding several people. Thus far it may be seen as an ülkücü riposte to the provocation of the previous day. And for that matter it would seem that this is how all those involved interpreted these two explosions, with nothing suggesting the extremes that were to follow. On 21 December 1978 two Töb-Der members who taught at the Kahramanmaraş industrial high school, Hacı Çolak and Mustafa Yüzbaşıoğlu, were killed on their way back home after work. That same evening, left-wing activists sought to avenge them. At 6:50 pm they went to the house of a judo instructor, Güngör Gençay, crying out, ' Güngör you fascist, out of there!'. On learning he was absent they dynamited his house.[54]

The massacre only really started the following day (on 22 December), when a funeral procession comprising Töb-Der members, CHP and far-left sympathizers and students from the industrial high school headed towards the Grand Mosque (Ulu Cami) for the funeral preceding the burial of the two teachers. About 140 policemen and soldiers patrolled the crowd of about 5000 people. After a minute of silence in front of the school, the crowd marched towards the mosque to the cries of 'Mustafas and Hacis never die!', 'Türkeş is a murderer!' and 'Let's find the killers, make them pay for that'. When the procession neared the mosque, a group blocked the entrance. Individuals (no doubt ülkücüs) alerted the faithful who had gathered for Friday prayers, 'The communists are coming! The communists are burning the Grand Mosque The soldiers are with us! Why are you stopping? Do you have no religion? They are taking our religion! March! Kill the communists!'.[55] Nearly 10,000 people then converged on the mosque to the cries of 'Communists back to Moscow!', 'Muslim Turkey!' and 'Murderous power, Ecevit is a murderer!'. Witness accounts state that chairs, bricks and stones were thrown at the funeral procession, breaking the windows of buildings along the route belonging to right-wing sympathizers.

In front of the Grand Mosque the situation took a turn for the worse. The forces of law and order were unable to contain the situation and killed one of the men blocking the access to the mosque. The group of members of left-wing political, trade union and student organizations then left, whilst those who had been barring their entrance to the mosque – mainly ülkücü activists and sympathizers – turned against the police. One of them exhorted his companions to resist the forces of law and order: 'Kill the left-wingers! If the police arrest you, shoot the police. If soldiers arrest you, turn and fire on them too!'.[56] Ülkücüs torched a police car and a minibus belonging to the State Water Board (Devlet Su İşleri), destroyed trucks from the Gölbaş gendarme commando squad, wrecked a shop belonging to a brother of one of the assassinated left-wing teachers and smashed the windows of the assistant chief of police's car, causing him a head injury.[57]

At 8 pm the 300 or so ülkücüs who were still present were chased off by a military squadron. They went to nearby Cyprus Square, where they torched the premises of the CHP, the TİKP, DİSK, the Textile Union, Töb-Der, Pol-Der and the Health Affairs Directorate (Sağlık İşleri Müdürlüğü). They also attacked shops belonging to Alevis and left-wing sympathizers. When the fire engines arrived they barred the way, chanting, 'Strike for Allah!' (*Allah için vurun!*).[58] They asked MHP sympathizers and those who supported right-wing parties to paint three moons (the MHP symbol) on their windows or else to write up the letters MHP.[59] In the Alevi neighbourhood of Yörük Selim, left-wing organizations and neighbourhood militias readied themselves to respond to ülkücü attacks. Small groups were formed that attacked inhabitants from the neighbouring district of Mağralı, which was known to be home to MHP sympathizers. Two people were killed, taking to three the number of deaths denounced by ülkücüs.[60] At nightfall, the forces of law and order managed to disperse the group stationed on Cyprus Square, but during the night ülkücü activists alerted the population, brandishing the threat of a large-scale attack that the Alevis and far-left groups were said to be preparing for the following day. Hundreds of people armed themselves with axes, knives, bludgeons, revolvers and rifles. Ülkücü activists, drawing on the mechanisms used by the militia to exert oversight over the neighbourhoods, were able to mobilize the Sunni population to take part in defence operations planned for the next day. On 23 December at 8 am the day started with the announcement, broadcast over the loudspeakers of the mosque and of the town authorities, of the funeral of the three ülkücü 'martyrs' killed the day before.[61] The governor of the province, Tahsin Soylu, was worried by the turn of events and decreed a curfew. But the town officials turned back the policeman who had come to announce this decision, and continued to broadcast calls to attend the funerals. They only stopped when the army intervened, but by then it was too late. At the end of the morning nearly 15,000 people packed into Uzunoluk Avenue, running between the Grand Mosque and Yörük Selim, chanting, 'Death to communists!, "We shall not leave our friends" blood on the ground, we shall avenge ourselves!'. The crowd attacked shops, as it had the day before. A gun store was pillaged, and then a group headed towards the Yörük Selim neighbourhood, but was stopped by the army which threatened to open fire. A crowd of between 4000 and 5000 people stayed there until evening, obliging the army to maintain the barrage they had erected. Meanwhile, several hundred masked individuals headed towards Yörük Selim by other routes. Altercations broke out between the far-left militias protecting the neighbourhood and assailants armed with firearms and dynamite. The assailants, unable to force their way in, beat a retreat.[62] But if the inhabitants of the centre of Yörük Selim were protected by armed men, this was not the case for those living around its edge. Several accounts provide an idea of how the attacks targeting isolated houses and inhabitants took place. Hüseyin Ün, an Alevi, explained:

> On Saturday 23 December 1978, we heard the noise of bullets from over by the hospital. We went out in front of our house to have a look. A group was coming towards us, armed with revolvers and all sorts of tools. We threw stones at them to keep them away. They fired at us. We took refuge in the house. At that moment soldiers arrived and dispersed the attackers. Then in the evening they left. The

attackers had seen the soldiers leave, and came back into the neighbourhood. They fired at our house with an automatic. Then they entered the house, lined us up, and opened fire. Kamil Gülşen, Zeynep Ün, and Yusuf Lakap were killed. They left Şakir and me for dead.[63]

Mahmut Duran, another person living on the edge of Yörük Selim, described a similar attack:

They came back after a short while. Around midday they fired from outside. Around twenty-five or thirty people lit bottles full of oil. They threw them through the windows. The house started to burn. They broke down the door and came inside. They were holding wooden sticks, axes, and revolvers. They pushed us outside. Then they opened fire. My son Mehmet Duran was killed.[64]

Other participants in the gathering on Uzunoluk Avenue decided to go to the neighbourhood of Serintepe, to the south-west of Yörük Selim. According to witness reports, municipal buses and minibuses took a large number of individuals from other parts of the town to Serintepe.[65] Once these people had assembled there, several ülkücüs called on them to launch an attack: 'all those who have arms, knives, don't stop, kill and cleanse our country of the Alevis', 'Those who love God and his Prophet, march!', 'Kill the communist Alevis!', 'Death to Alevis!', 'Don't let the Alevis live! Those who kill them will go to paradise!', 'Death to communists!', 'Communists back to Moscow!' and 'Long live Türkeş!'.[66] They separated into several groups, armed with axes and rifles to attack the inhabitants of the neighbourhood and the houses on the edge of Yörük Selim.[67] According to the accounts provided by those who escaped, torture was committed and the bodies of the dead mutilated[68] and pounded with stones.[69] In Yeni Mahalle, a group killed a certain Süleyman Metin and set his corpse on fire, before forcing his daughters to parade through the streets naked. The crowd surrounded them shouting, 'Let's make their roots disappear from Turkey! Whores, prostitutes! Ecevit would come and save you if he could! What can you do with such Alevis? Communists!'.[70]

The assailants demanded that people recite the *salavat*, one of the verses from the Koran, so as to identify Alevis. Only those who could do so were released.[71]

On 24 December the attacks spread to other neighbourhoods in town, such as Namık Kemal, which was now targeted by the assailants. According to Maviş Toklu, an inhabitant, it all started when 'around 10 AM a group of attackers, galvanised to action by the local mayor (*muhtar*) Mehmet Yemşen, started crying out: "God, God, we are going to destroy the communists! We shall crush the heads of communists, be they young or old!"'.[72] But on the same day there were numerous acts of revenge in Kahramanmaraş and the surrounding villages, where radical groups were more strongly present. These were mainly carried out by small groups overseen by far-left activists. Peasants from Sarıerik attacked farms in Sarıkatipler and Pakdiller belonging to Sunni families. At the end of the day an army battalion from Kayseri managed to enter the neighbourhood of the town which had hitherto been held by the militias.[73]

On 25 December, when the situation had returned to normal in Kahramanmaraş, acts of vengeance continued in the rural areas of the province. The houses of Sunnis and right-wing sympathizers were ransacked and then torched in the village of Emiroğlu, in Pazarcık. Osman Adı Andız and Hasan Şako, two Sunnis from the village of Akdemir, on finding they were unable to enter the town of Kahramanmaraş, which had been sealed off by the forces of law and order, halted in the village of Çiğili, where they were beaten, and Andız killed.[74] The following day parliament voted to impose a two-month state of martial law in thirteen provinces, including Kahramanmaraş.[75] The official figures for the events recorded 111 people killed and over 1000 wounded, together with 552 shops, 289 houses and 8 vehicles torched.

Analysis of how the massacre unfolded

The dynamic behind events in Kahramanmaraş can be explained in terms of the balance of political and union power on the ground, activities to capture local public resources and the limited state presence in the province. The lack of means available to the forces of law and order enabled the militias to take control of numerous neighbourhoods and to establish monopolistic positions there. Ülkücü militias were able to draw on the benevolent attitude of the town authorities, who delegated control over certain resources to the militias in exchange for their (often physical) participation in the struggle against the CHP and its local allies. In the opposing camp, far-left organizations oversaw the populations living in neighbourhoods where the majority supported the CHP and protected them from the exactions of ülkücü units and militias. If events in Kahramanmaraş were on such a scale, it was because the militias were able to replace the public authorities and get the inhabitants to take part in the mobilization in exchange for the protection they provided. Given that the forces of law and order were unable to ensure general security, irregular violence became an instrument of power and a means of levering mobilization.

Furthermore, the electoral inroads being made by the CHP meant that the control Nationalist Front coalition parties had hitherto exerted over local resources and positions was now coming under threat. When the CHP joined the government, this led to a reshuffling in the distribution of jobs in devolved state institutions. In the province of Kahramanmaraş, where it won the 1977 general election, local associations and unions supporting CHP activities benefited from its access to government positions. In the police, the left-wing trade union Pol-Der interfered in numerous appointments and so now found itself in a position of dominance over Pol-Bir. On the other hand, the AP's presence in the municipal arena enabled parties in the Nationalist Front coalition (and notably the MHP) to draw on municipal resources and positions. The Nationalist Movement thus extended its control over the municipal realm by guaranteeing the AP that there would be no social unrest in the town – if necessary by using force. This is what happened when the local Nationalist Movement lent its support to the head of the Pişkin factory, who called upon MİSK to re-establish order and get the DİSK-affiliated trade union closed down. The physically violent activities implemented by the ülkücüs provided them with a dominant position in the power relations opposing them to the new trade union. Violence was thus used as a means of action in local political contests, enabling each of the actors in the AP/MHP coalition to hang on to the positions they already held, and to conquer new ones.

The devolved institutions of state found themselves pulled apart into two opposing factions, and acted as the battleground for antagonistic associations with conflicting interests. The members of these associations politicized their professional practices, and the balance of power which held in 1978 – in favour of CHP-allied organizations – led them to compete with staff working in institutions where recruitment was in the hands of the towns authorities. This situation transpired particularly clearly on the morning of 23 December 1978, when policemen who had been sent out by the governor to establish a curfew during the funeral of the three ülkücüs killed the day before encountered the refusal to cooperate by municipal personnel. The ülkücü activists gathered near the Grand Mosque viewed the police as a politicized institution under party control. The ülkücüs facing the forces of law and order chanted their standard slogans ('Nationalist Turkey!', 'Death to communists!'), but they also targeted the police ('Communist police!').[76] Police officers suspected of being acquainted with Alevis or far-left organizations were chased and beaten. The same day an imam, perched on a vehicle belonging to the town's technical services, harangued the crowd: 'worthless policemen tortured our children! Heroic children of Muslim Turkey and Kahramanmaraş, take our revenge on the communists!'.[77] Municipal employees were involved in fights, as too were officials from devolved state institutions. Fevzi Onaç, the head of the Highways, Water, and Electricity Organisation (Yol Su Elektrik), and his colleagues were subsequently found guilty of having led assaults against the Pak-Tuz and Eser Bulgur factories, considered as ülkücü strongholds, and for having carried out gun attacks on neighbourhoods under ülkücü control.[78] After the events of December, high-ranking police officers, together with senior officials working in the Post Office and Telephone company, the Forestry Directorate, the State Education authority, secondary schools, technical secondary schools and the business secondary school, were suspected of having helped left-wing organizations[79] carry out their acts of revenge.

The repercussions of the massacre

The events in Kahramanmaraş had strong repercussions on Turkish political life. They took place at the end of 1978, at a time when all observers agreed that the Ecevit government, in office since the beginning of the year, was failing to restore the state's authority. On 2 January 1979 Minister of Interior Özaydınlı resigned under pressure.[80] Since early autumn 1978 the MHP had repeatedly declared itself in favour of establishing martial law.[81] The zeal with which the new government was arresting numerous ülkücü activists and putting them on trial would appear to have encouraged the Nationalist Movement to wish for an army intervention, being persuaded that it would work to its advantage if the CHP government were placed under army oversight. The available data is insufficient to ascertain whether the attacks in Kahramanmaraş resulted from autonomous initiatives by local sections of the Nationalist Movement, or whether the party 'allowed' or even encouraged the riots.[82] However, the fact that the beginning of events coincided with declarations by Nationalist Movement cadres calling for the proclamation of martial law is striking to say the least. On 26 December 1978, all the political parties, including those fiercely opposed to the idea a few days earlier, accepted the need to vote for martial law in thirteen provinces for a two-month period. Special military tribunals were set up,[83] and the army took up quarters in the towns. Regional commands were established to coordinate the action of all the forces of law and order along with the judicial institutions. The number of provinces placed under martial law rose each time parliament prolonged the army's mandate.[84] Once martial law was established, the army made numerous interventions in political debate, before then seizing power in September 1980. However, the army did not place the government under its oversight, at least not until the end of 1979. It let Ecevit govern, and the regional martial law commands devoted as much energy to arresting left-wing as right-wing activists. The Nationalist Movement in the province of Kahramanmaraş was recognized as responsible for the events.[85] Some 813 people faced charges at the trial which opened on 4 June 1979 in Adana,[86] with the death sentence being called for against 330 of them, including the head of the MHP section in the province.[87] Many of those standing trial were members of local ülkücü sections,[88] and nearly all of the death sentences passed were against ülkücüs.[89]

Yet the introduction of martial law did not put an end to the activities to capture resources or to the processes de-objectifying public institutions. Events in Kahramanmaraş even led to their escalation at the local level. Numerous Alevi families went back to their village of origin or else settled in the province's rural zones. According to Bölügiray, a quarter of the population in the district of Andırın, in the west of the province, was comprised of families who had migrated in the wake of events at Maraş. They settled in the zones overseen by left-wing militias, accepting their offer of protection all the more readily as the forces of law and order had failed to guarantee their security in the provincial capital.

Martial law did not act as a restraint on the militias and activists from the two camps. In the zones affected by the militia phenomenon, there was what Hamit Bozarslan calls a territorial 'fragmentation' or 'division':[90]

> The militia acted to set up sub-units comprising the same individuals, operating under the same military constraints, with obvious repercussions in the economy (controlling production and distribution networks), cultural affairs (the homogenisation of cultural resources), religion, and so on and so forth.[91]

Within these circumscribed territories, the militias exerted a monopoly over political and economic resources. They had the requisite means of violence to maintain their positions and acquire legitimacy with the population, who were convinced that the state was unable to ensure their protection. Although the level of violence dropped during the early months of martial law, the army was unable to prevent it rising again in the wake of confrontations between antagonistic groups. When Bölügiray took up his position as martial law commander in the south-east of the country in August 1979, his predecessor drew his attention to the personnel shortages, rendering it futile to try to re-establish security in the zone placed under his command.[92] Village inhabitants pooled money to buy weapons and reply to attacks from external militias. In city neighbourhoods with a strong Alevi presence, left-wing groups used the clamour triggered by events in Kahramanmaraş to step up their activities and impose armed control[93] over populations who placed greater faith in them than in the police, exposed to penetration by ülkücüs since the AP's return to power in November 1979.

In most cases the disconnect between local and national arenas was only partial, since the networks of collusion continued to operate, linking political and administrative staff in the antagonistic movements to local violence entrepreneurs. In addition to this, the national ambition of groups involved in the process of territorial fragmentation evaporated more rapidly amongst far-left organizations than it did amongst those from the Nationalist Movement.[94] Indeed, the MHP continued to expand the movement's geographical presence right up until the military intervention of 12 September 1980.

In 1979 and 1980 the use of violence as a means of political interaction became generalized. Groups external to the two movements took up arms in order to defend themselves or else take part in resource capture. Others affiliated to moderate political parties provided training in combat sports, or else created units to stand up to far-left and ülkücü sections. One such instance was the Akıncılar Association (Akıncılar Derneği), originally set up in 1975 as a straightforward youth association, and whose members tended to belong to the MSP, the Islamist party headed by Necmettin Erbakan. But faced with the electoral advances of the MHP and the way it was eating into the party's traditional electorate, the association's members decided to set up a series of structures along the same lines as the ülkücü model. Several associations were established such as the Akıncı Workers (Akıncı İşçiler), the Akıncı Officials (Akıncı Memurlar) and the Akıncı Athletes (Akıncı Sporcular) in order to oversee and expand the party's electorate. In 1979 there were 1200 Akıncılar sections in the country. On 22 November 1979 their general bureau was shut down, but the association was re-established in March 1980 under the new name of the Young Akıncı Association (Akıncı Gençler Derneği), headquartered in Konya, a province that was not under martial law. It then set up thirty or so armed action training camps, notably in Kayseri,[95] with the purpose of preparing 'the brothers in religion for the functions they will assume in the difficult struggle that is soon to come'.[96]

As of early 1980, the chief of army staff made an increasing number of declarations stating that the army would not remain inactive in the face of the unrest afflicting the country, and the threat that the army would intervene without parliamentary mandate started to take on definite shape. Organizations prepared for this by reinforcing their local positions. It was as if the anticipated military coup was encouraging actors from both action systems to step up their activities to capture resources and mobilize supporters in local arenas. The groups set up an increasing number of new municipal sanctuaries where they planned on repatriating their personnel in the event of military intervention. For the far left, these liberated zones were to act as the rear bases in the guerrilla warfare it planned on conducting once the army took power. Mahmut, a member of the Dev-Yol military apparatus, gave the following explanation:

> We were talking about Fatsa, and well, Demirel sent a new governor to Fatsa who organised Operation Nokta, sending in tanks, helicopters, and boats, and with masked fascists guiding the forces of law and order. Fikri [Sönmez, the mayor] was taken into custody. So we were pretty sure the coup was imminent and tried to set up organisations in the countryside. As of 1980 we tried to set up an organisation in Adana, along an axis running from Tunceli to Artvin, and along another passing through Malatya, Sivas, and Ordu, with an axis parallel to the Mediterranean, and one parallel to the Black Sea. We insisted especially on the axes parallel to the seas. Over the course of 1979 and 1980 we set up Revolutionary War Units (Devrimci Savaş Birliği, DSB) for the towns, and Armed Resistance Units (Silahlı Direniş Birlikleri, SDB) for rural guerrilla operations.[97]

For the ülkücüs, the local positions they controlled held out the possibility of negotiating with the army to share power with the government to be set up in the wake of the military intervention. This tactic seemed reasonable in the light of past experience, for though the 1960 and 1971 coups had led to a redistribution of power in the central institutions of state, the local power relations and equilibriums had been largely unaffected. For the organizations from the two conflicting movements, the social, political and economic positions they held in local arenas acted as a guarantee that they would retain their control over accumulation mechanisms in the event of military intervention. For the MHP, they were to be used as a way to establish the party as an essential partner for the military.

But the coup of 12 September 1980 was unparalleled in its scale and violence. The National Security Council, contrary to the expectations of the MHP, did not recognize the Nationalist Movement as a credible partner. As for the far-left organizations, directly affected by the systematic arrests being carried out by the army, they failed to establish any real urban or rural guerrilla campaign. Nor did they manage to involve the population, the vast majority of whom seemed to accept the strong-handed military coup as a necessary stage in re-establishing the authority of the state in the wake of the confrontations between antagonistic groups that had been leaving nearly twenty people dead nationwide every day.

Violence as a means of legitimizing the military coup

The military coup of 12 September 1980 strikes many observers as a natural outcome of the crisis. It is argued that the number of victims (over twenty people killed every day over the summer of 1980), the spread of violence as a mode of political action, the institutional deadlock (as embodied by parliament's inability to elect a new president of the republic after ninety-six votes between April and July 1980), and, as of 1979, the scale of the economic crisis, led irremediably to the army's intervention. This view of events is, however, only partially correct, since it legitimizes the intervention as a precondition for ending the 'chaos', without enquiring into how the military institution may have used the political crisis and the accompanying violence sustaining it.

The claim here is clearly not that the military was waiting for an opportunity to come to power. The military could not, indeed, have intervened if a grand coalition between the CHP and the AP had been established in 1973 or 1977, if a president had been elected in 1980 or if there had been effective and stable governments in the 1970s. But growing violence undeniably served as a justification for the military to take power.

Rather than seeing the escalation and spread of violence and the resulting ungovernability as principles explaining why the military intervention occurred, I believe they are better viewed as elements used to legitimize and justify the coup to the population and to the country's international allies and creditors.[98] Hence the effects of violence on political contest also need to be interpreted in the light of how violence provided the army with an opportunity to acquire a central position. The military intervention was not the product of violence; it was the violence which provided the military with the opportunity to implement an alternative social and political programme, one that excluded the 1970s politicians and the protagonists in the mechanisms leading up to the military intervention. And so if we are to understand how the mobilization by radical groups and the attendant violence increased the army's influence over political contest up until the moment it seized power, then we need to look at the relationship between military and civilian circles prior to its intervention.[99]

The state of martial law approved by parliament in the wake of the Kahramanmaraş massacre, and its extension to an increasing number of provinces each time it was prolonged, enabled the army to intervene directly in the political contest as of 1979. When the AP returned to power in November 1979, at the head of a minority government, the influence of the army became considerable. On 27 December 1979 the military staff sent Present Korutürk a warning letter (*uyarı mektubu*), urging the government to put an end to the 'anarchy' (*anarşi*), 'terror' (*terör*) and 'divisions' (*bölücülük*), and indicating that should it fail to do so, the army would take the necessary steps to remedy the situation itself. On 2 January 1980 the president of the republic summoned Bülent Ecevit and Süleyman Demirel to inform them of the military's position and the contents of this letter. The next day the *Hürriyet* newspaper published substantial excerpts from it. Demirel, who had been prime minister for a bit less than a month, then had a string of meetings with the military staff to whom he submitted each decision he planned on implementing.

Changes taking place in the international (and especially regional) political context in late 1979 – with the USSR intervening in Afghanistan, and Iran rising up against the Shah – pushed Turkey's international creditors to support its economy so as to prevent it from succumbing to political instability. The IMF and its intermediary the United States extended Turkey the largest loans it had ever hitherto agreed. In exchange for this the government undertook to reform the country's economy. On 24 January 1980 Demirel presented a series of measures: the Turkish lira was devalued by 32.7 per cent and its exchange rate was now allowed to float on a daily basis; salaries were frozen and agricultural subsidies scrapped; the country significantly reduced customs duties, foreign investment was encouraged and foreign trade was liberalized. This programme, which had been given prior consent by the military, was the work of Turgut Özal, who at the time was secretary of state to the prime minister. Özal had been a member of the State Planning Organisation (Devlet Planlama Teşkilatı) during the 1960s, before joining the World Bank in the early 1970s, going on to be the coordinator for Sabancı Holding, one of the largest economic groups in Turkey. He was exactly the type of person on whom the military would rely during their three years in power from 1980 to 1983, and he went on to become economic affairs adviser to the prime minister up until 14 June 1982, when he founded the Motherland Party (Anavatan Partisi), before going on to win the general elections marking the return to civilian power.

The announcement and implementation of these measures added to the worsening social climate. Rising unemployment and inflation led to an increasing number of strikes, and demonstrations were staged to protest against the decisions of 24 January, drawing hundreds of thousands of people out onto the streets. The CHP leader Bülent Ecevit was against these measures. He argued that the social unrest they would inevitably spark would render them inoperative – unless one imagined they were implemented by a military regime, something he suspected the army of wanting to do. The joint chief of staff appeared to share this opinion, and a few years later declared to a journalist who had come to interview him, Mehmet Ali Birand, that he was persuaded that the measures of 24 January would have been to no effect had the army not taken the necessary steps. Yet in early 1980 the military staff stated it wished to privilege a civilian solution to the country's economic and social difficulties, calling on Turkey's two main political parties to set up a government of national unity. But once the measures of 24 January had been proclaimed, the CHP could no longer envisage entering into an alliance with the AP without running the risk of being deserted by part of its electorate. For its part the MSP withdrew the parliamentary support it had been providing the Demirel government since November. In a press conference on 13 March 1980, the MSP leader, Erbakan, declared he wanted to 'let the government stew', and would thus back any vote of no confidence brought against one of its ministers.[100]

Between January and September 1980, the army waited for the right moment to intervene, sending an increasing number of ultimatums to the politicians, which did nothing to end the institutional deadlock. Notes taken by Kenan Evren, the joint chief of staff, on 24 May 1980, show that he had been envisaging the possibility of a military intervention since the spring,[101] at a time when no candidate was able to gather enough votes in parliament to be elected president of the republic. Whilst the lack of reliable information on the subject makes it impossible to arrive at a detailed understanding of the decision processes within the military staff, it was clearly operating under a series of constraints, waiting in particular until international creditors extended the country new credit lines before acting. A first opportunity arose in early July 1980, when the CHP brought a vote of no confidence against the government, which would necessarily precipitate early elections if it fell since the parliamentary balance of power precluded setting up a new coalition government. The military staff anticipated that the government would find itself in the minority before 11 July.[102] On 17 June the Flag Plan (Bayrak Planı) was drawn up,[103] and all army commands received the order to intervene at 4 am on 11 July. But the Demirel government managed to win the vote of no-confidence, while renewed negotiations to obtain further loans dragged on in Paris. The violence peaked in July and August 1980. The army then seized the opportunity that presented itself in September. During an MSP public meeting, held on 6 September, militias wearing commando uniforms paraded in the streets of Konya, calling for the introduction of sharia, the liberation of Jerusalem and an end to secularity in Turkey, booing when the national anthem was sung. A CHP public meeting was planned for the coming days, and the DİSK trade union confederation called for a general strike. Many observers feared that the country was about to go up in flames. In the night of 11 to 12 September a National Security Council took power, made up of the Joint Head of Staff Kenan Evren, together with the army, navy and air force heads of staff. The military shut down all political parties, all trade unions and 23,667 associations. They suspended parliamentary activity, and most politicians found themselves behind bars; 650,000 people were taken into custody, the use of torture became widespread and a purge was conducted of the public sector.[104]

The army implemented a genuine social and economic revolution. It transformed the country's political economy, set up a security regime[105] and established institutions and measures enabling it to maintain its influence over political contest for many years to come. It promoted a Turko-Islamic ideology intended to guarantee the population conformed to the order it embodied, and relied on business leaders, who were amongst the main beneficiaries of its intervention. Unions were shut down, wages were reduced and union rights were severely restricted. The country went from being a redistributive planned economy based on comparatively broad social and civic rights to an ultra-liberal model whose efficiency was underpinned by the implementation of a political system based on security, and in which the army subsequently occupied a central place for over twenty years.

CONCLUSION

The general view of the second half of the 1970 tends to present the period as a parenthesis, brought to a close by the military intervention of 12 September 1980. Antagonistic radical mobilizations, endowed with a similar capacity for disrupting the social order and political contest, are said to have initiated an uncontrollable process of escalating violence; this, it is argued, triggered the failure of the state, which found itself unable to maintain order and infested by political parties that were more interested in distributing state sinecures than in seeking to govern the country. The 'disruptions' of the 1970s are thus presented as stemming from the degeneration of the political regime grounded in the 1961 Constitution that the coup of 12 March 1971 failed to redress due to the laxity of the measures adopted. In this view of things, the political elites' inability to deal with the crisis, the political parties' increasing drift towards clientelism and the continuing escalation of violence and social disruption left the army – *qua* guarantor of the autonomy and continuity of state – as the sole institution capable of re-establishing order and re-asserting the sovereignty of state.

Yet this interpretation of the period does not stand up to analysis, especially since there was nothing exceptional about the use made of the state by social and political forces during the 1970s. We have seen how practices to penetrate the state and capture its resources reach back to the beginning of the Republic, and perhaps beyond, and how the shift to a multi-party system, by destabilizing any lasting hold over state positions, merely modified the forms this phenomenon took. Given the historical continuity of these practices, the field of state needs to be seen as a place for accumulation, mobilization and competition between the actors involved in capturing its resources. When the military took power in 1980, this in no way put an end to activities to penetrate the state, and instead merely brought about a change of those involved. When the army handed power back to the civilians in 1983, the new institutional positions it now enjoyed gave it an advantage in the struggle to access public resources; the indirect control it exerted over political life up until the early 2000s meant that the political parties were obliged to work with the army, having to either rely upon its institutions or else obtain its certification in order to secure state revenue streams. Furthermore, condemnation of the links that held during the 1970s between the public sector and criminal milieus did little to hide the fact that this type of collusion continued to exist after the military coup. As of 1984, coalitions were set up between members of the security institutions (the army, police and intelligence services), politicians (ministers and MPs) and entrepreneurs in intermittent violence (reconverted *ülkücü* activists, militia members and tribal groups) in order to capture the security revenue streams generated by the war against the PKK in the south-east of the country. These predatory forms of collusion were often confined in geographical scope, but links between official sectors, political parties and criminal or mafia networks continued to exist. And whilst, under the tutelage of the army, the actors involved changed between 1980 and the early 2000, the ways in which the state was used did not, as we have seen over the course of this study.

And so this work helps shed light on how institutions in Turkey operate on a routine basis. For instance, it shows that there was nothing 'deviant' about the activities carried out by conflicting groups to penetrate the state in the 1970s. Equally, it sets out certain avenues of enquiry for arriving at a better understanding of the political trajectory taken by Republican Turkey, emphasizing in particular interpenetration of the party political and State fields as an attested historical fact. Once in government, political parties hold all the cards they need to take up and appropriate state positions and siphon off its resources on a massive scale. Since parties are essential partners for social forces working to access public resources (companies, trade unions, interest groups and so on), they are in a position to build up broad coalitions and thereby reinforce their power. Within this context political – or more specifically party political – rationales are a key factor in how the society and economy are regulated. These avenues of enquiry could be explored by carrying out systematic studies of the links between the state and party political fields in Turkey, privileging relational analysis of the exchanges and flows between actors and leaving to one side any static examination of how the Turkish 'political regime' functions, where this latter approach cannot fail to disappoint any observers attentive to the multiple configurations it has assumed over time.

Lastly, the case of Turkey can be used to further our understanding of political crises in which a state loses its capacity to exert its monopoly over the legitimate use of symbolic and physical violence. We have seen how the MIIP copied state penetration practices that were absolutely run-of-the-mill for a governing party in Turkey. We have also seen how the innovative aspect of its activity resided in the way it used its positions to spread the conflict and radicalize it by using violence, within a socio-economic context in which the state did not have the requisite means to stamp it out. The activities conducted by ülkücüs and far-left groups to capture resources thus enabled them (each in their own way) to become one with state institutions and modify the structural constraints incumbent upon them. As a counterpart to this, they influenced how these institutions operated on a daily basis by politicizing their members' practices. Public institutions thus became arenas for conflicts of interest (political, economic, professional etc.) where these were connected with the political divides imported by the mobilized groups. These institutions thereby lost their objectivity towards users, who were obliged to place themselves in the hands of the organizations involved in resource capture so as to draw on the redistribution of those resources or benefit from their protection. It was within this specific context that violent practices tended to become generalized across social sectors. Thus the level of violence peaked whenever the MHP had access to the central institutions of state but was excluded from accessing public resources at the local level. Hence the spread of violence may be interpreted as indicative of a general modification in the rules of political context, in which all the actors tended to take up the use of violence within their resource accumulation strategies. By the end of the decade mobilization, resource capture and the use of violence had become the three main forms of political action employed by ülkücü and far-left groups, as well as by an increasing number of moderate groups, parties and actors who did not wish to be sidelined.

The approach taken in these pages towards the Turkish crisis has been based on close observation of the tactical activities deployed by various protagonists in the institutions of state and in the streets. The results obtained suggest that particular attention needs to be paid to the crisis strategies certain actors adopt (and to those strategies they adopt within the crisis). It has also emphasized how the initiatives of the Nationalist Movement significantly influenced the way these processes transpired. The various lines of action adopted by the Nationalist Movement – which may be summarized as a three-pronged strategy of *electoral involvement, capturing public resources and armed violence* – furthered its tactic of accessing power whilst intensifying the crisis mechanisms it was drawing on to reinforce its positions. And so furthering our understanding of political crises such as that which Turkey experienced in the second half of the 1970s involves analysis of the ways in which the practices of mobilized groups help modify the formal and informal rules governing social contests.

NOTES

Introduction

1. See Hamit Bozarslan, 'Le chaos après le déluge? Notes sur la crise turque des années 70', *Cultures et Conflits*, 24–25, winter-spring 1996–7, pp. 73–97.
2. The set of extremist right-wing organizations discussed in this work forms what is commonly referred to as the Nationalist Movement, a network of organizations based around a political party, the Nationalist Movement Party (Milliyetçi Hareket Partisi, MHP), which sought to control and politicize the electorate within different professional sectors. In Turkey the organizations and members of the Movement called themselves *ülkücüs* (idealists). That is why the Nationalist Movement is described here as an 'ülkücü action system'. Both terms will be used indiscriminately to designate the network of organizations built up by the MHP as of the second half of the 1960s. The direct translation of *ülkücü* (idealist) and *ülkü* (ideal) would have been too confusing for the English reader unfamiliar with the Turkish political context and unsettling for the Turkish reader. In English, 'idealist', indeed, doesn't indicate the fact that these ülkücü activists and movements were part of the far right. The choice has thus been made to use the Turkish *ülkücü* (and *ülkücüs* in the plural).
3. 'Bir öğrenci öldürüldü … Sokak savaşı oldu', *Milliyet*, 17 January 1977, p. 1.
4. '40°C in Adana. As hot as Africa. No water, ongoing power cuts, darkness and anarchy are taking hold everywhere.' Quoted by N. Bölügiray, *Sokaktaki Asker, Bir Sıkıyönetim Komutanının 12 Eylül Öncesi Anıları*, Istanbul, Milliyet Yayınları, 1989.
5. H. F. Güneş, 'Türkiye'de terör, anarşi ve mücadele yolları', *Polis Magazin*, 15, 8, 1980, pp. 8–13.
6. The press regularly published 'terror' and 'anarchy statistics'. A press review mentioned in the memoirs of Commander Nevzat Bölügiray gave: 'Statistics for terror in Turkey between 6 January 1978 and 21 August 1979: 9034 acts of terror and anarchy. 2016 people killed. 9227 people injured, of whom 465 students, 109 teachers, 226 workers, 66 policemen, 16 officers, NCOs, and soldiers, 5 judges, and 1089 people of various professions. 1000 people died in 1978. 87 people were assassinated over the month of August 1978, but by August 1979 this number had risen to 147.' N. Bölügiray, *Sokaktaki Asker, op. cit.,* p. 18.
7. S. Haffner, *Defying Hitler. A Memoir*, New York, Picador, 2000, p. 101.
8. The CHP was set up by Mustafa Kemal. During the 1970s it took up the centre-left ground under the leadership of Bülent Ecevit, and was the dominant governing party from 7 January to 18 September 1974, from 22 June to 21 July 1977 and from 15 January 1978 to 12 November 1979.
9. 'Türkeş: "komünizm, Ecevit iktidarının kanatları altında"', *Hergün*, 10 July 1978, p. 1; 'Komünistler halk savaşı hazırlıyor', *Hergün*, 27 August 1978, p. 1; 'MHP Lideri Türkeş, "bölücü ve komünistler iç savaş yaratmak istiyor"', *Hergün*, 11 February 1979, p. 1.
10. 'Devlet Kars'a giremiyor', *Hergün*, 26 October 1978, pp. 1 and 7.

11 'Faşist teröre karşı savaşalım', *Devrimci Yol*, 20, 31 July 1978.
12 'The fascist dogs shall pay for each of their crimes and their massacres! The working people must respond to each of their ignoble attacks. The blood of the dead shall not remain on the ground!', *Devrimci Yol*, 21, 21 August 1978, p. 1.
13 'Türkeş: "sıkıyönetim derhal ilân edilerek anarşi durdurulmalı"', *Cumhuriyet*, 5 October 1978, pp. 1 and 9; 'MHP sıkıyönetim istedi', *Hergün*, 5 October 1978, p. 1.
14 There were seven successive governments between 1974 and 1980: the Ecevit government (CHP, MSP) from 17 January to 18 November 1974, the İrmak government from 17 November 1974 to 31 March 1975, the first Nationalist Front government (AP, MSP, MHP, CGP) from 31 March 1975 to 22 June 1977, the second Ecevit government (CHP) from 22 June 1977 to 21 July 1977, the second Nationalist Front government (AP, MSP, MHP) from 21 July 1977 to 5 January 1978, the third Ecevit government (CHP, DP, independents) from 15 January 1978 to 12 November 1979 and the Demirel government (AP) from 12 November 1979 to 12 September 1980.
15 O. Müftüoğlu, *1960'lardan 1980'e Türkiye Gerçeği*, Istanbul, Patika Yayınları, 1989.
16 M. A. Birand, H. Bilâ and R. Akar, *12 Eylül. Türkiye'nin miladı*, Istanbul, Doğan Kitap, 2006, p. 122.
17 Bölügiray, *Sokaktaki Asker, op. cit.*; K. Bulutoğlu, *Bunalim ve Çikiş*, Istanbul, Tekin Yayınları, 1980.
18 The two antagonistic movements may be viewed as action systems, where this expression designates networks of organizations in which 'the social insertion of political militants… may be detected in numerous systems of belonging, sketching out characteristic configurations in alliances between organisations, even though these "alliances" are neither formal nor official'. The officialization of the links created 'legitimises the claim made by leaders to represent a social group or a set of social groups said to have common interests, facilitating the spread of shared beliefs regarding social life, thereby making it easier for militants to progress from one position in their career to another'. See J. Lagroye, B. François and F. Sawicki, *Sociologie Politique*, Paris, Presses de Sciences Po and Dalloz, 2002, pp. 291–2.
19 The MHP took part in the so-called 'Nationalist Front' coalition governments (Milliyetçi Cephe), from 31 March 1975 to 22 June 1977, and from 21 July 1977 to 5 January 1978. In the general election of 14 October 1973 it won 3.38 per cent of the vote and three parliamentary seats, enabling it to obtain two ministries in the first Nationalist Front coalition government that was set up by the Justice Party (Adalet Partisi, AP) to marginalize the CHP, which had come first in the elections. The improved performance of the MHP in the general election of 5 June 1977 (winning 6.42 per cent of the vote and 16 seats) brought it five ministries in the second Nationalist Front government (21 July 1977–5 January 1978).
20 Z. Kırdemir, *Devrim bize yakışırdı*, Istanbul, Ozan Yayıncılık, 2004.
21 M. A. Birand, *12 eylül. Saat: 04.00*, Istanbul, Karacan Yayınları, 1985.
22 Anthony Giddens argues that 'rules cannot be conceptualised apart from resources, which refer to the modes whereby transformative relations are actually incorporated into the production and reproduction of social practices. Structural properties thus express forms of domination and power'. A. Giddens, *The Constitution of Society*, Oakland, University of California Press, 1984, p. 18.
23 For a critique of the idea of state autonomy, see the works by George Steinmetz, and especially George Steinmetz, 'The myth and the reality of an autonomous

state: Industrialists, junkers and social policy in imperial Germany', *Comparative Social Research*, 12, 1990, pp. 239-93.
24 See in particular M. Heper, *The State Tradition in Turkey*, Northgate, The Eothen Press, 1985, and 'The state, religion and pluralism: The Turkish case in comparative perspective', *British Journal of Middle Eastern Studies*, 18, 1, 1991, pp. 38-51; Ş. Mardin, 'Power, civil society and culture in the Ottoman Empire', *Comparative Studies in Society and History*, 11, 3, June 1969, pp. 258-81; E. Özbudun, *Social Change and Political Participation in Turkey*, Princeton, New Jersey, Princeton University Press, 1976.
25 P. Dumont, *Mustafa Kemal invente la Turquie moderne*, Paris, Complexe, 2006.
26 See for example L. L. Roos and N. P. Roos, *Managers of Modernisation: Organizations and Elites in Turkey (1950-1969)*, Cambridge, Harvard University Press, 1971, and A. Özman, 'Law, ideology and modernisation in Turkey: Kemalist legal reforms in perspective', *Social and Legal Studies*, 19, 1, March 2010, pp. 67-84.
27 Feroz Ahmad argues that 'the notion of an Islamic state was anathema to Mustafa Kemal and his supporters. They viewed such a state as the way to maintain the status quo and perpetuate the backwardness of Turkey. For their part, the Kemalists wanted to see Turkey transformed into a modern nation state which, in the words of Mustafa Kemal (Atatürk), would "live as an advanced and civilised nation in the midst of contemporary civilisation". Such a nation would have to be secular and rational, emphasising science and modern education in order to create a modern industrial economy'. F. Ahmad, *The Making of Modern Turkey*, London, Routledge, 1993, p. 53.
28 The army intervened on 27 May 1960 against the government of the Democrat Party, accused of drifting too far towards authoritarianism, on 12 March 1971 against the 'fratricidal conflict and economic and social disorder [threatening] the future of the Republic of Turkey', on 12 September 1980 against ungovernability and civil war, and against an 'Islamist' government in the 'velvet' coup of 28 February 1997. Jacob Landau, referring to the coups of 1960 and 1971, argues that the former was essentially a coup against a majority party which was neglecting reform and modernization, whilst the latter sought to reduce the violent activities being carried out by radical groups. J. M. Landau, *Radical Politics in Modern Turkey*, Leiden, E. J. Brill, 1974, p. 288. Landau also quotes F. Ahmad, *The Turkish Experiment in Democracy, 1950-1975*, Boulder, Co., Westview Press, 1977, p. 205. For a critical analysis of this interpretation, see G. Dorronsoro and B. Gourisse, 'The Turkish army in politics. Institutional autonomy, the formation of social coalitions, and the production of crises', *Revue française de science politique*, 65, 4, 2015, pp. 609-31.
29 The idea of the *tertius gaudens* (the rejoicing third) was originally developed by Georg Simmel, before being taken up by Charles Tilly to describe the role played by the state in its interactions with mobilized groups. See G. Simmel, *Sociology: Enquiries into the Construction of Social Forms*, Leiden, Brill, 2009, and C. Tilly, *From Mobilisation to Revolution*, Reading, MA, Addison-Wesley Publishing Company, 1978.
30 The Turkish state was not totally penetrated by radical groups. Indeed, a system of public sector recruitment based on competitive exams existed, even though it was often circumvented or gamed. Certain state sectors were less affected by this politicization, diplomacy being a good example, with diplomats' professional culture and social recruitment limiting the hold parties had over their practices. Other sectors, particularly strategic ones, were more directly targeted by radical groups, such as institutions in charge of law and order (the police), as well as those pertaining

to places of protest (universities, high schools etc.) and to the accumulation of resources (the Ministry of Customs and Monopolies).
31 When the MHP was in government the ülkücü Confederation of Nationalist Workers Unions (Milliyetçi İşçi Sendikaları Konfederasyonu, MİSK) established its hold in nearly all public-sector companies in order to lend its backing to management and to silence left-wing trade unionists, by force if necessary. The local section thereby obtained the right to select personnel, who were recruited from amongst ülkücü milieus in town.
32 M. Dobry, *Sociologie des crises politiques*, Paris, Presses de la FNSP, 1992, p. 154.
33 As Jean-Louis Briquet and Gilles Favarel-Garrigues observe, 'possession of know-how and the use of violence in many... cases serve as a bargaining chip in negotiating with the public authorities', J-L Briquet and G. Favarel-Garrigues, *Organised Crime and States: The Hidden Face of Politics*, Palgrave MacMillan, The Sciences Po Series in International Relations and Political Economy, New York, 2010, p. 5.

Chapter 1

1 J. S. Migdal, *State in Society: Studying How States and Societies Transform and Constitute One Another*, Cambridge, Cambridge University Press, 2001.
2 And so to a certain extent 'actors are found neither in nor outside the State. Rather, all actors, depending on circumstance, sometimes participate within a statist dimension and sometimes turn away from it'. J.-F. Bayart, *The State in Africa: The Politics of the Belly*, London, Polity, 2009 [1993], p. 254.
3 Ibid., p. 20.
4 S. Faroqhi, 'Political initiatives "from the bottom up" in the sixteenth- and seventeenth-century Ottoman Empire: Some evidence for their existence', in G. M. Hans (ed.), *Osmanistiche Studien zur Wirtschafts- und Sozialgeschichte: In Memoriam Vanco Boskov*, Wiesbaden, Otto Harrasowitz, 1986, 'Political tensions in the Anatolian countryside around 1600: An attempt at interpretation', in J.-L. Bacqué-Gramont et al., 'Festschrift for Robert Anhegger', *Varia Turcica*, 9, 1987, and 'Political activity among Ottoman taxpayers and the problem of Sultanic legitimation (1570–1650)', *Journal of the Economic and Social History of the Orient*, 35, 1992, pp. 1–39.
5 Meeker shows that 'the military, treasury and judicial officials were members of a special class without ties to the lands and people they governed'. M. E. Meeker, *A Nation of Empire. The Ottoman Legacy of Turkish Modernity*, Berkeley and Los Angeles, University of California Press, 2002, p. 114.
6 Jean-François Bayart notes that it 'transpires that the Empire was far less intrusive than myths of "Oriental despotism" would suggest. It knew for instance how to accommodate local situations and reproduced Byzantium's pragmatic approach to laisser-faire, both in trade and in the monetary field. Its interventionism was "selective" and sought primarily to safeguard the supply of Istanbul'. J.-F. Bayart, *L'Islam républicain. Ankara, Téhéran, Dakar*, Paris, Albin Michel, 2010, p. 40.
7 Meeker argues that in the early nineteenth century 'like the Sultan, the Agha was also a ruler, only in miniature. He, too, had a grand house, many wives, many children, many followers, armed supporters, a resident imam, a resident mosque, a hospital, and a jail'. M. E. Meeker, *Social Practice and Political Culture in the Turkish Republic*, Istanbul, The Isis Press, 2004, p. 181.

8   S. J. Shaw, 'Local administrations in the tanzimat', in D. Y. Hakki (ed.), *150. yılında Tanzimat*, Ankara, Türk Tarih Kurumu Yayınları, 1992, pp. 33–49, quoted by M. Aymes, 'Affaires courantes pour marcheurs d'empire. Le métier d'administrateur dans les provinces ottomanes au XIXe siècle', *Genèses*, 72, 2008, p. 4.
9   Ibid., p. 10.
10 M. Heper, *The State Tradition in Turkey*, Northgate, The Eothen Press, 1985, p. 42.
11 R. Kasaba, 'A time and a place for the nonstate: Social change in the Ottoman Empire during the long nineteenth century', in J. S. Migdal, A. Kohli and V. Shue (eds), *State, Power and Social Forces: Domination and Transformation in the Third World*, Cambridge, Cambridge University Press, 1994, pp. 207–30.
12 M. E. Meeker, *A Nation of Empire*, op. cit., p. xxii.
13 J. F. Bayart, *The State in Africa: The Politics of the Belly*, op. cit., p. 246.
14 M. E. Meeker, *A Nation of Empire*, op. cit., p. 256.
15 The idea here is not to suggest that there was any determinism at work in the passage from the Empire to the Republic but rather to inscribe the Republic within the historical matrix formed by 'the concatenation of the Empire with the Republic', by identifying the synchronic and diachronic interactions of which it was constituted. See J.-F. Bayart, *Les Études postcoloniales, un carnaval académique*, Paris, Karthala, 2010.
16 M. Heper, *The State Tradition in Turkey*, op. cit., p. 55.
17 The law also states that lists of those not selected were to be examined, and that those who had not been opposed to the nationalist cause would be deemed to have resigned, and would receive the appropriate salary. See M. Heper, *The State Tradition in Turkey*, op. cit., p. 56.
18 Ibid., pp. 56–7.
19 M. Heper, *The State Tradition in Turkey*, op. cit., pp. 69–70.
20 L. V. Thomas and R. N. Frye, *The United States and Turkey and Iran*, Cambridge, The MIT Press, 1965, p. 163.
21 M. Heper, *The State Tradition in Turkey*, op. cit., p. 4.
22 C. Koçak, 'Parliament membership during the single-party system in Turkey (1925–1945)', *European Journal of Turkish Studies*, 3, 2005, p. 37. Koçak also notes that the other seats in parliament were generally held by military officers and retired high-ranking public officials, who had no particular ties with the constituency they represented and changed constituency from one election to another. Ibid., p. 38.
23 As of 1950 each new government carried out 'purges' of the public administration involving the marginalization of members appointed by the previous government. The officials in question were retired, reassigned to subaltern positions or else nominated as some form of adviser whose opinion was never taken into account.
24 G. Şaylan, 'Cumhuriyet bürokrasisi', in *Cumhuriyet Dönemi Türkiye Ansiklopedisi*, vol. 2, Istanbul, İletişim Yayınları, 1983, p. 305. See too Ö. Bozkurt, *Memurlar. Türkiye'de kamu bürokrasinin sosyolojik görünümü*, Ankara, TODAİE, 1980; G. Şaylan, *Türkiye'de kapitalizm, bürokrasi ve siyasal ideoloji*, Ankara, TODAİE, 1972; F. Ahmad, *Modern Türkiye'nin Oluşumu*, Istanbul, Kaynak Yayınları, 2006.
25 For discussion of the laws pertaining to public administration passed by the DP, see M. Heper, *The State Tradition in Turkey*, op. cit., pp. 110–11.
26 G. Şaylan, 'Cumhuriyet bürokrasisi', op. cit., p. 306.
27 C. Sönmez, *Ülkücü bir Kaymakam Vardı*, Ankara, Ajans-Türk Matbaası, 1965, pp. 34–53.
28 G. Şaylan, 'Cumhuriyet bürokrasisi', op. cit., p. 306.

29 Ibid., p. 307.
30 I. Sunar, *State and Society in the Politics of Turkey's Development*, Ankara, AÜSBF, 1975, pp. 137-9.
31 E. Kalaycıoğlu, '1960 sonrası türk politik hayatına bir bakış: demokrasi neo-patrimonyalizm ve istikrar', in E. Kalaycıoğlu and A. Y. Sarıbay, *Türkiye'de Politik Değişim ve Modernleşme*, İstanbul, Alfa Yayınları, 2000, p. 393.
32 M. Heper, *The State Tradition in Turkey, op. cit.*, p. 93.
33 R. Culpan, 'Bürokratik sistemin yozlaşması', *Amme İdaresi Dergisi*, 13, 33, 1980; C. Tutum, 'Yönetimin siyasallaşması ve partizanlık', *Amme İdaresi Dergisi*, 9, 29, 1976.
34 The twelve MPs in question were appointed ministers or secretaries of state in the CHP government.
35 '40 ilin valisi değişiyor', *Milliyet*, 3 February 1978, pp. 1 and 9.
36 'Istanbul Toplum Polis Müdürü görevden alındı', *Milliyet*, 3 February 1978, p. 9.
37 'Tekin Istanbul valisi, Atabek emniyet genel müdürü oldu', *Milliyet*, 8 February 1978, p. 1.
38 '26 ilin valisi merkez valiliğine alındı', *Milliyet*, 13 February 1978, p. 1.
39 'Emniyet örgütünde yeni terfi ve atamalar yapıldı', *Cumhuriyet*, 8 July 1978, p. 5.
40 '38 kaymakam görev yeri değiştirildi', *Cumhuriyet*, 31 July 1978, p. 5.
41 'MC döneminde görevlendirilen 11 000 vekil öğretmenin işlerine son verildi', *Cumhuriyet*, 20 July 1978, p. 1. The article describes the surprising situations in certain schools in the west of the country, in which there were thirty or so teachers for about sixty pupils.
42 '220 kaymakamın görev yeri yine değişiyor', *Cumhuriyet*, 19 July 1980, pp. 1 and 9.
43 K. Barkey, *Bandits and Bureaucrats. The Ottoman Route to State Centralisation*, Ithaca and New York, Cornell University Press, 1994, pp. 195-203.
44 F. Bovenkerk et Y. Yeşilgöz, 'Urban knights and rebels in the Ottoman Empire', in C. Fijnaut and L. Paoli, *Organised Crime in Europe. Concepts, Patterns and Control Policies in the European Union and Beyond*, Dordrecht, Springer, 2004, p. 207.
45 E. Bilginer, *Babalar Senfonisi*, Istanbul, Cep Yayınları, 1990, p. 18.
46 G. Dorronsoro, 'Les politiques ottomane et républicaine au Kurdistan à partir de la comparaison des milices Hamidiye et *korucu*: modèles institutionnels, retribalisation et dynamique des conflits', *European Journal of Turkish Studies*, 2006, p. 5, https://journals.openedition.org/ejts/778 (consulted on 17 January 2021).
47 E. Massicard, '"Gangs in Uniform" in Turkey: Politics at the Articulation between Security Institutions and the Criminal World', in Jean-Louis Briquet and Gilles Favarel-Garrigues, *Organised Crime and States: The Hidden Face of Politics*, New York, Palgrave MacMillan, The Sciences Po Series in International Relations and Political Economy, 2010, p. 61.
48 G. Dorronsoro, 'Les politiques ottomane et républicaine au Kurdistan', *op. cit.*, p. 1.
49 Ibid., p. 25.
50 Ibid., p. 31.
51 Ibid., p. 9.
52 Gilles Dorronsoro observes that 'in the case of *korucu*, the salary was especially important given that the economy in the south-east had been completely devastated in the 1980s and 1990s due to insecurity and the low level of State investment (other than in the military). In absolute terms the *korucu* were paid about 230 dollars and, under certain conditions, they benefited from the public sector welfare system'. G. Dorronsoro, 'Les politiques ottomane et républicaine au Kurdistan', *op. cit.*, p. 22.
53 Ibid., p. 9.

54 Ibid., p. 13.
55 The organization had been active since 1911, but only came into official existence on 5 August 1914.
56 P. Stoddard, *The Ottoman Government and the Arabs, 1911 to 1918. A Preliminary Study of the Teskilat-i-Mashusa*, doctoral thesis, Princeton University, 1963.
57 See in particular D. Ganser, *Les Armées secrètes de l'OTAN: réseaux Stay-Behind, Gladio et terrorisme en Europe de l'Ouest*, Brussels, Éditions Demi Lune, 2007.
58 See for example E. Kiliç, *Özel Harp Dairesi*, Istanbul, Timaş Yayınları, 2010.
59 É. Massicard, ' "Gangs in Uniform" in Turkey: Politics at the articulation between security institutions and the criminal world', *op. cit.*, p. 62.
60 Ibid., p. 94.
61 H. Bozarslan, 'Le chaos après le déluge ?', *op. cit.*, p. 9.
62 'proletarianization of the economy' is here used to refer to the phenomenon whereby the number and proportion of workers in the active population both increase, where this is generally accompanied by an increase in the secondary sector's share of national output.
63 M. Özay, 'Turkey in crisis: Some contradictions in the Kemalist development strategy', *International Journal of Middle East Studies*, 15, 1, February 1983.
64 Ibid., p. 54.
65 Ibid., p. 51.
66 Ibid., p. 50.
67 Ibid., p. 52.
68 S. Pamuk, 'Political economy of industrialisation in Turkey', *MERIP Reports*, 93, January 1981, p. 26.
69 Ibid., p. 27.
70 A. A. Cecen, A. S. Doğruel and F. Doğruel, 'Economic growth and structural change in Turkey 1960-1988', *International Journal of Middle East Studies*, 26, 1, Feburary 1994, p. 38.
71 The State Planning Organisation (Devlet Planlama Teşkilatı) was set up on 30 September 1960. See J. P. C. Carey and A. G. Carey, 'Turkish agriculture and the five-year development plans', *International Journal of Middle East Studies*, 3, 1, January 1972, p. 47.
72 M. Özay, 'Turkey in crisis', *op. cit.*, p. 54.
73 A. A. Cecen, A. S. Doğruel and F. Doğruel, 'Economic growth and structural change in Turkey 1960-1988', *op. cit.*, p. 38.
74 Ibid., p. 28.
75 Ibid.
76 Ibid., p. 40.
77 Ibid.
78 Ibid., p. 39.
79 M. Özay, 'Turkey in crisis', *op. cit.*, p. 55.
80 A. A. Cecen, A. S. Doğruel and F. Doğruel, 'Economic growth and structural change in Turkey 1960-1988', *op. cit.*, p. 44.
81 'Batılılar türk ekonomisi için özel plan hazırlıyor', *Milliyet*, 1 December 1978, pp. 1 and 9; '4'ler 150 milyon dolarlık ivedi yardımistiyor', *Milliyet*, 12 April 1979, pp. 1 and 7.
82 'IMF, 450 milyon dolar kredi açtı', *Milliyet*, 17 March 1978, pp. 1 and 8.
83 A. A. Cecen, A. S. Doğruel and F. Doğruel, 'Economic growth and structural change in Turkey 1960-1988', *op. cit.*, p. 47.

84 'Türk ekonomisinin ağustos başında ferahlama dönemine girmesi bekleniyor', *Milliyet*, 25 June 1979, p. 9.
85 'IMF'den 224 milyon dolar bugün geliyor', *Cumhuriyet*, 30 January 1980, pp. 1 and 6; 'Hükümet dış kredi bekleyişi içinde', *Cumhuriyet*, 4 February 1980, pp. 1 and 11.
86 A. A. Cecen, A. S. Doğruel and F. Doğruel, 'Economic growth and structural change in Turkey 1960-1988', *op. cit.*, p. 47.
87 S. Pamuk, 'Political economy of industrialisation in Turkey', *op. cit.*, p. 27.
88 See *Türkiye İstatistik Yıllığı*, 1973, Ankara, 1974, Başbakanlık Devlet İstatistik Enstitüsü, pp. 29 and 37, and *Genel nüfüs Sayimi*, Ankara, 1975, Başbakanlık Devlet İstatistik Enstitüsü, p. 1.
89 A. A. Cecen, A. S. Doğruel and F. Doğruel, 'Economic growth and structural change in Turkey 1960-1988', *op. cit.*, p. 39.
90 E. Kongar, *İmparatorluktan Günümüze Türkiye'nin Toplumsal Yapısı*, Istanbul, Cem Yayınevi, 1978, pp. 369-72.
91 M. Heper, *Geckondu Policy in Turkey. An Evaluation with a Case Study of Rumelihisarüstü Squatter Area in Istanbul*, Istanbul, Boğaziçi University Publications, 1978, p. 12.
92 Ibid., p. 13.
93 M. Ozay, 'Turkey in crisis', *op. cit.*, p. 59.
94 M. Heper, *Geckondu Policy in Turkey*, *op. cit.*, p. 13.
95 F. Yavuz, R. Keleş and C. Geray, *Şehircilik: Sorunlar, Uygulama ve Politika*, Ankara, Ankara Üniversitesi, 1973, p. 591.
96 Ö. Ozankaya, *Türk Devrimi ve Yüksek Öğretim Gençliği*, Ankara, SBF Yayınları, 1978.
97 The six universities existing at that time were the Istanbul University (Istanbul Üniversitesi), which acquired its current form in 1922, Istanbul Technical University (Istanbul Teknik Üniversitesi), founded in 1928, Ankara University (Ankara Üniversitesi), founded in 1946, Ege University (Ege Üniversitesi) in Izmir, founded in 1955, the Middle East Technical University (Orta Doğu Teknik Üniversitesi) in Ankara, founded in 1956 and Atatürk University (Atatürk Üniversitesi) in Erzurum, founded in 1957. To this have to be added the six universities making up the Institute for Public Administration for Turkey and the Middle East (Türkiye ve Orta Doğu Amme İdaresi Enstitüsü, TODAİE), founded in 1953.
98 The Black Sea Technical University (Karadeniz Teknik Üniversitesi) was founded in Trabzon in 1963, Hacettepe University (Hacettepe Üniversitesi) in Ankara in 1967; Bosphorus University (Boğaziçi Üniversitesi) was created in 1971 (established on the former Robert College campus, founded in 1863), Çukurova University (Çukurova Üniversitesi) in 1973, Diyarbakır University (Diyarbakır Üniversitesi) in 1973; the University of Anatolia (Anadolu Üniversitesi) at Eskişehir was founded in 1975, Bursa University (Bursa Üniversitesi) in 1975, the University of the Republic (Cumhuriyet Üniversitesi) in Sivas in 1975, Euphrates University (Fırat Üniversitesi) in Elazığ in 1975, the University of 19 May (19 Mayis Üniversitesi) at Samsun in 1975 and Seljuk University (Selçuk Üniversitesi) at Izmir in 1977.
99 Celalettin Can, *Bağımsızlık, Demokrasi ve Sosyalizm Mücadelesinde Gençlik*, vol. 1, 1974-1980, Istanbul, Boran Yayınevi, 1999, pp. 265-74.
100 Ibid., p. 266.
101 B. W. Beeley, 'The Turkish village coffeehouse as a social institution', *Geographical Review*, 60, 4, October 1970, pp. 475 and 481.
102 H. Bozarslan, 'Le chaos après le déluge ?', *op. cit.*, p. 8.
103 H. Bozarslan, *Histoire de la Turquie contemporaine*, *op. cit.*, p. 53.

104 C. Eroğlu, *Demokrat Parti. Tarihi ve İdeolojisi*, Ankara, İmge Kitabevi, 2003.
105 Four independent candidates were elected and the Democratic Party (Demokratik Parti) had only one single seat.
106 G. Dorronsoro, *Que veut la Turquie ? Ambitions et stratégies internationales*, Paris, Autrement, 2009, p. 62.
107 E. Akbay, 'Türk polisin iç yüzü', *Polis Magazin*, 15, 2, 1980, pp. 10–21.
108 Semi-structured interview with Sıtkı Öner (Pol-Der) on 3 May 2006 in Ankara.
109 E. Akbay, 'Türk polisin iç yüzü', *op. cit.*
110 In January 1979, the General Directorate of Security announced a vast programme to train 5000 new police officers per year. The objective was to 'reach Western standards of four policemen per 1000 inhabitants'. See 'Türkiye'de bin kişiye bir polis düşüyor', *Cumhuriyet*, 23 January 1979, pp. 1 and 11.
111 S. Öner, *Halkın Polisi. Pol-Der Anıları*, Istanbul, İletişim Yayınları, 2003, p. 25.
112 H. F. Güneş, 'Türkiye'de terör, anarşi ve mücadele yolları', *Polis Magazin*, 15, 8, 1980, pp. 8–13.
113 E. Akbay, 'Türk polisin iç yüzü', *Polis Magazin*, 15, 1, 1980, pp. 8–12.
114 D. Della Porta, 'Police knowledge and protest policing: Some reflections on the Italian case', in D. Della Porta and H. Reiter (eds), *Policing Protest. The Control of Mass Demonstration in Western Democracies*, Minneapolis, University of Minnesota Press, 1998.
115 N. Bölügiray, *Sokaktaki Asker, op. cit.*, pp. 70–1.
116 Ibid., p. 159.
117 Ibid., p. 39.
118 See P. Bruneteaux, *La Violence d'État dans un régime démocratique: les forces de maintien de l'ordre en France. 1880-1980*, doctoral thesis in political science, University Paris 1, 1993, pp. 427–50.
119 Ibid., p. 434.
120 *Polis. Vatandaşın can, mal ve namusunu korur, devlet güvenliğini sağlar, trafiği murakabe eder, demokratik nizamın kanun dışı hareketlerle bozulmasını önler*, no place of publication indicated, 1970.
121 In neighbouring Hatay province there were 500 police officers for 500,000 inhabitants.
122 N. Bölügiray, *Sokaktaki Asker, op. cit.*, p. 254.
123 Ibid., p. 272.
124 Ibid., p. 46.
125 E. Akbay, 'Türk polisin iç yüzü', *op. cit.*, pp. 10–21.
126 N. Bölügiray, *Sokaktaki Asker, op. cit.*, p. 255.
127 'Denge Suçlular lehine bozuluyor', *Milliyet*, 27 February 1977, p. 7.
128 N. Bölügiray, *Sokaktaki Asker, op. cit.*, p. 221.
129 Ibid., 178.
130 Ibid., p. 357.
131 In November 1979 Bölügiray introduced a system for training special teams (Özel Timler): an intervention team, a photographic team, a bomb disposal team, a team specialized in gas, a heavy artillery team and so on. Whilst these teams met with only partial success, this needs to be weighed against the police shortages in the province.
132 N. Bölügiray, *Sokaktaki Asker, op. cit.*, p. 150.
133 S. Öner, *Halkın Polisi. Pol-Der Anıları, op. cit.*, p. 39.
134 Ibid.

Chapter 2

1. The new constitution consecrated freedom of expression and association. Articles 22 and 23 of the 1961 Constitution asserted the freedom of the press and condemn censorship, article 28 consecrated the right of assembly and demonstration and article 29 that of association. Articles 46 and 47 recognized the right to found a trade union without prior authorization as well as the right to strike. Article 56 stipulated that political parties – 'indispensable entities of democratic political life' – could be freely set up, provided that their activities and policy programmes did not run counter to 'human rights and freedoms', the principles of the secular republic and 'the State's territorial and national integrity' (art. 57): http://www.anayasa.gen.tr/1961constitution-amended.pdf (consulted on 7 January 2021).
2. M. Belge, 'Türkiye İşçi Partisi', in *Cumhuriyet Dönemi Türkiye Ansiklopedisi*, Istanbul, İletişim Yayınları, 1983, p. 2120.
3. E. Aydınoğlu, *Türkiye Solu. 1960–1980*, Istanbul, Versus Yayınları, 2007, pp. 39–42.
4. Rıza Kuas was the leader of the Lastık- İş rubber workers union as of 1954, Kemal Nebioğlu was the leader of the Gıda-İş trade union of food industry workers, İbrahim Güzelce a member of the Türk-İş board and head of the transport workers union, Avnı Erakalın a textile union official, Ahmet Muslu head of the chocolate industry workers union, Hüseyin Ulubaş head of the tobacco workers union, Saffet Göksözoğlu was the leader of the pharmaceutical industry union, Salih Özkarabay the head of the press union, and Adnan Arıkan the leader of the drivers union.
5. E. Aydınoğlu, *La Gauche turque dans les années soixante (1960–1971)*, doctoral thesis in political science, University Paris 1, April 1993.
6. On the strength of its trade union roots the party's founders were able to declare that 'the Workers Party of Turkey is the only party in our history to be founded directly by workers'. This was only partly true for, in 1951, all the founding members of the Democratic Labour Party (Demokrat İşçi Partisi) were workers, apart from its leader. The founding members of the Fatherland Party (Vatan Partisi), established in 1954, were also all workers, with the exception of Doctor Hikmet Kıvıcımlı. See E. Aydınoğlu, *Türkiye Solu. 1960–1980, op. cit.*, p. 89.
7. Ibid., p. 2121.
8. Of whom 32.4 per cent were workers, 20.3 per cent small-scale farmers, 19 per cent shopkeepers and tradesmen, 9.24 per cent farm labourers and 4.75 per cent students. See A. Ünsal, *Parti ouvrier de Turquie*, doctoral thesis in political science, University Paris 1,1970, p. 297.
9. A. Ünsal, *Türkiye İşçi Partisi (1961–1971). Umuttan yalnızlığa*, Istanbul, Tarih Vakfı Yurt Yayınları, 2002.
10. The legal existence of the TİİKP only lasted until the coup of 12 March 1971.
11. Celalettin Can, *Bağımsızlık, Demokrasi ve Sosyalizm Mücadelesinde Gençlik, op.cit.*, p. 61.
12. Ibid., p. 64.
13. *Türkiye Gerçekleri ve Terörizm*, Ankara, Babşakanlık Basımevi, 1973, pp. 26–8.
14. The THKP-C proclaimed that it drew its inspiration from the Tupamaros movement in Uruguay and Carlos Marighella's Popular revolutionary avant-garde in Brazil.
15. R. Margulies and E. Yıldızoğlu, 'Trade unions and Turkey's working class', *MERIP Reports*, 121, 'State terror in Turkey', February 1984, p. 17.

16 F. Ahmad, *The Turkish Experiment in Democracy, 1950–1975*, Boulder, CO, Westview Press, 1977, p. 148.
17 The banning of the TİP led a whole generation of activists to disengage from politics, including numerous academics and intellectuals who had been involved with the party ever since it was set up. See N. Monceau, 'Les intellectuels mobilisés: le cas de la fondation d'histoire de Turquie', in G. Dorronsoro (ed.), *La Turquie conteste. Mobilisations sociales et régime sécuritaire*, Paris, CNRS, 2005, p. 114.
18 Gilles Dorronsoro argues that 'because the backing of Western States was required, the Army were unable to directly control the political field, for example by banning on a lasting basis political parties and electoral contest. The Army thus had to refrain from sponsoring candidates, for the political contest had a genuine aspect of competition and the military never managed to impose their choice on the electors. Lastly, the price paid on the international stage for the coups was such that indirect control became systematised'. G. Dorronsoro, 'Introduction: mobilisations et régime sécuritaire', *La Turquie conteste, op. cit.*, p. 14.
19 F. Tachau and M. Heper, 'The state, politics, and the military in Turkey', *Comparative Politics*, 16, 1, October 1983, p. 23.
20 A. E. Turan, *Türkiye'de Seçmen Davranışı. Önceki Kırılmalar ve 2002 Seçimi*, Istanbul, Istanbul Bilgi Üniversitesi Yayınları, 2004, p. 86.
21 TÖB went on to become one of the most powerful associations in the public sector, under the name of the All Teachers Union and Solidarity Association (Tüm Öğretmen Birleşme ve Dayanışma Derneği, Töb-Der).
22 R. P. Nye, 'Civil-military confrontation in Turkey: The 1973 presidential election', *International Journal of Middle East Studies*, 8, 2, April 1977, p. 213.
23 The TSİP leadership therefore decided to bring out another *Kitle* Journal. The two journals were known as the 2.5-lira *Kitle* and the 5-lira *Kitle*. See I. Alpat, *Türkiye Solu Sözlüğü*, Istanbul, Mayı Yayınları, 2003, p. 163.
24 Ibid., p. 139.
25 *Sosyalizm ve Toplumsal Mücadeleler Ansiklopedisi*, vol. 7 (1960–80), Istanbul, İletişim Yayınları, 1988, p. 2236.
26 Ibid., p. 2234.
27 Ibid.
28 Ibid., p. 2236.
29 This step led to the departure of the Tek Bank-Is, Cağdas Gida-Is, İlerici Yapı-Is and Özgür Haber-Is unions, who were all opposed to this directive.
30 Thus enabling the Revolutionary Teachers Group (Devrimci Öğretmen Grubu) to win a growing number of Töb-Der sectional elections as of 1977.
31 *Sosyalizm ve Toplumsal Mücadeleler Ansiklopedisi, op. cit.*, pp. 2246–7.
32 S. Öner, *Halkın polisi. Pol-Der Anıları*, Istanbul, İletişim Yayınları, 2003, p. 94.
33 N. Çalışkan, *ODTÜ Tarihçe. 1956–1980*, Ankara, Arayış Yayınları, 2002, p. 293.
34 In her work about the Polish opposition during the Cold War, Osa shows how maintaining a dormant 'opposition network' in Poland between 1956 and 1980 enabled a rapid rise in mobilization once Solidarity emerged in 1980. M. Osa, *Solidarity and Contention, Networks of Polish Opposition*, Minneapolis, University of Minnesota Press, 2003.
35 *Sosyalizm ve Toplumsal Mücadeleler Ansiklopedisi, op. cit.*, p. 2237.
36 Ibid., pp. 2252–3.
37 A. Yılmaz, *Bu Tarih Bizim*, Istanbul, Devrim Dergisi Yayınları, 2006, pp. 88–96.

38 Semi-structured interview with Mahmut (Dev-Yol) on 10 May 2006 in Ankara. When interviewees are named by first name only, these are pseudonyms.
39 In the summer of 1978, however, its Istanbul's section broke off and set itself up as the Revolutionary Left (Devrimci Sol, Dev-Sol).
40 Semi-structured interview with Mahmut (Dev-Yol) on 10 May 2006 in Ankara.
41 Semi-structured interview with Ergun (VP) on 22 March 2006 in Istanbul.
42 Kasaba is the former name of the neighbourhood of Turgutlu in Manisa.
43 'DİSK yönetiminin seçimlerdeki tutumu', *Devrimci Yol*, 2, 15 May 1977, p. 11.
44 'Seçimler, TİP ve Tavrımız', *Devrimci Yol*, 2, 15 May 1977, p. 12.
45 'Gençlik örgütü değil, besleme bir naylon örgüt: İGD', *Devrimci Yol*, 3, 1 June 1977, p. 4.
46 '*Devrimci Yol* dergisinin seçimler konusundaki tesbitlerini ve oportünist-revisyonist siyasi taktiği eleştireceğiz', *Halkın Kurtuluşu*, 58, 1 June 1977, p. 1.
47 '*Halkın Kurtuluşu*'nun siyasi şaşkınlığı', *Devrimci Yol*, 4, 15 June 1977, p. 8.
48 '*Aydınlık*, oportünist fırsatçı tavırlar ve spekülasyonlarla devrimci harekete kara çalıyor', Ibid., p. 9.
49 '*Halkın Yolu* yalandan ne umuyor?', *Devrimci Yol*, 14, 3 February 1978, p. 15.
50 'TSİP Revisyonistlerinin Epengle işçilerine ihaneti', *Halkın Sesi*, 1, 15 April 1975, p. 4.
51 'TSİP revisyonistlerinin maskesini indirelim', *Halkın Sesi*, 14, 15 July 1975, p. 8.
52 'İGD'li revizyonistler Bursa'da devrimcilere ve TİP'lilere saldırdılar', *Halkın Sesi*, 66, 20 July 1976, p. 8.
53 'Amerikan uşağı MHP, AP, CGP'ye, Rus uşağı TİP'e oy verme Hesap sor!', *Halkın Sesi*, 111, 31 May 1977, p. 1.
54 "*Devrimci Yol*'cular İTÜ'de gençliği bölüyor', *Halkın Sesi*, 141, 27 December 1977, p. 6.
55 "*Devrimci Yol* katilleri açıklamalıdır', *Halkın Sesi*, 150, 28 February 1978, p. 3.
56 Semi-structured interview with Mahmut (Dev-Yol) on 10 May 2006 in Ankara.
57 The activities of this association sought to get the military officers behind the 12 September 1980 putsch put on trial.
58 The members of the committee who were relieved of their functions, retired from the army and sent on diplomatic postings abroad were: Alparslan Türkeş (New Dehli), Orhan Kabibay (Brussels), Orhan Erkanlı (Mexico), Münir Köseoğlu (Stockolm), Mustafa Kaplan (Lisbon), Muzaffer Karan (Oslo), Şefik Soyuyüce (Copenhagen), Fazıl Akkoyunlu (Kabul), Rifat Baykal (Tel Aviv), Dündar Taşer (Rabat), Numan Esin (Madrid), İrfan Solmazer (The Hague), Muzaffer Özdağ (Tokyo) and Ahmet Er (Libya). Orhan Erkanlı, *Anılar ... Sorunlar ... Sorumlular*, Istanbul, Baha Matbaası, 1972, 158.
59 F. S. Sanlı, *Türk Milliyetçiliğin Siyasetleşması – CKMP'den MHP'ye 1965–1969*, Ankara, Ülkü Ocakları Eğitim ve Kültür Vakfı, 2020.
60 Orhan Erkanlı, *Anılar ... Sorunlar ... Sorumlular*, op. cit., 158.
61 H. Poulton, *Top Hat, Grey Wolf and Crescent. Turkish Nationalism and the Turkish Republic*, London, Hurst and Company, 2006, p. 139.
62 M. Çalık, *MHP Hareketi. 1965–1980*, Ankara, Cedit Neşriyat, 1995, p. 92.
63 A. Türkeş, *Dokuz Işık*, Istanbul, Hamle Yayınevi, undated.
64 The term *Başbuğ* means leader in old Turkish, but its connotations are similar to those of the terms *Duce*, *Führer* and *Caudillo* used elsewhere.
65 T. Bora and K. Can, *Devlet Ocak Dergah – 12 Eylül'den Günümüze Ülkücü Hareket*, Istanbul, İletişim Yayınları, 1999, p. 48.
66 *Ülkücü Komando Kampları. AP Hükümeti'nin 1970'te Hazırlattığı MHP Raporu*, Istanbul, Kaynak Yayınları, 1978.

67 T. Feyizoğlu, *Fırtınalı Yıllarda Ülkücü Hareket*, İstanbul, Ozan Yayıncılık, 2000, p. 28.
68 Ibid., p. 30.
69 Ibid., p. 34.
70 Ibid., p. 32.
71 The BÜD continued to enjoy formal legal existence, however, taking over from the Ülkü Hearths in various places.
72 Semi-structured interview on 3 July 2008 with Remzi Çayir, a former member of the ÜOD, and then of the ÜGD and the ÜYD.
73 According to the indictment drawn up for the MHP trial, 'during the period of activity of the Ülkücü Youth Associations (Ülkücü Gençlik Dernekleri, ÜGD) 107 associations were opened on 30 May 1978, 288 on 30 June 1978, 119 on 30 July 1980, 32 on 30 August 1978, 41 on 30 September 1978, 21 on 30 October 1978 and 46 on 30 November 1978, together with 81 dependent libraries. The fact that 654 agencies were set up in such a short period of time betrays the fact that the ÜOD associations which had been shut down continued their activities under a different name'. See *T. C. Ankara-Çankırı-Kastamonu İlleri Sıkıyönetim Komutanlığı Askeri Savcılığı. Iddianame: MHP ve Ülkücü Kuruluşlar*, drawn up by Nurettin Soyer, military prosecutor under martial law, 1981, p. 68. Several precautions are required in using data from the indictment, for the allegations against the MHP were presented in such a way as to secure a guilty ruling. One cannot be suspicious enough of a document produced by a military tribunal whose sole purpose was to shut down a party identified as one of the main troublemakers having led to the military intervention. We need to be careful not to take up without checking data produced by a judicial institution. One indication in the publication of Alparslan Türkeş's defence during the trial suggests that the indictment may be a useful source for our argument. Rather than denying the allegations made against the party, Türkeş's position was to recognize them while arguing that these activities were conducted to protect the state from the communist threat by showering it with personnel loyal to the country's independence (*Milliyetçi Hareket Partisi ve Ülkücü Kuruluşlar Davası. Sorgu. Alparslan Türkeş*, Istanbul, Mayaş Matbaacılık Yayın, 1982). He never accused the prosecutor of having produced false documents. The information available in the indictment may thus be used for our argument while being compared, whenever possible, to that available in other sources.
74 Ibid., p. 139.
75 http://www.fes.de/fulltext/bueros/istanbul/00253015.htm (consulted on 2 February 2014).
76 *T. C. Ankara-Çankırı-Kastamonu İlleri Sıkıyönetim Komutanlığı Askeri Savcılığı*, op. cit., p. 65.
77 It is hard to assess the exact number of MHP activists, as public-sector workers were banned by law from taking part in party political activities. Many public-sector workers were members of ülkücü associations even though they were unable to be party activists. What counted was not so much being a party member as taking part in the Nationalist Movement. When it came down to it, it made little difference whether one participated in specifically party activities as opposed to those of its sister associations, which benefited non-officially from the networks of sociability, training programmes, support and special privileges the party provided.
78 There were specific structures for women in all Nationalist Movement organizations.
79 *T. C. Ankara-Çankırı-Kastamonu İlleri Sıkıyönetim Komutanlığı Askeri Savcılığı*, op. cit., p. 142.

80 Ibid.
81 Ibid., p. 158.
82 Namık Kemal Zeybek was the MHP candidate for Bursa in the 1977 general elections, Ramiz Ongun was head of the party's youth wing from 31 December 1974 to 21 November 1975, succeeded by Türkmen Onur from 21 November 1975 to 3 October 1977, Mustafa Öztürk was head of the Kayseri Ülküm section in 1974 and 1976, Lokman Abbasoğlu was Ülkü-Köy deputy chairman and board member, Sami Bal ran the ÜOD between January 1975 in January 1976, Abdullah Alay headed the Bursa section for a while, and Abdullah Kiliç ran the Karabük section in 1975.
83 *T. C. Ankara-Çankırı-Kastamonu İlleri Sıkıyönetim Komutanlığı Askeri Savcılığı, op. cit.*, p. 226.
84 Ibid.
85 All in all, between January 1978 and September 1980, about thirty people were officially 'instructors' (*eğitimci*) and local *Hergün* correspondents. Ibid., p. 135.
86 The information about ülkücü bureaus is taken from *T. C. Ankara-Çankırı-Kastamonu İlleri Sıkıyönetim Komutanlığı Askeri Savcılığı, op. cit.*, pp. 140–2.
87 Ibid., p. 230.
88 Ibid., p. 240.
89 Ibid., p. 243.
90 Ibid., pp. 221–2.
91 Ibid., p. 221.
92 Ibid., p. 245.
93 O. Grojean, *La Cause kurde, de la Turquie vers l'Europe. Contribution à une sociologie de la transnationalisation des mobilisations*, doctoral thesis in political sociology, Paris, EHESS, 2008, p. 104.
94 F. Aslan and K. Bozay, *Graue Wölfe Heulen Wieder. Türkische Faschisten und Ihre Vernetzung in der BRD*, Münster, Unrast, 2000, p. 184.
95 Ibid.
96 O. Grojean, *La Cause kurde, op. cit.*, p. 105. Olivier Grojean also notes that as of '1973 the presence of these associations in over thirty German towns and five other European countries (France, Belgium, Netherlands, Austria, and Switzerland) meant that Türkeş' party was the Turkish organisation with the widest presence in Europe'. Ibid.
97 He was replaced by Enver Altaylı, whose substitute member he became, at a MHP European council congress held in late December 1975. See F. Aslan and K. Bozay, *Graue Wölfe Heulen Wieder, op. cit.*, p. 186.
98 *T. C. Ankara-Çankırı-Kastamonu İlleri Sıkıyönetim Komutanlığı Askeri Savcılığı, op. cit.*, pp. 71–2.
99 O. Grojean, *La cause kurde, op. cit.*, p. 105.
100 E. Özcan, *Türkische Immigrantenorganisationen in des Bundesrepublik Deutschland*, Berlin, Hitit Verlag, 1989, p. 191, quoted in Ibid.
101 See O. Grojean, *La Cause kurde, op. cit.*, p. 105.
102 F. Aslan and K. Bozay, *Graue Wölfe Heulen Wieder, op. cit.*, p. 187.
103 *Hürriyet*, 18 January 1980, quoted in Ö. Ertekin, *Türkische Immigrantenorganisationen, op. cit.*, p. 179, and in O. Grojean, *La Cause kurde, op. cit.*, p. 106.
104 *T. C. Ankara-Çankırı-Kastamonu İlleri Sıkıyönetim Komutanlığı Askeri Savcılığı, op. cit.*, pp. 75, 266.
105 F. Aslan and K. Bozay, *Graue Wölfe Heulen Wieder, op. cit.*, p. 188.

106 T. C. Ankara-Çankırı-Kastamonu İlleri Sıkıyönetim Komutanlığı Askeri Savcılığı, op. cit., p. 255.
107 O. Grojean, La Cause kurde, op. cit., p. 106.

Chapter 3

1 A resource is taken here to mean anything that an individual or a group may draw upon to pursue a course of action in order to obtain an asset or a position they covet.
2 The dollar was worth 14.12 Turkish lira (TL) in 1975, 16.32 in 1976, 17.85 in 1977, 25 in 1978 and 35.70 in 1979. The exchange rates of the Turkish lira since 1975 may be consulted on the website of the Turkish central bank at: http://www.tcmb.gov.tr/
3 T. C. Ankara – Çankırı – Kastamonu İlleri Sıkıyönetim Komutanlığı Askeri Savcılığı, op. cit., pp. 189–200.
4 D. McAdam, S. Tarrow and C. Tilly, Dynamics of Contention, Cambridge, Cambridge University Press, 2001, p. 157.
5 T. C. Ankara – Çankırı – Kastamonu İlleri Sıkıyönetim Komutanlığı Askeri Savcılığı, op. cit., pp. 137 and 246.
6 Between 2 February and 4 December 1978, Ramiz Ongun received over 2 million Turkish lira, or a bit over $80,000. Ibid., pp. 216, 225, 227, 228 and 248.
7 Ibid., p. 96.
8 Ibid., pp. 208–18.
9 Ibid., p. 216.
10 Ibid.
11 In the accounts drawn up by the party, total expenditure for 1975 stood at 9,326,802 Turkish lira, but inspectors appointed by the prosecutor discovered several invoices that the party had not included in its accounts. Ibid., p. 200.
12 The equivalent of $32,000 in 1978, $16,985 in 1979 and $11,428 in 1980.
13 Ibid., p. 227.
14 Ibid., p. 223.
15 Ibid., pp. 223–4.
16 Ibid., p. 226.
17 T. C. Ankara – Çankırı – Kastamonu İlleri Sıkıyönetim Komutanlığı Askeri Savcılığı, op. cit., p. 109.
18 Ibid., p. 204.
19 Ibid., p. 211.
20 Ibid.
21 Ibid., pp. 219–20.
22 Ibid., p. 105.
23 In March 1979 the dollar was worth TL25.50.
24 In January 1980 the dollar was worth TL35.70.
25 T. C. Ankara – Çankırı – Kastamonu İlleri Sıkıyönetim Komutanlığı Askeri Savcılığı., op. cit., p. 231.
26 Ibid., p. 215.
27 Ibid.
28 Ibid., p. 203.
29 Ibid., p. 204. The largest donors for the second campaign were Ülkü-Bir (the ülkücü teacher association), Ülkü-Tek (the ülkücü technician association), Ülküm (the ülkücü public-sector worker association) and the ÜGD. Ibid., pp. 211–14.

30 Alparslan Türkeş opened an account with Commerzbank in 1970 in order to finance the setting up of a printing and press company (Matbaa ve Gazetecilik İşletmesi) which worked to publish and distribute ülkücü publications in Europe. A letter written by Türkeş states that this account contained DM30,000 before the company was set up. Two other accounts were used to pool financial contributions from ülkücüs in Germany, one with the Deutschbank in Cologne and the other with the Köln-Bank für Gemeinwirtschaft (BFG). See *T. C. Ankara – Çankırı – Kastamonu İlleri Sıkıyönetim Komutanlığı Askeri Savcılığı*, op. cit., p. 261.
31 Ibid., p. 74.
32 '1 dolar = 17,85 TL', *Milliyet*, 2 March 1977, p. 1.
33 *T. C. Ankara – Çankırı – Kastamonu İlleri Sıkıyönetim Komutanlığı Askeri Savcılığı*, op. cit., p. 262.
34 Ibid., p. 266.
35 Ibid.
36 Semi-structured interview with Ergun (VP) in Istanbul on 22 March 2006.
37 'Değerli dostlar', *Ürün Sosyalist dergi*, 5th year, 10, 55, January 1979, p. 2.
38 Semi-structured interview with Ergun (VP) in Istanbul on 22 March 2006.
39 The first issue of *Devrimci Yol* was sold for 3 lira; this went up to 5 lira as of 1978.
40 Semi-structured interview with Mustafa (Kurtuluş) on 2 May 2006 in Ankara.
41 '1 şubat 1978'e kadar Devrimci Yol'un kampanyasına gelen bağışlar', *Devrimci Yol*, 15, 3 February 1978, p. 10.
42 Semi-structured interview with Tevfik (Dev-Yol) on 10 May 2006 in Ankara.
43 Semi-structured interview with Kutay (Dev-Genç) on 2 May 2006 in Ankara.
44 Semi-structured interview with Yusuf (VP) on 3 May 2006 in Ankara.
45 Semi-structured interview with Tuncay (Dev-Genç) on 11 May 2006 in Ankara.
46 Semi-structured interview with Mahmt (Dev-Yol) in Ankara on 10 May 2006. According to İrfan the situation was different at Dev-Sol, reputed for being more violent, where the central body and local sections would often supply weapons: '*And how much would a weapon cost? It depended – a revolver could cost TL3500, that's two months' salary nowadays. The organization bought them for the more important cadres, but in general it was up to the local branches, the purchase could be ... spontaneous, for example, young people in a neighbourhood would pool their savings to buy a weapon. If big operations were being organized, then the organization, the centre could send specific weapons.*' Semi-directive interview with Irfan (Dev-Yol, Dev-Sol, Dev-Yol) on 27 May 2006 in Istanbul.
47 Semi-structured interview with Irfan (Dev-Yol, Dev-Sol, Dev-Yol) on 27 May 2006 in Istanbul.
48 Semi-structured interview with Mustafa (Kurtuluş) on 2 May 2006 in Ankara.
49 N. Ethuin, 'De l'idéologisation de l'engagement communiste. Les écoles du PCF (1970–1990)', *Politix*, 16, 63, 2003, p. 152.
50 M. Çalık, *MHP Hareketi. 1965–1980*, op. cit., pp. 137–40.
51 Semi-structured interview with Ömer (ÜOD, ÜGD, ÜYD, MHP) at the headquarters of the Ankara section of the party on 15 May 2007.
52 Kurt Karaca was also widely read (*Milliyetçi Türkiye-Milliyetçi Toplum Düzen – The Order of Nationalist Turkey and Society*). Amongst those surveyed, eighteen people said they had encouraged to read *Mein Kampf*, as well as Hitler's political testament. Ibid.
53 Semi-structured interview with Mehmet Şandır, an MP and former deputy leader of the MHP, editor of *Hergün* and head of the party's educational programmes from 1977 to 1980, on 5 April 2007 at the MHP headquarters in Ankara.

54 T. C. *Ankara – Çankırı – Kastamonu İlleri Sıkıyönetim Komutanlığı Askeri Savcılığı*, op. cit., p. 137.
55 H. Poulton, *Top Hat, Grey Wolf and Crescent. Turkish Nationalism and the Turkish Republic*, op. cit., p. 156.
56 Members of DİSK trade unions were able to follow more centralized training programmes, drawn up by the confederation or specific union. It is also known that DİSK and certain unions published training pamphlets. See *Sosyalizm ve Toplumsal Mücadeleler Ansiklopedisi*, op. cit., p. 538.
57 N. Bölügiray, *Sokaktaki Asker*, op. cit., p. 237.
58 Semi-structured interview with Yusuf (VP) in Ankara on 3 May 2006.
59 'Kitle eğitiminde dikkat edilmesi gereken noktalar', *Devrimci Yol*, 1, 1 May 1977, p. 15.
60 Ibid.
61 'Marksist teorinin ve teorik eğitimin önemi üzerine', *Devrimci Yol*, 1, 1 May 1977, pp. 13-15.
62 'Marksist felsefe eğitimi üzerine', *Devrimci Yol*, 3, 1 June 1977, pp. 14-15.
63 'Ekonomi politik ve eğitim üzerine', *Devrimci Yol*, 5, 1 July 1977, p. 14.
64 'Emperyalizm', *Devrimci Yol*, 15, 21 February 1978, pp. 12-13.
65 'Kapitalist olmayan yol: Leninst Devrim Teorisinin inkârı', *Devrimci Yol*, 4, 15 June 1977, pp. 6-7.
66 'İleri Demokrasi ve T "K" P', *Devrimci Yol*, 5, 1 July 1977, pp. 8-9.
67 'Sosyalist sistemin parçalanması ve Sovyet Çin Kutuplaşmasında tavır', *Devrimci Yol*, 8, 15 July 1977, pp. 7-8; 'Sosyalist sistemin parçalanması ve Sovyet Çin Kutuplaşmasında tavır (II)', *Devrimci Yol*, 7, 1 August 1977, pp. 8-9; 'Sosyalist sistemin parçalanması ve Sovyet Çin Kutuplaşmasında tavır (III)', *Devrimci Yol*, 8, 1 September 1977, p. 9.
68 'Türkiye'de kürt meselesi ve devrimci hareketin görevleri', *Devrimci Yol*, 9, 19 September 1977, pp. 8-11; 'Türkiye'de kürt meselesi ve devrimci hareketin görevleri (2)', *Devrimci Yol*, 10, 21 October 1977, pp. 12-15.
69 '"Sömürgecilik" tartışmaları üzerine', *Devrimci Yol*, 16, 20 March 1978, pp. 10-12; '"Sömürgecilik" tartışmaları üzerine (II)', *Devrimci Yol*, 17, 1 May 1978, pp. 12-13.
70 'Faşizm ve faşizme karşı mücadele sorunu', *Devrimci Yol*, 12, 1 December 1978, pp. 8-9; 'Faşizm ve faşizme karşı mücadele sorunu üzerine (2)', *Devrimci Yol*, 13, 15 January 1978, pp. 8-11.
71 'Honduras devrimin yolu', *Devrimci Yol*, 5, 1 July 1977, pp. 10-11.
72 'Şili halkın faşizme karşı direnişi', *Devrimci Yol*, 9, 19 September 1977, pp. 12-13.
73 'Yaşasın Nikaragua halkın devrimci mücadelesi', *Devrimci Yol*, 22, 20 September 1978, pp. 12-13.
74 'İran'da faşist Şah yönetimine karşı devrimci mücadele yükseliyor', *Devrimci Yol*, 19, 20 June 1978, pp. 14-15.
75 'Pakistan. Genel seçimlerden sonraki gelişmeler', *Devrimci Yol*, 3, 1 June 1977, pp. 16-17; 'Pakistanda'ki askeri darbe ve yeni sömürgecilik üzerine', *Devrimci Yol*, 8, 15 July 1977, p. 16.
76 'Ho Şi Minh', *Devrimci Yol*, 8, 1 September 1977, p. 16, 'Mao Zedung (1893- ...)', *Devrimci Yol*, 9, 19 September 1977, p. 16.
77 Semi-structured interview with Haldun (Dev-Genç) on 21 March 2006 in Istanbul.
78 Ibid.
79 Semi-structured interview with Mustafa (Kurtuluş) on 2 May 2006 in Ankara.
80 Semi-structured interview with Tamer (HK) on 10 May 2006 in Ankara.

81 *Ülkücü Komando Kampları. AP Hükümeti'nin 1970'te Hazırlattığı MHP Raporu*, Istanbul, Kaynak Yayınları, 1978, p. 20.
82 Ö. Tanlak, *İtiraf. Eski bir ülkücü MHP'yi anlatıyor*, Istanbul, Kaynak Yayınları, 1996, p. 72.
83 Semi-structured interview with Mehmet Şandir (MHP) on 5 April 2007 in Ankara.
84 'TİİKP'nin, Toroslarda silahlı eylem eğitimi yaptiği haberleri alınıyor', *Milliyet*, 25 February 1977, p. 7.
85 Semi-structured interview with Ergun (VP) on 22 March 2006 in Istanbul.
86 Semi-structured interview with Haldun (Dev-Genç) on 21 March 2006 in Istanbul.
87 Ibid.
88 L. Wacquant, 'L'habitus comme objet et méthode d'investigation. Retour sur la fabrique du boxeur', *Actes de la recherche en sciences sociales*, 184, 2010, p. 114.
89 B. Pudal, *Prendre parti: pour une sociologie historique du PCF*, Paris, Presses de la FNSP, 1989, p. 292.
90 Semi-structured interview with Ömer (MHP) on 15 May 2007 in Ankara.
91 B. Caymaz and E. Szurek, 'La révolution au pied de la lettre. L'invention de "l'alphabet"', *European Journal of Turkish Studies*, 6, 2007, https://journals.openedition.org/ejts/1363 (consulted on 17 January 2021).
92 Several studies have brought out the significance of using 'passwords' and specific vocabulary in group identification, especially in black ghettos in the United States and amongst 'yobs'. See W. Labov, *Language in the Inner City: Studies in the Black English Vernacular*, Philadelphia, University of Pennsylvania Press, 1977; G. Mauger and C. Fossé-Poliak, 'Les loubards', *Actes de la recherche en sciences sociales*, 50, 1983.
93 'Yes, in Halkın Kurtuluşu when addressing someone we said Hoca, Bacı', semi-structured interview with Tamer (HK) on 10 May 2006 in Ankara.
94 Semi-structured interview with Tevfik (Dev-Yol) on 10 May 2006 in Ankara.
95 Semi-structured interview with Tamer (HK) on 10 May 2006 in Ankara.
96 B. Hibou, *Anatomie politique de la domination*, Paris, La Découverte, 2011, p. 59.
97 The ülkücü's moustache, eyebrows and hairline represented the three moons of the MHP emblem, which was also meant to indicate his proximity to Islamic values.
98 Semi-structured interview with Kutay (Dev-Genç) on 2 May 2006 in Ankara.
99 Semi-structured interview with Metin (TİP) on 11 May 2006 in Ankara.
100 Semi-structured interview with Tevfik (Dev-Yol) on 10 May 2006 in Ankara.
101 Ibid.
102 M. Çalık, *MHP Hareketi. 1965–1980, op. cit.*, p. 140.
103 M. Van Bruinessen, *Türklük, Kürtlük, Alévilik-Etnik ve Dinsel Kimlik Mücadeleleri*, İstanbul, İletişim Yayınları, 2002, p. 120.
104 B. Gürel, *Political Mobilisation in Turkey in the 1970's. The Case of the Kahramanmaraş Incidents*, doctoral thesis, Boğaziçi University, Atatürk Institute for Modern Turkish History, 2004, pp. 55–6.
105 *T. C. Ankara – Çankırı – Kastamonu İlleri Sıkıyönetim Komutanlığı Askeri Savcılığı, op. cit.*, p. 105.
106 Semi-structured interview with Mustafa (Kurtuluş) on 2 May 2006 in Ankara.
107 Ibid.
108 Semi-structured interview with Tevfik (Dev-Yol) on 10 May 2006 in Ankara.
109 Semi-structured interview with Tamer (HK) on 10 May 2006 in Ankara.
110 Semi-structured interview with Kutay (Dev-Genç) on 2 May 2006 in Ankara.
111 Semi-structured interview with Faruk (ÜYD) on 2 June 2007 in Istanbul.
112 Semi-structured interview with Metin (TİP) on 11 May 2006 in Ankara.

113 Semi-structured interview with Tamer (HK) on 10 May 2006 in Ankara.
114 *Şehitler Olmez*, Istanbul, Hamle kitabevi (date of publication not given), pp. 1571-3.
115 T. C. Ankara – *Çankırı – Kastamonu İlleri Sıkıyönetim Komutanlığı Askeri Savcılığı*, *op. cit.*, p. 105.
116 Ibid.
117 Ibid.
118 M. Çalık, *MHP Hareketi. 1965-1980*, *op. cit.*, p. 144.
119 Semi-structured interview with Nejat (Kurtuluş) on 4 May 2006 in Ankara.
120 Semi-structured interview with Tamer (HK) on 10 May 2006 in Ankara.
121 C. Koçak, *Türkiye'de Milli Şef Dönemi. 1938-1945*, Istanbul, İletişim Yayınları, 2010, p. 225.
122 See A. Türkeş, *Dokuz Işık ve Türkiye*, Istanbul, Hamle Yayınevi, 1965.
123 A. Türkeş, *Dokuz Işık ve Türkiye*, *op. cit.*
124 Ibid.
125 'Komünizme karşı set Milliyetçi Hareket. Kapılma hiç hayale ver oy'unu hilal'e', in *Sosyalizm ve Toplumsal Mücadeleler Ansiklopedisi*, vol. 7 (1960-1980), Istanbul, İletişim Yayınları, 1988, p. 518.
126 A. Türkeş, *Yeni Ufuklara Doğru*, Istanbul, Kutluğ Yayınları, 1974, chapter headed 'İç ve dış tehditler'.
127 A. Türkeş, *Yeni Ufuklara Doğru*, *op. cit.*
128 DİSK also published an undated pamphlet headed 'We are downing tools against fascist attacks' (Faşist saldırılara karşı işi birakıyoruz). See *Sosyalizm ve Toplumsal Mücadeleler Ansiklopedisi*, *op. cit.*, Appendix, p. 549.
129 Ibid., p. 2248.
130 Slogans against fascism were chanted in turn with various others, the most popular of which were 'Revolution is the only path' (*Tek yol devrim*), 'Long live socialism' (*Yaşasın Sosyalizm*), 'Freedom to the people' (*Halklara özgürlük*), 'The red sun shall rise' (*Kızıl güneş doğacaktır*), 'Use water, work the land' (*Su kullanın, toprak işleyenin*) and 'Shut down the MİT [National Intelligence Organisation], the counter-guerrilla, the MHP, and the ÜYD!' (*Mit, Kontgerilla, ÜYD MHP kapatılsın!*).
131 M. Çalık, *MHP Hareketi. 1965-1980*, *op. cit.*, pp. 137-40.
132 Ibid., p. 140.
133 Ibid.

Chapter 4

1 N. Bölügiray, *Sokaktaki Asker, Bir Sıkıyönetim Komutanının 12 Eylül Öncesi Anıları*, Istanbul, Milliyet Yayınları, 1989, p. 212.
2 Ibid., p. 213.
3 M. Dobry, *Sociologie des crises politiques*, *op. cit.*, p. 154.
4 The MHP refused to take part in the Demirel government which took office in November 1979, preferring to lend parliamentary support. This conditional support for the minority government enabled it to negotiate with the AP to obtain state positions.
5 This first Nationalist Front Government was composed of the AP, the MSP (Milli Selâmet Partisi – National Salvation Party), the CGP (Cumhuriyetçi Güven Partisi – Republican Reliance Party) and the MHP.

6 The CHP won 41.4 per cent of the vote and 213 seats, the AP 36.9 per cent and 189 seats, the MSP 8.6 per cent and 80 seats, the MHP 6.4 per cent and 16 seats, and the CGP 1.9 per cent and 3 seats.
7 The government was composed of ministers from the AP, MHP and MSP, and could count on the support of 229 members of parliament.
8 Alparslan Türkeş was deputy prime minister, Şadi Somuncuoğlu minister of State, Gün Sazak minister for customs and monopolies, Cengiz Gökçek minister for health and Agah Oktay Güner minister for trade.
9 *T. C. Ankara – Çankırı – Kastamonu İlleri Sıkıyönetim Komutanlığı Savcılığı, op. cit.,* p. 135.
10 Ö. Tanlak, *İtiraf. Eski bir ülkücü MHP'yi anlatıyor, op. cit.,* p. 133.
11 *T. C. Ankara – Çankırı – Kastamonu İlleri Sıkıyönetim Komutanlığı Askeri Savcılığı, op. cit.,* p. 118.
12 Ibid., p. 131.
13 Ibid., p. 103.
14 Ibid., p. 130.
15 Ibid., p. 113.
16 Ibid., p. 117.
17 Ibid., p. 113.
18 A report drawn up by ülkücü associations and called 'The situation in schools in the beginning of 1980' refers to state educational establishments in which activists were certain to be awarded their diploma. Ibid., p. 110.
19 Ibid., p. 89.
20 The Cabinet decision of 23 March 1979, number 7/17339, set out in paragraph 13 of article 8 of the disciplinary statutes of the Security Organization, states that 'the fact of being a member of a political party, acting for or against a political party, or taking part in political activities shall be punished by dismissal'.
21 Article 7 of law no. 657 on state officials stipulates that 'officials may not be members of a political party. They shall not behave in such a way as to disadvantage or privilege a political party or an individual; in carrying out their functions they shall act without any distinction between language, religion, race, gender, political opinion, or philosophical or religious ideas'. Article 125 of the law on state officials sets out the disciplinary sanctions (being fired) for any who withhold information or documents containing information that might contravene the law.
22 *T. C. Ankara – Çankırı – Kastamonu İlleri Sıkıyönetim Komutanlığı Askeri Savcılığı, op. cit.,* pp. 155–6.
23 Ibid., p. 133.
24 Ibid., p. 138.
25 Ibid., pp. 167–8.
26 Ibid., p. 132.
27 Şadi Somuncuoğlu was minister of state in the second Nationalist Front government.
28 Ibid., p. 94.
29 Ibid.
30 Ibid., p. 169.
31 Ibid., p. 131.
32 Ibid., p. 97.
33 Ö. Tanlak, *İtiraf. Eski Ülkücü MHP'yi Anlatıyor, op. cit.,* p. 15.
34 Ibid., p. 21.
35 Ibid., p. 37.

36 T. C. Ankara – Çankırı – Kastamonu İlleri Sıkıyönetim Komutanlığı Askeri Savcılığı, op. cit., p. 98.
37 Extract from a semi-structured interview with Yusuf (VP) on 3 May 2006 in Ankara.
38 F. Ahmad, *Modern Türkiye'nin Oluşumu, op. cit.*, p. 157; G. Şaylan, 'Cumhuriyet Bürokrasisi', in *Cumhuriyet Dönemi Türkiye Ansiklopedisi*, Istanbul, İletişim Yayınları, 1983, p. 306.
39 N. Bölügiray, *Sokaktaki Asker, op. cit.*, pp. 27–8.
40 Ibid., p. 206.
41 B. Gürel, *Political Mobilisation in Turkey in the 1970s, op. cit.*
42 Ibid., pp. 147–8.
43 General Evren, who was chief of staff at the time, told Mehmet Ali Birand that 'there might have been ideological influences in Harbiye, in the military academies, in the ranks. And these ideological pressures led to groups being built up in the Army. This happened at the War Academy (Harp Okulu). Altercations took place between students. … At the Piyade Academy two lieutenants, lieutenants following the courses there, struck a gendarme on duty during an incident in Istanbul. And afterwards they escaped. They went abroad. In other words the Army had started to fragment too. It was inevitable as I told you'. See M. A. Birand, H. Bilâ and R. Akar, *12 Eylül Türkiye'nin Miladi, op. cit.*, p. 78.
44 For discussion of the claims to be apolitical, see P. Juhem, *SOS-Racisme. Histoire d'une mobilisation 'apolitique'. Contribution à l'analyse des transformations des représentations politiques après 1981*, Doctoral thesis in political science, University Paris 10-Nanterre, 1998.
45 B. Gürel, '"Communist Police!" The state in the 1970s Turkey', *Journal of Historical Studies*, 2, 2004, p. 7.
46 Ç. Yiğenoğlu, *Sakıncalı Kadın Polis Nurhan Varlı'nın Anıları*, İstanbul, Çağdaş Yayınları, 1995, p. 41.
47 Ibid., p. 44.
48 Ibid., p. 60.
49 'It happened a few months after the declaration of martial law. A police team had been sent out to settle disputes between leftists and right-wing people. I arrived shortly after, and what I saw was unimaginable. The policemen had joined in the fight, i.e. the Pol-Der officers and the Pol-Bir officers were fighting one another to protect those who were fighting.' See N. Bölügiray, *Sokaktaki Asker, op. cit.*, p. 51.
50 Ibid., p. 87.
51 Ibid., p. 123.
52 Yunus Emre was a thirteenth-century Turkish poet.
53 S. Öner, *Halkın polisi. Pol-Der Anıları, op. cit.*, p. 86.
54 'I was doing my nightly round when I suddenly heard the sound of gunfire in a street where right-wing people lived. On getting there I saw two young people running away. A police team had arrived before me, and so I did not get involved. But the policemen called out the inhabitants who had asked for assistance and started hitting them. Some were taken into custody.' Account reported in N. Bölügiray, *Sokaktaki Asker, op. cit.*, p. 33.
55 Ibid.
56 He condemns the fact that the police and army called social-democrats 'dirty leftists' and 'communists', and right-wing people 'dirty rightists', 'fascists', and 'reactionaries'. Ibid., p. 226.
57 Ibid., p. 133.

58 These events left 111 dead and over 1000 injured. In addition to this, 552 shops, 289 houses and 8 vehicles were torched. See B. Gürel, *Political Mobilisation in Turkey in the 1970s, op. cit.*, p. 124.
59 Ibid.
60 N. Bölügiray, *Sokaktaki Asker, op. cit.*, p. 50.
61 Ibid., p. 153.
62 H. Bozarslan, 'Le phénomène milicien: une composante de la violence politique en Turquie des années 1970', *Turcica*, 31, 1999, p. 207.
63 P. Aksakal, *Fatsa Gerçeği*, Ankara, Penta Yayıncılık, 2007, pp. 40 and 125.
64 Ibid., pp. 125–6.
65 Two attacks were made on Fikri Sönmez during the election campaign by members of the local MHP section.
66 The municipality forced a prostitute elected to a people's committee to resign. See P. Aksakal, *Fatsa Gerçeği, op. cit.*, pp. 133–4.
67 Ibid., p. 134.
68 H. Bozarslan, 'Le phénomène milicien', *op. cit.*, p. 235.
69 Nearly 800 people were arrested when the army intervened in July 1980.
70 P. Aksakal, *Fatsa Gerçeği, op. cit.*, p. 97.
71 The resistance committees were initially composed of Dev-Yol activists and sympathizers, and recruited their members in the neighbourhoods, compelling the inhabitants to take turns on guard duty patrolling the frontiers of the zone under their control. Ibid., p. 32.
72 'Fatsa'da olay yok, ama halk tedirgin', *Cumhuriyet*, 11 July 1980, pp. 1 and 9.
73 'Fatsa operasyonu: 300 kişi gözaltına', *Cumhuriyet*, 12 July 1980, pp. 1 and 5.
74 P. Aksakal, *Fatsa Gerçeği, op. cit.*, p. 107.
75 'Fatsa'daki maskeliler ülkücü militanlardı', *Cumhuriyet*, 12 July 1980, pp. 1 and 9.
76 H. Bozarslan, 'Le phénomène milicien', *op. cit.*, p. 235.
77 The governor of Ordu was thus pleased to announce that 'people who had been unable to go back to Fatsa for two years [can] return'. See 'Operasyon sonrası Fatsa', *Cumhuriyet*, 15 August 1980, p. 10.
78 'Devlet Kars'a giremiyor', *Hergün*, 26 October 1978, pp. 1 and 7.
79 Ş. Aslan, *1 Mayıs Mahallesi. 1980 Öncesi Toplumsal Mücadeleler ve Kent*, Istanbul, İletişim yayınları, 2004.
80 H. Metin, *Geckondu Policy in Turkey. An Evaluation with a Case Study of Rumelihisarüstü Squatter Area in Istanbul*, Istanbul, Boğaziçi University Publications, 1978.
81 Ş. Aslan, *1 Mayıs Mahallesi, op. cit.*, p. 87.
82 DİE Nüfus İstatistikleri, 2001.
83 Ş. Aslan, *1 Mayıs Mahallesi, op. cit.*, p. 106.
84 Ibid., p. 107.
85 Ibid., pp. 114–15.
86 Semi-structured interview with Haldun (Dev-Genç) on 21 March 2006 in Istanbul.
87 '1) Dwellings must be healthy and comfortable. They must be fairly large and have a garden. 2) They must be cheap and practical, 3) With transport links, 4) They must be part of the town, 5) Education and health services need to be set up in the neighbourhood along with cultural institutions, 6) Places need to be created for socialisation and to encourage neighbourly relations.' See Ş. Aslan, *1 Mayıs Mahallesi, op. cit.*, p. 120.
88 Ibid., p. 121.

89 Ibid., p. 130.
90 Ibid., p. 155.
91 In answer to the question: 'Which neighbourhoods in Istanbul were held by left-wing groups, and which by right-wing groups?', Şadi answered: 'Beşiktaş left, Şişli right ... Beyazit right, Zeytinburnu left, Kağıthane left ... '; and Metin stated that 'the neighbourhoods of Gaziosmanpaşa and of Alibeyköy, in Europe, and of Umraniye and Kartal, in Asia, were workers' neighbourhoods, where there were factories, and there the left was strong, places with migrants [göçmen], where most of the population was Alevi. Aksaray and Üsküdar were right wing, and fairly dangerous for the Socialists. In Ankara, Tuzluçahir, an Alevi migrant neighbourhood, was held by the left, whereas out Ulus way it was fascist, as was Bahçelievler too. To the South Kavaklidere, Çankaya, and Gazi were more luxurious neighbourhoods, it was different, people there voted liberal or CHP'. Semi-structured interviews conducted with Şadi on 15 March 2006 in Istanbul and with Metin (TİP) on 11 May 2006 in Ankara.
92 According to Yusuf, 'the fascist neighbourhoods [were] Hasköy, Keçiören, Demetevler, Bahçelievler, Balgat, part of Kayaş, and Mamak'. Semi-structured interview conducted with Yusuf (VP) on 3 May 2006 in Ankara.
93 Hamit Bozarslan refers to a Justice Party report, made public on 26 May 1978 (before the departure of the ülkücüs), in which the town of Kars – with the exception of the neighbourhoods of Yeni Mahalle and Cumhuriyet Mahallesi – is presented as a liberated zone. H. Bozarslan, 'Le phénomène milicien', *op. cit.*, p. 240.
94 Justice Party report (no indication of date or page number), quoted by Hamit Bozarslan in Ibid.
95 N. Ilıcak, *Makaleler II, 1978*, Istanbul, Kervan Yayınları, 1980, p. 444.
96 N. Bölügiray, *Sokaktaki Asker, op. cit.*, p. 217.
97 This was frequently the case elsewhere too 'in Ankara, for example, guards were posted every night ... In Tuzluçahir for example. Dev-Yol was the most powerful outfit in the neighbourhood, but together with Dev-Yol and Kurtuluş we defended the neighbourhood against the fascists'. Semi-structured interview with Yusuf (VP) in Ankara on 3 May 2006.
98 H. Bozarslan, 'Le phénomène milicien', *op. cit.*, p. 212.
99 N. Bölügiray, *Sokaktaki Asker, op. cit.*, p. 26.
100 Ş. Aslan, *1 Mayıs Mahallesi, op. cit.*, p. 125.
101 In Turkish mythology Ergenekon is the country from which the Turks originated, and that they are said to have left in order to settle in Central Asia and Asia Minor.
102 H. Bozarslan, 'Le phénomène milicien', *op. cit.*, p. 209.
103 The *Cumhuriyet* newspaper is centre-left and supported the CHP, directing most of its criticism against the MHP (described as fascist) and right-wing parties (the AP and MSP).
104 Semi-structured interview with (Dev-Genç) on 21 March 2006 in Istanbul.
105 *T. C. Ankara – Çankırı – Kastamonu İlleri Sıkıyönetim Komutanlığı Askeri Savcılığı, op. cit.*, pp. 105–6.
106 'We must make contact with trusted people and religious leaders. That will win us their confidence and make them favourably disposed towards us. ... In order to win over the hearts of district inhabitants, it is important for instance to carry the shopping bags of the elderly on their way back home from the markets and to accompany them back to their home. We have to oblige our ülkücüs and our sympathizers to attend the religious seminars given by the religious leaders in

the neighbourhood. We need to make sure that all ülkücüs attend Friday prayers. Organisation leaders (section or neighbourhood cadres, etc.) shall perform the five daily prayers. A room shall be set aside for prayer in each association.' Ibid., p. 105.
107 Ibid.
108 The book of Dede Korkut is a series of epic episodes of the Oghuz, the ancestors of Western Turks (the Turks of Turkey, the Azeris, the Turkmens etc.), and it sets out the moral values and pre-Islamic beliefs of the nomadic Turks.
109 These and the following elements are taken from *T. C. Ankara – Çankırı – Kastamonu İlleri Sıkıyönetim Komutanlığı Askeri Savcılığı, op. cit.*, p. 106.
110 For a discussion of how mobilized actors may compel public authorities to recognize them as privileged partners, see D. McAdam, 'Tactical innovation and the pace of insurgency', *American Sociological Review*, 48, 1983.
111 Ş. Aslan, *1 Mayıs Mahallesi, op. cit.*, p. 159.
112 Ibid., p. 161.
113 Ibid., p. 163.
114 Ibid., p. 179.

Chapter 5

1 Zald and Usem have shown how the tactics deployed by one protagonist can help shape the tactical possibilities open to rivals. See M. N. Zald and B. Usem, 'Movement and countermovement interaction: Mobilization, tactics, and state involvement', in J. MacCarthy and M. N. Zald (eds), *Social Movement in an Organizational Society*, Morristown, Transaction Books, 1987, pp. 247–72.
2 The mechanisms which can be observed at Tariş were transferable. Other conflicts that received less media coverage show similar mechanisms being used to extend left-wing mobilization to multiple sectors in reaction to MHP tactics. This was the case with a protest movement centred on the Antbirlik cooperative in Antalya, and the Pişkin cotton mill (Pişkinler İplik Fabrikası) in Kahramanmaraş, where the ülkücü trade union confederation MİSK managed to intervene in the distribution of jobs. It is because of the extensive media coverage and thus the existence of numerous accounts of events that the Tariş conflict has been chosen as a case study.
3 On 1 October 1977 the minister for education, called upon to explain increased violence in 'schools', admitted that administrative staff received bribes in exchange for enrolling certain students. See E. Akyıldız, 'Millî Eğitim Müdürü: "Anarşık olaylardan okul yöneticileri sorumludur,"' *Milliyet*, 1 October 1977, p. 4.
4 'Eğitim enstitüsü sınavları ülkücülerin baskısı altında yapıldı', *Milliyet*, 10 November 1977, p. 8.
5 Ş. Ketenci, 'Eğitim. Sorunlar daha da büyükerek bu yıla aktarıldı', *Cumhuriyet*, 2 January 1979, supplement, p. 3.
6 'Ayın aynası', *Öğretmen Dünyası*, 5, May 1980, pp. 32–3. The recent build-up of MHP presence at the institute had led to requests by teachers who were Justice Party sympathizers to be transferred. The study I have conducted of national newspapers has thrown up several such situations. This gives a more nuanced picture of relations between AP and ülkücü personnel, who did not work together as systematically as might otherwise be thought.
7 Ibid.

8 Ibid.
9 'Ayın aynası', *Öğretmen Dünyası*, 6, June 1980, pp. 31-2.
10 Ibid.
11 Ibid.
12 'Ayın aynası', *Öğretmen Dünyası*, 8, August 1980, pp. 31-2.
13 According to Bülent Forta, 'This antidemocratic appointment ran into opposition due to a student boycott, the refusal of teachers to give lessons, and workers' strikes. Eventually Hasan Tan did not remain as rector and a new rector was appointed who was accepted by the entire university.' See N. Çalışkan, *ODTÜ Tarihçe, 1956-1980, op. cit.*, p. 304.
14 Ibid., p. 173.
15 Ibid., p. 195.
16 Ibid., p. 196.
17 Ibid., p. 197.
18 'ODTÜ'deki forumda yeni rektör istenmedi', *Milliyet*, 16 February 1977, pp. 1 and 7.
19 N. Çalışkan, *ODTÜ Tarihçe, 1956-1980, op. cit.*, p. 199.
20 'ODTÜ öğretim üyeleri siyasal iktidarlarca atanan yöneticilere karşı çıktı', *Milliyet*, 18 February 1977, pp. 1 and 10.
21 N. Çalışkan, *ODTÜ Tarihçe 1956-1980, op. cit.*, p. 198.
22 Ibid., p. 200.
23 Semi-structured interview in Istanbul with Ahmet (ODTÜ-ÖTK) on 2 June 2007.
24 N. Çalışkan, *ODTÜ Tarihçe 1956-1980, op. cit.*, p. 202.
25 'Rektör Tan, ODTÜ'yü 15 gün kapattı', *Milliyet*, 24 February 1977, p. 6.
26 N. Çalışkan, *ODTÜ Tarihçe 1956-1980, op. cit.*, pp. 202-4.
27 Ibid., p. 217.
28 Ibid., p. 218.
29 Ibid., p. 250.
30 Ibid.
31 Ibid.
32 Ibid., p. 228.
33 Ibid., pp. 229-30.
34 'ODTÜ'de çıkan olaylarda 3'ü ağır 35 öğrenci yaralandı', *Milliyet*, 3 December 1977, p. 8; 'Bazı işçilerin işine son vermek için ODTÜ'de personelin ad listesi çıkartılıyor', *Milliyet*, 4 December 1977, pp. 1 and 6.
35 The ODTÜ Students Families Solidarity Association (ODTÜ Öğrenci Ailerleri Dayanışma Derneği) played a particularly active part in this campaign, calling on students not to attend classes for as long as their safety could not be ensured.
36 Or in Michel Dobry's terminology 'the linking up of spheres of confrontation or, to put that differently, arenas or places of competition specific to various sectors'. M. Dobry, *Sociologie des crises politiques, op. cit.*, p. 143.
37 Ibid.
38 In 1972 the Nationalist movement set up the Association of the Ülkücü Teachers Union (Ülkücü Öğretmenler Birliği Derneği, Ülkü-Bir), and then in 1973 the Ülkücü Technical Staff Association (Ülkücü Teknik Elemanlar Derneği, Ülkü-Tek). On entering government in 1975 the movement diversified the number of sites where it was present and active. It established the Association of Ülkücü Officials (Ülkücü Memurlar Derneği, Ülküm), the Association of Ülkücü Villagers (Ülkücü Köylüler Derneği, Ülkü-Köy), the Union of Ülkücü Craftsmen (Ülkücü Esnaflar Birliği, Ülkü-Es), the Union of the Ülkücü Financiers and Economists Association (Ülkücü

39 T. C. Ankara – Çankırı – Kastamonu İlleri Sıkıyönetim Komutanlığı Askeri Savcılığı, op. cit., p. 82.

Maliyeciler ve İktisatçılar Derneği Birliği, Ümid-Bir) and the University Assistants Mutual Support Association (Üniversiteli Asistanlar Yardımlaşma Derneği, Ünay). The Pol-Bir association in the police opened in 1976.

39 T. C. Ankara – Çankırı – Kastamonu İlleri Sıkıyönetim Komutanlığı Askeri Savcılığı, op. cit., p. 82.
40 The results obtained in this study invalidate the idea put forward by Richard Katz and Peter Mair that party political organizations distance themselves from 'civil society' on becoming an integral part of the State. It is when the MHP was in government that it devoted most effort to expanding and coordinating the activities of ülkücü associations. See P. Mair, 'Party organisations: From civil society to the state', in R. Katz and P. Mair (eds), *How Parties Organise. Change and Adaptation in Party Organisations in Western Democracies*, London, Sage, 1994; R. Katz and P. Mair, 'Changing models of party organisation and party democracy. The emergence of the cartel party', *Party Politics*, 1, 1, 1995.
41 T. C. Ankara – Çankırı – Kastamonu İlleri Sıkıyönetim Komutanlığı Askeri Savcılığı, op. cit., p. 96.
42 The alignment of far-left protest movements always took place as part of a second phase, once the ülkücü organizations had helped transform the protest sites into bipolar spheres of contest.
43 D. McAdam, S. Tarrow and C. Tilly, *Dynamics of Contention, op. cit.*, p. 57.
44 For Charles Tilly and Sidney Tarrow, 'Certification occurs when a recognised external authority signals its readiness to recognise and support the existence and claims of a political actor', in C. Tilly and S. Tarrow (eds), *Contentious Politics*, Oxford: Oxford University Press, 2006, p. 75.
45 'Decertification withdraws recognition and commitments of future support', Ibid.
46 As Edward Walsh observes about the Three Mile Island protest movement, campaigns involve a range of actors with different levels of involvement in the movement, and hoping for different beneficial outcomes. See E. J. Walsh, 'Resource mobilisation and citizen protest in communities around Three Mile Island', *Social Problems*, 29, 1, 1981, pp. 1–21.
47 'Tariş'in yeni Genel Müdürü Ertan göreve başladı', *Milliyet*, 7 July 1977, pp. 1 and 10.
48 '19. Demirel'in politikalarına bir örnek: Tariş', http://www.devrim-ciyol.org/Devrimci%20Yol/kitaplar/kitap10_a33.htm (consulted on 2 February 2014).
49 Ibid.
50 'Tariş'te 1 600 işçi direnişe geçti', *Cumhuriyet*, 19 January 1980, pp. 1 and 11.
51 'Tariş işçileri bazı bölümleri işgal etti', *Cumhuriyet*, 9 February 1980, pp. 1 and 11.
52 N. Çalışkan, *ODTÜ tarihçe 1956–1980, op. cit.*, p. 271.
53 'Tariş olayları dün de Istanbul'da protesto edildi', *Cumhuriyet*, 25 January 1980, pp. 1 and 11.
54 'Tariş olayları dün de Istanbul'da protesto edildi', *op. cit.*
55 'Tariş'ten işçi çıkarmalar sürüyor, Gültepe'de yaralanan polis öldü', *Cumhuriyet*, 10 February 1980, pp. 1 and 11.
56 'Izmir'de olaylar sürdü, AP binası bombalandı', *Cumhuriyet*, 12 February 1980, pp. 1 and 11.
57 Chapter 7 looks at the ways in which militias of ülkücü groups and of far-left extra-parliamentary movements managed to get the population to take part in physically violent activities.
58 M. Dobry, *Sociologie des crises politiques, op. cit.*, p. 141.
59 Ibid., p. 143.
60 Ibid., p. 239.

Chapter 6

1. H. Bozarslan, 'Le phénomène milicien', *op. cit.*, p. 194.
2. M. N. Zald, 'Looking backward to look forward: Reflections on the past and future of the resource mobilisation research program', in A. D. Morris and C. Mc Clurg Mueller (eds), *Frontiers in Social Movement Theory*, New Haven, Yale University Press, 1992.
3. F. F. Piven and R. A. Cloward, *Poor People's Movements: Why They Succeed, How They Fail*, New York, Vintage, 1977.
4. C. Tilly, *From Mobilisation to Revolution*, *op. cit.*
5. For a discussion of the idea of repertoires of collective action, see S. Tarrow, 'State and opportunities: The political structuring of social movements', in D. McAdam, J. D. McCarthy and M. N. Zald (eds), *Comparative Perspectives on Social Movements. Political Opportunities, Mobilising Structures, and Cultural Framings*, Cambridge, Cambridge University Press, 1996.
6. http://www.byegm.gov.tr/YAYINLARIMIZ/AyinTarihi/ (consulted on 2 February 2014).
7. *Cumhuriyet 1977*, Istanbul, Cumhuriyet Yayınları, 1977; *Cumhuriyet 1978*, Istanbul, Cumhuriyet Yayınları, 1978; *Cumhuriyet 1978-1979*, Istanbul, Cumhuriyet Yayınları, 1979; *Cumhuriyet 1979-1980*, Istanbul, Cumhuriyet Yayınları, 1980; *1976 Ansiklopedik Yilliği*, Istanbul, Hürriyet Yayınları, 1977; *1977 Ansiklopedik Yilliği*, Istanbul, Hürriyet Yayınları, 1978; *1978 Ansiklopedik Yilligi*, Istanbul, Hürriyet Yayınları, 1979; *1979 Ansiklopedik Yilliği*, Istanbul, Hürriyet Yayınları, 1977; *Milliyet 76*, Istanbul, Milliyet Yayınları, 1977; *Milliyet 77*, Istanbul, Milliyet Yayınları, 1978; *Milliyet 78*, Istanbul, Milliyet Yayınları, 1979; Ünsal, Artun and İlnur Çevik, *Turkey Almanac 1979*, Istanbul, Turkish Daily News Publications, 1979.
8. *Şehitler Ölmez*, Istanbul, Hamle kitabevi, 15 volumes, undated.
9. The first May Day celebration, held the previous year, had attracted nearly 200,000 people to the same square, without any serious incidents being reported. The second gathering took place against a radically different backdrop. General elections were to be held the following month, which the CHP had every chance of winning. As election day drew near, DİSK, Töb-Der and nearly all the revolutionary groups decided to support Ecevit and turn May Day into a show of left-wing strength. DİSK invited all the far-left organizations to take part in the public meeting called on Taksim Square. When the day came, uniformed and plainclothes officers from the forces of law and order took up positions around the square and in the buildings overlooking it. The first groups of marchers started arriving at 1 pm and the DİSK security unit, overwhelmed by the number of people present, was rapidly unable to filter access to the square. Nearly 500,000 people attended the meeting. Scarcely had the head of DİSK started speaking when a gunshot rang out, followed by two others. The crowd panicked. A moment later gunshots were heard coming from four different places. According to witnesses these were fired from the Intercontinental hotel and the water board building (*Sular İdaresi*). The forces of law and order intervened, tanks entered the square and thirty-four people were crushed to death, either by the vehicles or by the crowd. See M. A. Birand, H. Bila and R. Akar, *12 Eylül Türkiye'nin miladi*, *op. cit.*, pp. 49-52.
10. '"Hamido", 2 torunu ve gelini posta ile gelen paketin patlaması sonucu öldüler', *Milliyet*, 18 April 1978, pp. 1 and 12; 'Malatya'da en az 700 işyeri tahrip edildi, CHP il Merkezi de yakıldı', *Milliyet*, 19 April 1978, pp. 1 and 8.

11 '11 aylık icraatın sonucu: 943 ölü', *Hergün*, 1 December 1978, p. 1. The Nationalist Movement denounced the government, accusing it of having failed to take action to maintain security ever since taking office in January 1978. See in particular '7 aylık Ecevit iktidarı döneminde anarşi bilancosu: ölü: 460', *Hergün*, 1 August 1978, p. 1; 'Kan yurdu kapladı', *Hergün*, 10 August 1978, p. 1; '10 aylık anarşi bilançosu: 870 ölü', *Hergün*, 1 November 1978, p. 1.
12 M. A. Birand, H. Bilâ and R. Akar, *12 Eylül Türkiye'nin miladi, op. cit.*, p. 109.
13 Ibid., p. 71.
14 'Balgat Katliamıyla ilgili olarak bir ülkücü yakalandı', *Cumhuriyet*, 15 August 1978, pp. 1 and 5; 'Balgat katliamı sanıkları savcıya, silahlı eylem için örgüt kurduklarını açıkladılar', *Cumhuriyet*, 12 October 1978, pp. 1 and 9.
15 Ibid.
16 '6 TİP'li hunharca öldürüldü', *Cumhuriyet*, 10 October 1978, pp. 1 and 5.
17 'Doçent Cömert öldürüldü, eşi yaralandı', *Cumhuriyet*, 12 July 1978, pp. 1 and 5.
18 'Belediye otobüsüne ateş aşan ülkücüler 2 yurttaşı öldürüldü', *Cumhuriyet*, 8 August 1978, pp. 1 and 4.
19 'Aksaray ilçesinde terör yaratan sağ görüşlü 37 kişi tutuklandı', *Cumhuriyet*, 9 October 1978, pp. 1 and 5.
20 'MHP Şişli İlçe Gençlik Kolu Başkanı ve 3 arkadaşı 7 kişiyi öldürmekten sanık olarak tutuklandı', *Cumhuriyet*, 19 September 1978, pp. 1 and 9.
21 '13 ayrı suça katılan MHP Şişli İlçe Gençlik Kolu Başkanı ve arkadaşı idam cezası ile yargılanacak', *Cumhuriyet*, 11 October 1978, pp. 1 and 9.
22 For examples of actions organized by ülkücü 'commandos', see: 'Kahramanmaraş'taki bombalamaların sanığı 12 ülkücünün yargılanması bugün Ankara'da başlıyor', *Cumhuriyet*, 12 October 1978, pp. 1 and 9; 'Ankara'da ETKO üyesi 7 ülkücü tutuklandı', *Cumhuriyet*, 29 November 1978, pp. 1 and 9; '23 ülkücü için savcı, 5–10 yıl arası hapis istedi', *Milliyet*, 16 November 1978, p. 1; 'Ülkücü sanık Veli Can Oduncu 7 kişiyi öldürdüğünü itiraf etti', *Milliyet*, 23 February 1979, pp. 1 and 9.
23 'Sanık komandolar Maltepe'de silâhları ÜGD, Beykoz'da da MHP Gençlik Kolu Başkanlarından aldıklarını anlattılar', *Cumhuriyet*, 22 October 1978, pp. 1 and 9.
24 'Yakalanan 7 ülkücü silahları MHP'li yöneticilerden aldıklarını açıkladılar', *Cumhuriyet*, 27 October 1978, p. 5.
25 'İskilip MHP II. Başkanı 2 tabanca, tüfek ve dinamitlerle yakalandığı bildirildi', *Cumhuriyet*, 27 October 1978, p. 5.
26 'Elbistan Ülkü-Bir Başkanı yasa dışı eylem düzenlemek suçundan tutuklandı', *Milliyet*, 3 December 1978, p. 9.
27 'Kadirli ÜGD başkanı cinayet sanığı olarak tutuklandı', *Cumhuriyet*, 10 December 1978, pp. 1 and 5.
28 'MİSK'te bomba yapıldığı saptandı, MHP binası arandı', *Cumhuriyet*, 19 July 1979, pp. 1 and 11; 'MİSK genel başkanı ile 2 yönetici sıkıyönetimce gözaltına alındı', *Cumhuriyet*, 21 July 1979, p. 6.
29 'Denizli MİSK Bölge Başkanı bomba yaparken elleri koptu, Istanbul'da 5 yere patlayıcı madde atıldı', *Cumhuriyet*, 4 January 1980, p. 7.
30 'The situation in Kırşehir is as follows: the left has been eliminated in all the schools. We control all the neighbourhoods in town, as well as all the factories'. See T. C. *Ankara – Çankırı – Kastamonu İlleri Sıkıyönetim Komutanlığı Askeri Savcılığı, op. cit.*, p. 336.
31 Ibid., pp. 348–91.

32 In Adana the MHP won 2.16 per cent of the votes cast in the elections for municipal head, and 3.43 per cent in those for the town council; in Osmaniye it won 28.21 per cent and 29.19 per cent respectively of the votes cast; in Ceyhan it scored 7.14 per cent and 7.69 per cent; and in Kozan 16.87 per cent and 17.64 per cent.
33 Semi-structured interview with Mahmut (Dev-Yol) on 10 May 2006 in Ankara. Mahmut was one of those in charge of organizing Dev-Yol's armed activities, especially after the coup of 12 September.
34 D. Ergil, *Türkiye'de Terör ve Şiddet*, Ankara, Turhan Kitabevi, 1980, pp. 105–70.
35 Ibid., p. 131.
36 B. Gourisse, 'Penser les relations entre politisation et passage par l'université: le cas turc (1971–1980)', *Critique internationale*, 50, 2011, pp. 39–53.
37 The available sources do not provide any information about the social category of the victims of fighting between radical groups after 1 January 1980. The almanacs published by the national newspapers either did not come out at the end of 1980 or else did not provide information about events subsequent to the coup of 12 September.
38 In the various sources used here the 'public-sector workers' does not include police officers, primary school teachers, secondary school teachers or all categories of teaching staff in places of further education.

Chapter 7

1 Semi-structured interview with Nejat (Kurtuluş) 4 May 2006 in Ankara.
2 Semi-structured interview with Celal (Vatan Partisi) 9 May 2006 in Ankara.
3 Semi-structured interview with Şadi (Sürekli Devrim) 15 March 2006 in Istanbul.
4 Semi-structured interview with Mahmut on 10 May 2006 in Ankara.
5 'Kozan'daki sağ-sol çatışmasında bir genç öldürüldü', *Milliyet*, 25 November 1978, p. 9.
6 Certain headlines are revelatory: 'Gaziantep'teki liselilerin çatışmada bir işçi tabancayla vurularak öldü', *Milliyet*, 7 January 1977, p. 6; 'Ankara'da 1 öğrenci öldürüldü, 2'si ağır 13 genç yaralandı', *Milliyet*, 25 February 1977, p. 7.
7 'MHP'liler Çine'de CHP ve Töb-Der binalarına saldırıldı, çatışmada bir liseli öldü', *Milliyet*, 18 April 1977, p. 1.
8 *Cumhuriyet* reported an incident in Kırşehir on 14 July 1978 involving machine-gun fire. The article states that several ülkücüs fired from their vehicle at a group of students, wounding twenty-three people. The following month *Cumhuriyet* reported that two people were killed and fourteen others wounded when a town bus was caught in ülkücü gunfire. In August it reported an attack on a funeral procession by a 'commando unit', but according to the information given in the article in question, it was carried out by a handful of armed militants. 'Kırşehir'de komando saldırısı: 23 yaralı var', *Cumhuriyet*, 15 July 1978, pp. 1 and 9; 'Belediye otobüsüne ateş aşan ülkücüler 2 yurttaşı öldürüldü', *Cumhuriyet*, 8 August 1978, pp. 1 and 4; 'Komando cenaze alayına ateş açtı', *Cumhuriyet*, 13 August 1978, pp. 1 and 5.
9 Semi-structured interview with Celal (Vatan Partisi) 9 May 2006 in Ankara.
10 Semi-structured interview with Metin (TİP) in Ankara on 11 May 2006.
11 'Bir öğrenci öldürüldü … Sokak Savaşı oldu', *Milliyet*, 17 January 1977, p. 1.
12 N. Koçak, 'Yurtlararası savaş sabaha kadar sürdü', *Milliyet*, 1 April 1977, pp. 1 and 7.
13 'Adana yurdunda 1 işçi öldürüldü', *Milliyet*, 2 March 1977, pp. 1 and 7.

14 'Atatürk Üniversitesi süresiz kapatıldı', *Milliyet*, 13 January 1977, p. 6.
15 Semi-structured interview with Kutay (Dev-Yol) on 2 May 2006 in Ankara.
16 Semi-structured interview with Irfan (Dev-Yol, Dev-Sol, then Dev-Yol) on 27 May 2006 in Istanbul.
17 'Kahramanmaraş'ta gizli örgütün bomba ve belgeleri ele geçti', *Milliyet*, 23 April 1978, p. 8; 'Kahramanmaraş Savcısı: "Gizli örgütün merkezi Ankara'dadır"', *Milliyet*, 27 April 1978, p. 9; 'Ankara'da ETKO üyesi 7 ülkücü tutuklandı', *Cumhuriyet*, 29 November 1978, pp. 1 and 9.
18 The book *Dış Politika ve Kıbrıs* (Foreign Policy and Cyprus) designated dynamite, *Türkiye Tarihi* (History of Turkey) a large-calibre automatic weapon, *Büyük Türkiye* (Great Turkey) a 7.65mm firearm, *Konuşmalar* (Speeches) a Smith and Wesson, *Leninizm-Komünizm* a 6.35mm firearm and *Diğerleri* (The Others) an automatic weapon. See *T. C. Ankara – Çankırı – Kastamonu İlleri Sıkıyönetim Komutanlığı Askeri Savcılığı, op. cit.*, p. 285.
19 Ibid., p. 291.
20 Abdullah Çatlı was first involved in legal Ülkü Hearth bodies, before becoming one of the main organizers of the Nationalist Movement's violent activities in Ankara.
21 *T. C. Ankara – Çankırı – Kastamonu İlleri Sıkıyönetim Komutanlığı Askeri Savcılığı, op. cit.*, p. 314.
22 Ibid., p. 308.
23 Ibid., pp. 308–9.
24 Ibid.
25 Ibid., p. 312.
26 Ibid., p. 341.
27 Ibid., p. 342.
28 Ibid., p. 345.
29 G. Favarel-Guarrigues, 'Mafia violence and political power in Russia', in Jean-Louis Briquet and Gilles Favarel-Garrigues, *Organised Crime and States: The Hidden Face of Politics, op. cit.*, p. 159.
30 Ö. Tanlak, *İtiraf. Eski bir Ülkücü MHP'yi Anlatıyor, op. cit.*, pp. 58–9.
31 Ibid., p. 14.
32 Ibid.
33 V. Volkov, 'Les entreprises de violence dans la Russie postcommuniste', *Politix*, 13, 49, first quarter 2000, p. 57.
34 H. Bozarslan, 'Le phénomène milicien', *op.cit.*, pp. 185–244.
35 Ibid., p. 197.
36 B. Gürel, *Political Mobilisation in Turkey in the 1970s, op. cit.*, p. 53.
37 Ibid., p. 101.
38 H. Bozarslan, 'Le phénomène milicien', *op. cit.*, p. 205.
39 In the same way as Mafia groups had been able to take advantage of a situation enabling them to 'take charge' of violence in late nineteenth-century Sicily. Pezzoni argues that 'in Sicily not only did the private use of violence spread, but organised groups also appeared which took charge of violence. Violence thus became a means to access resources, an instrument for economic accumulation and political struggle'. P. Pezzino, 'La mafia, l'État et la société dans la Sicile contemporaine (XIXe et XXe siècles)', *Politix*, 13, 49, first quarter 2000, p. 20.
40 H. Bozarslan, 'Le phénomène milicien', *op. cit.*, p. 208.
41 Ibid., p. 209.

42　Hamit Bozarslan notes that 'the ungovernability reigning in the centre was a decisive asset for the militia, enabling it to *effectively* convince the group that the State was not able to meet their need for protection. The State thus withdrew from other domains, being unable to meet the other needs of the group such as social advancement, power-sharing, etc.'. Ibid., p. 225.
43　C. Tilly, 'War making and state making as organized crime', in P. B. Evans, D. Rueschmeyer and T. Skocpol (eds), *Bringing the State Back In*, Cambridge: Cambridge University Press, 1985, p. 171.
44　H. Bozarslan, 'Le phénomène milicien', *op. cit.*, p. 227.
45　B. Gürel, *Political Mobilisation in Turkey in the 1970's*, *op. cit.*, p. 65.
46　'"Kahrolsun gerici çalışma yasası!", "Kahrolsun toplumsal ihanet anlaşması!", "Faşizme ölüm, halka hürriyet!"', *Halkın Kurtuluşu*, 136, 20 November 1978.
47　B. Gürel, *Political Mobilisation in Turkey in the 1970's*, *op. cit.*, p. 46.
48　Ibid., p. 47.
49　M. İ. Erdost, *Faşizm ve Türkiye 1977–1980*, Ankara, Nur Yayınları, 1995, pp. 218–19.
50　'Özaydınlı: "bombalı paketler ve gizli örgütler saptandı"', *Milliyet*, 20 April 1978, pp. 1 and 8; 'Kahramanmaraş'ta gizli örgütün bomba ve belgeleri ele geçti', *Milliyet*, 23 April 1978, p. 8.
51　'Kahramanmaraş'ta bir milletvekili, oğlunu tutuklayan yargıcı tartak-ladı', *Milliyet*, 22 April 1978, p. 8.
52　M. A. Birand, H. Bilâ and R. Akar, *12 Eylül Türkiye'nin miladi*, *op. cit.*, p. 80.
53　B. Gürel, *Political Mobilisation in Turkey in the 1970's*, *op. cit.*, p. 106.
54　Ibid., p. 107.
55　Ibid., pp. 109–11.
56　B. Gürel, '"Communist Police!" The state in the 1970s Turkey', *op. cit.*, p. 9.
57　B. Gürel, *Political Mobilisation in Turkey in the 1970's*, *op. cit.*, pp. 109–11.
58　bid.
59　Ibid., p. 112.
60　'Kahramanmaraş'ta 3 kişi öldü, işyerleri tahrip edildi, 39 kişi yaralandı', *Milliyet*, 23 December 1978, p. 9.
61　M. A. Birand, H. Bilâ and R. Akar, *12 Eylül Türkiye'nin miladi*, *op. cit.*, p. 83.
62　B. Gürel, *Political Mobilisation in Turkey in the 1970's*, *op. cit.*, pp. 114–15.
63　Ibid.
64　Ibid., pp. 116–17.
65　Ibid.
66　Ibid.
67　Murat Bozkurt, an Alevi who lived in Serintepe, provided the following account: 'we were in İmam Ergönül's house. They surrounded the house and broke the windows. After that they went away. But a few minutes later they came back. They attacked the house and tried to make their way in through the roof. They inserted burning rags. They threw explosives. We and the women and children were screaming and trying to protect ourselves. Another group tried to break down the door. … The attackers broke into the house. They started hitting us with sharp tools and sticks, axes, swords. We were covered in our own blood, they insulted us. We were surrounded by our echoing cries …. They killed İmam, Hüseyin, and Güllü Ergönül, and Hacı Bektaş Bozkurt, and Mahmut Ünal. Some of us were seriously wounded.' Ibid., pp. 117–18.
68　In an article published in *Milliyet* on 26 Dec., the journalist notes that the bodies often bore traces of mutilation and torture: 'Ölü sayısının 100'ün üstüne çıkacağı anlaşılıyor', *Milliyet*, 26 December 1978, pp. 1 and 9.

69 B. Gürel, *Political Mobilisation in Turkey in the 1970's, op. cit.*, pp. 119.
70 Ibid., pp. 120–1.
71 The *salavat* is an Arabic formula calling for the holy blessing of the Prophet Muhammad during prayer or in times of peril.
72 Ibid., p. 121.
73 'Ölü sayısı 76'a çıktı', *Milliyet*, 25 December 1978, p. 1.
74 B. Gürel, *Political Mobilisation in Turkey in the 1970's, op. cit.*, pp. 121–2.
75 Martial law was also declared in Adana, Ankara, Bingöl, Elazığ, Erzincan, Erzurum, Gaziantep, Istanbul, Kars, Malatya, Sivas and Urfa.
76 B. Gürel, '"Communist police!" The state in the 1970s Turkey', *op. cit.*, p. 9.
77 Ibid.
78 B. Gürel, *Political Mobilisation in Turkey in the 1970's, op. cit.*, pp. 147–8.
79 Ibid.
80 'Özaydınlı istifa etti', *Milliyet*, 3 January 1979, p. 9; 'Hasan Fehmi Güneş, İçişleri Bakanı oldu', *Milliyet*, 14 January 1979, pp. 1 and 12.
81 The party declared itself in favour of martial law at a meeting of its general board held on 2 October 1978. 'MHP Sıkyönetim istedi', *Hergün*, 3 October 1978, pp. 1 and 7. On 14 October *Hergün* listed the MHP's demands: '1 – Sıkıyönetim ilânı, 2 – Güvenlik mahkemeleri, 3 – Erken seçime didilmeli', *Hergün*, 14 October 1978, pp. 1 and 7.
82 On 21 December 1978 Türkeş granted an interview to the IKA press agency in which he warned that 'the government will fall, perhaps tomorrow, perhaps before tomorrow': 'Türkeş: "Hükümetin düşmesi belki yarın, belki yarından da yakındır"', *Hergün*, 22 December 1978, pp. 1 and 7.
83 '6 sıkıyönetim Mahkemesi kuruldu', *Milliyet*, 28 December 1978, pp. 1 and 9.
84 The Turkish parliament prolonged the state of martial law every two months up until the coup on 12 September 1980. 'Milli Güvenlik Kurulu'nun tasviyesi ile Hükümet sıkıyönteimin 2 ay daha uzatılmasını kararlaştırdı', *Cumhuriyet*, 24 February 1979, pp. 1 and 11.
85 The explosive device which was set off at the Çiçek Cinema was apparently placed there by an ETKO member. 'Maraş olaylarını başlatan bombalamayı bir ülkücü üstlendi', *Cumhuriyet*, 17 January 1979, p. 1.
86 '330 kişi için idam istenen dava bugün başlıyor', *Milliyet*, 4 June 1979, p. 9.
87 V. Özkoçak, 'İlk gün 250 sanığın kimliği saptandı', *Milliyet*, 5 June 1979, p. 6.
88 Ç. Yiğenoğlu, 'Kahramanmaraş olayları davasında dün MHP'li 2 avukat, "mahkemeye saygısızlık" gerekçesiyle duruşma dış bırakıldı', *Milliyet*, 16 June 1979, p. 13; 'Kahramanmaraş davasında, Sakarya ve Yenimahalle sanıklarının sorguları yapıldı', *Milliyet*, 20 June 1979, p. 13; 'Kahramanmaraş davasında Namık Kemal Mahallesi ve Erkenez Çayı olayı sanıklarının sorguları yapıldı', *Milliyet*, 26 June 1979, p. 9.
89 'K.Maraş katliamı davası sonuçlandı. 22 sanık ölüm cezasına çarptırıldı', *Cumhuriyet*, 9 August 1980, pp. 1 and 9.
90 H. Bozarslan 'Le phénomène milicien', *op. cit.*, p. 222.
91 Ibid., p. 227.
92 N. Bölügiray, *Sokaktaki Asker, op. cit.*, p. 21.
93 According to Kutay, 'after Kahramanmaraş Alevis became anti-fascists almost automatically'. Semi-structured interview with Kutay (Dev-Yol) on 2 May 2006 in Ankara.
94 The number of far-left organizations rocketed in 1979 and 1980 due to the increasing frequency with which sections and sub-units were breaking free.

95 S. Yalçın, 'Kayseri'de silahlı bir Akıncı Gençlik kampı hikayesi', *Hürriyet*, 2 September 1980.
96 Ibid.
97 Semi-directive interview with Mahmut (Dev-Yol) on 10 May 2006 in Ankara.
98 The United States approved and even supported the military intervention. See in particular G. Dorronsoro, *Que veut la Turquie ?, op. cit.*, p. 60.
99 B. Gourisse, 'What politics does to the army: Divisions and reconfigurations to the military institution in the 27 May 1960 coup in Turkey', *Middle Eastern Studies*, 58, 1, 2022, pp. 70–86.
100 H. Bozarslan, *Histoire de la Turquie contemporaine, op. cit.*, p. 65.
101 Evren noted: '1st army/Selimiye: all the army commanders and academy commanders felt that intervention was the only solution'. See M. A. Birand, *12 Eylül Saat: 04:00*, Istanbul, Karacan Yayınları, 1985, p. 33.
102 Ibid.
103 Ibid.
104 For a discussion of the effects of the military coup of 12 September 1980, see M. A. Birand, H. Bilâ, and R. Akar, *12 Eylül Türkiye'nin miladi, op. cit.*
105 For discussion of this point see G. Dorronsoro (ed.), *La Turquie conteste, op. cit.*, and 'Réflexions sur la causalité d'un manque: pourquoi y a-t-il si peu de mobilisations en Turquie?', September 2001, http://www.ceri-sciences-po.org.

OUTLINE CHRONOLOGY OF EVENTS (1961-1980)

13 February 1961: Founding of the Workers Party of Turkey (Türkiye İşçi Partisi, TİP) by a group of nine trade union leaders who had broken away from the Türk-İş trade union confederation.

9 July 1961: Proclamation of the new constitution, setting up freedom of the press (articles 22 and 23), freedom of assembly and demonstration (article 28), and freedom of association (article 29); trade unions could be set up without prior authorization (articles 46 and 47); political parties, the 'indispensable entities of democratic political life', could be freely set up (article 56) provided that their activities and policies did not run counter to 'human rights and freedoms', the principles of the secular republic or 'the State's territorial and national integrity' (article 57).

22 and 23 February 1964: Conference of the Republican Villager Nation Party (Cumhuriyetçi Köylü Millet Partisi, CKMP). It was here that Alparslan Türkeş joined the party as inspector general. He was tasked with identifying members who had remained loyal to its former chairman, Osman Bölükbaşı.

31 July and 1 August 1965: Extraordinary conference of the CKMP. Alparslan Türkeş was elected party chairman with 698 votes, against 516 for the outgoing chairman, Ahmet Oğuz.

10 October 1965: General elections won by the Justice Party (Adalet Partisi, AP) with 52.87 per cent of the votes cast. The Republican People's Party (Cumhuriyet Halk Partisi, CHP) turned in its worst ever electoral performance (28.7 per cent), whilst the Workers Party of Turkey won 3 per cent of the votes cast, making it the first far-left party to enter parliament, with fourteen seats.

17 December 1965: Founding of the Federation of Opinion Clubs (Fikir Kulüpleri Federasyonu, FKF).

March 1966: The first Ülkü Hearth (*Ülkü ocağı*) was set up in the Law Faculty at Ankara University on the initiative of the chairman of the CKMP's youth wing, Namık Kemal Zeybek.

January 1967: The Confederation of Progressive Trade Unions of Turkey (Devrimci İşçi Sendikaları Konfederasyonu, DİSK) was set up. In its founding charter the DİSK emphasized the need to use all constitutionally authorized means, and in particular to conduct the struggle for workers' rights within the political arena. It rapidly became the main organization for left-wing social movements.

29 February 1968: Founding of the Ülkücü Youth Organisation (Genç Ülkücüler Teşkilatı, GÜT).

January 1969: FKF conference. Representatives of the National Democratic Revolution movement (Milli Demokratik Devrim, MDD), who were opposed to the policy adopted by TİP representatives of winning power via parliament, won control of the federation. The new leadership team concluded their presentation of their motion by chanting 'Long live civil wars' ('*Yaşasın Hak Savaşları*').

8–9 February 1969: Adana conference of the CKMP, which became the Nationalist Movement Party (Milliyetçi Hareket Partisi, MHP).

26 April 1969: The Ülkü Hearths at the Literature, Law, and Forestry Faculties of Istanbul University, and at the Istanbul College of Architecture and Lighting Engineering (Istanbul Işık Mühendislik ve Mimarlık Yüksek Okulu), joined to form the Union of Ülkü Hearths (Ülkü Ocakları Birliği), in the presence of MHP chairman, Alparslan Türkeş.

15 May 1969: The Ankara Union of Ülkü Hearths (Ankara Ülkü Ocağı Birliği) was created, comprising the Ülkü Hearths at the Faculties of Law, Medicine, and Political Science at Ankara University.

23 June 1970: The Confederation of Nationalist Workers Unions (Milliyetçi İşçi Sendikaları Konfederasyonu, MİSK) was set up by members of the Nationalist Movement.

January 1971: Mahir Çayan, Yusuf Küpeli and Münir Aktolga resigned from the editorial committee of the MDD's journal, *Aydınlık Sosyaslist Dergi* (*ASD*). They founded the *Kurtuluş* journal (*Liberation*), in which they pronounced themselves in favour of urban guerrilla activity, going on to found the Kurtuluş Group (Kurtuluş Grubu). This changed its name to the Peoples Liberation Party-Front of Turkey (Türkiye Halk Kurtuluş Partisi-Cephesi, THKP-C) on kidnapping Israel's consul general, Ephraïm Elrom, on 17 May 1971. Its members demanded the release of all Marxist-Leninist activists and that the THKP-C's first bulletin be read out on radio for three days; they killed the consul when the authorities refused to comply with these demands.

4 March 1971: The Peoples Liberation Army of Turkey (Türkiye Halk Kurtuluş Ordusu, THKO) came into official existence with the kidnapping of four American officers in Ankara. The THKO called for armed struggle, presented as a war to free the Turkish people and for an independent Turkey, to be conducted against the forces of capital, parliamentarianism and neocolonialism. It presented itself as drawing on the combined influence of Palestinian resistance and South American national liberation models.

12 March 1971: The army sent a communiqué to the AP government demanding that Prime Minister Demirel resign and his government be dissolved; he left office immediately.

26 April 1971: Martial law was proclaimed in eleven Turkish provinces.

May 1971: The Islamist National Order Party (Milli Nizam Partisi, MNP) was shut down, which had been founded by Necmettin Erbakan in 1969. It reopened on 11 October 1972 as the National Salvation Party (Milli Selâmet Partisi, MSP).

July 1971: The TİP was shut down and its cadres sent to prison.

7–8 February 1972: Setting up of the Communist Party of Turkey – Marxist-Leninist/ Workers and Peasants Liberation Army of Turkey (Türkiye Komünist Partisi – Marxist Leninist/Türkiye İşçi Köylü Kurtuluş Ordusu, TKP-ML/TİKKO). The group called for civil war (*halk savaşı*) and armed struggle (*silahlı mücadele*) 'organised in the villages, for red political power in the rural regions'. Its activities were interrupted by a large-scale operation conducted by the security forces in May 1973 in which the entire TİKKO executive committee was arrested. On 18 May its leader, İbrahim Kaypakkaya, died in Diyarbakir prison after being tortured for several days.

15 February 1972: Setting up of the Turkish Ülkücüs Organisation (Türk Ülkücüler Teşkilatı, TÜT) in Çankırı.

6 May 1972: THKO cadres Deniz Gezmiş, Hüseyin İnan and Yusuf Aslan were arrested. They were executed on 6 May 1972 after being sentenced to death on 9 October 1971 by martial law tribunals.

18 May 1972: Bülent Ecevit elected as chairman of the CHP.

22 December 1972: Setting up of the Association of the Great Ideal (Büyük Ülkü Derneği, BÜD) in Kayseri.

15 September 1973: The Association of Ülkü Hearths (Ülkü Ocakları Derneği, ÜOD) was set up in Bursa by Ramiz Ongun, a MHP youth organization cadre.

14 October 1973: General elections won by the CHP with 33.3 per cent of the votes cast. The AP came second with 29.8 per cent, whilst the MHP won 3.4 per cent and three seats in parliament.

November 1973: Setting up of the Istanbul Higher Education Cultural Association (Istanbul Yüksek Öğrenim Kültür Derneği, İYÖKD), in which far-left movements were soon in the majority.

26 January–17 November 1974: Coalition government comprising the CHP and the MSP.

8 April 1974: Setting up of the Ankara Higher Education Democratic Association (Ankara Demokratik Yüksek Öğrenim Derneği, ADYÖD), in which the radical left-wing movements were in the majority.

1974: Setting up of Halkın Yolu ('People's Path'), a group run by former members of the THKP-C sections in Istanbul, Izmir, Trabzon, Denizli and Kars. The group went on to found a journal called *Militan Gençlik* (*Militant Youth*), and then another called *Halkın Yolu* (*People's Voice*) in 1975.

14 May 1974: The Turkish parliament passed the draft law for a general amnesty to be granted to political personnel and activists imprisoned in the wake of the coup of 12 March 1971.

22 June 1974: Founding of the Socialist Workers Party of Turkey (Türkiye Sosyalist İşçi Partisi, TSİP).

20 July 1974: Military intervention in Cyprus, condemned by NATO, but greeted with virtually unanimous approval in Turkey.

20 January 1975: Setting up of the far-left Association for Union and Solidarity between Officials (Tüm-Der).

21 January 1975: Founding of the Fatherland Party (Vatan Partisi, VP) by associates of Hikmet Kıvılcımlı, a communist intellectual.

23 February 1975: Founding of the Labour Party of Turkey (Türkiye Emekçi Partisi, TEP) by Mihri Belli, a long-standing member of the Turkish Communist Party.

31 March 1975-22 June 1977: First Nationalist Front government (Milliyetçi Cephe Hükümeti), composed of the AP, MSP, MHP and CGP (Cumhuriyetçi Güven Partisi, Republican Reliance Party).

17 May 1975: Setting up of the Pol-Der (Polis Derneği) police association. From the outset the leadership team wanted the association to be a model of a 'people's police' (*halkın polisi*). It denounced the demands of the 'fascists', abuses of power by the recently formed Nationalist Front government and the torture used by certain policemen against members of 'progressive' organizations.

1 May 1975: Founding of the second Workers Party of Turkey (Türkiye İşçi Partisi, TİP) by Behice Boran and Sadun Aren.

30 Main 1975: Founding of the Socialist Revolution Party (Sosyalist Devrim Partisi, SDP) by former TİP chairman Mehmet Ali Aybar.

2 February 1976: Setting up of the Halkın Kurtuluşu group ('People's Liberation'), which endeavoured to embody the Maoist legacy of Deniz Gezmiş' THKO. By the end of the decade this group acted as the main proponent in Turkey of Enver Hodja's so-called 'Albanian' theses.

June 1976: Setting up of the Kurtuluş group (Liberation) by former members of the THKP-C (to which the new group's name directly referred), which broke away from the Higher Education Associations (Yüksek Öğrenim Dernekleri) over diverging interpretations of texts written by Mahir Çayan, the THKP-C leader who had been assassinated by security forces in 1972.

August 1976: Setting up of the Federation of Revolutionary Youth Associations (Devrimci Gençlik Dernekleri Federasyonu, DGDF) in the wake of a rapprochement between the Istanbul Higher Education Association (Istanbul Yüksek Öğrenim Derneği, İYÖD), the Ankara Higher Education Association (Ankara Yüksek Öğrenim Derneği, AYÖD) and the Higher Education Cultural Associations (Yüksek Öğrenim Kültür Dernekleri) of Izmir, Bursa, Adana, Sakarya, and Erzurum.

13 February 1977: The board of governors at the Middle East Technical University (Orta Doğu Teknik Üniversitesi, ODTÜ) elected Hasan Tan as rector. Tan was a member of the governing body of the Intellectuals Association and viewed as an MHP sympathizer. A student boycott started, lasting until the rector resigned on 22 June 1977.

1 May 1977: Labour Day public meeting held on Taksim Square in Istanbul, organized by DİSK. The trade unionists invited all organizations opposed to the Nationalist Front government to join the march. The meeting ended in a bloodbath in which thirty-four people were killed as a result of an outbreak of panic when gunshots were fired into the crowd.

May 1977: The DGDF published the first issue of its journal *Revolutionary Path* (*Devrimci Yol*, better known under its abbreviated form, *Dev-Yol*), adopting this as the federation's name.

5 June 1977: General elections won by the CHP with 41.38 per cent of the votes cast. The AP came second with 36.88 per cent, ahead of the MSP (8.56 per cent), the MHP (6.42 per cent), the CGP (1.87 per cent) and the Democratic Party (Demokratik Parti, DP [1.85 per cent]).

15 June 1977: Opening of the Ülkücü Youth Association (Ülkücü Gençler Derneği, ÜGD) in Konya, ahead of the junta's closing down of the ÜOD.

22 June-21 July 1977: Provisional government of Bülent Ecevit, which failed to win a parliamentary vote of confidence.

21 July 1977-5 January 1978: Second Nationalist Front government (İkinci Milliyetçi Cephe), comprised of the AP, MSP and MHP.

16 March 1978: A bomb was set off by ülkücüs at Istanbul University.

1 May 1978: The Istanbul section of Dev-Yol broke away from the organization to form Devrimci Sol (Revolutionary Left).

17-18 June 1978: The MHP founded the Federation of Turkish Democratic Ülkücü Associations in Europe (Avrupa Demokratik Ülkücü Türk Dernekleri Federasyonu, ADÜTDF), or Turkish Federation (Türk Federasyonu), headquartered in Schwarzenborn in Germany. This had 220 associations in Europe, 170 of which were in Germany, and numbered over 33,000 members.

11 July 1978: Bedrettin Cömert, a lecturer at Hacettepe University in Ankara, was assassinated by ülkücü activists.

7 August 1978: Three ülkücüs (including the head of a local ÜOD section) opened fire from a car on a public bus in the Mamak neighbourhood in Ankara, killing two people and wounding fourteen others.

10 August 1978: A group of ülkücüs opened fire with a machine gun on a coffeehouse in the Balgat neighbourhood in Ankara, wounding fourteen people and leaving five others dead.

3-4 September 1978: In Sivas, ülkücüs spread the rumour that the Alibaba Mosque had been attacked by Alevis, triggering a mass attack against Alevi populations in the town, conducted under the orders of ülkücüs.

9 October 1978: Seven TİP members were tortured and then assassinated by ülkücü activists in the Bahçelievler neighbourhood in Ankara.

December 1978: Shutting down of the Association of Ülkü Hearths.

22-25 December 1978: In Kahramanmaraş, the Alevi community was targeted by part of the town's Sunni population, under the orders of members of local ülkücü organizations. After three days of confrontation, official figures put the number of dead at 111, with over 1000 people injured; 552 shops, 289 houses, and 8 vehicles were torched.

26 December 1978: Martial law was declared in the thirteen provinces to be hardest hit by confrontations between radical groups, namely Adana, Ankara, Elazığ, Bingöl, Erzincan, Malatya, Erzurum, Gaziantep, Istanbul, Kahramanmaraş, Kars, Urfa and Sivas. The state of martial law was prolonged and expanded up until the coup of 12 September 1980.

28 September 1979: Cevat Yurdakul, the head of the Directorate of Security in Adana and a member of Pol-Der, was assassinated by an ülkücü activist.

14 October 1979: Fikri Sönmez, a tailor from the town of Fatsa and Dev-Yol member, stood as an independent candidate in the municipal elections and won.

12 November 1979–12 December 1980: Minority AP government.

27 December 1979: The military staff sent Present Korutürk a warning letter (*uyarı mektubu*), demanding that the government put an end to the 'anarchy' (*anarşi*), 'terror' (*terör*), and 'divisions' (*bölücülük*), and indicating that, if it failed to do so, the army would take the necessary steps.

24 January 1980: Demirel presented a series of measures to liberalize the economy. The Turkish lira was devalued by 32.7 per cent and its exchange rate was now allowed to float on a daily basis; salaries were frozen and agricultural subsidies scrapped. The country opened up to foreign capital by significantly reducing customs duties. Foreign investment was encouraged and foreign trade liberalized.

9 March 1980: The courts shut down the ÜGD. Its members set up a new structure, the Association of the Ideal Path (Ülkü Yolu Derneği, ÜYD), headquartered in a province unaffected by martial law (in Nevşehir).

3 July 1980: Çorum events. Ülkücü units took control of the town's main entry and exit points, and an increasing number of shootings were carried out against Alevi populations. Hundreds of shops and dwellings were pillaged and then torched, as were the buildings of the local branches of the major newspapers and television stations. Calm was restored when an MHP MP and the governor of the province came to an agreement to reopen the town.

11 July 1980: Operation Point (*Nokta Operasyonu*). The 'liberated' town of Fatsa came to an end at 4:15 AM when three gendarmerie commando squadrons entered the town, together with troops from Ordu Province Commandership, a mechanised infantry battalion, and policemen.

6 September 1980: militias wearing commando uniforms paraded in the streets of Konya during an MSP public meeting, calling for the introduction of sharia, the liberation of Jerusalem, and an end to secularity in Turkey, booing when the national anthem was sung.

12 September 1980: military coup. A National Security Council took power, made up of Joint Head of Staff Kenan Evren, together with the Army, Navy and Air Force heads of staff. The military shut down all political parties, all trade unions and 23,667 associations. They suspended parliamentary activity, and conducted a systematic wave of arrests of activists and cadres from ülkücü and far-left organizations. Most political personnel were arrested, 650,000 people were taken into custody, the use of torture became widespread and a purge was conducted of the public sector.

BIBLIOGRAPHY

Sources

Alpat, İnönü, *Türkiye Solu Sözlüğü*, Istanbul, Mayı Yayınları, 2003.
Can, Celalettin, *Bağımsızlık, Demokrasi ve Sosyalizm Mücadelesinde Gençlik*, vol. 1, 1974–1980, Istanbul, Boran Yayınevi, 1999.
Belge, Murat, 'Türkiye İşçi Partisi', in *Cumhuriyet Dönemi Türkiye Ansiklopedisi*, Istanbul, İletişim Yayınları, p. 2120.
Bölügiray, Nevzat, *Sokaktaki Asker, Bir Sıkıyönetim Komutanının 12 Eylül Öncesi Anıları*, Istanbul, Milliyet Yayınları, 1989.
Genel Nüfus Sayımı, Ankara, 1975, Başbakanlık Devlet İstatistik Enstitüsü. http://www.anayasa.gen.tr/1961constitution-amended.pdf (consulted on 7 January 2021).
http://www.byegm.gov.tr/YAYINLARIMIZ/AyinTarihi/ (consulted on 2 February 2014).
Nüfus İstatistikleri, Ankara, 2001, Başbakanlık Devlet İstatistik Enstitüsü.
Öner, Sıtkı, *Halkın Polisi. Pol-Der Anıları*, Istanbul, İletişim Yayınları, 2003.
Polis. Vatandaşın Can, Mal ve Namusunu Korur, Devlet Güvenliğini Sağlar, Trafiği Murakabe Eder, Demokratik nizamın Kanun Dışı Hareketlerle Bozulmasını Önler, no place of publication indicated, 1970.
Şaylan, Gencay, 'Cumhuriyet Bürokrasisi', in *Cumhuriyet Dönemi Türkiye Ansiklopedisi*, vol. 2, Istanbul, İletişim Yayınları, 1983, pp. 298–308.
Şehitler Ölmez, 15 volumes, Istanbul, Hamle kitabevi, undated.
T. C. Ankara-Çankırı-Kastamonu İlleri Sıkıyönetim Komutanlığı Askeri Savcılığı. *Iddianame: MHP ve Ülkücü Kuruluşlar*, drawn up by Nurettin Soyer, military prosecutor under martial law, 1981.
Tanlak, Ömer, *İtiraf. Eski Bir Ülkücü MHP'yi Anlatıyor*, Istanbul, Kaynak Yayınları, 1996.
Türkeş, Alparlsan, *Dokuz Işık ve Türkiye*, Istanbul, Hamle Yayınevi, 1965.
Türkeş, Alparslan, *Dokuz Işık*, Istanbul, Hamle Yayınevi, undated.
Türkeş, Alparslan, *Yeni Ufuklara Doğru*, Istanbul, Kutluğ Yayınları, 1974, chapter headed '"İç ve dış tehditler'.
Türkiye İstatistik Yıllığı, 1973, Ankara, 1974, Başbakanlık Devlet İstatistik Enstitüsü.
Ülkücü Komando Kampları. AP Hükümeti'nin 1970'te Hazırlattığı MHP Raporu, Istanbul, Kaynak Yayınları, 1978.
Ünsal, Artun and İlnur Çevik, *Turkey Almanac 1979*, Istanbul, Turkish Daily News Publications, 1979.
Yiğenoğlu, Çetin, *Sakıncalı Kadın Polis Nurhan Varlı'nın Anıları*, İstanbul, Çağdaş Yayınları, 1995.
Yılmaz, Adil, *Bu Tarih Bizim*, Istanbul, Devrim Dergisi Yayınları, 2006.

Periodicals

'1 - Sıkıyönetim İlânı, 2 - Güvenlik Mahkemeleri, 3 - Erken Seçime Didilmeli', *Hergün*, 14 October 1978, pp. 1 and 7.

'1 dolar = 17,85 TL', *Milliyet*, 2 March 1977, p. 1.

'1 şubat 1978'e Kadar Devrimci Yol'un Kampanyasına Gelen Bağışlar', *Devrimci Yol*, 15, 3 February 1978, p. 10.

'10 Aylık Anarşi Bilançosu: 870 Ölü', *Hergün*, 1 November 1978, p. 1.

'11 Aylık İcraatın Sonucu: 943 Ölü', *Hergün*, 1 December 1978, p. 1.

'13 Ayrı Suça Katılan MHP Şişli İlçe Gençlik Kolu Başkanı ve Arkadaşı İdam Cezası İle Yargılanacak', *Cumhuriyet*, 11 October 1978, pp. 1 and 9.

'19. Demirel'in Politikalarına bir Örnek: Tariş', http://www.devrim-ciyol.org/Devrimci%20Yol/kitaplar/kitap10_a33.htm (consulted on 2 February 2014).

1976 Ansiklopedik Yilliği, Istanbul, Hürriyet Yayınları, 1977.

1977 Ansiklopedik Yilliği, Istanbul, Hürriyet Yayınları, 1978.

1978 Ansiklopedik Yilligi, Istanbul, Hürriyet Yayınları, 1979.

1979 Ansiklopedik Yilliği, Istanbul, Hürriyet Yayınları, 1980.

'220 Kaymakamın Görev Yeri Yine Değişiyor', *Cumhuriyet*, 19 July 1980, pp. 1 and 9.

'23 Ülkücü İçin Savcı, 5-10 Yıl Arası Hapis İstedi', *Milliyet*, 16 November 1978, p. 1.

'26 İlin Valisi Merkez Valiliğine Alındı', *Milliyet*, 13 February 1978, p. 1.

'330 Kişi için Idam Istenen Dava Bugün Başlıyor', *Milliyet*, 4 June 1979, p. 9.

'38 Kaymakam Görev Yeri Değiştirildi', *Cumhuriyet*, 31 July 1978, p. 5.

'4'ler 150 Milyon Dolarlık İvedi Yardımistiyor', *Milliyet*, 12 April 1979, pp. 1 and 7.

'40 İlin Valisi Değişiyor', *Milliyet*, 3 February 1978, pp. 1 and 9.

'6 Sıkıyönetim Mahkemesi Kuruldu', *Milliyet*, 28 December 1978, pp. 1 and 9.

'6 TİP'li Hunharca Öldürüldü', *Cumhuriyet*, 10 October 1978, pp. 1 and 5.

'7 Aylık Ecevit İktidarı Döneminde Anarşi Bilancosu: Ölü: 460', *Hergün*, 1 August 1978, p. 1.

'Adana Yurdunda 1 Işçi Öldürüldü', *Milliyet*, 2 March 1977, pp. 1 and 7.

Akbay, Ertuğrul, 'Türk Polisin İç Yüzü', *Polis Magazin*, 15, 1, 1980, pp. 8-12.

Akbay, Ertuğrul, 'Türk Polisin İç Yüzü', *Polis Magazin*, 15, 2, 1980, pp. 10-21.

'Aksaray İlçesinde Terör Yaratan Sağ Görüşlü 37 Kişi Tutuklandı', *Cumhuriyet*, 9 October 1978, pp. 1 and 5.

Akyıldız, Erhan, 'Millî Eğitim Müdürü: "Anarşık Olaylardan Okul Yöneticileri Sorumludur"', *Milliyet*, 1 October 1977, p. 4.

'Amerikan Uşağı MHP, AP, CGP'ye, Rus Uşağı TİP'e oy Verme Hesap Sor! ', *Halkın Sesi*, 111, 31 May 1977, p. 1.

'Ankara'da 1 Öğrenci Öldürüldü, 2'si Ağır 13 Genç Yaralandı', *Milliyet*, 25 February 1977, p. 7.

'Ankara'da ETKO Üyesi 7 Ülkücü Tutuklandı', *Cumhuriyet*, 29 November 1978, pp. 1 and 9.

'Atatürk Üniversitesi Süresiz Kapatıldı', *Milliyet*, 13 January 1977, p. 6.

'*Aydınlık*, Oportünist Fırsatçı Tavırlar ve Spekülasyonlarla Devrimci Harekete Kara Çalıyor', *Devrimci Yol*, 4, 15 June 1977, p. 9.

'Ayın Aynası', *Öğretmen Dünyası*, 5, May 1980, pp. 32-3.

'Ayın Aynası', *Öğretmen Dünyası*, 6, June 1980, pp. 31-2.

'Ayın Aynası', *Öğretmen Dünyası*, 8, August 1980, pp. 31-2.

'Balgat Katliamı Sanıkları Savcıya, Silahlı Eylem İçin Örgüt Kurduklarını Açıkladılar', *Cumhuriyet*, 12 October 1978, pp. 1 and 9.

'Balgat Katliamıyla İlgili Olarak Bir Ülkücü Yakalandı', *Cumhuriyet*, 15 August 1978, pp. 1 and 5.
'Batılılar Türk Ekonomisi için Özel Plan Hazırlıyor', *Milliyet*, 1 December 1978, pp. 1 and 9.
'Bazı İşçilerin İşine Son Vermek İçin ODTÜ'de Personelin Ad Listesi Çıkartılıyor', *Milliyet*, 4 December 1977, pp. 1 and 6.
'Belediye Otobüsüne Ateş Aşan Ülkücüler 2 Yurttaşı Öldürüldü', *Cumhuriyet*, 8 August 1978, pp. 1 and 4.
'Bir Öğrenci Öldürüldü … Sokak Savaşı Oldu', *Milliyet*, 17 January 1977, p. 1.
Cumhuriyet 1977, Istanbul, Cumhuriyet Yayınları, 1977.
Cumhuriyet 1978–1979, Istanbul, Cumhuriyet Yayınları, 1979.
Cumhuriyet 1978, Istanbul, Cumhuriyet Yayınları, 1978.
Cumhuriyet 1979–1980, Istanbul, Cumhuriyet Yayınları, 1980.
'Değerli Dostlar', *Ürün Sosyalist dergi*, 5th year, 10, 55, January 1979, p. 2.
'Denge Suçlular Lehine Bozuluyor', *Milliyet*, 27 February 1977, p. 7.
'Denizli MİSK Bölge Başkanı Bomba Yaparken Elleri Koptu, Istanbul'da 5 Yere Patlayıcı Madde Atıldı', *Cumhuriyet*, 4 January 1980, p. 7.
'Devlet Kars'a Giremiyor', *Hergün*, 26 October 1978, pp. 1 and 7.
'*Devrimci Yol* Dergisinin Seçimler Konusundaki Tesbitlerini ve Oportünist-Revisyonist Siyasi Taktiği Eleştireceğiz', *Halkın Kurtuluşu*, 58, 1 June 1977, p. 1.
'*Devrimci Yol* Katilleri Açıklamalıdır', *Halkın Sesi*, 150, 28 February 1978, p. 3.
'*Devrimci Yol*'cular İTÜ'de Gençliği Bölüyor', *Halkın Sesi*, 141, 27 December 1977, p. 6.
'DİSK Yönetiminin Seçimlerdeki Tutumu', *Devrimci Yol*, 2, 15 May 1977, p. 11.
'Doçent Cömert Öldürüldü, Eşi Yaralandı', *Cumhuriyet*, 12 July 1978, pp. 1 and 5.
'Eğitim Enstitüsü Sınavları Ülkücülerin Baskısı Altında Yapıldı', *Milliyet*, 10 November 1977, p. 8.
'Ekonomi Politik ve Eğitim Üzerine', *Devrimci Yol*, 5, 1 July 1977, p. 14.
'Elbistan Ülkü-Bir Başkanı Yasa Dışı Eylem Düzenlemek Suçundan Tutuklandı', *Milliyet*, 3 December 1978, p. 9.
'Emniyet Örgütünde Yeni Terfi ve Atamalar Yapıldı', *Cumhuriyet*, 8 July 1978, p. 5.
'Emperyalizm', *Devrimci Yol*, 15, 21 February 1978, pp. 12–13.
'Faşist Teröre Karşı Savaşalım', *Devrimci Yol*, 20, 31 July 1978.
'Faşizm ve Faşizme Karşı Mücadele Sorunu Üzerine (2) ', *Devrimci Yol*, 13, 15 January 1978, pp. 8–11.
'Faşizm ve Faşizme Karşı Mücadele Sorunu', *Devrimci Yol*, 12, 1 December 1978, pp. 8–9.
'Fatsa Operasyonu: 300 Kişi Gözaltına', *Cumhuriyet*, 12 July 1980, pp. 1 and 5.
'Fatsa'da Olay Yok, Ama Halk Tedirgin', *Cumhuriyet*, 11 July 1980, pp. 1 and 9.
'Fatsa'daki Maskeliler Ülkücü Militanlardı', *Cumhuriyet*, 12 July 1980, pp. 1 and 9.
'Gaziantep'teki Liselilerin Çatışmada Bir Işçi Tabancayla Vurularak Öldü', *Milliyet*, 7 January 1977, p. 6.
'Gençlik Örgütü Değil, Besleme bir Naylon Örgüt: İGD', *Devrimci Yol*, 3, 1 June 1977, p. 4.
Güneş, Hasan Fehmi, 'Türkiye'de Terör, Anarşi ve Mücadele Yolları', *Polis Magazin*, 15, 8, 1980, pp. 8–13.
Güneş, Hasan Fehmi, 'Türkiye'de Terör, Anarşi ve Mücadele Yolları', *Polis Magazin*, 15, 8, 1980, pp. 8–13.
'"Hamido", 2 Torunu ve Gelini Posta ile Gelen Paketin Patlaması Sonucu Öldüler', *Milliyet*, 18 April 1978, pp. 1 and 12.
'*Halkın Kurtuluşu*'nun Siyasi Şaşkınlığı', *Devrimci Yol*, 4, 15 June 1977, p. 8.
'*Halkın Yolu* Yalandan ne Umuyor? ', *Devrimci Yol*, 14, 3 February 1978, p. 15.

'Hasan Fehmi Güneş, İçişleri Bakanı Oldu', *Milliyet*, 14 January 1979, pp. 1 and 12.
'Ho Şi Minh', *Devrimci Yol*, 8, 1 September 1977, p. 16.
'Honduras Devrimin Yolu', *Devrimci Yol*, 5, 1 July 1977, pp. 10-11.
'Hükümet Dış Kredi Bekleyişi İçinde', *Cumhuriyet*, 4 February 1980, pp. 1 and 11.
'İGD'li Revizyonistler Bursa'da Devrimcilere ve TİP'lilere Saldırdılar', *Halkın Sesi*, 66, 20 July 1976, p. 8.
'İleri Demokrasi ve TKP', *Devrimci Yol*, 5, 1 July 1977, pp. 8-9.
'İlk Gün 250 Sanığın Kimliği Saptandı', *Milliyet*, 5 June 1979, p. 6.
'IMF, 450 Milyon Dolar Kredi Açtı', *Milliyet*, 17 March 1978, pp. 1 and 8.
'IMF'den 224 Milyon Dolar Bugün Geliyor', *Cumhuriyet*, 30 January 1980, pp. 1 and 6.
'İran'da Faşist Şah Yönetimine Karşı Devrimci Mücadele Yükseliyor', *Devrimci Yol*, 19, 20 June 1978, pp. 14-15.
'İskilip MHP II. Başkanı 2 Tabanca, Tüfek ve Dinamitlerle Yakalandığı Bildirildi', *Cumhuriyet*, 27 October 1978, p. 5.
'Istanbul Toplum Polis Müdürü Görevden Alındı', *Milliyet*, 3 February 1978, p. 9.
'Izmir'de Olaylar Sürdü, AP Binası Bombalandı', *Cumhuriyet*, 12 February 1980, pp. 1 and 11.
'K.Maraş Katliamı Davası Sonuçlandı. 22 Sanık Ölüm Cezasına Çarptırıldı', *Cumhuriyet*, 9 August 1980, pp. 1 and 9.
'Kadirli ÜGD Başkanı Cinayet Sanığı Olarak Tutuklandı', *Cumhuriyet*, 10 December 1978, pp. 1 and 5.
'Kahramanmaraş Davasında Namık Kemal Mahallesi ve Erkenez Çayı Olayı Sanıklarının Sorguları Yapıldı', *Milliyet*, 26 June 1979, p. 9.
'Kahramanmaraş Davasında, Sakarya Ve Yenimahalle Sanıklarının Sorguları Yapıldı', *Milliyet*, 20 June 1979, p. 13.
'Kahramanmaraş Savcısı: "Gizli Örgütün Merkezi Ankara'dadır"', *Milliyet*, 27 April 1978, p. 9.
'Kahramanmaraş'ta 3 Kişi Öldü, İşyerleri Tahrip Edildi, 39 Kişi Yaralandı', *Milliyet*, 23 December 1978, p. 9.
'Kahramanmaraş'ta bir Milletvekili, Oğlunu Tutuklayan Yargıcı Tartakladı', *Milliyet*, 22 April 1978, p. 8.
'Kahramanmaraş'ta Gizli Örgütün Bomba ve Belgeleri Ele Geçti', *Milliyet*, 23 April 1978, p. 8.
'Kahramanmaraş'taki Bombalamaların Sanığı 12 Ülkücünün Yargılanması Bugün Ankara'da Başlıyor', *Cumhuriyet*, 12 October 1978, pp. 1 and 9.
'Kahrolsun Gerici Çalışma Yasası! ', 'Kahrolsun Toplumsal İhanet Anlaşması!', 'Faşizme Ölüm, Halka Hürriyet!', *Halkın Kurtuluşu*, 136, 20 November 1978.
'Kan Yurdu Kapladı', *Hergün*, 10 August 1978, p. 1.
'Kapitalist Olmayan Yol: Leninst Devrim Teorisinin İnkârı', *Devrimci Yol*, 4, 15 June 1977, pp. 6-7.
Ketenci, Şükran, 'Eğitim. Sorunlar Daha da Büyükerek bu Yıla Aktarıldı', *Cumhuriyet*, 2 January 1979, supplement, p. 3.
'Kitle Eğitiminde Dikkat Edilmesi Gereken Noktalar', *Devrimci Yol*, 1, 1 May 1977, p. 15.
'Kırşehir'de Komando Saldırısı: 23 Yaralı Var', *Cumhuriyet*, 15 July 1978, pp. 1 and 9.
Koçak, Namık, 'Yurtlararası Savaş Sabaha Kadar Sürdü', *Milliyet*, 1 April 1977, pp. 1 and 7.
'Komando Cenaze Alayına Ateş Açtı', *Cumhuriyet*, 13 August 1978, pp. 1 and 5.
'Komünistler Halk Savaşı Hazırlıyor', *Hergün*, 27 August 1978, p. 1.

'Komünizme karşı set Milliyetçi Hareket. Kapılma Hiç Hayale Ver Oy'unu Hilal'e', in *Sosyalizm ve Toplumsal Mücadeleler Ansiklopedisi*, vol. 7 (1960-1980), Istanbul, İletişim Yayınları, 1988, p. 518.
'Kozan'daki Sağ-Sol Çatışmasında Bir Genç Öldürüldü', *Milliyet*, 25 November 1978, p. 9.
'Malatya'da en Az 700 İşyeri Tahrip Edildi, CHP İl Merkezi de Yakıldı', *Milliyet*, 19 April 1978, pp. 1 and 8.
'Mao Zedung (1893-...)', *Devrimci Yol*, 9, 19 September 1977, p. 16.
'Maraş Olaylarını Başlatan Bombalamayı Bir Ülkücü Üstlendi', *Cumhuriyet*, 17 January 1979, p. 1.
'Marksist Felsefe Eğitimi Üzerine', *Devrimci Yol*, 3, 1 June 1977, pp. 14-15.
'Marksist Teorinin ve Teorik Eğitimin Önemi Üzerine', *Devrimci Yol*, 1, 1 May 1977, pp. 13-15.
'MC Döneminde Görevlendirilen 11 000 Vekil Öğretmenin İşlerine Son Verildi', *Cumhuriyet*, 20 July 1978, p. 1.
'MHP Lideri Türkeş: "Bölücü ve Komünistler İç Savaş Yaratmak İstiyor"', *Hergün*, 11 February 1979, p. 1.
'MHP Şişli İlçe Gençlik Kolu Başkanı ve 3 Arkadaşı 7 Kişiyi Öldürmekten Sanık Olarak Tutuklandı', *Cumhuriyet*, 19 September 1978, pp. 1 and 9.
'MHP Sıkyönetim İstedi', *Hergün*, 3 October 1978, pp. 1 and 7.
'MHP Sıkıyönetim İstedi', *Hergün*, 5 October 1978, p. 1.
'MHP'liler Çine'de CHP ve Töb-Der Binalarına Saldırıldı, Çatışmada Bir Liseli Öldü', *Milliyet*, 18 April 1977, p. 1.
'Milli Güvenlik Kurulu'nun Tasviyesi ile Hükümet Sıkıyönetimin 2 Ay Daha Uzatılmasını Kararlaştırdı', *Cumhuriyet*, 24 February 1979, pp. 1 and 11.
Milliyet 76, Istanbul, Milliyet Yayınları, 1977.
Milliyet 77, Istanbul, Milliyet Yayınları, 1978.
Milliyet 78, Istanbul, Milliyet Yayınları, 1979.
'MİSK Genel Başkanı Ile 2 Yönetici Sıkıyönetimce Gözaltına Alındı', *Cumhuriyet*, 21 July 1979, p. 6.
'MİSK'te Bomba Yapıldığı Saptandı, MHP Binası Arandı', *Cumhuriyet*, 19 July 1979, pp. 1 and 11.
'ODTÜ Öğretim Üyeleri Siyasal İktidarlarca Atanan Yöneticilere Karşı Çıktı', *Milliyet*, 18 February 1977, pp. 1 and 10.
'ODTÜ'de Çıkan Olaylarda 3'ü Ağır 35 Öğrenci Yaralandı', *Milliyet*, 3 December 1977, p. 8.
'ODTÜ'deki Forumda yeni Rektör İstenmedi', *Milliyet*, 16 February 1977, pp. 1 and 7.
'Ölü Sayısı 76'a Çıktı', *Milliyet*, 25 December 1978, p. 1.
'Ölü Sayısının 100'ün Üstüne Çıkacağı Anlaşılıyor', *Milliyet*, 26 December 1978, pp. 1 and 9.
'Operasyon Sonrası Fatsa', *Cumhuriyet*, 15 August 1980, p. 10.
'Özaydınlı İstifa Etti', *Milliyet*, 3 January 1979, p. 9.
'Özaydınlı: "Bombalı Paketler ve Gizli Örgütler Saptandı"', *Milliyet*, 20 April 1978, pp. 1 and 8.
'Pakistan. Genel Seçimlerden Sonraki Gelişmeler', *Devrimci Yol*, 3, 1 June 1977, pp. 16-17.
'Pakistanda'ki Askeri Darbe ve Yeni Sömürgecilik Üzerine', *Devrimci Yol*, 8, 15 July 1977, p. 16.
'Rektör Tan, ODTÜ'yü 15 Gün Kapattı', *Milliyet*, 24 February 1977, p. 6.

'Sanık Komandolar Maltepe'de Silâhları ÜGD, Beykoz'da da MHP Gençlik Kolu Başkanlarından Aldıklarını Anlattılar', *Cumhuriyet*, 22 October 1978, pp. 1 and 9.
'Seçimler, TİP ve Tavrımız', *Devrimci Yol*, 2, 15 May 1977, p. 12.
'Şili Halkın Faşizme Karşı Direnişi', *Devrimci Yol*, 9, 19 September 1977, pp. 12-13.
'"Sömürgecilik" Tartışmaları Üzerine', *Devrimci Yol*, 16, 20 March 1978, pp. 10-12.
'"Sömürgecilik"'Tartışmaları Üzerine (II)', *Devrimci Yol*, 17, 1 May 1978, pp. 12-13.
'Sosyalist Sistemin Parçalanması ve Sovyet Çin Kutuplaşmasında Tavır', *Devrimci Yol*, 8, 15 July 1977, pp. 7-8.
'Sosyalist Sistemin Parçalanması ve Sovyet Çin Kutuplaşmasında Tavır (II)', *Devrimci Yol*, 7, 1 August 1977, pp. 8-9.
'Sosyalist Sistemin... (III)' *Devrimci Yol*, 8, 1 September 1977, p. 9.
'Tariş İşçileri Bazı Bölümleri İşgal Etti', *Cumhuriyet*, 9 February 1980, pp. 1 and 11.
'Tariş Olayları Dün de Istanbul'da Protesto Edildi', *Cumhuriyet*, 25 January 1980, pp. 1 and 11.
'Tariş'in Yeni Genel Müdürü Ertan Göreve Başladı', *Milliyet*, 7 July 1977, pp. 1 and 10.
'Tariş'te 1 600 İşçi Direnişe Geçti', *Cumhuriyet*, 19 January 1980, pp. 1 and 11.
'Tariş'ten İşçi Çıkarmalar sSürüyor, Gültepe'de Yaralanan Polis Öldü', *Cumhuriyet*, 10 February 1980, pp. 1 and 11.
'Tekin Istanbul Valisi, Atabek Emniyet Genel Müdürü Oldu', *Milliyet*, 8 February 1978, p. 1.
'TİİKP'nin, Toroslarda Silahlı Eylem Eğitimi Yaptiği Haberleri Alınıyor', *Milliyet*, 25 February 1977, p. 7.
'TSİP Revisyonistlerinin Epengle İşçilerine İhaneti', *Halkın Sesi*, 1, 15 April 1975, p. 4.
'TSİP Revisyonistlerinin Maskesini İndirelim', *Halkın Sesi*, 14, 15 July 1975, p. 8.
'Türk Ekonomisinin Ağustos Başında Ferahlama Dönemine Girmesi Bekleniyor', *Milliyet*, 25 June 1979, p. 9.
'Türkeş: "Hükümetin Düşmesi Belki Yarın, Belki Yarından da Yakındır"', *Hergün*, 22 December 1978, pp. 1 and 7.
'Türkeş: "Komünizm, Ecevit İktidarının Kanatları Altında"', *Hergün*, 10 July 1978, p. 1.
'Türkeş: "Sıkıyönetim Derhal İlân Edilerek Anarşi Durdurulmalı"', *Cumhuriyet*, 5 October 1978, pp. 1 and 9.
'Türkiye'de Bin Kişiye bir Polis Düşüyor', *Cumhuriyet*, 23 January 1979, pp. 1 and 11.
'Türkiye'de Kürt Meselesi ve Devrimci Hareketin Görevleri (2)', *Devrimci Yol*, 10, 21 October 1977, pp. 12-15.
'Türkiye'de Kürt Meselesi ve Devrimci Hareketin Görevleri', *Devrimci Yol*, 9, 19 September 1977, pp. 8-11.
'Ülkücü Sanık Veli Can Oduncu 7 Kişiyi Öldürdüğünü İtiraf Etti', *Milliyet*, 23 February 1979, pp. 1 and 9.
'Yakalanan 7 Ülkücü Silahları MHP'li Yöneticilerden Aldıklarını Açıkladılar', *Cumhuriyet*, 27 October 1978, p. 5.
Yalçın, Soner, 'Kayseri'de Silahlı Bir Akıncı Gençlik Kampı Hikayesi', *Hürriyet*, 2 September 1980.
'Yaşasın Nikaragua Halkın Devrimci Mücadelesi', *Devrimci Yol*, 22, 20 September 1978, pp. 12-13.
Yiğenoğlu, Çetin, 'Kahramanmaraş Olayları Davasında Dün MHP'li 2 Avukat, "Mahkemeye Saygısızlık" Gerekçesiyle Duruşma Dış Bırakıldı', *Milliyet*, 16, June 1979, p. 13.

Studies

Ahmad, Feroz, *The Making of Modern Turkey*, London, Routledge, 1993.
Ahmad, Feroz, *Modern Türkiye'nin Oluşumu*, Istanbul, Kaynak Yayınları, 2006.
Ahmad, Feroz, *The Turkish Experiment in Democracy, 1950-1975*, Boulder, CO, Westview Press, 1977.
Aksakal, Pertev, *Fatsa Gerçeği*, Ankara, Penta Yayıncılık, 2007.
Aslan, Fikret and Kemal Bozay, *Graue Wölfe Heulen Wieder. Türkische Faschisten und Ihre Vernetzung in der BRD*, Münster, Unrast, 2000.
Aslan, Şükrü, *1 Mayıs Mahallesi. 1980 Öncesi Toplumsal Mücadeleler ve Kent*, Istanbul, İletişim yayınları, 2004.
Aydınoğlu, Ergun, *La Gauche turque dans les années soixante (1960-1971)*, doctoral thesis in political science, University Paris 1, April 1993.
Aydınoğlu, Ergun, *Türkiye Solu. 1960-1980*, Istanbul, Versus Yayınları, 2007.
Aymes, Marc, 'Affaires courantes pour marcheurs d'empire. Le métier d'administrateur dans les provinces ottomanes au XIXe siècle', *Genèses*, 72, 2008, pp. 4-25.
Barkey, Karen, *Bandits and Bureaucrats. The Ottoman Route to State Centralisation*, Ithaca and New York, Cornell University Press, 1994, pp. 195-203.
Bayart, Jean-François, *L'Islam républicain. Ankara, Téhéran, Dakar*, Paris, Albin Michel, 2010.
Bayart, Jean-François, *Les Études postcoloniales, un carnaval académique*, Paris, Karthala, 2010.
Bayart, Jean-François, *The State in Africa: The Politics of the Belly*, London, Polity, 2009 [1993].
Beeley, Brian W., 'The Turkish Village Coffeehouse as a Social Institution', *Geographical Review*, 60, 4, October 1970, pp. 475-93.
Bilginer, Engin, *Babalar Senfonisi*, Istanbul, Cep Yayınları, 1990.
Birand, Mehmet Ali, *12 Eylül Saat: 04:00*, Istanbul, Karacan Yayınları, 1985.
Birand, Mehmet Ali, Hikmet Bilâ and Rıdvan Akar, *12 Eylül. Türkiye'nin Miladı*, Istanbul, Doğan Kitap, 2006.
Bölügiray, Nevzat, *Sokaktaki Asker, Bir Sıkıyönetim Komutanının 12 Eylül Öncesi Anıları*, Istanbul, Milliyet Yayınları, 1989.
Bora, Tanıl and Kemal Can, *Devlet Ocak Dergah - 12 Eylül'den Günümüze Ülkücü Hareket*, Istanbul, İletişim Yayınları, 1999.
Bovenkerk, Frank and Yücel Yeşilgöz, 'Urban knights and rebels in the Ottoman empire', in Cyrille Fijnaut and Letizia Paoli (eds), *Organised Crime in Europe. Concepts, Patterns and Control Policies in the European Union and Beyond*, Dordrecht, Springer, 2004, pp. 2013-24.
Bozarslan, Hamit, 'Le chaos après le déluge? Notes sur la crise turque des années 70', *Cultures et Conflits*, 24-25, winter-spring 1996-7, pp. 73-97.
Bozarslan, Hamit, 'Le phénomène milicien: une composante de la violence politique en Turquie des années 1970', *Turcica*, 31, 1999, pp. 185-244.
Bozkurt, Ömer, *Memurlar. Türkiye'de Kamu Bürokrasinin Sosyolojik Görünümü*, Ankara, TODAİE, 1980.
Briquet, Jean-Louis and Gilles Favarel-Garrigues, *Organised Crime and States: The Hidden Face of Politics*, New York, Palgrave MacMillan, The Sciences Po Series in International Relations and Political Economy, 2010.

Bruneteaux, Patrick, *La Violence d'État dans un régime démocratique: les forces de maintien de l'ordre en France. 1880–1980*, doctoral thesis in political science, University Paris 1, 1993.
Bulutoğlu, Kenan, *Bunalim ve Çikiş*, Istanbul, Tekin Yayınları, 1980.
Çalık, Mustafa, *MHP Hareketi. 1965–1980*, Ankara, Cedit Neşriyat, 1995.
Çalışkan, Nurettin, *ODTÜ Tarihçe. 1956–1980*, Ankara, Arayış Yayınları, 2002.
Caymaz, Birol and Emmanuel Szurek, 'La révolution au pied de la lettre. L'invention de "l'alphabet"', *European Journal of Turkish Studies*, 6, 2007, https://journals.openedition.org/ejts/1363 (consulted on 17 January 2021).
Cecen, A. Aydın, A. Suut Doğruel and Fatma Doğruel, 'Economic Growth and Structural Change in Turkey 1960–1988', *International Journal of Middle East Studies*, 26, 1, 1994, pp. 37–55.
Clark, Carey, Jane Perry and Carey Andrew Galbraith, 'Turkish Agriculture and the Five-Year Development Plans', *International Journal of Middle East Studies*, 3, 1, January 1972, pp. 45–58.
Culpan, Refik, 'Bürokratik Sistemin Yozlaşması', *Amme İdaresi Dergisi*, 13, 33, 1980.
Della Porta, Donatella, 'Police knowledge and protest policing: Some reflections on the Italian case', in Donatella Della Porta and Herbert Reiter (eds), *Policing Protest. The Control of Mass Demonstration in Western Democracies*, Minneapolis, University of Minnesota Press, 1998.
Dobry, Michel, *Sociologie des crises politiques*, Paris, Presses de la FNSP, 1992.
Dorronsoro, Gilles, 'Les politiques ottomane et républicaine au Kurdistan à partir de la comparaison des milices Hamidiye et *korucu*: modèles institutionnels, retribalisation et dynamique des conflits', *European Journal of Turkish Studies*, 5, 2006, https://journals.openedition.org/ejts/778 (consulted on 17 January 2021).
Dorronsoro, Gilles, *Que veut la Turquie? Ambitions et stratégies internationales*, Paris, Autrement, 2009.
Dorronsoro, Gilles, 'Réflexions sur la causalité d'un manque: pourquoi y a-t-il si peu de mobilisations en Turquie?', *Les dossiers du CERI*, 2001, https://www.sciencespo.fr/ceri/sites/sciencespo.fr.ceri/files/artgd_0.pdf.
Dorronsoro, Gilles and Gourisse Benjamin, 'The Turkish Army in Politics. Institutional autonomy, the formation of social coalitions, and the production of crises', *Revue française de science politique*, 65, 4, 2015, pp. 609–31.
Dumont, Paul, *Mustafa Kemal invente la Turquie moderne*, Paris, Complexe, 2006.
Erdost, Muzaffer İlhan, *Faşizm ve Türkiye 1977–1980*, Ankara, Nur Yayınları, 1995.
Ergil, Doğu, *Türkiye'de Terör ve Şiddet*, Ankara, Turhan Kitabevi, 1980.
Eroğlu, Cem, *Demokrat Parti. Tarihi ve İdeolojisi*, Ankara, İmge Kitabevi, 2003.
Ethuin, Nathalie, 'De l'idéologisation de l'engagement communiste. Les écoles du PCF (1970–1990)', *Politix*, 16, 63, 2003, pp. 145–68.
Faroqhi, Suraiya, 'Political activity among Ottoman taxpayers and the problem of Sultanic legitimation (1570–1650)', *Journal of the Economic and Social History of the Orient*, 35, 1992, pp. 1–39.
Faroqhi, Suraiya, 'Political initiatives "from the bottom up" in the sixteenth- and seventeenth-century Ottoman empire: Some evidence for their existence', in Hans Georg Majer (ed.), *Osmanistiche Studien zur Wirtschafts- und Sozialgeschichte: In Memoriam Vanco Boskov*, Wiesbaden, Otto Harrasowitz, 1986, pp. 24–33.
Faroqhi, Suraiya, 'Political tensions in the Anatolian countryside around 1600: An attempt at interpretation', in Jean-Louis Bacqué-Gramont *et al.*, 'Festschrift for Robert Anhegger', *Varia Turcica*, 9, 1987, pp. 116–30.

Favarel-Guarrigues, Gilles, 'Mafia violence and political power in Russia', in Jean-Louis Briquet and Gilles Favarel-Garrigues, *Organised Crime and States: The Hidden Face of Politics*, The Sciences Po Series in International Relations and Political Economy, New York, Palgrave MacMillan, 2010, pp. 147–71.

Feyizoğlu, Turhan, *Fırtınalı Yıllarda Ülkücü Hareket*, İstanbul, Ozan Yayıncılık, 2000.

Ganser, Daniele, *Les Armées secrètes de l'OTAN: réseaux Stay-Behind, Gladio et terrorisme en Europe de l'Ouest*, Brussels, Éditions Demi-Lune, 2007.

Giddens, Anthony, *The Constitution of Society*, Oakland, University of California Press, 1984.

Gourisse, Benjamin, 'What Politics does to the Army: Divisions and reconfigurations to the military institution in the 27 May 1960 Coup in Turkey', *Middle Eastern Studies*, 58, 1, 2022, pp. 70–86.

Gourisse, Benjamin, 'Enquête sur les relations entre politisation et études supérieures: le cas turc (1971–1980) ', *Critique internationale*, 50, 2011, pp. 39–53.

Grojean, Olivier, *La Cause kurde, de la Turquie vers l'Europe. Contribution à une sociologie de la transnationalisation des mobilisations*, doctoral thesis in political sociology, Paris, EHESS, 2008.

Gürel, Burak, '"Communist Police!" The state in the 1970s Turkey', *Journal of Historical Studies*, 2, 2004, pp. 1–18.

Gürel, Burak, *Political Mobilisation in Turkey in the 1970's. The Case of the Kahramanmaraş Incidents*, doctoral thesis, Boğaziçi University, Atatürk Institute for Modern Turkish History, 2004.

Haffner, Sebastian, *Defying Hitler. A Memoir*, New York, Picador, 2000.

Heper, Metin, *Geckondu Policy in Turkey. An Evaluation with a Case Study of Rumelihisarüstü Squatter Area in Istanbul*, Istanbul, Boğaziçi University Publications, 1978.

Heper, Metin, 'The state, religion and pluralism: The Turkish case in comparative perspective', *British Journal of Middle Eastern Studies*, 18, 1, 1991, pp. 38–51.

Heper, Metin, *The State Tradition in Turkey*, Northgate, The Eothen Press, 1985.

Hibou, Béatrice, *Anatomie politique de la domination*, Paris, La Découverte, 2011.

Ilıcak, Nazlı, *Makaleler II, 1978*, Istanbul, Kervan Yayınları, 1980.

Juhem, Philippe, *SOS-Racisme. Histoire d'une mobilisation 'apolitique'. Contribution à l'analyse des transformations des représentations politiques après 1981*, Doctoral thesis in political science, University Paris 10-Nanterre, 1998.

Kalaycıoğlu, Ersin, '1960 Sonrası Türk Politik Hayatına bir Bakış: Demokrasi Neo-Patrimonyalizm ve İstikrar', in Ersin Kalaycıoğlu and Yaşar Sarıbay, *Türkiye'de Politik Değişim ve Modernleşme*, İstanbul, Alfa Yayınları, 2000, pp. 387–412.

Kasaba, Reşat, 'A time and a place for the nonstate: Social change in the Ottoman empire during the long nineteenth century', in Joel S. Migdal, Atul Kohli and Vivienne Shue (eds), *State, Power and Social Forces: Domination and Transformation in the Third World*, Cambridge, Cambridge University Press, 1994, pp. 207–30.

Katz, Richard and Peter Mair, 'Changing models of party organisation and party democracy. The emergence of the cartel party', *Party Politics*, 1, 1, 1995, pp. 5–28.

Kiliç, Ecevit, *Özel Harp Dairesi*, Istanbul, Timaş Yayınları, 2010.

Kırdemir, Zeki, *Devrim bize yakışırdı*, Istanbul, Ozan Yayıncılık, 2004.

Koçak, Cemil, 'Parliament membership during the single-party system in Turkey (1925–1945)', *European Journal of Turkish Studies*, 3, 2005, https://journals.openedition.org/ejts/497 (consulted on 17 January 2021).

Koçak, Cemil, *Türkiye'de Milli Şef Dönemi. 1938–1945*, Istanbul, İletişim Yayınları, 2010.

Kongar, Emre, *İmparatorluktan Günümüze Türkiye'nin Toplumsal Yapısı*, Istanbul, Cem Yayınevi, 1978.
Labov, William, *Language in the Inner City: Studies in the Black English Vernacular*, Philadelphia, University of Pennsylvania Press, 1977.
Lagroye, Jacques, Bastien François and Frédéric Sawicki, *Sociologie politique*, Paris, Presses de Sciences Po and Dalloz, 2002.
Landau, Jacob M., *Radical Politics in Modern Turkey*, Leiden, E. J. Brill, 1974.
Mair, Peter, 'Party organisations: From civil society to the state', in Richard Katz and Peter Mair (eds), *How Parties Organise. Change and Adaptation in Party Organisations in Western Democracies*, London, Sage, 1994, pp. 1–22.
Mardin, Şerif, 'Power, civil society and culture in the Ottoman empire', *Comparative Studies in Society and History*, 11, 3, June 1969, pp. 258–81.
Margulies, Ronnie and Ergin Yıldızoğlu, 'Trade unions and Turkey's working class', *MERIP Reports*, 121, 'State terror in Turkey', February 1984, p. 17.
Massicard, Elise, '"Gangs in uniform"' in Turkey: Politics at the articulation between security institutions and the criminal world', in Jean-Louis Briquet and Gilles Favarel-Garrigues (eds), *Organised Crime and States: The Hidden Face of Politics*, New York, Palgrave MacMillan, The Sciences Po Series in International Relations and Political Economy, 2010, pp. 41–71.
Mauger, Gérard and Claude Fossé-Poliak, 'Les loubards', *Actes de la recherche en sciences sociales*, 50, 1983, pp. 49–68.
McAdam, Doug, 'Tactical innovation and the pace of insurgency', *American Sociological Review*, 48, 1983, pp. 735–54.
McAdam, Doug, Sidney Tarrow and Charles Tilly, *Dynamics of Contention*, Cambridge, Cambridge University Press, 2001.
Meeker, Michael E., *A Nation of Empire. The Ottoman Legacy of Turkish Modernity*, Berkeley and Los Angeles, University of California Press, 2002.
Meeker, Michael E., *Social Practice and Political Culture in the Turkish Republic*, Istanbul, The Isis Press, 2004.
Mehmet, Özay, 'Turkey in crisis: Some contradictions in the Kemalist development strategy', *International Journal of Middle East Studies*, 15, 1, February 1983, pp. 47–66.
Migdal, Joel S., *State in Society: Studying How States and Societies Transform and Constitute One Another*, Cambridge, Cambridge University Press, 2001.
Monceau, Nicolas, 'Les intellectuels mobilisés: le cas de la fondation d'histoire de Turquie', in Gilles Dorronsoro (ed.), *La Turquie conteste. Mobilisations sociales et régime sécuritaire*, Paris, CNRS, 2005, pp. 109–26.
Müftüoğlu, Oğuzhan, *1960'lardan 1980'e Türkiye Gerçeği*, Istanbul, Patika Yayınları, 1989.
Nye, Roger P., 'Civil-military confrontation in Turkey: The 1973 presidential election', *International Journal of Middle East Studies*, 8, 2, April 1977, pp. 209–28.
Osa, Maryjane, *Solidarity and Contention, Networks of Polish Opposition*, Minneapolis, University of Minnesota Press, 2003.
Ozankaya, Özer, *Türk Devrimi ve Yüksek Öğretim Gençliği*, Ankara, SBF Yayınları, 1978.
Özbudun, Ergun, *Social Change and Political Participation in Turkey*, Princeton, New Jersey, Princeton University Press, 1976.
Özcan, Ertekin, *Türkische Immigrantenorganisationen in des Bundesrepublik Deutschland*, Berlin, Hitit Verlag, 1989.
Özman, Aylin, 'Law, ideology and modernisation in Turkey: Kemalist legal reforms in perspective', *Social and Legal Studies*, 19, 1, March 2010, pp. 67–84.

Pamuk, Şevket, 'Political economy of industrialisation in Turkey', *MERIP Reports*, 93, January 1981, pp. 26–30.
Pezzino, Paolo, 'La mafia, l'État et la société dans la Sicile contemporaine (XIXe et XXe siècles) ', *Politix*, 13, 49, 2000, pp. 13–33.
Piven, Frances Fox and Richard A. Cloward, *Poor People's Movements: Why They Succeed, How They Fail*, New York, Vintage, 1977.
Poulton, Hugh, *Top Hat, Grey Wolf and Crescent. Turkish Nationalism and the Turkish Republic*, London, Hurst and Company, 2006.
Pudal, Bernard, *Prendre parti: pour une sociologie historique du PCF*, Paris, Presses de la FNSP, 1989.
Roos, Leslie L. and Noralou P. Roos, *Managers of Modernisation: Organizations and Elites in Turkey (1950–1969)*, Cambridge, Harvard University Press, 1971.
Sanlı, Ferit Salim, *Türk Milliyetçiliğin Siyasetleşmesı – CKMP'den MHP'ye 1965–1969*, Ankara, Ülkü Ocakları Eğitim ve Kültür Vakfı, 2020.
Şaylan, Gencay, *Türkiye'de Kapitalizm, Bürokrasi ve Siyasal İdeoloji*, Ankara, TODAİE, 1972.
Shaw, Stanford J., 'Local administrations in the Tanzimat', in Hakki Dursun Yıldız (ed.), *150. yılında Tanzimat*, Ankara, Türk Tarih Kurumu Yayınları, 1992, pp. 33–49.
Simmel, Georg, *Sociology: Enquiries into the Construction of Social Forms*, Leiden, Brill, 2009.
Sönmez, Cemil, *Ülkücü bir Kaymakam Vardı*, Ankara, Ajans-Türk Matbaası, 1965, pp. 34–53.
Sosyalizm ve Toplumsal Mücadeleler Ansiklopedisi, vol. 7 (1960–80), Istanbul, İletişim Yayınları, 1988.
Steinmetz, George, 'The myth and the reality of an autonomous state: Industrialists, junkers and social policy in imperial Germany', *Comparative Social Research*, 12, 1990, pp. 239–93.
Stoddard, Philip, *The Ottoman Government and the Arabs, 1911 to 1918. A Preliminary Study of the Teskilat-i-Mashusa*, doctoral thesis, Princeton University, 1963.
Sunar, İlkay, *State and Society in the Politics of Turkey's Development*, Ankara, AÜSBF, 1975, pp. 137–9.
Tachau, Frank and Metin Heper, 'The state, politics, and the military in Turkey', *Comparative Politics*, 16, 1, October 1983, pp. 17–33.
Tarrow, Sidney, 'State and opportunities: The political structuring of social movements', in Doug McAdam, John D. McCarthy and Mayer N. Zald (eds), *Comparative Perspectives on Social Movements. Political Opportunities, Mobilising Structures, and Cultural Framings*, Cambridge, Cambridge University Press, 1996, pp. 41–61.
Thomas Lewis, V. and Richard N. Frye, *The United States and Turkey and Iran*, Cambridge, The MIT Press, 1965.
Tilly, Charles, *From Mobilisation to Revolution*, Reading, MA, Addison-Wesley Publishing Company, 1978.
Tilly, Charles, 'War making and state making as organized crime', in Peter Evans, Dietrich Rueschmeyer and Theda Skocpol (eds), *Bringing the State Back In*, Cambridge: Cambridge University Press, 1985, pp. 169–91.
Tilly, Charles and Sidney Tarrow, *Contentious Politics*, Oxford: Oxford University Press, 2006.
Turan, Ali Eşref, *Türkiye'de Seçmen Davranışı. Önceki Kırılmalar ve 2002 Seçimi*, Istanbul, Istanbul Bilgi Üniversitesi Yayınları, 2004.
Türkiye Gerçekleri ve Terörizm, Ankara, Babşakanlık Basımevi, 1973.

Tutum, Cahit, 'Yönetimin Siyasallaşması ve Partizanlık', *Amme İdaresi Dergisi*, 9, 4, 1976, pp. 9–32.

Ünsal, Artun, *Parti ouvrier de Turquie*, doctoral thesis in political science, University Paris 1, 1970.

Ünsal, Artun, *Türkiye İşçi Partisi (1961–1971). Umuttan Yalnızlığa*, Istanbul, Tarih Vakfı Yurt Yayınları, 2002.

Van Bruinessen, Martin, *Türklük, Kürtlük, Alévilik-Etnik ve Dinsel Kimlik Mücadeleleri*, İstanbul, İletişim Yayınları, 2002.

Volkov, Vadim, 'Les entreprises de violence dans la Russie postcommuniste', *Politix*, 13, 49, 2000, pp. 57–75.

Wacquant, Loic, 'L'habitus comme objet et méthode d'investigation. Retour sur la fabrique du boxeur', *Actes de la recherche en sciences sociales*, 2010, 184, pp. 108–21.

Walsh, Edward J., 'Resource mobilisation and citizen protest in communities around three mile island', *Social Problems*, 29, 1, 1981, pp. 1–21.

Yavuz, Fehmi, Rüşen Keleş and Cevat Geray, *Şehircilik: Sorunlar, Uygulama ve Politika*, Ankara, Ankara Üniversitesi, 1973.

Zald, Mayer N., 'Looking backward to look forward: Reflections on the past and future of the resource mobilisation research program', in Aldon D. Morris and Carol Mc Clurg Mueller (eds), *Frontiers in Social Movement Theory*, New Haven, Yale University Press, 1992, pp. 326–48.

Zald, Mayer N. and Bert Usem, 'Movement and countermovement interaction: Mobilisation, tactics, and state involvement', in John MacCarthy and Mayer N. Zald (eds), *Social Movement in an Organisational Society*, Morristown, Transaction Books, 1987, pp. 247–72.

INDEX

Accumulation 5, 8, 10, 21, 31, 45, 57–83, 140, 162, 167, 169
action system 3, 33–4, 40–1, 46, 56–7, 61, 64, 74–5, 82, 85, 97, 106, 121, 128, 161
Adalet Partisi (AP) 7, 14, 22–5, 35, 37, 38, 40, 47, 86, 87, 91, 108, 115, 117–18, 124, 127–9, 132–3, 152–3, 158–9, 163–4
Alevi 7, 73, 74, 96, 100, 102, 124, 139, 149–50, 153–61
Ankara Yüksek Öğrenim Derneği (AYÖD) 109
anti-communism 24–5, 46–8, 65, 78–3, 113, 124, 126, 149–50, 154–7, 159
anti-fascism 1, 33–35, 40–1, 45–6, 62, 68, 81, 94–7, 110, 116–19, 141–4, 154–5
Aren Sadun 36, 39
Army 4, 14, 16, 23, 33, 38–39, 46–7, 79, 93–4, 97, 103, 121, 125, 134, 156, 157, 159, 160, 161–8
Atsız Nihal 74, 78
autonomy of the state 10, 14, 89, 167
Avrupa Demokratik Ülkücü Türk Dernekleri Federasyonu (ADÜTDF) 55
Aybar Mehmet Ali 36, 39

Başbuğ 47, 71, 90
Belli Mihri 35, 39
Bir Mayis Mahallesi. *See* May Day neighbourhood
Bölügiray Nevzat 27, 29–30, 94, 96–7, 103, 160–1
Bölükbaşı Osman 47
Boran Behice 36, 39
Boycott 89–90, 109–11, 117
Büyük Ülkü Derneği (BÜD) 49, 51, 145–6, 154

capture of public resources 5, 6, 8, 10, 12, 14, 83, 86, 90, 93, 94, 106, 107, 121, 139, 152, 158, 160, 161, 162, 167–9
Çayan Mahir 36, 37, 42, 44, 67, 98
coalition government 2–3, 13–14, 22–4, 31, 39, 55, 86–7, 107, 124, 126–7, 132–3, 152, 158–9, 163, 165. *See also* Nationalist Front government
Committee of National Union 46–7, 79
Constitutional Court 37, 55
coup
  27 May 1960 13, 22, 33, 38, 47, 79, 94, 162
  12 March 1971 14, 34, 36–7, 39–40, 44, 48–9, 70, 94, 121, 162, 167
  12 September 1980 3–4, 8, 16, 28, 34, 40, 46, 51, 68, 94, 106, 122–5, 129, 130,137–8, 152, 161–2, 165, 167
crisis (politcal, economic)
  economic 2, 10, 18, 24, 26, 163
  political 3, 4–5, 83, 162, 167, 169
Cumhuriyet Halk Partisi (CHP) 1, 11–14, 21–5, 38–41, 45, 47, 49–50, 87, 89–93, 95, 98, 100, 110, 114, 116, 125–8, 130, 132–3, 141, 150, 152–9, 163–5
Cumhuriyetçi Güven Partisi (CGP) 24
Cumhuriyetçi Köylü Millet Partisi (CKMP) 23, 46–9, 78–9
Cumhuriyetçi Parti (CP) 38
Cyprus 23–5

delegation of state's functions 10, 15–17, 21, 150, 158
Demirel Süleyman 14, 38, 40, 69, 87, 99, 127, 162–5
Democrat Party (DP). *See* Demokrat Parti
Demokrat Parti (DP) 12–13, 18, 21–2, 38, 152
Demokratik Parti 24

de-objectivation of the state 6, 8, 85–6, 97, 106, 139, 152, 160
Devrimci Gençlik Dernekleri Federasyonu (DGDF) 42–3
Devrimci Gençlik Federasyonu (Dev-Genç) 35–7, 41–3, 62, 64, 68, 81, 110
Devrimci İşçi Sendikaları Konfederasyonu (DİSK) 35, 38–40, 45, 48, 50, 112, 116–18, 153, 156, 158, 165
Devrimci Sol (Dev-Sol) 63, 77, 144
Devrimci Yol (Dev-Yol) 42–3, 45, 62, 63, 66–7, 72, 74–5, 77, 81, 98–100, 134, 143–4, 162
Directorate of Security 14, 26, 28, 30, 41, 88, 91–3, 97, 105, 137, 146
distribution of public resources 5, 10, 12, 17, 21, 24–5, 51, 57, 85–6, 91, 99, 158, 167, 168

Ecevit, Bülent 23–5, 38, 40–1, 87, 100, 124–6, 155, 157, 159–60, 163–4
educational institute 88–9, 143
elite
    bureaucratic 13
    local 11–12, 15
    political 167
    social 9–10, 21
    traditional 17, 31, 152
Erbakan, Necmettin 23, 39, 54, 161, 164
escalation in violence 3, 8, 123, 125–6, 128, 138, 140, 152, 163, 167
Esir Türkleri Kurtarma Ordusu (ETKO) 124, 144, 154
ethos 71–8

Fatsa 98–100, 105, 151, 162
Fikir Kulüpleri Federasyonu (FKF) 35–7
1 May 1977 124, 126, 153

gecekondu 20–1, 53, 62, 104, 118, 135
general election
    15 October 1961 22, 23
    10 October 1965 22, 35, 40
    12 October 1969 22, 23, 38, 47, 153
    14 October 1973 23, 39, 47, 87, 152, 153
    5 June 1977 24, 39, 87, 153–4, 158
Germany 21, 54–5, 60–1, 78–9
Gezmiş Deniz 36, 42
Gladio network 16

governor 10–12, 14, 28, 92, 97–8, 105, 128, 156, 159, 162
Guerrilla 37, 44, 134, 162
Gültekin Necati 93, 115
Güneş, Hasan Fehmi 27
Gürsel Cemal 38, 47

Habitus 28, 57, 76, 119
Halkın Kurtuluşu (HK) 45, 69, 72, 74, 102, 153
Halkın Yolu (HY) 42
hall of residence 20–1, 49, 51, 53, 66–7, 89, 100, 103, 111–12, 135, 142–3
High school 28, 40, 64, 68, 70, 81–2, 88, 93, 104, 108–9, 135–6, 143, 155

İlerici Gençlik Derneği (İGD) 42
industrialization 18–20
infiltration of public institutions 6, 13, 14, 33, 89, 150, 152
İnönü, İsmet 22–3, 38, 79
intellectuals 1, 15–16, 33–4, 65, 109
International Monetary Fund (IMF) 2, 19, 163
Istanbul University 37, 41, 91, 140–1
İstanbul Yüksek Öğrenim Kültür Derneği (İYÖKD) 41–2

Justice Party. *See* Adalet Partisi

Kadrolaşma. *See* infiltration of public institutions
Kahramanmaraş massacre 2, 7, 13, 25, 51, 94, 96, 124–5, 139, 152–3, 155–65
Kaymakam. *See* sub-governor
Kıvılcım Hikmet 39
Korutürk Fahri 39, 111, 163

liberated
    zone 100–3, 105–6, 123, 142–3, 150–1, 162
    institution 88, 108

Maoism 37, 42–3, 45–6, 103
martial law 2, 25, 27, 37–9, 48–9, 52, 88, 94, 96–7, 103, 119, 125, 134, 158–61, 163
Marxist Leninist Silahlı Propaganda Birliği (MLSPB) 44, 143

May Day neighbourhood 100–3, 105–6
Militia 3, 7, 16, 25, 48, 100, 103–6, 121, 124, 127, 134, 136, 139–40, 143, 148–52, 156–8, 160–1, 165, 168
Milli Birlik Komitesi (MBK). *See* Committee of National Union
Milli Demokratik Devrim (MDD) 35–6, 39, 41
Milli Güvenlik Konseyi (MGK). *See* National Security Council
Milli Nizam Partisi (MNP) 23, 38–9
Millet Partisi (MP) 21, 35
Milli Selâmet Partisi (MSP) 23–5, 39, 54, 91, 92, 128–9, 132, 161, 164–5
Milliyetçi Cephe hükümeti. *See* Nationalist Front government
Milliyetçi İşçi Sendikaları Konfederasyonu (MİSK) 50, 54, 59, 112, 127, 147, 148, 153–4, 158
Ministry of Customs and Monopolies 14, 52, 55, 87, 91
Ministry of Education 13, 88
muhtar 12, 93, 99, 103, 106, 137, 157

National Security Council 162, 165
Nationalist Front government 14, 24–5, 40, 50, 52, 55, 58, 86–7, 95, 102, 108–9, 113, 116, 125–7, 148
North Atlantic Treaty Organization (NATO) 16, 23, 34, 81–2
notable 9, 11–12, 15, 17, 21, 150

Öner Sıtkı 26–7, 95
Orta Doğu Teknik Üniversitesi (ODTÜ). *See under* university
Ottoman Empire 4, 8–12, 15–17, 65, 74
Özal Turgut 164

palestinian training camp 44, 70
pan-Turanism 78–9
pan-Turkism 46–7, 78–9
Partya Karkerên Kurdistan (PKK) 16, 134, 168
Perinçek Doğu 36–7, 39, 42, 45, 70
police 3, 6, 14–15, 25–30, 40–1, 50–1, 53, 72, 74, 76, 80, 85–6, 88, 91, 93–101, 103, 108, 111–12, 117–19, 128, 136–7, 140, 142, 144–8, 153, 155–9, 161, 168

Polis Birliği (Pol-Bir) 50, 95–6, 158
Polis Derneği (Pol-Der) 26, 41, 50, 93, 95–7, 124, 146, 156, 158
Politicization 4, 6, 8, 14, 21, 27, 40, 43, 85–7, 89, 91, 93–7, 99, 101, 103, 105, 139, 149, 159, 168
Press 13, 22, 54–5, 102, 110, 113, 118, 122–3, 126, 138, 141–2, 147, 164, 170
proletarianization 10, 17, 20, 31

radicalization 23, 28, 118, 124, 128, 168

Sazak Gün 52, 87
Somuncuoğlu Şadi 91
Sosyalist Devrim Partisi (SDP) 39
student(s) 6, 20–1, 33–7, 39–44, 48, 51, 53, 62–9, 79, 81–2, 88, 90, 94, 97, 102, 104, 107–18, 136–7, 140–3, 155
subcontracting 15–16, 18
sub-governor 12–14, 16, 90, 98, 105–6, 128

Tan Hasan 107–14
tanzimat 10–11
Tüm Öğretmenler Birleşme ve Dayanışma Derneği (Töb-Der) 40, 50, 65, 109, 141, 155–6
Tüm Öğretmen Sendikası (TÖS) 38
Türk İntikam Tugayı (TİT) 124
Türk Ülkücüler Teşkilatı (TÜT) 49
Türk Yıldırım Ordusu (TYO) 124
Türkeş, Alparslan 23, 33, 46–56, 58, 60, 64–5, 69, 71, 78–80, 87, 90, 92, 154–7
Türkiye Emekçi Partisi (TEP) 39, 61
Türkiye Halk Kurtuluş Ordusu (THKO) 37, 41–2, 44
Türkiye Halk Kurtuluş Partisi-Cephesi (THKP-C) 37, 41–2, 44, 67, 98
Türkiye İhtilalci İşçi Köylü Partisi (TİİKP) 37, 39, 70
Türkiye İşçi Partisi (TİP) 23, 33–9, 45, 47–8, 61, 64, 78, 126
Türkiye Komünist Partisi (TKP) 34, 42–3, 45, 62, 67
Türkiye Komünist Partisi – Marxist Leninist/Türkiye İşçi Köylü Kurtuluş Ordusu (TKP-ML/TİKKO) 37, 41

Türkiye Memurlar Birleşme ve Dayanışma Derneği (Tüm-Der) 40
Türkiye Sosyalist İşçi Partisi (TSİP) 39, 42, 45, 61

Ülkü Ocakları Birliği (ÜOB) 48
Ülkü Ocakları Derneği (ÜOD) 49, 51, 58–9, 126, 144
Ülkü Yolu Derneği (ÜYD) 49, 51, 58–9, 76, 144
ülkücü bureaus 53–4, 59–60, 66, 104, 115
Ülkücü Gençler Derneği (ÜGD) 49, 51, 59, 127, 144, 146, 147, 154
Ülkücü Hanımlar Derneği (Ülkü-Han) 50, 59
Ülkücü Kamu Görevliler ve Memurlar Derneği (Ülküm) 50, 59, 90
Ülkücü Kamu Görevlileri Güçbirliği Derneği (Ülküm-Bir) 50
Ülkücü Köylüler Derneği (Ülkü-Köy) 50
Ülkücü Öğretmenler Birliği Derneği (Ülkü-Bir) 93, 109, 115, 117, 154

United States of America 25, 34, 36, 40, 73–5, 81–2, 137
university
  Ankara University 37, 48
  Istanbul Technical University 45, 91, 126
  Istanbul University 20, 37, 41, 91, 140
  Middle East Technical University 13, 41, 43, 45, 81, 107, 109–14, 117
urbanization 10, 17, 20, 31
Union of Soviet Socialist Republics (USSR) 24, 34, 79, 163

vali. *See* governor
Vatan Partisi (VP) 39

World Bank 19, 164

Yurdakul Cevat 41, 97, 137, 146
yurt. *See* hall of residence

Zeybek Namık Kemal 48, 65

www.ingramcontent.com/pod-product-compliance
Lightning Source LLC
Chambersburg PA
CBHW062219300426
44115CB00012BA/2133